The Transformation of Capacity
in International Development

The Transformation of Capacity in International Development

Afghanistan and Pakistan (1977–2017)

Avideh K. Mayville

ANTHEM PRESS

Anthem Press
An imprint of Wimbledon Publishing Company
www.anthempress.com

This edition first published in UK and USA 2020
by ANTHEM PRESS
75–76 Blackfriars Road, London SE1 8HA, UK
or PO Box 9779, London SW19 7ZG, UK
and
244 Madison Ave #116, New York, NY 10016, USA

British Library Cataloguing-in-Publication Data
A catalogue record for this book is available from the British Library.

Library of Congress Cataloging-in-Publication Data
Library of Congress Control Number: 2019952769

ISBN-13: 978-1-78527-155-7 (Hbk)
ISBN-10: 1-78527-155-5 (Hbk)

This title is also available as an e-book.

This book is dedicated to my parents, who devoted their lives to making my dreams possible and for allowing me to think that getting a PhD was a normal thing to do. I would never have achieved anything in life if it were not for your love, support, encouragement, and belief in my abilities. I have been so lucky to have you both. This is your accomplishment.

CONTENTS

CONTENTS   ix

FIGURES

ACKNOWLEDGMENTS

I am truly lucky to have had so many great mentors, teachers, and fundamentally incredible humans inspiring me to commit my life to learning, scholarship, and service. I would like to thank some of them here.

From preschool to college: Ms. Peggy Sanford, Ms. Lane, Mrs. Torpy, Mrs. Kerri Cook, Ms. Allison Bailey, Mrs. Linda Holloway, Mr. Seth DeRose, and Mrs. Christy Edgar. You have devoted your lives not only to your subjects but also to the potential and mess of unfiltered youth. Thank you for being the first teachers who made a difference in my life.

To the faculty at St. Mary's College of Maryland—a truly magical place of undergraduate learning by the river. Dr. Michael J. G. Cain, thank you for being my first real mentor, encouraging my curiosity, making me feel like my questions mattered, and for not letting me get away with surface-level answers. Dr. Dustin Howes—may you rest in peace. You brought a passion into the classroom, a creativity toward your discipline, and a commitment toward your students that I seek to emulate in my own career. Dr. Sahar Shafqat—for demonstrating the importance of activism as a scholar. Dr. Kate Norlock— the funniest philosopher I have ever met. Dr. Iris Ford—it is ironic that my first introduction to sociology was from an anthropologist!

Thank you to the IPCR faculty in the School of International Service at American University (AU) who have dedicated their lives to peace. Dr. Abdul Aziz Said—the legend who has inspired generations, myself included—your wisdom made the pursuit of knowledge mystical. Dr. Anthony Wanis St. John, who stepped in near the end of my time at AU and became an unexpected mentor as I raced to finish my thesis.

Thank you to my doctoral committee who were instrumental in the development of this project. Dr. Agnieszka Paczynscka and Dr. Lester Kurtz—your feedback has been critical in making my work stronger. Dr. John G. Dale: you are the model of mentor, teacher, researcher, critic, scholar, practitioner, leader, colleague, facilitator, mediator, and friend that I will forever strive to emulate in my life and career. I have no idea how you do it all. Thank you for investing your time in me as I've found my voice as a scholar. I will be forever grateful for your insight and guidance, particularly as I navigated a complex topic during a trying time in my life.

My ACP family—who bore witness my early mornings and cheered me on throughout the trials and turmoil involved in the construction of this beast.

Thank you also to Dr. Mark Frezzo, the editor of this series, for being a true colleague in helping me to navigate the book publishing world. Your guidance has been invaluable and the future of young scholars (and of scholarship) depends on the mentorship of those who have walked the path before us. I also thank the reviewers who provided feed-back on this manuscript before publication.

Finally, I think it is important to acknowledge the artists of sound whose rhymes and melodies fueled me through many days of reading, writing, coding, note taking, figure drawing, head wringing, and exasperated dance breaks: Oddisee, Jamiroquai, Basement Jaxx, Daft Punk, Grace Jones, Gil Heron, Hiromi, Lloyd Miller, Breakbot, Flight Facilities, Flamingosis, Nightmares on Wax, and countless others.

Chapter One

INTRODUCTION

USAID often engages with governments that lack the capacity for full country ownership (my emphasis), *even if there is political will to address development challenges fomenting violent extremism and/or insurgency. In other places, capacity may exist, but demonstrated political will is lacking. Ultimately, USAID must leverage and further develop local capacity and good governance principles, such as transparency and accountability, to respond to drivers of violent extremism and/or insurgency.—USAID Policy Task Team (PTT) publication, "The Development Response to Violent Extremism and Insurgency." (USAID 2011a, 10)*

Capacity development remains one of the most "slippery" and unsatisfactory concepts in development—"a refuge for the scoundrel," as one colleague recently noted. There is no agreed definition, there is no formal academic body of knowledge discussing it and there are no university courses teaching it. (Tesky 2011, 44)

Introduction

Much of the aid to developing countries in recent decades has fallen under the broad umbrella of building capacity. Buzzwords such as "capacity building" and "capacity development" have permeated the development discourse and are employed in a variety of ways, typically identified as an issue, a need, and a solution to the challenges of "growth and progress." Furthermore, the wide-ranging and all-encompassing nature of the usage of the term "capacity" obscures how exactly it is manifested in projects. For this reason, there is a need for clarification of the concept of capacity, in both its theoretical origins and the way in which it has been applied as a project of development.

With this aim in mind, this project explores a particular case of the transformation of capacity as a concept and a practice within international development, tracing the relationship between this transformation and the rise of transnational militancy in Afghanistan and Pakistan. I situate my analysis of this transformation through a close examination of the policies and projects to build capacity in these two countries between 1977 and 2017, implemented by the largest institutional donor driving them—the United States Agency for International Development (USAID).

As we near the end of the second decade in this new century, the donor community faces significant global security challenges. In spite of a concentrated so-called Global War on Terror, global terrorism continues to threaten the livelihoods of individuals, communities, and the system of states. As these security challenges become more complex, so does development. Nearly eighty years removed from the Universal Declaration of Human Rights, this century is also marked by a greater call for the integration of human rights approaches to development practice by the major development institutions. This project examines the transformation of capacity within this context—amid a world increasingly defined by growing global security concerns and greater calls for human rights approaches to development.

This research tackles a complex web of questions. First of all, what is capacity? How and why has it gained salience in the donor discourse on development and what does its emergence show us about the transformation of development projects and donor methods? Furthermore, does the transformation of the concept actually reveal changes in USAID's frameworks for development? If not, what does capacity mask?

Considering the cases of Afghanistan and Pakistan, we must also ask, what does this transformation show us about human rights approaches to development, particularly in the context of development in so-called fragile or failed states? Can we determine a relationship between the continued efforts of donors to build capacity and the rise of transnational Islamic militancy in Afghanistan and Pakistan? Why do capacity development efforts fail, particularly in so-called fragile state contexts, and what implications does this failure have on the relationships and networks surrounding development and transnational militancy and on the relevance and legitimacy of the state? Finally, what does USAID's efforts to build capacity reveal about how donors attempt to craft the state? How does this empirical example inform our sociological understanding of statebuilding processes and the role and function of the development agency within the context of bilateral relationships?

I argue that capacity is actually a *discursive tool* of statemaking that reveals the flow of international and transnational power in the construction and circumvention of the state—as a site for the intersection of globalization and capitalist development. My research also sheds light on the discursive significance and function of major development concepts as they relate to competing narratives and agendas within Western frameworks for progress. This project exposes the tensions in donor discourses and agendas on the cultivation of markets, prioritization of human rights, and concerns over security threats as they coalesce under the umbrella of development and are obscured through the language of capacity.

I also specifically ask what the relationship is between the transformation of capacity and the rise of the security–development nexus in donor activity *and* transnational militancy in Afghanistan and Pakistan over the past forty years. I argue that donors fail to recognize their role in relationships of development within project methodology designed to build capacity and superficially conceive of how to construct relationships and networks for sustained centralized governance. This argument is significant because it is central to understanding how donor efforts at statebuilding and counterinsurgency fundamentally fail as donors attempt to build capacity through superficially and ideologically conceiving of relationships and networks of power.

In this introductory chapter, I begin by providing a brief background on my case selection and conclude with an overview of my methodology and introduction to the chapters that follow. However, before diving into the background of this case, I highlight the following story not only to display and illuminate the tension between donor objectives for global security and development but also to provide some context for the challenges facing USAID and other donors in the development of Afghanistan and Pakistan.

USAID Vaccination Campaign or CIA Plot?

On September 11, 2001, Osama bin Laden planned and executed an act of terrorism against the United States that spawned a new era in global politics and US foreign policy: the so-called Global War on Terror. After the Taliban refused to hand over bin Laden, the United States led an international coalition of military forces into Afghanistan. This manhunt turned into a two-decades-long war that saw the rise of new forms of collaboration, cooperation, and integration of international military, humanitarian, and development efforts. On May 2, 2011, a decade after the 9/11 attacks, US Special Operations forces penetrated Pakistani airspace from a base in Afghanistan and assassinated Osama bin Laden in his home in Abbottabad, Pakistan. Chased out of Afghanistan by coalition forces, bin Laden had eventually settled in Abbottabad, located in the heart of Khyber Pakhtunkhwa (a province of Pakistan in the tribal belt near Afghanistan) less than a mile from Pakistan's top military academy (Sherwell 2011), begging questions about how such a high-profile and wanted militant leader could go unnoticed by the government of Pakistan (GOP).

Following bin Laden's assassination, the GOP commissioned a report investigating the events surrounding (1) the failure of Pakistan to capture bin Laden on their own soil and (2) the events surrounding his assassination by US Special Operations forces. The report, subsequently known as the Abbottabad Report, was leaked to the media by Al Jazeera in 2013. The report recommended trying Dr. Shakil Afridi, a Pakistani doctor and district health officer of Khyber Agency who had worked with Save the Children on a USAID-funded vaccination campaign program in the areas near Abbottabad, for treason (Abbottabad Commission 2013, 110–14). Why was this local doctor and aid worker to be tried for treason? Nine days before the assassination, Dr. Afridi had visited the compound in which bin Laden and his family were in hiding and, while turned away at the door, was able to obtain a name to contact the head of the household so that he could return to complete the vaccinations (ibid., 115). This name happened to belong to bin Laden's courier, which when identified by CIA agents led to the attack and subsequent assassination the following week (Mullaney and Hassan 2015).

In the report, Dr. Afridi claimed while being interrogated that he was recruited by the CIA through USAID (Abbottabad Report 2013, 115). Whether or not the CIA had actually infiltrated USAID or Save the Children is contested and unknown, but claims that the CIA manipulated a vaccination campaign for intel gathering seriously angered public health experts in the United States who worried this incident would cause a rise in local suspicion toward aid workers in other developing countries. In the tribal regions of Pakistan, there is already considerable hostility to vaccination campaigns, where some village imams claim that polio vaccines are a part of a Western plot to sterilize Pakistani Muslims. In January 2013, the deans of 12 public health schools wrote a letter to the Obama administration demanding that it cease using health workers in covert operations, citing the resurgence of polio in Pakistan—to which the CIA agreed to comply. Meanwhile, the Taliban has a death warrant out for Afridi. "He is now top of our list," Pakistan Taliban spokesperson Ehsanullah Ehsan said, gruesomely adding, "We will cut him into pieces when and where we manage to reach him" (Sayah 2012).

I present this example as it demonstrates how US counterterrorism priorities took precedence and also manipulated development project activities. This incident not only was damaging to the ability of any group to conduct public health campaigns in rural areas (consider that while he was an international healthcare worker, Dr. Afridi was also a local resident of the areas he worked in) but also increased stigma and suspicion around aid workers and development activity. In examining the capacity-building efforts of USAID in Afghanistan and Pakistan, I explore these nuances surrounding the donor challenge of development and the rise of transnational militancy. I do so to show that donor efforts to build capacity in these contexts are extremely delicate and are contingent upon building relationships and networks based on trust and the cultivation of a shared framework for development.

Case Background

The empirical basis for this project consists of an examination of USAID's work in Afghanistan and Pakistan. Why USAID? As a government development agency that has been in existence since the 1960s, USAID occupies a unique role in the international development space. It has existed and evolved through cycles of development discourse, from the initial thrust of modernization with industrialization and poverty reduction tactics to structural adjustment and global market integration. Following the Bretton Woods Agreement in 1944, the United States led the charge on international development and aid. As a US foreign policy tactic, aid was fashioned not only to combat the perceived threat of communism—to reduce poverty and facilitate the development of Third World states—but also to prevent the spread of communism and create foreign markets for the United States to increase capitalist production and the profitability of US-based corporations. Part of this process resulted in the establishment of three organizations in the 1950s that would eventually converge to unite as the USAID in 1961 (2017e). While now many countries have their own national development agencies, the scale of USAID's operations is unparalleled, in part due to the United States' investment in the agency as furthering foreign policy interests.

USAID is also uniquely situated in Afghanistan and Pakistan. During the Cold War and Soviet occupation of Afghanistan, USAID's activity provided a vantage point from which to deepen the understanding of the United States' relationship to Pakistan, its attempts to contain the spread of communism, and the nascent beginnings of a budding nexus of military and development activities. After September 11, 2001 (9/11), the United States conjured an international military coalition to hunt Osama bin Laden in the War on Terror and invaded Afghanistan. As a consequence, USAID and other development agencies embarked on the coordination of an unprecedented effort to reconstruct and develop the capacity of the Afghan state in a struggle to contain the spread of Islamic global militancy that continues to this day.

Most institutions of development present their approaches to Afghanistan and Pakistan separately, as distinct states, or as part of the Middle East or South Asian region. USAID designates Afghanistan and Pakistan together as its own special region, alongside Europe and Eurasia and the Middle East. USAID explicitly states that the countries are vital to US national security and cite the security and governance challenges in each country as reasons for sustained efforts in development. In this way, their institutional approach to Afghanistan and Pakistan is unique and explicitly linked to US foreign policy interests. While this blatantly political logic may not raise eyebrows among practitioners, it still raises important questions about the nature of projects of capacity as projects of development assistance are inextricably linked to foreign policy interests.

Afghanistan and Pakistan share fundamental challenges as states; their past, present, and future are inextricably linked. The colonial demarcation of their shared border by the British has fomented and complicated ethnic and tribal conflicts that inherently disrupt efforts to adapt to the territoriality of a state system. In the border regions, tribal affiliations and loyalties take precedence over ethnicity-based or nationalist sentiments unless threatened by foreign invasion, serving as a continual source of conflict and a hotbed of global insurgent activity. The internal state dynamics of each country are complex and volatile and impact the politics and internal conflict dynamics of the other. It has been over a century since Afghanistan has been spared from foreign military intervention, with central rule shifting largely among warring Pashtun and also Tajik tribes. The state of Pakistan, parts of which used to fall under undemarcated territory between British India and Afghanistan, has spent much of its existence negotiating the role of the military in the central government, with enduring Punjab dominance.

Pakistan has been relying on foreign aid to meet public expenditures and to build infrastructure and institutional capacity of the state since its inception (Shirazi et al. 2010, 853). With the exception of the period of Taliban rule in the 1990s, Afghanistan has remained dependent on donor regimes, replicating the cycle of aid dependence the country experienced during the Soviet period (Minkov and Smolynec 2010). Yet, from the Cold War and the Soviet occupation of Afghanistan to the US-led War on Terror after 9/11, the centralization and expansion of state authority has remained an elusive objective for the foreign invaders and donors seeking to manage threats in the region.

As an ideological battleground between communism and capitalism, Islamic fundamentalism and liberal democracy, Afghanistan and Pakistan have become home to transnational insurgency networks whose objectives are global in reach and whose agendas and activities over the years have involved collusion with donor agencies and organizations, foreign governments, as well as the central government and militaries of both countries. These relationships have developed convoluted networks and structures that provide incentives for opportunism and have resulted in pervasive and chronic systemic state corruption. Furthermore, the continuous situation of conflict, particularly during the Soviet occupation of Afghanistan, facilitated an Afghan refugee situation in Pakistan that strengthened and granted legitimacy to transnational networks and infrastructure circumventing the state, providing an ideal site from which insurgent groups can carry out agendas against the central governments of both countries and foreign governments. Donors that seek to build capacity for the purpose of expanding the reach and legitimacy of governing institutions face significant challenges in both Afghanistan and Pakistan.

Furthermore, the prevalence of transnational militant networks built upon Pashtunwali, a cultural and social code that places value on *autonomy*, *loyalty*, *hospitality*, and *revenge*, fundamentally challenges the attempted expansion and reach of centralized state institutions. The reality of transnational militancy, sustained by such groups as the Taliban and Haqqani Network, has led to a situation where development assistance efforts in many cases require partnering with state military or security forces, foreign governments, or local militias. This complicates development project efforts to build capacity and compromises the cultivation of "local ownership" of the very institutions that donors seek to build (Goodhand and Sedra 2010, 595). Often the poorest areas of the country, which are also those least affected by insurgency, are overlooked as candidate sites for programs, and the decisions to allocate development assistance—usually to areas that are prone to insurgency—are politically motivated. This increasing role of foreign militaries in development initiatives supports a "rescue industry," in which security becomes a prerequisite for development activities (Ryerson 2012, 68). In Chapter 5, I highlight the history of USAID's efforts in Afghanistan and Pakistan, situating foreign-led development during the Cold War alongside the transformation of Islamic and Marxist insurgencies into transnational militant networks of today, as well as the implications this example has for donors' capacity-building efforts.

These convoluted and polluted hierarchies of loyalty prevent centralized state institutions from gaining a foothold, commanding loyalty and establishing legitimacy in subnational environments. Particularly in Afghanistan (which harbors a greater degree of fragmentation than Pakistan), nationalist sentiments have historically only successfully been invoked to unify warring groups to dispel foreign invaders under the banner of Islam (though the face of this banner has not been consistent over time) (Blatt et al. 2009, 20; 25–6). However, this nationalism (if it can accurately be called that) in Afghanistan has historically been divorced from the centralization of institutions. A culture of autonomy is fundamental to tribal existence, and this point is key in framing the donor challenge of building the capacity of a central government to manage power dynamics and threats of transnational militancy. I unpack these messy issues in Chapter 5 to explore the core of the capacity problem facing donors, particularly in relation to states battling transnational militancy.

Methodology

This book exposes and deconstructs the transformation of the capacity project within the development discourse, illuminating the relationship between human rights, security, insurgency, terrorism, and the development of so-called fragile states. I take an inductive approach and carry out this task through a discursive institutional analysis of development projects, focusing on the USAID in Afghanistan and Pakistan as a case study. The agency's initiatives provide a wide-angled empirical wellspring of project and policy literature from which to examine the donor community's attempts to build capacity.

My objectives in this project are fourfold:

1. reveal the narratives behind the capacity project, as well as the forces behind the transformation of the concept in theory and in practice;
2. examine donor methodologies that set the framework for integrating "capacity development" into development projects;

3. contextualize the donor capacity project in states harboring transnational militant groups; and
4. examine the reach (and limits) of donor operation to build capacity within subnational spaces.

This discursive institutional analysis of capacity involves an examination of donor discourses. Donor discourse occurs within many spaces and scales of operation. Much discursive institutional analysis is used as an analytical tool to shed light on institutions and processes of institutionalization. Indeed, this project does shed light on the development institution itself and processes of knowledge production within development institutions. However, this type of discursive analysis focuses not merely on USAID as an institution or specific process of institutionalization but on how a concept gains salience both within and among a set of diverse cooperative institutions and stakeholders.

Through this process of gaining salience, the relationships, networks, and tensions of power become exposed at varying scales—in global agenda-setting processes, in implementing global agendas within institutional policies and methodologies, and in project implementation. Further, an examination of how a major development concept gains salience illuminates the distance (and overlap) between donor and recipient spaces of discourse and operation. A discursive deconstruction of capacity also reveals the variation in how major concepts are interpreted within institutional frameworks and the tension caused by this discursive diversity in how donors, military, and other stakeholders coordinate the implementation of programs in the development of so-called fragile states in situations of terrorism and insurgency.

The sample of documents I selected and reviewed is wide-ranging, but most pertain to USAID programming in Afghanistan and Pakistan between 1977 and 2017. I examined documents produced by USAID, private contractors, and consulting firms, as well as implementing partners on USAID projects and initiatives. My sample includes activity/project/program overviews, annual reports, assessments, audit reports, design and implementation plans, evaluations/final evaluation reports, periodic reports, reports to Congress, and strategic planning documents. My initial selection included 761 documents, 189 of which I physically copied and converted into PDF format from USAID's physical archives at the National Archives and Records Administration (NARA) of the United States, located at the University of Maryland, College Park, and 572 downloaded from the Development Experience Clearinghouse (DEC) online.

The DEC is "USAID's institutional memory, spanning over 50 years; including documents, images, video and audio materials (DEC 2017)." With the passage of ADS Chapter 540 in 2012, it became required for all documents and development assistance activity descriptions produced or funded by USAID to be submitted for inclusion in the DEC database, making it the largest online resource of USAID-funded technical and programmatic documentation (USAID 2012a). The DEC is housed under USAID's Knowledge Services Center. I reduced this sample further for analysis, and I discuss this process as well as the parameters of my selection throughout this book, particularly in Chapter 6 on USAID's statecraft in Afghanistan and Pakistan.

This lengthy process of document selection was largely one of familiarizing myself with the nature of the literature available, as well as the scope of programming and projects over the years of USAID activity. I proceeded in this way also to ensure that, first of all, in the course of my own analysis, I would be better able to situate the stylistic and formulaic attributes of USAID's institutional discourse surrounding the notions and usage of capacity and, secondly, that my selection of documents covered a representative range of projects. From the sample I collected, I further reduced my selection to roughly 200 documents for a more thorough review and coded 94 using NVivo textual analysis software. Nevertheless, given the nuanced nature of my research objectives, I conducted my analysis of this coded data manually. I created spreadsheets to track the selection of projects, as well as specific project *activities*, *assumptions* behind projects and activities, *justifications* for projects, *needs* identified (both donor and beneficiary), *impediments* to project success, *objectives*, *outcomes*, donor *agenda/strategy*, donor shortcomings, and recipient framing surrounding the concept of capacity in the project literature.

There are two important aspects to note about the documents I reviewed. First, the sample skews largely toward programming after 9/11. I rely heavily on bilateral assistance program evaluations and assessments for projects during the Soviet occupation of Afghanistan and more on evaluations and reports on specific projects post-2000. There are a few reasons for this. The sheer scope of assistance is much greater post-2000 than it was during the 1980s, paralleling the globalization of the architecture of the donor space and due to the (donor-identified) need for development in Afghanistan post-ISAF invasion in order to prevent a Taliban resurgence. US bilateral assistance to both Afghanistan and Pakistan largely waned in the 1990s, so projects during this period were mostly closing out by the mid-1990s, save for a few small-scale humanitarian programs.

Additionally, while I focused my collection of documents on specific projects, programs, and initiatives over the past forty years, I also reviewed evaluations of bilateral programming in both countries from the beginning of bilateral assistance in the 1950s (I cover most of this in Chapter 5). From 1950 until roughly 1990, evaluations of individual projects and programs were largely included in evaluations of bilateral programming as a whole, primarily because processes of producing monitoring and evaluation (M&E) reports on the progress and outcomes of individual projects were not as institutionalized in development practice as it is today. This, to some extent, has to do with both the transformation of the relationship between individual projects and bilateral assistance strategy and the transformation of development project methodologies. Especially between 1950 and 1990, individual projects were largely tied to multiyear bilateral assistance programs, with evaluations and assessments contracted to evaluate these multiyear bilateral assistance programs that involved multiple projects. These evaluations are hundreds of pages long, review specific projects, and examine the reasons behind successes and failures.

The second important aspect to note is that while I kept my selection of documents fairly even in terms of projects conducted in both Afghanistan and Pakistan, my analysis leans heavily toward Afghanistan post-9/11. Primarily, the task of development is much more significant and challenging in Afghanistan than it is in Pakistan (or most other countries in the world for that matter). I devote much of Chapter 5 to describing the context of global wars, tribal feuds, migration of militant fighters, and integration of foreign Islamic extremism into the Pashtun social fabric, as well as the institutionalization of covert transnational networks in the final decades of the twentieth century. I do not intend to introduce those points here, but make a mere mention to highlight the complexity of the situation. Perhaps most critically influencing my analysis is the fact that the militaries of the donor community defeated the existing Taliban government, making the task of development that much more challenging than in a state such as Pakistan, which actually has a functioning central government (regardless of the challenges this government faces). Donor coordination reached a new, unprecedented level following the US-led invasion of Afghanistan after 9/11. Donor coordination in Pakistan has never been to the extent that it has been in Afghanistan, because the central GOP has been a legitimate party to negotiations and agreement of bilateral assistance, whereas in Afghanistan, donors sought to build a government with which they would have this kind of engagement.

There are also some general limitations regarding the nature of the documents I examined. Donor processes of M&E generally fail to measure the long-term impact of development projects. Evaluations and audits are usually conducted within a year of programming. This time frame limits donors' framing of impact. This is in no small part a budget issue. Conducting preprogram assessments, audits, evaluations, and so on is a part of program budget, supplied by donor governments, and so there are budget cycle restrictions on the presentation of outcomes and findings. Periodic reports and annual reports will note successes and challenges to programs, but as these documents are produced for funders (institutions representing the various publics funding donor governments), the focus is usually to highlight outcomes or "achievements" in a manner that is almost completely without context outside of the project (e.g., presenting the number of participants in a training, or certificates awarded, or the number of specific types of office equipment provided) and does not necessarily indicate actual impact. In some of my analysis, I found that project documents were extremely vague or provided a very poor presentation of the challenges faced in implementation, with virtually no context of the outcomes. This is not to say that there are no critical evaluations but that the project literature has its limitations in explaining the reality surrounding the launching, implementation, and evaluation of projects. My attempts to contextualize this project literature in my own analysis involved a review of other types of literature—books and articles authored by scholars, policymakers, and practitioners, as well as military and news reports—to better gauge the impacts of projects and situate the project literature.

A final limitation of this research has to do with my examination of the evolving infrastructure of social relations within which the production and transformation of capacity is embedded. Chapter 3 explores and reveals shifts in how donors conceptualize capacity in policy and practice through an analysis of USAID literature over the past forty years. In Chapter 5, I explain the macro-historical Cold War context that defined USAID's initial development experiments in Afghanistan and Pakistan, culminating in the transformation of transnational militant networks that house the insurgencies of today. I provide this context largely through an examination of secondary data. I do this to situate my analysis of how USAID and other donors *apply* projects of capacity in states battling insurgencies that are steeped in an infrastructure of transnational networks. This infrastructure of networks is critical to fully understanding both the production and limitations of how donors conceptualize social transformation in environments they are far removed from—a key point of my project.

However, the shifts in how capacity is conceptualized and implemented are a result of the *ebb and flow* and a *shifting of forms* of power within and among the infrastructure of states, supranational organizations, multinational corporations, and other transnational actors and organizations. Obviously, as a bilateral development agency that is an extension of the US government, an examination of USAID's role must consider how the United States allocates funding and policy directives for development that are then carried out through USAID and also a consideration of how the United States both engages with and reacts to major historical events. Some of this context is provided throughout this project and within the longitudinal evaluations on US bilateral programming—but this is mostly specific to Afghanistan and Pakistan—which I argue represent a crossroads of global conflict. That said, a full analysis of these major shifts within USAID's policies and how they are embedded within other relations of power is an area for further research that would strengthen our overall understanding of the discursive shifts I identify throughout this project. These are the limits of the inductive approach.

Instead, in Chapter 2 I situate USAID's positioning more broadly within the development space. I define and describe the primary institutional actors within this space and explain some of the dynamics of operation. I do not, however, fully explain the transformations of the networks of power within this space over the past four decades. That said, taking an inductive analytical approach to institutional discourse as a method does reveal important points about the movement of power.

First, a discursive institutional analysis reveals the *actual* (and not just theorized) shifts in the conceptualization and implementation of concepts within policy and in practice. Sometimes these discursive shifts reveal changes in the composition and configuration of institutional actors involved in constructing agendas and how institutions (and which institutions) implement these agendas within strategic frameworks and in their work on the ground. This is significant as it displays important *transformations in the networks of power* surrounding both agenda-setting processes and how those agendas get implemented on the ground. I identify and trace roughly four macro-historical phases in which I situate the transformation of capacity as concept throughout this project (Figure 7.1 offers a visual summary of these phases). However, while illuminating shifts within discourse and institutional networks, discursive analysis does not *fully* explain the power dynamics and timing of these shifts or USAID's role and positioning throughout these shifts.

That said, the analysis of concepts within institutional discourse allows us to *identify and recognize* when shifts have occurred as either separate from or in alignment with other macro-historical shifts in networks of power. The inductive approach provides actual substance from which to conceptualize or challenge grand theories of power or speculation behind major shifts in geopolitical climate and infrastructure. This is especially true when considering the framing of relationships around capital—a limiting and shallow framework for approaching social transformation that is pervasive throughout scholarly, policy, and practitioner literature, which I expand upon in greater detail in Chapters 3,

4, and 6. Thus, as we continue to examine new impacts, networks, and forms of power, we must also consider the institutionalization of discourse, especially within policy, as a meaningful source from which to examine power.

Overview of Chapters

In Chapter 2, I highlight the influences of modernization on the development space and situate the emergence of capacity within modernization scholarship. As capacity has evolved and transformed through various epistemological frameworks, I elaborate on the tensions among actors behind the creation of development knowledge in terms of which actors and what forms of knowledge gain salience, which is inherently tied to notions of expertise among donors and in the development space. In particular, tensions among scholars and practitioners reveal an epistemological battle occurring among those producing knowledge on development. In this same vein, I define the variation of organizations and institutions that operate in the development space, highlighting primary areas of donor collaboration in which capacity gained salience and where international agendas for aid are set.

In Chapter 3, I trace the evolution of capacity in donor policy and practice through a review of institutional frameworks and project literature on capacity. I identify methodologies of capacity development and detail how USAID's framework has changed from one that was capital-centric and system-based for national development to one that is adapting performance-based models of private sector organizational growth to public sector institutions. Through this review, I find that capacity development has become ingrained within the institutional methodologies for development projects. Finally, a major weakness in the donor framework for capacity development is its understanding of the *enabling environment* context, which either enables or disables the building of the capacity of individuals and organizations supporting the cohesive national development efforts of the state. This is an issue and a weakness in how donors frame and attempt to cultivate relationships with recipients to build capacity, particularly in the twenty-first century as global security has increasingly become an issue of development.

Chapter 4 examines the relationship between capacity and the concept of fragility, couching the relationship between these two concepts of practice within a sociological framework for the capacity project, underscoring the centrality of the state to projects of capacity. The chapter highlights two cases of community-building programs as capacity building in cases situated in the Global North, explaining capacity as the construction of a habitus or as seen through a shifting of frames. Though these frameworks are limiting in the application of this particular case—the foreign-led development of two countries—they draw attention to three major themes of the capacity project: state power, community, and social capital. In juxtaposing these theoretical frameworks of the capacity project, I turn to the state as an entity that donors seek to build by constructing relationships and networks through projects, teasing out relevant narratives on state formation and how relationships and networks surrounding capital and coercion comprise the material basis of the state. I then relate the project of statebuilding and the cultivation of state capacity to the designation of fragility and rising influence of military frameworks for development, examining the role of the development agency (USAID) in counterinsurgency operations. The chapter concludes with an overview of USAID's frameworks for fragility and human rights-based approach (HRBA) for programming, considering the situation of counterinsurgency in fragile states. Ultimately, I argue that these discursive relationships are significant and serve to mask a broader donor-driven project to construct the state in the name of capacity building.

In Chapter 5, I explain the complexity of the situation in Afghanistan and Pakistan and the implications this complexity has with regard to the question of capacity and the spaces within which transnational militant networks operate. The question of building capacity "for what?" in both countries is intertwined with a multitude of hard-to-measure factors: the impact of partitioning, the population/tribal dynamics, as well as teasing out the effects of global conflict, waves of migration (refugee and Arab ideologues/fighters), covert relationships of state and militant groups, and foreign financing. I also draw attention to systems of capacity that already exist or have been built by militant groups such as the Haqqani Network, who essentially govern a transnational territory, provide services, run businesses, and build infrastructure. Development is but a piece of this story, and this context is necessary in order to situate capacity as a concept as well as to display its role (in development agendas) and meaning (in projects).

In Chapter 6, I expand on the development context of Afghanistan and Pakistan from the previous chapter, as well as the weaknesses I identify in the donor capacity development methodologies from Chapter 3, to examine the capacity project in practice in Afghanistan and Pakistan. Capacity development in states combating transnational militancy is ultimately a project of statebuilding by donors. I invoke and expand upon Monika Krause's (2014) discussion of the production of projects and the commodification of beneficiaries and James C. Scott's conception of statecraft, explaining USAID's attempts to gain social capital to build capacity as a general failure by donors to understand the sources of power at varying scales of operation. I identify four elements of donor statecraft based on my analysis of USAID projects, highlighting themes in development activities and objectives of donor projects that aim to build the capacity of the state. I also highlight how the apparent "shifts" in USAID's capacity development methodologies (which mirror shifts in the donor discourse) are theoretically insufficient to make sense of the empirical reality of development in Afghanistan and Pakistan.

Impact and Conclusion

This project is intended for scholars and practitioners alike, although the level of detail to which I expand upon issues of macro-historical context, transnational militancy, and the development–security nexus, as well as processes of donor knowledge production, agenda setting, and methodologies is likely beyond the appetite of those primarily concerned with setting immediate, actionable policy. In an attempt to reconcile theory and practice, this project will be the first of its kind to examine the evolution of a major development concept—that of capacity—as a project of development in the most challenging of contexts. Furthermore, this project contributes to a body of knowledge that employs an analysis of institutional discourse as a method for (1) understanding the emergence and production of salient topics within the donor discourse on development, (2) exploring the gaps between frameworks for programming and projects as they are implemented, and (3) bridging the scholar–practitioner divide in the field of international development by engaging with institutional literature surrounding policy and projects.

This project has important implications for those seeking to advance HRBAs to development, particularly within so-called fragile states and within situations of counter-insurgency. The transformation of capacity as a concept within institutional frameworks and projects demonstrates how the pervasiveness of an obscure, yet salient concept works in ways to also conflate and manipulate narratives for progress and relationships surrounding development. As we consider HRBAs within the context of global security concerns, it is imperative to acknowledge the way in which the usage of major concepts surrounding development problems clouds both the tensions and the opportunities for establishing clearer, coordinated, and collaborative approaches to development problems.

An important theme in this project surrounds notions of *ownership* and the distance between *spaces of operation* with regard to the development of capacity. Ownership, according to USAID reports, refers to many things—influence to sway or determine outcomes, ability to maintain a continued source of financing, taking responsibility for processes surrounding projects, demonstrating social empowerment and autonomy, and maintaining external perceptions of authenticity—to name only the most prominent. This question of ownership and guiding the management of society is at the heart of the challenge of development *and* of building (capacity), and of expanding the reach of centralized state institutions, particularly in states contending with threats of trans-national militancy. The scale to which donors are able to reach and penetrate commu-nities housing militant networks operating on subnational and transnational scales is a significant component of this ownership challenge of development processes. It is my intention that this research will inform those with a genuine interest in (1) taking on the ubiquitous concepts of the development discourse and to challenge (and take own-ership of) the failures of the donor community; (2) contributing to the scholarship on state formation processes, through the examination of a major bilateral development agency; (3) contributing to a constructive dialogue among scholars, practitioners, and policymakers on the relevance of the state model of centralized political structures in managing global threats and transnational militancy; and (4) working toward a more real-istic and thoughtful human rights-based framework from which we conceive of capacity.

Chapter Two

DEVELOPMENT AGENDAS AND DONOR SPACES: *HOW CAPACITY GAINED SALIENCE*

What is the space within which donors operate? And what is the scale of the space in which donors operate? These questions matter in considering how to situate the emergence of capacity as a problem of development and its evolution into a project of development encompassing many different issue areas. This situating involves not only an examination of the ideological environment from which the issue of capacity was born but also scrutiny into the transformation of the actual development space—the institutions and actors—that both produce and establish agendas and frameworks for projects and also serve as vessels for the implementation of the policies of donors, which in USAID's case is the US government.

Later on in this book, I trace the evolution of *transnational militant networks of resistance* in conjunction with the integration of military and development activities during the Cold War. While Western donors cultivated transnational humanitarian and military networks to contain the Soviet influence coming from Afghanistan, Arab financiers also capitalized on the construction of a transnational infrastructure to support radical Islamic elements of the Afghan struggle against the Soviets. This period of Western funding of transnational networks to bifurcate the communist threat coming from the state established and legitimized the relationships of transnational militant resistance that evolved into the present-day campaign of Global Jihad stemming from the region.

The space in which donors produce knowledge, collaborate, facilitate relationships, and create agendas transcends national boundaries of operation and encompasses a multitude of actors and organizations operating on various scales. Broadly speaking, the scale of donor operation is extensive, but it is also limited. Through access to Pakistani state officials and Mujahideen leaders, the scale of donor operation during the Cold War extended into Afghanistan without donors ever having to establish relationships with the Soviet-occupied central government or even most of the Mujahideen leaders. Pakistan's ISI, through their relationships with militant leaders, granted the Pakistani state access to subnational spaces and transnational scales of operation across Afghanistan and Pakistan. This access was previously also granted to European humanitarian groups working directly with Mujahideen leaders during the Soviet occupation of Afghanistan. Traditional Organisation for Economic Co-operation and Development's (OECD) Development Assistance Committee (DAC) donor institutions and agencies, such as the USAID, have been unable to develop sustainable relationships with operators in subnational and transnational spaces that harbor networks of resistance and militancy.

This chapter travels miles away from those spaces detailed in the following chapters to examine the space within which USAID and other traditional donors actually do operate, in part to highlight the distance between their scales of operation. To situate donor tactics to build state capacity and combat transnational militancy, I highlight the influences, tensions, and dynamics of the space of development within which donors operate. This chapter opens with a discussion of the impact of modernization on the space of development policy and practice. I situate the emergence of capacity within the scholarship of modernization theorists who shaped the spaces of development practice. As a by-product of their predatory notions of development, the concept of capacity emerged as a component of the political development of postcolonial states and as a donor scheme of systemization to strengthen political institutions in order to encourage the expansion of industrial and agricultural markets. As the missionary-esque rally cry of modernization gave way to the disoriented and fragmented discourses of globalization, capacity only became more salient as a practice and in the discourses among scholars, policy makers, practitioners, and within the project frameworks of donor institutions. In tracing the emergence of capacity within modernization theory, I identify the two main themes of capacity driving development practice: *systemization* and *performance* (of individuals, organizations, and institutions).

The second part of this chapter builds on this context and highlights the professional and epistemological disparities and tensions within notions of expertise on development and how these disparities have become institutionalized within the architectural foundation of donor spaces. There is a big difference between the expertise:

1. That private contractors claim on subject areas such as "good governance," as actionable, technical, and billable projects that follow institutional frameworks and meet governmental agendas;
2. That scholarly notions of what the promotion of "good governance" means in the context of global power dynamics; and
3. What locals actually perceive to be "good governance" when their leaders appear to be more accountable to donor purse strings than to local populations.

These are just a few examples. This variation in epistemological and professional subspaces of operation obscures the transformation of shallow and vague concepts, such as capacity, and prevents critical notions from impacting spaces of practice. Furthermore, the architecture of institutions and actors who claim ownership on the production processes of knowledge on what constitutes "development" operate in spaces that are vastly distanced from the local populations that are the subjects of this practice. This variation and tension of subspaces, as well as the distance in scales of operation between actors in donor spaces and those living in recipient states, is at the core of the challenge of building capacity in practice, particularly in states challenged and targeted by transnational militancy.

In this section, I also highlight the situation of "International Development Studies" (IDS) as an example of a *space of contention* where the tensions between a wide range of contributing actors play out in the production of knowledge that influences development practice. I address these dynamics of knowledge production, highlighting the work of critical development scholars who engage in an analysis of institutional discourses in the development space. I also engage in a discussion on the general exclusion of scholarly work in the production of knowledge used in spaces of practice, emphasizing scholarship that engages with institutional literature as a way to integrate critical scholarship in spaces of practice and transform relatively unchallenged notions of capitalist expansion in development strategy. This project, in part, aims to help fill this void in IDS scholarship through an application of critical frameworks to expose and address theoretical and practical shortcomings in capacity development methodologies employed by donors, with USAID as the primary example.

The final part of this chapter breaks down the development space as it relates to the processes surrounding the *setting of international agendas* on development in order to situate the growing salience of capacity. I carry out this task by (1) defining the primary donor systems in the development space, in order to contextualize and situate the case of USAID as an agency of practice, and (2) highlighting the evolving dynamics within and among the primary donor systems, in particular that of OECD/DAC member dominance in the agenda-setting discourse, and the role and situation of emerging actors in the development space. I identify five primary areas of international cooperation facilitated by global governing institutions such as the UN that have resulted in agendas and agreements throughout the latter half of the twentieth century that are global in scope:

1. Conflict and Human Rights
2. Trade and Global Finance
3. Military and Global Security
4. Environment and Global Sustainability
5. Global Development and Aid Effectiveness (the first four areas are embedded within, depoliticized, and culminate in this fifth area of cooperation)

I trace the construction of global agendas within these spaces of donor collaboration within which capacity has gained salience, leading to declarations and agreements calling for the creation of donor policy and institutional frameworks for implementation such as the USAID frameworks that I reviewed in the introductory chapter.

Modernization and the Birth of Development: Security, Human Rights, and the Discursive Emergence of Capacity

USAID's 50-year track record is an impressive experience base. The underlying development theory has evolved each decade, from modernization and Rostow's stages of economic growth, through Human Capital theory and the Basic Needs approach, to the neo-liberal Washington Consensus for policy-based conditionality in the 1990s, to the more recent focus on civil society, democracy, sustainable development, and country leadership. Each development theory informed and influenced USAID capacity development programs in each period. Programs shift between an emphasis on individual leadership and technical expertise, government institutions implementing 5-year plans, empowering the poorest of the poor, strengthening private enterprise, and empowering political balance through civil society. Although this has not produced "the" answer, it provides a rich vein of experience.—*USAID Country Systems Strengthening: Beyond Human and Organizational Capacity Development.* (Gillies and Alvarado 2012, 8)

How do theoretical concepts gain salience in spaces of practice? In considering the transformation and growing salience of a concept within a space of practice, one must first examine the context of the space from which it emerges. In this chapter, I highlight *dynamics and processes* of donor agenda-setting through an examination of the types of actors, organizations, and institutions involved in knowledge production, as well as of the *spaces* within which donors collaborate. I contend with diverse forms of literature: scholarly or academic, institutional, policy, and practitioner. How scholars engage with spaces of development practice has varied over time—from the heyday of modernization theorists-turned-political advisors to the relative exclusion of critical postmodern, postcolonial, and feminist scholarship from spaces of policy and practice. Within this context, capacity has gone from a tangential concept in modernization theories to a fully formed area of development practice. When considering the future of HRBA to development and global security, this context matters.

The influence of modernization on spaces of development practice cannot be ignored. The foundation of the donor space is built upon institutions that have carried out modernist notions of progress and assigned designations of value and distinction to the subjects or "beneficiaries" of their efforts. With the establishment of the Bretton Woods institutions, the institutionalization of global inequality took on an applied global form. This inequality was built into the very institutional configuration—the World Bank and International Monetary Fund (IMF)'s structures are based on membership subscriptions, both reinforcing first-world influence in setting institutional agendas and facilitating trade relationships that resulted in import dependency and a strengthening of first-world national currencies (McMichael 2005, 58). In this very brief section, I selectively highlight some of the modernist influences that have shaped the transformations of discourse within the development space, as well as shaped the frameworks behind capacity. This provides some important context for understanding the relationships between development agencies such as USAID and their beneficiaries and also emphasizes the distance in scales of operation between the processes that culminated in donor-driven theories of progress and beneficiary existence.

The ideological birth of development can be traced to the nineteenth century. Cowen and Shenton (1995) situate this birth as the *intentional establishment of a set of managerial tactics* (they call it a *trusteeship*) to cope with social disorder. From the beginning, *schemes of systemization* have been a hallmark of the discourse. Comte (1851) referred to a natural clashing between processes of progress and order, arguing that there existed natural laws of social evolution. Progress was unyielding and messy, and development was the proactive application of order to chaotic progress (Lenzer 1983 329, 341–42). Mill (1859) also highlights the problematic contradiction between progress, which he also refers to as "reform" and order, or "stability." He proposed the "stationary state" as a model of the way in which development could counteract the mayhem of progress (297). Durkheim (1893) focused on notions of social order, suggesting how "primitive" societies can "transition" into industrial capitalist societies. List (1856) proposed management by the state as an answer to the question of how to *do* development, to *achieve* progress. List argued that the state should take on the task of the "constructive development" of agrarian societies, which he theorized would lead to a universal harmony among nations (but only in Europe), and an eventual "civilizing of barbarian nationalities" (263). It is easy to see how grand schemes for development have been influenced and informed scholarly notions of state planning and development. The work of these nineteenth-century scholars set the stage for the modernist discourses of the twentieth century in conceiving of modes of progress. Echoes of List, in particular, are only too evident in development discourse surrounding Bretton Woods.

Scholars of the twentieth century, notably not only political scientists but also some economists, were instrumental to the institutionalization of modernization schemes as development. Particularly within the bipolar geopolitical climate of the Cold War, these scholars-turned-policy advisors furthered the institutionalization of global inequality and linear progress during the construction of the donor architecture that shaped the donor space. Rostow (1959) proposed *stages* of economic growth, Weber (1905) and Inkeles (1969) identify "rationality" as a core component of modernity, Parsons (1964) and Huntington (1971) deconstruct modern society and modernization processes, Lipset (1959) and later Huntington (1991) espouse economic development as a *condition* for democracy, and Wallerstein (1974) explained world-systems theory with a designation of "core" and "periphery"—these are but a few examples of the scholarship on notions of progress that set the discourse for development *and* established global distinctions among populations *within that discourse.*

As industrialized, modern First World nations assisted the postcolonial states on their path toward "progress," the ways of "traditional" societies, as well as any critical perspectives or animosity displayed toward modernization processes suddenly became obstacles to be overcome through modernization processes (Gilman 2004, 198). One of the MIT modernization scholars, Lucian Pye, even advocated for the role of the military in modernization processes, noting that it was the force most likely to provide "stability" and could help overcome the "psychological problems" associated with decolonization and modernization, as well as provide functional training for future *modernist societies* (Gilman 2004, 187). It is quite striking that notions of integrating military and development activity appear here in the theoretical speculation of what methods may bring about progress and what this might look like in practice. The way in which development is framed by Pye even during this period is foretelling of the integration of security and development activities in stabilization and counterinsurgency operations of today.

Yet, inherent within these frameworks stemming from political scientists and economists are also calls for the prioritization of human rights—claims that political and civil rights are prerequisites for economic development, based on the assumption that political and social conditions play a role in either assisting or impeding the rise of per capita income (Pritchard 1989, 329). Practitioner networks advocating for HRBAs to development today note that when the UN was established in 1945, its stated purposes meant that the organization was expected to apply HRBAs to all aspects of its work and claim that "development" has been ideologically misinterpreted by the superpowers during the Cold War, prioritizing certain rights over others (IHRN et al. 2008). In considering the dissonance between the foundational legacy of human rights narratives within modernist frameworks for development and the actual practice of development (particularly since human rights narratives serve to justify the establishment and legitimacy of global governance institutions such as the UN), discursive analyses are particularly relevant in the work of bridging the gaps between narratives and approaches of practice.

These narratives of progress also carried forth an undertone of altruism, a moral obligation of countries with advanced industrial economies to "help" underdeveloped societies. This sentiment was so pervasive that it even became part of the national narrative of the United States. An important example of this is the United States President Truman's historic 1949 inaugural speech and call for a "bold new program for *making the benefits* of *our scientific advances* and *industrial progress available* for the *improvement* and *growth* of *underdeveloped areas*" (Truman 1949, Esteva 1987, 7, italics my own). This speech helped to lay the groundwork for the reinforcement power of the political narrative in development projects, ingraining divisive designations of developing societies, solidifying the Western role as savior, and justifying the need for intervention. Sachs (1992) cites Truman's speech extensively as fundamental to the key concepts of the development discourse postwar, which in and of itself is illuminating in understanding processes of development knowledge production. A full discussion of these theoretical foundations of the donor space is beyond the scope of this project, but acknowledging this context is critical in sourcing the transformation of capacity as a development concept, as well as the contradictions between security and rights narratives within frameworks for development. So where did "capacity" actually come from?

In the scholarship of the nineteenth and most of the twentieth centuries, there are scant references to "capacity" as a stand-alone concept. This is because it is a concept that is only given substance in the context of political frameworks for systems of power, in particular regarding markets and capital. Durkheim (1893) provides vague references to capacity as it relates to state and markets, referring to "productive capacity" (12), "sovereign capacity" (52), "capacity of common consciousness to steer individuals in a collective direction" (105), remarking notably that "capacity for the means of production" is one way in which the development of the state is limited. Marx references individual human capacity for labor (1986 [1867]), labor-power as a collective capacity itself (1986 [1875]), productive capacity (1986 [1867]), the transformation of personal capacity into objective wealth (1986 [1858]), and capacity as excess of the capitalists' ability to dispose of their own labor (1986 [1858]). Shannon (1958) makes a connection between "capacity for self-government" as being related to "level of development." These references provide some basic notions of how capacity was being conceptualized at various scales—individual, organizational, and state—which notably is not that different from those in present-day capacity development methodologies. Additionally, we already see here a relationship between "capacity" and *capital*, *labor*, and *wealth*, even in the context of the state.

The term "capacity building" first started appearing in applied literature in the 1950s and 1960s, referring to the provision of technical assistance to build the self-help abilities of rural communities through training, research, and counterpart relationships (Smillie 2001, 8). While the term itself was not popularized in the international development discourse at this time, some practitioners assert that capacity-building activities were actually taking place, citing the building of public sector institutions during the 1950s as an example of such activity (Morgan 1994, 14). The modernization theorists/political advisors of MIT sought to engage these community development methods as a tactic to guarantee village compliance with the dictates of the center, ultimately adapting tactics intended to preserve the traditions of local communities with the modernization of traditional societies through the centralization of institutions (Immerwahr 2015, 62–63). This is significant—as from the very beginning the application of the capacity-building project model to international development demonstrates a very real tension between the need to dictate compliance (which is on a basic level, particularly in "fragile" states—an issue of security) and preserving the traditions of local communities (ensuring their rights).

During this postwar period until the financial crisis of the 1970s, the development of postcolonial societies carried forth the agenda of modernization. This agenda was marked by the intertwining of "economic growth" and "political development" as conjoined processes to ensure the centralization of the state—the site of political development that would ensure and enable the management of economic growth. Parsons (1964) actually references "capacity" in the context of the ability of *systems* to *adapt*:

> Adaptation should mean ... the capacity of a living system. This capacity includes an active concern with mastery ... the ability to change the environment to meet the needs of the system ... the ability to survive in the face of its unalterable features ... the capacity to cope with broad ranges of environmental factors, through adjustment (and)/or active control ... the capacity to cope ... with uncertainty (and) instability. (340)

Parsons's definition begins to get at some notion of the role of the *environment* not only as a factor of capacity but also as a *site or object* to be managed and controlled through state planning schemes. References to capacity evolved within this modernist discourse on political development, institutions, and systems. Throughout these references, there are hints of rights and security narratives with capacity within the conceptualization of the political system of the state.

Lipset (1958) argued that *"legitimacy* involves the capacity of a political system to engender and maintain the belief that existing political institutions are the most appropriate or proper ones for the society ... (which) affects its capacity to survive ... crises" (86). While Lipset wrote of democracy, it is notable because this reference to capacity alludes to the relationship between state and society—of the system to manage society's perception of it. He later references the importance of *capacity of political systems* regarding maintaining *political moderation* (ibid., 97). In both references, capacity refers to the ability of the state, in one instance as a *measure of legitimacy* and in the other instance regarding *ability to maintain order*—though arguably, the two are related—in both cases framing the relationship between the duty-bearers and the rights-holders. Lucian Pye

(1965) also extensively references various forms of capacity within the context of political development:

1. ... capacity of "political system" (Pye 1965, italics my own: 1)
2. ... capacity of "authoritative government structures" (1)
3. "... capacity of a country to equip itself with *such modern cultural artifacts* as political parties, civil and rational administrations, and legislative bodies" (6) (*note the reference to processes of systemization*[1])
4. "... capacity to maintain certain kinds of public order, to mobilize resources for a specific range of collective enterprises, and to make and uphold effectively types of international commitments" (7)
5. "... capacity for purposeful and orderly change" (9)
6. "... capacity to control social change ... to maintain order" (10)
7. "the capacity to claim resources and to mobilize and allocate them ... (in a way that does not threaten) popular support" (10)
8. "... capacity of political system. In a sense capacity is related to the outputs of a political system and the extent to which the political system can affect the rest of the society and economy" (12)
9. "Capacity is also closely associated to governmental performance and the conditions which affect such performance" (12)
10. "Capacity ... the sheer magnitude, scope and scale of political and government performance" (12)
11. "... capacity means effectiveness and efficiency in the execution of public policy" (12)
12. "... capacity is related to rationality in administration and a secular orientation toward policy" (12)
13. "Pressure for greater equality (as a) challenge (to) ... the capacity of the system" (12)
14. "... the problems of capacity are generally related to the performance[2] of the authoritative structures of government ..." (13)

There is an inherent assumption within this language that society has a *need* to be managed, for the betterment of society, and that the capacity of centralized institutions is fundamental to order and progress. To be clear, this work does not argue that there is not a need to manage society, particularly given the global risks facing humanity. However, this is a language that assumes an uneasy relationship between the duty-bearers and the rights-holders, presuming a shared vision for progress between the two, except for when the two conflict, which is when the duty-bearers must exercise the "capacity to control social change and maintain order" (10). In this vision, the cultivation of state capacity

---

1. Author's note.
2. Interestingly, present-day capacity development methodologies of donor institutions employ performance-based models of organizational growth. I expand upon this further in Chapter 3, section four. In Pye's definition of "political development," we see numerous references to issues of "government performance."

is first and foremost for the purpose of order and control, with the assurance of human rights as a secondary objective, presumably one that should be inherent within the state-propelled vision for progress.

In this breakdown of definitions, Pye effectively instantiates capacity as a component of political development. These definitions also largely reflect the concerns that defined the nineteenth-century discourse regarding the reconciliation of *order* and *progress*—the capacity of the state or system of governance to keep order, maintain stability, manage change, and perform "tasks" of governance consistent with the modern understanding of the state. We see with Pye's definitions a demonstration of the salience of two major themes of development which the advancement of capacity has served to depoliticize: *performance* of public sector institutions and *systemization* for state planning purposes. These themes remain at the core of development practice and donor attempts to build capacity.

Expertise and the Tensions of Development Knowledge Production

In this section, I highlight the professional and epistemological disparities and tensions as they relate to the knowledge production processes of the development space. Concepts such as capacity development, which has become salient in the global discourse and a major component of international agendas, have resulted from various processes of knowledge production. The *practice* of development and the production of knowledge that seeks to deconstruct, evaluate, and guide this practice are in some ways both distinct and overlapping professional spaces. A large part of the growing salience and institutionalization of concepts within development involves a consideration of these dynamics. These processes of knowledge production—both technical and theoretical—provide the skeleton and the flesh of development. Furthermore, the production of capacity and the process of its gaining salience in discourse, knowledge, agendas, and frameworks demonstrate the manifestation of professional and epistemological tensions[3] between the spaces within which scholars and practitioners operate.

The production of knowledge on development takes place in many different spaces—within universities, think tanks, development agencies and institutions, in the private sector, international nongovernmental organizations (INGOs), individual actors, among others. I distinguish primarily between the space of *development practice* and *scholarship*, the convergence of which has morphed into a field of scholar-practitioners producing knowledge in IDS. A wide range of dynamics influence knowledge production processes (professional and epistemological, as well as of politics and power—on national, international, and transnational scales). I highlight some of these tensions through a discussion on the field of IDS, which emerged from convergences between scholars and practitioners of the development space. In this project, I contend mostly with the literature produced from the space of development practice, in part to highlight its distance from the dynamics of the realities within which beneficiaries operate. The production of projects that carry

---

3. Particularly, in methodological frameworks, writing style and format, terminology, and so on.

out the subsequent capacity development methodologies reveals similar, but different tensions surrounding notions of distinction as they relate to the processes and objectives of development projects, which I discuss in the following chapter.

As noted in the previous section and the introduction, political scientists and economists largely drove forward the initial notions of capacity as relating to political development (systemization and performance, also later social capital) and markets (capital). There is no one profile or background that defines the present-day "scholar" of development— university academics, independent researchers, government advisors and officials, NGO activists, community workers, policy makers, corporate economists, and even independent filmmakers have all contributed to scholarship on development. However, having such a wide array of actors contributing to scholarship in a field changes the very notion of what scholarship is and what constitutes legitimate knowledge. Institutional literature does not focus explicitly on their methods of modernization and notions of "under-development," but instead have espoused popular notions of capitalist progress relatively unquestioningly. This lack of distinction among actors contributing to the "scholarship" of IDS and processes of knowledge production institutionalizes the depoliticization of development work, particularly in practitioner spaces.

Traditionally, the scholar writes in his or her own voice and, above all, seeks to com-municate the objective truth and reality of the topic, the object, or whatever "thing" it is they seek to understand and shed light on. The question of the purpose of scholarship and the role of the scholar is one that is too broad to be addressed in this project, but the one important distinction about the scholar I seek to highlight is on the subject of their affiliations, resources, and positioning regarding the subject matter. Above all, the scholar operates from a position of relative autonomy, their research *open-ended*, embarking on projects of inquiry that are not as constrained by their affiliations. The institution and even the practitioner conduct research that is constrained and subject to political strategy, national budget constraints, and public opinion, resulting in, as Gilbert Rist notes, a religious-like faith in capitalist progress (Rist 2002).

Donor institutions and agencies have missions, visions, and make value statements justifying their work. The World Bank sets out to "end extreme poverty" and "promote shared prosperity" (World Bank 2017a). In addition to the "eradication of poverty," the United Nations Development Programme (UNDP) works toward the "reduction of inequalities and exclusion" (UNDP 2017a). The DAC has the mandate to "pro-mote development cooperation to contribute to sustainable development … pro-poor economic growth and poverty reduction" (OECD 2017). In this same vein, USAID's stated mission is to "end extreme poverty and promote resilient, democratic societies while advancing our security and prosperity" (USAID 2017a). Just about all of these institutions and agencies also have nominally committed to taking HRBAs to develop-ment as well, linking these objectives of eradicating poverty, exclusion, vulnerability, and conflict to the violation of human rights.

The literature produced by a development agency, financial lending institution (FLI), or supra-governing body, while sometimes authored by one individual, is meant to represent and support the voice, mission, and values of the organization. Therefore, in the produc-tion of institutional literature, there exists a level of accountability that is interwoven with the politics of the relationships that enable the institution's work and resources. These include relationships with other actors—other donor entities, beneficiaries, exogenous beneficiaries, and, of course, with governments. Institutional literature—annual reports, assessments, planning documents, evaluations, so on—generally follows a standardized format developed to *brand* the literature as a product of the institution and is intended to display progress toward the institutional objectives. Institutional literature, while distinct from scholarship, is written in a format that denotes expertise, effectively claiming ownership of knowledge on practice-based concepts such as capacity building.[4]

Furthermore, the contributions of critical scholars are largely ignored not only from spaces of practice but also from within their own fields, in part due to the marginalized nature of discourse analysis research. Presently, these spaces of practice and scholarship operate in relatively distinct spheres and it is in the production of scholarship on development that they converge. Yet this space is dominated by practitioners and scholars whose work remains marginalized within their own disciplines. Dimitri Della Faille, a Canadian sociologist, highlights the work of development "discourse analysts," who he argues share a rejection of mainstream analysis of underdevelopment but remain marginalized in their own fields. Della Faille also notes that these scholars may not even brand themselves as "discourse analysts" but perhaps as "critical development scholars" (Della Faille 2011, 217). Unfortunately, these disagreements in methodological branding contribute to the marginalization of academic scholars as producers of knowledge on development. While discursive distinctions matter, debates on discursive designations that occur within the already narrow tunnels of academe only serve to further fog their voices from penetrating practitioner-dominated spaces, where these designations are not as hotly contested.

A number of the authors Della Faille reviews discuss these notions of expertise in spaces of practice. In particular, James Ferguson's (1994) work on what he calls the "anti-politics machine" of the bureaucratization and depoliticization of development in Lesotho examines World Bank reports, portraying development literature as belonging to a genre of its own. In Della Faille's review of Ferguson's work on development literature, he notes, "it (the literature) has the appearance of scientific research, written by highly trained specialists, using graphs and statistics, quoting other research, making use of complex concepts, yet has no connection to reality, which it does not attempt to represent truthfully" (Della Faille 2011, 255). Della Faille notes that Ferguson (1994) portrays development literature as "creative writing" that exists for the purpose of justifying the existence of development agencies and the use of government money (Della Faille 2011, 230). Krause (2014) makes a similar argument with the "Good Project," asserting that projects of humanitarian relief are actually a form of production within a field and that agencies must produce "good projects" in order to justify and continue their existence. Krause does not conduct a discursive analysis per se, but the notions of *production* to justify *continued production* (of projects) within spaces of development practice are consistent here.

---

4. These claims of knowledge ownership by donors also create tensions with beneficiaries in project implementation, though that is the subject matter of the following chapter.

There is no shortage of literature by critical development scholars decrying the production of knowledge by institutions and practitioners in the development space. Escobar (1988) defines this "professionalization" as the politics of truth construction, which in the context of development was the application of knowledge in existing disciplines to Third World problems (430). In a study on the framing of military aid in Egypt as "developing the private sector and pluralism," Mitchell (2002) decries the development discourse as "wish(ing) to present itself as a detached centre of rationality and intelligence ... (with) The relationship between West and non-West ... constructed (as) ... The West possess(ing) the expertise, technology and management skills that the non-West is lacking" (156). This seeming objectivity is evident throughout the discourse—in terminological labels such as "developed," "underdeveloped," "developing," "fragile," "failed," "beneficiary," in so-called measurements of wealth and forms of governance, and especially in the literature stressing the need to build "capacity."

Escobar also highlights how the reality of the so-called Third World is constructed by economists, planners, nutritionists, and demographers, among other experts (Escobar 1992, Escobar 1994, and see also Illitch 1977 and Mitchell 2002). These "development experts" who work in institutional environments as "cosmopolitan intellectuals" not only are framed as having the knowledge and expertise to designate "underdeveloped" societies and define "cultures of poverty" but are also *morally obligated* to "help the poor" and to facilitate a modernized construction of human progress (Lewis 1966, Hannerz 1990, Klitgaard 1990). Watts (1995) portrays development actors as "scribes," oversee(ing) "the production and reproduction of knowledge and practices which purport to measure well-being and poverty, national growth and standards of living, who negotiate the re-entry of national economies into the world market through the science of adjustment, who attempt to 'mobilize' and 'animate' peasants in the name of basic needs" (56).

Other scholars address the issue of how institutional literature substantiates both policy agendas and projects from a framework that legitimizes need and justifies intervention. Tristen Naylor, an international relations scholar at the London School of Economics, who also is the managing director at a public and corporate diplomacy advisory firm, published an article on the use of power and pity[5] in the international development discourse specifically on narratives surrounding Afghanistan. Naylor notes that when determining need, classifications matter: "Categories like 'developed' and 'developing' or contextual descriptors like 'stable' and 'insecure,' temporal imperatives like 'dire' and 'pressing,' classifications like 'vulnerable or marginalized' are discursive predicates that have naturalized and stabilized in general understandings of the world" (Naylor 2011, 183). Naylor goes on to note that vulnerability becomes technocratic, suffering becomes measured and qualified, making intervention not only possible but also justified (Naylor 2011, 185–86). Naylor's work is in line with and references Boltanski's *Distant Suffering*, particularly in how the spectator's general identification with those who suffer translates into meriting political intervention based on the sentiment of pity (Boltanski 1999, 155–56).

---

5. In the spirit of Hannah Arendt's "Politics of Pity" (1965).

One notable difference about my work from other discourse analysts is that I do not place my focus on revealing discursive constructions of need. That is not to say that the discursive construction of the *situation* of development (e.g., "fragility") or presentation of the *context* within which beneficiaries (and needs) are portrayed in agendas, frameworks, and projects is irrelevant, but rather that this is one aspect of understanding the usage and function of practice-based concepts such as capacity. This scholarship on how the broad range of actors tied to the donor community discursively construct the "reality" of development and the "needs" of beneficiaries is useful and relevant in exposing the production (and reproduction) of relationships of global inequality. However, the task of deconstructing the production of practice-based concepts such as capacity involves more of a focus on defining the relationships and epistemological frameworks surrounding the *discursive processes of distinction* that result in the production of concepts that gain salience in spaces of practice.

I expand upon this (see Figure 2.1) by providing a visual representation of the various professional and epistemological frameworks at play in the production of knowledge in development practice. Particularly, in the spaces of development practice (and IDS) the epistemological and professional positionings of actors influence the production of knowledge and also notions of expertise that are employed by institutions. It is for this reason that literature produced by donor institutions and exogenous beneficiaries[6] of development projects on the broader concepts of development, such as capacity building, must not be viewed as presenting facts about what capacity is or is not but as representative of underlying shifts in policy that determine the ideological course of donor behavior and development practice. Broad concepts written about as technical subject matter, such as capacity building, actually serve as textual mechanisms that further institutionalize and legitimize the expertise of political institutions, including its ideological underpinnings, and contribute to the depoliticization of the development work.

The *scholar* of "international development," most notably scholars of traditional disciplines such as sociology, anthropology, economics, or political science, largely occupies an outside role in this present-day development space. The dismissiveness the traditional scholar has faced from spaces of practice and private industry is not to be ignored. I distinguish here between the scholar-practitioner (whose primary career is scholarship) and the practitioner-scholar (whose primary career is as a practitioner). The writing of some on both sides influences policy, but typically scholar-practitioners place less focus on having their work impact policy. Practitioner-scholars—individuals whose educational training may be in a practitioner-oriented field such as Strategic Studies, Development Economics, Global Finance, Peacebuilding or Dispute Resolution, to name a few examples—are those who have spent their careers as practitioners and may also produce literature that straddles the boundary between academic scholarship and practitioner literature. In Figure 2.1, I present both the primary professional affiliations and the epistemological frameworks of actors within the applied and scholarly fields of development.

---

6. Further detail on the exogenous beneficiary in the next section.

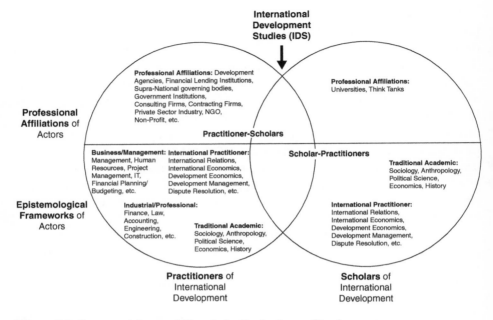

Figure 2.1 Spaces and Actors of Knowledge Production on Development.

The literature produced by practitioners, overall, is not very useful for understanding the shifting meanings of capacity that has taken place since its initial conception. The practitioner-scholar may write from their personal experience working for an agency or contractor but will write independently of their institution from a position of relative autonomy. The position of autonomy is what they have in common with the traditional scholar. However, much of the practitioner literature on capacity-building is the result of task forces affiliated with institutions or agencies of development determining where there is a need in terms of development knowledge. Capacity development is one of these areas.

The practitioner literature appears more scholarly in nature than the institutional literature (e.g., Brinkerhoff 2007, Eade 1997, Morgan 1994, Smillie 2001, etc.). It identifies trends in the development work of capacity building, presents questions and criticisms, and offers suggestions for ways to improve the work—however, this literature does not contextualize the work and issues of building capacity from a macro-sociohistorical lens, nor does it address questions regarding the macro-systemic framework that justifies the building of capacity. The focus of literature produced by IDS practitioner-scholars is generally narrowly *issue-* and *activity* oriented, intended for an audience of practitioners, and thus fairly devoid or uncritical of any complex theoretical frameworks that would serve to situate the issues or activities at hand. Providing a theoretical framework or macro-historical context is not integral to the objectives of this literature, as the literature is intended to improve the work and processes of the practice.

This is demonstrated in the practitioner literature on capacity building (ibid.). The very terms of "capacity building" and "capacity development" are concepts that emerged from spaces of practice, which I provide a greater explanation of in the following chapters. Naylor (2011) actually identifies the narrative of "capacity development" as one of two dominant narratives[7] that characterize and justify the activities that are the product of institutionalization processes of the development practice. Naylor argues that "capacity development" is a focus common to the activities of all actors, and especially so in relation to the issues of aid effectiveness and cooperation among actors (Naylor 2011, 187–90). I address and confirm this assertion later in section three of this chapter in my review of international agendas on development.

There is a divide among development and policy practitioners and academic analysts that exists in many spaces of practice. However, in the case of international development I argue this is in large part due to the *institutionalization of anti-intellectualism* in spaces of practice that is in the business of reducing notions of liberal capitalist progress to the production of isolated *issue-oriented technical knowledge*, and *claims ownership on the expertise* of the definitions of progress it puts forth. Furthermore, the academic discourse on development has largely dealt with macro-scale issues regarding the *utility* and *productive or destructive impact* of aid, begging theoretical questions about the work of development that are hardly addressed in institutional literature.

While there are those who cross over between the space of development work and the academic realm, those who are more entrenched on either side rarely engage with the other. "Practitioners often do not read what scholars write, considering it all too often lengthy, opaque, heavily footnoted, and unconcerned with operational implications ... Scholars, on the other hand, read little that is written by practitioners and even less that is written for practitioners" (Nair 2013, 634). If there is a battle between practitioners and academics on ownership of knowledge and expertise regarding notions of progress, then the institutional infrastructure of the development apparatus largely dominates in practice, begging the question of the role and strategy of academic scholars in development.

Della Faille's (2011) work identifies two primary objectives of scholarship in international development: (1) ideational and interventionist and (2) descriptive, reflective, and informative. The first type of writing has ambitions of social change, reform, and radical transformation in international relations and global trade, while the second type generally tends to be in regard to the nature of developing, sometimes bringing to light previously unacknowledged or marginal voices. This work attempts to be a combination of both by exposing the textual application and mechanisms of capacity building, a broad concept in practice. Empirical and descriptive analysis on the "work" of development and the functions of discursive labels that command and direct the discourse of the practice is an area in which academic scholars may make objective claims regarding the knowledge production that could impact its direction without pandering to the political interests of policy makers and institutional actors within the donor space.

---

7. The second narrative Naylor identifies is in the characterization of development projects as responses to locally identified needs—framing development activities in terms of their strengths as organizations—to support infrastructure, economic development, and government capacity (Naylor 2011, 190).

Traditional Donor Systems and the Development Space

In the last section, I reviewed some of the professional and epistemological tensions that exist in the production of knowledge on development. In this section, I define the various forms of institutions and actors in spaces of practice. The first task in situating the role of capacity in international development is actually defining the environment from which it has emerged. This is an important task because spaces of practice are made up of various actors, organizations, and institutions that all make claims in their work about what capacity is, why it is important, and how to build it. These claims are made in global conferences that set international agendas, in institutional methodological frameworks for programming, in the creation of policy and in policy analysis, in institutional reports and country development plans, as well as in project and policy evaluations and assessments. These distinctions matter in how the positioning of the author presents and portrays *knowledge*, especially in establishing who claims the title of "expert," in determining who designates need, and ultimately who the beneficiaries and recipients are. The relationship between the composition and dynamics of actors points to a framework for defining not only what capacity is but also what capacity is for.

The international development space is made up of a diverse array of actors—each individual and organization with its own framework for understanding and explaining the work of development. It is a space comprised of practitioners, policy makers, journalists, private sector actors, government officials, subject matter experts, peacebuilders, mediators, reformers and activists, academics, and countless others. It is a space where international FLIs, development agencies, humanitarian INGOs, global and regional governing bodies and regulatory institutions, as well as national governments interface and work together in the name of development. The composition of the individuals and actors operating in the development space denotes a complexity that hinders the attempt to understand the role of capacity in the agendas and frameworks of development.

Tracing the sources of transformation of capacity building within the development space is in direct relation to the line of inquiry regarding the rise of development as a profession and industry within this space, essentially composed of subfields and other industries displayed in Figure 2.1. The process of professionalization is also a process of institutionalization of the traditional donor architecture, which reproduces relationships of inequality that impact the dynamics of the field itself and the objectives and activities of those working within it. The development space, and convergence of professions within it, did not evolve from a single framework, and the relationships surrounding development certainly do not exist in isolation of history.

The present-day dynamics of the field were set immediately following World War II. There were significant shifts in the international order during this time. The victors of the Global North organized and established a cooperative structure and political and economic arrangement for international development and aid. The Bretton Woods Agreement established a landmark system for global monetary and exchange rate management, setting the US dollar as the global currency—equivalent to the gold standard, and resulting in the founding of the IMF and the World Bank (McMichael 2012, 58–60).

The United Nations also came into being in 1945 following the devastation of World War II with one central mission: the maintenance of international peace and security (UN Charter, Chapter 1). For the first time, altruism took global form. The Universal Declaration of Human Rights boldly declared all lives were equal, sparking a global debate about intervention as the stage was being set for institutionalizing forms of intervention in postcolonial states, in the name of human rights and development.

Concurrently, the US Marshall Plan marked funds in order to rebuild and develop a war-ravaged Europe, setting in motion a historical initiative of foreign aid and cooperation larger in scope than any other in history (McMichael 2012, 57–58). The Marshall Plan marked the first significant international development initiative, as a form of soft power that assuaged the foreign policy anxieties of the United States, fresh from a war to prevent the spread of fascism. While the Soviet Union was an ally during the war, the potential spread of Communism was a very real policy concern. During this time, the Organization for European Economic Cooperation (OEEC), the parent organization of the OECD, was formed in order to help administer the Marshall Plan aid (OECD History 2017).

The Marshall Plan set important precedents for international aid. Processes of building national capitalist economies that would be active participants in an international marketplace were provided as a framework for development. Conditions were set by donors for beneficiaries in order to receive aid, and the dissemination of aid was determined not solely by need but also by political leaning and ally relationships during the war. Aid was explicitly established as a political mechanism to prevent the global spread of communist ideology. The seeds for a field of international development were thus firmly rooted in a policy of establishing international stability and preventing the rise of a competing global ideology.

Development assistance has changed much since the postwar period when aid was coming primarily from governments and a few large multilateral institutions, and the sources and flow of resources are difficult to track. Since there are so many actors in the development space, situating USAID's objectives, activities, and relationships within this complex web is integral to making any substantive claims regarding its significance and impact on the transformation of capacity. I have created Figure 2.2 to visually display sources of aid in what I call Donor Systems in the Development Space.

This figure shows where donors and actors of aid fall in terms of resource flows and the agenda-setting processes for projects of development. The primary distinction among the flow of donor aid is between Official Development Assistance (ODA), which is sourced from national governments, and non-ODA aid, which is private. While the majority of ODA comes from DAC member countries, which are located predominantly in the Global North, the presence and contribution of non-DAC countries have been increasing since the 1990s and commanding more attention as nontraditional actors have become increasingly involved in global aid. This dynamic I address more fully later but is not the focus of this section. Additionally, while the actors under the private/non-ODA aid umbrella operate with their own agendas for aid, there are no overarching collaborative agenda-setting processes for private aid and thus not as impactful as the development agenda set by ODA actors.

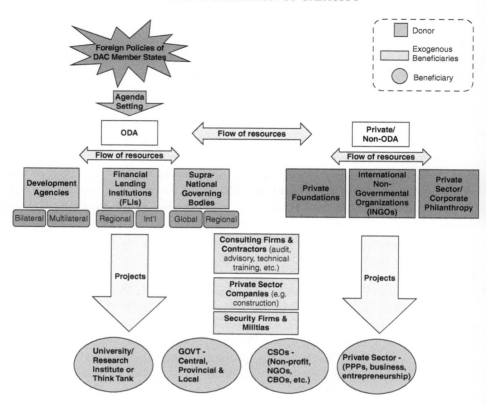

Figure 2.2 Donor Systems in the Development Space.

The historical role and influence of DAC is significant, as its members determine the course of the ODA agenda through international meetings to discuss the major development issues of the time. DAC was originally DAG, the Development Assistance Group, established in 1960 under the OEEC as a forum for consultations among aid donors on assistance to less-developed countries (OECD 2006a). The DAC currently has 30 member states, almost all located in the Global North. Membership is only open to states, though the World Bank, IMF, and UNDP participate as observers. The DAC has the mandate to "… promote development co-operation and other policies so as to contribute to sustainable development, including pro-poor economic growth, poverty reduction, improvement of living standards in developing countries, and a future in which no country will depend on aid" (OECD 2017).

The DAC member states, displayed in the map in Figure 2.3 (Australian Department of Foreign Affairs and Trade 2017), play an important role in ODA—they set the agenda of aid and their member countries fund development agencies, FLIs, and supra-national governing bodies—the primary types of ODA donors. Below, I provide brief definitions and overviews of these donors, as well as their scales of operation within the donor space.

Figure 2.3 OECD/DAC Member States.

Development Agencies

The development agency umbrella includes primarily not only bilateral agencies such as USAID, DFID, SIDA, or JICA but also some multilateral development agencies, such as the World Health Organization and the World Food Programme. It is important here to note that the relationship between bilateral national development agencies, such as USAID, and the donor country's ministry of foreign affairs or equivalent department of state varies widely by country, and this relationship shifts over time along with the evolving dynamics of government and transitions in leadership. Some agencies are actually departments within a government ministry and only engage in very limited or issue-specific programming, while others have evolved out of and/or have been folded back into a government ministry (i.e., Israel's MASHAV, Brazil's ABC, Canada's CIDA, Luxembourg's LuxDev, etc.). Furthermore, the reach and scope of most bilateral national development agencies are very limited. Among the category of bilateral development agencies, USAID is distinct and arguably the most significant institutional actor given that its contribution toward development assistance consistently surpasses every other bilateral development agency. Since development agencies are inherently tied to donor governments, the scope of their agendas and scales of operation is limited to that of the donor government, though sometimes potentially extended through collaboration with other types of organizations.

Regarding multilateral development agencies, I make an intentional distinction between development agencies and FLIs, which are also multilateral. Multilateral development agencies do not provide loans for projects or initiatives, and traditionally they do not overtly address questions of governance or the political or economic policy and structure of a recipient country. I include UN-established multilateral development agencies in this category because these are agencies tasked with specific missions for international aid or development, such as the eradication of hunger or gender equality and women's empowerment. While bilateral agencies such as USAID have some overtly political aims, those aims have generally been within the framework of an explicitly development-oriented agenda. I also distinguish between UN agencies, with specific issue-oriented missions, and the UN itself, which has a mission of international peace and security and operates as a supranational governing body.

Financial Lending Institutions

FLIs are multilateral international and regional institutions that provide loans for projects and provide a policy framework for monetary policy in developing countries. FLIs are both multilateral and bilateral. The most notable FLIs are not only the World Bank and the IMF but also regional development banks such as the European Investment Bank, Islamic Development Bank (IsDB), African Development Bank (AfDB), Asian Development Bank (ADB), and the Inter-American Development Bank (IADB). FLIs are the largest source of development finance in the world, typically lending between $30 and $40 billion to low- and middle-income countries each year (BiC 2017). There is much controversy about the impact FLIs actually have on the development of countries.

While loans to finance investment projects and policy reforms in developing countries are intended to reduce poverty and encourage economic development, many have caused widespread environmental and social damage on natural habitats, displaced communities, and indigenous peoples.

The governance structure of FLIs varies. The World Bank Group (WBG) and IMF operate under the UN system, and both have boards of governors who determine the policy of the institutions. Governors come primarily from one professional background: typically ministers of finance or of development or governors of a country's central bank, representing each member country. The governors at the bank also delegate specific duties to boards of directors, a group of 25 executive directors (EDs) who are in charge of all operations within their respective agencies. These EDs are either elected or directly appointed by the governors, and voting power is determined by the subscription percentage of each member country. The United States has the highest percentage of voting power at both the WBG and the IMF, with 15–20 percent of directors having voting share (World Bank 2017b, IMF 2017a).

Supranational Governing Bodies

These bodies set international and regional policy and agendas for political and economic cooperation and development. Some of these bodies have subarms devoted specifically to development or humanitarian aid work, but this is not their overarching purpose even though development activities comprise important components of their missions. Supranational governing bodies seek to define global issues and also espouse an architecture for the political and economic governance of states that is intended to prevent conflict, encourage participation in the global economy, and maintain the stability of the current international system.

Examples of supranational governing bodies include the UN, the EU, OECD, the World Trade Organization (WTO), as well as other regional trade and governance organizations. I divided these bodies into two main categories, those concerned with markets and trade and those concerned with governance, human rights, and global security. There is collaboration among these bodies at the highest level in the coordination and agenda-setting of policy that determines the direction of international relations. They facilitate international conferences that set agendas such as the Millennium Development Goals (MDGs) or the 2030 Sustainable Development Agenda, which are then carried out by development agencies, international FLIs and also impacts the donor focus and activities of non-ODA donors.

Private / Non-ODA Aid

Private/non-ODA aid consists of aid coming from foundations, INGOs, and the private sector. These donors are typically unaffiliated with governments and do not face the same bureaucratic hurdles that ODA does but maintain fewer mechanisms and processes for accountability and is therefore less trackable. Private aid has increased substantially since the 1990s, far surpassing ODA in sheer amount of resources allocated for aid.

A recent estimate by Hudson Institute's Index of Global Philanthropy and Remittances shows private aid as being more than five times the amount of ODA (Hudson Institute 2016). That said, the issues of gaps in data and the lack of methodological standardization of private development assistance present a significant challenge in understanding the reach and impact of this aid. This means that any understanding we have of impact is largely incomplete and requires further research and evaluation.

Of the private aid that has been tracked, the majority is sourced from the United States, and much of this aid does not go to "least developed nations" but rather to "emerging developing countries" like China, India, South Africa, or Brazil or to global programs designed to address specific issues such as battling the spread of diseases (Pratt et al. 2012). Private aid donors operate largely outside of the space of government bureaucracy, but they are also not immune from politics. While there is no centralized data tracking for private aid, some organizations are making attempts to track this economic engagement for politically strategic purposes. The Hudson Institute, which I referenced earlier, is a nonprofit founded in 1961 to "promote American leadership and global engagement for a secure, free, and prosperous future by … help(ing to) manage strategic transitions to the future through interdisciplinary studies" (Hudson Institute 2018). The institute has been publishing an index since 2006 to try and measure private and public foreign aid. Notably, the institute was founded by Herman Khan, a US political strategist known for applying game theory to situations of nuclear war and theorizing postnuclear reality (Schwartz 1991, 7).

The Institute's 2016 report showed that of US economic engagement with developing countries, US ODA accounts for only 9 percent, with philanthropy (12 percent), remittances (30 percent), and private capital flows or foreign direct investment (49 percent) accounting for 91 percent of US economic engagement (Hudson Institute 2016, 9). That said, while private capital flows and remittances may be a component of the economic development of a country, I do not count these categories as part of "foreign aid," since they are not explicitly tied to ODA and their objectives may lie outside of the framework of development practice. However, these figures do place development assistance into the broader context of overall financial flows from donor countries, adding a new element to contextualize the impact of aid and, importantly, recipient impressions of donors.

While private aid does not play much of a role in setting international development agendas, and private aid actors are uncoordinated and decentralized, the issues they choose to focus on both shed light on trends within aid (since private aid actors often have to work with ODA actors and institutions) and also display themes in the development discourse. Private aid is sole-issue oriented, with agendas ranging from addressing one or two specific issues such as maternal health or water and sanitation to general and vaguely defined objectives such as challenging inequality, achieving social justice, and advancing human achievement.

That said, while it is relevant to acknowledge the growing role of private aid in development assistance, it will not play an important role in this particular project. While private aid surpasses ODA aid overall, it accounts for only a small portion of development assistance in Afghanistan and Pakistan—never rising above over 1 percent of assistance in Afghanistan, and reaching 6 percent at its peak in Pakistan (average is 1 percent) during the years that private aid has been tracked (UNOCHA 2017).

Exogenous Beneficiaries

Exogenous beneficiaries of aid consist of the consulting firms, private sector companies, and contractors whose business exists due to the situation of development. Their mere existence demonstrates how the professionalization of the development practice has enabled the flourishing of subindustries that exist for the purpose of gaining contracts from ODA agencies and institutions. The exogenous beneficiaries of aid neutralize the political activities of development as technical and discrete matters. Their work is essentially specialized in building the architecture of the development space's vision of progress and to profit from the wreckage of societies ravaged by war and international conflict.

Consulting firms and private sector companies—most based in the United States—such as Checci Consulting, Chemonics Inc., John Snow Incorporated, Tetra Tech, Inc., DAI, Aecom, Deloitte, KPMG, PWC, and so on—all claim expertise in areas such as "infrastructure development," "human rights and governance," "economic development," "rule of law and security," "training and technical assistance," "capacity building for local institutions," "supply chain solutions," "program design, implementation and management," and so on. These companies are the exogenous beneficiaries of development assistance and bid for multimillion dollar contracts to implement development projects for ODA donors such as USAID. They claim technical expertise on development and benefit from the depoliticizing of aid and situations of conflict. Additionally, security contractors such as Blackwater have raked in millions from the US government in assisting with the implementation of development infrastructure projects, with US contractors winning the lion's share of contracts, subsequently stirring up controversy over issues of accountability and incident reporting (Center for Public Integrity 2014, Orlina 2016, USAID 2010, Economist 2017). While these subindustries of aid have no explicit role in designating aid agendas, their existence and the controversies surrounding the mismanagement of ODA have further legitimized criticisms of development aid and impacted DAC member dynamics, particularly US dominance, among donors.

In this section, I have provided an overview of the primary actors and organizations within the development space, as well as the kind of issues they engage with. Within this project I contend primarily with the work and literature of traditional OECD/DAC donors, as that is the space within which USAID primarily operates, and in the context of Afghanistan and Pakistan this cadre of donors dictates the trajectory of development. The scope of OECD/DAC donor operation is global, but the actual scale of their operation does not reach subnational spaces—a point elaborated upon in Chapters 5 and 6. In the following section, I build upon this framework of primary players and discuss dynamics and spaces of international coordination and how these spaces have contributed to a globalizing of the donor architecture within the development space. It is within the spaces of international collaboration and agenda-setting in which the concept of capacity has gained salience.

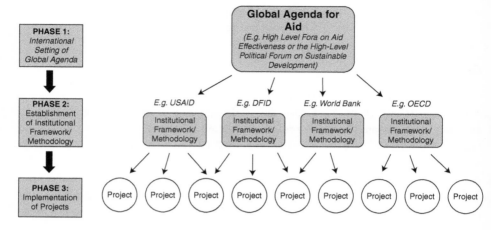

Figure 2.4 Discursive Phases of Development Concepts.

The Globalization of the Donor Architecture and the Salient Obscurity of Capacity

Dynamics in the development space have changed over the years as the world has become increasingly globalized and new spaces for international collaboration have emerged, entrenching donor relationships and making the architecture of these relationships more complex. It is from within these spaces that capacity has gained traction as a practitioner-based concept of development, pervasive in global agendas and institutional frameworks. In the past 30 years, the donor space has also become saturated with nontraditional actors (so-called emerging donor states from the Global South as well as private aid). While these actors are increasingly gaining access to traditional donor spaces of collaboration and agenda-setting, OECD/DAC member states still dominate.

There are three discursive phases from which to trace the emergence and evolution of capacity: (1) in global agendas for aid, (2) the subsequent institutional frameworks that are developed to carry out this agenda, and (3) in the actual projects of development (Figure 2.4). This section contends with phase one and the way in which capacity became salient in the international agenda for aid (an analysis of phases two and three— USAID's frameworks for capacity in policy frameworks, methodologies for practice, and projects—is addressed in the following chapters).

Throughout the post-World War II period, the aid architecture was largely dominated by the OECD/DAC member states of the Global North. However, during the Cold War, the Soviet Union offered an alternative model to development, with Afghanistan serving as the testing grounds for an ideological battle between capitalist democracy and Soviet communist development agendas. When the bipolar world of the Cold War gave way, there was little to prevent the architecture of a Western-dominated donor system from becoming increasingly globalized in agenda-setting processes, institutionalizing an interdependency among states committed to global development.

Coming off the implosion of the communist model, the capitalist countries of the Global North pushed forth a template for development during the 1990s that touted a model of Western democratic governance and trade liberalization for the globalization of markets as the method by which to integrate so-called developing countries into the global economic order. The establishment of the WTO in 1995 with the Marrakesh Agreement advanced the institutional infrastructure, pushing forth this vision of development. This period of time during the 1990s through the early 2000s saw an increase in multilateral cooperation and a shift in discourse away from a narrative of *aid for development* to *aid for trade*, which placed a further emphasis on the importance of development cooperation and financing (Connolly and Sicard 2012, Iorio 2012, 5).

Consequently, at the turn of the twenty-first century, the UN convened the largest ever gathering of world leaders to redefine its role and vision. These meetings culminated in the establishment of an ambitious 15-year agenda for the new century: the MDGs. In order to advance this agenda and address issues of coordination and effective aid management, the OECD organized four conferences known as the High Level Fora on Aid effectiveness: Rome (2002), Paris (2005), Accra (2008), and Busan (2011). The purpose of these conferences was to build "consensus on goals and funding for international cooperation ... (and to set) rules for the conduct of cooperation" (Grimm et al. 2009, 5). However, global development and aid coordination are historically newer areas for international collaboration. I assert that this space is in part a culmination of the globalization of other primary issue areas for international collaboration. Historically, states and institutions convene for the purpose of addressing identified global issues or risks, such as climate change, mass violence, and to establish systems of agreement and cooperation.

I have identified five primary areas that have generated international cooperation on a global scale: (1) Conflict and Human Rights, (2) Trade and Global Finance, (3) Military and Global Security, (4) Environment and Global Sustainability, and (5) Global Development and Aid Effectiveness. Global Development and Aid Effectiveness is the newest area of cooperation that has, to a large extent, been a result of convergence over the four other primary issue areas, as well as a consequence of the significant increase in actors and non-DAC/OECD donors operating in the development space, causing a need for coordination. Traditional spaces for donor collaboration (e.g., World Bank, OECD annual meetings, etc.) excluded many of the nontraditional actors involved in development work from participation and placed more focus on the direction of the institutions rather than the direction of global development. Additionally, issues of human rights, conflict, sustainability, and the integration of markets into a global economy are embedded within agendas for development, with the goal that as countries "develop" and "catch up," they will have the ability to manage risks and issues within their own societies, thus global issues will decrease and become more manageable (Iorio 2012, 5). This has not been the case in practice, but it is the underlying drive behind much of the development agenda.

The primary spaces for donor collaboration, planning, and agenda-setting are international meetings, workshops, and conferences, usually resulting in declarations, agendas, and agreements for cooperation (Figure 2.5). It is outside the aim of this project to provide a comprehensive review of these spaces and the literature ratifying and legalizing international cooperative efforts. However, trends in international cooperation

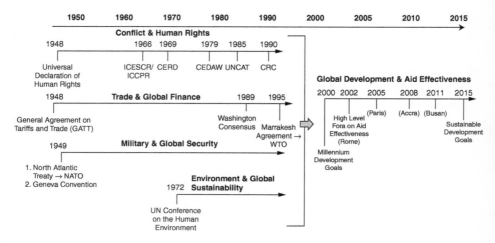

Figure 2.5 Primary Areas of Donor Collaboration.

shed light on the transformation of capacity within the development discourse as capacity is a pervasive issue appearing throughout the five primary areas of international cooperation.

The OECD High Level Fora conferences showcased some landmark firsts in the spaces of donor coordination. The first conference in Rome was attended by 150 delegates including representatives from recipient country governments who were included for the first time as equals to OECD donor governments and multilateral organizations. A few years later in Paris, 500 delegates attended, including Brazil, India, and China as observers among other "middle-income countries." Busan was the largest of the conferences, with 3,000 participants including actors from the private sector, philanthropic foundations, civil society, and think tanks. These meetings resulted in declarations and agendas for action, cementing the importance of capacity development as a core component of all international development activities.

While capacity as a concept has been in the development literature since the 1970s, it became notably so in the 1990s, when the issue of the capacity of partners came to the forefront of the development dialogue. However, capacity building really began gaining traction as a priority of the international development agenda in the 2000s alongside the focus on global development and aid effectiveness, and that is the primary focus of this section. The importance of focusing on building capacity in developing nations is littered throughout the core MDG documents, the agendas and frameworks resulting from the High Level Fora on Aid Effectiveness, and the more recent 2015 sustainable development goals (SDGs). Capacity development has become a core component of development strategies on national, regional, and international levels, displaying an institutionalization of the concept within development agendas.

The frameworks developed by development agencies, FLIs, and even the supranational governing bodies are largely influenced by the agendas and agreements resulting from international meetings, which have a ripple effect on how each body incorporates capacity into its own policy and agenda. There is a great difference, for example, between

UNDP frameworks on capacity development and how the WTO frames capacity as part of its agenda on *aid for trade*.

The first High Level Fora meeting resulted in the Rome Declaration, which pointed to capacity-building activities as integral to development effectiveness (OECD 2003). Supporting the capacity development of partner countries is further emphasized in the Paris Declaration's five principles to make aid more effective (OECD 2008b). The Paris Declaration also defines the role of donors and partner countries in capacity development: "Capacity development is the responsibility of partner countries, with donors playing a *support* role ... Partner countries commit to integrate specific capacity strengthening objectives in national development strategies, and Donors commit to ... aligning their analytic and financial support with partners' capacity development objectives and strategies" (OECD 2008c).

The Accra Agenda also emphasized the importance of capacity development for partner countries, in order to "build the ability of countries to manage their own futures" (OECD 2008a) through identifying on six capacity development priorities: (1) civil society and private sector, (2) national, sector, and thematic strategies, (3) technical cooperation, (4) enabling environment—addressing systemic impediments, (5) country systems, and (6) fragile situations. This Agenda spawned a partnership between the DAC, the Southern-led Capacity Development alliance, and the Learning Network for Capacity Development (LenCD) to implement these priority areas.

Subsequent international conferences and workshops were organized to implement the High Level Fora agendas, specifically on the issue of capacity development. Building upon the Accra Agenda, the Bonn Workshop on Capacity Development in 2008 identified six areas of action supporting two major premises: (1) that capacity development is critical for *sustainable development* and *national ownership* and (2) that capacity development is primarily a *developing country responsibility* (OECD 2008d). I pause here to draw attention to a theme in the transformation of capacity that I expand upon further in my analysis of institutional methodologies to build capacity: the placement by donors of the responsibility of *development processes* (specifically to build capacity) on the recipient. This donor shirking of responsibility is intended to make processes of development appear less didactic and to present development as a process that is actually owned and driven by beneficiaries and not by donor purse strings. Even so, determining what playing a "supportive" role actually means in the context of granting beneficiaries ownership has presented donors with significant challenges.

The Bogota High Level Meeting in 2010, as well as the Cairo Consensus and Bangkok Call to Action on Technical Cooperation for Capacity Development in 2011 further support the premises of the 2008 Bonn Workshop. The latter (Bangkok Call to Action) argues for the need to reform the practices of "technical cooperation," which is largely what accounts for capacity development activity. The statement builds upon the Accra Agenda and the "Cairo Consensus," calling for the "meaningful exist(ence)" of ownership in technical cooperation activities, with built-in quality-assurance mechanisms, characterized by a diversity of actors and targeting all levels of capacity (human capital, institution-building and business processes, as well as the enabling environment) (LenCD 2011a, LenCD 2011b, OECD 2010a). Here we see that theoretically, operating from a framework of inclusivity with enhanced monitoring mechanisms in place should enable the cultivation of capacity in beneficiaries at multiple levels (individual, organizational, and environmental).

The last High Level Fora conference resulted in the Busan Partnership Agreement for Effective Development Cooperation, which highlighted the necessity of capacity development for sustainable development, although by this time there had already been several international conferences specifically on capacity development. At Busan, the thematic session on capacity development highlighted both crucial aspects for successful capacity development and the next steps (OECD 2011, 105–6).

The thematic session highlighted the following three aspects in particular:

1. Ownership, political commitment, and sustained political engagement and leadership are critical for effective capacity development.
2. A strong national vision and focusing capacity development on clear national priorities, as well as the role of nonstate actors in the development process.
3. Highlighting knowledge exchange and peer learning as powerful mechanisms for capacity development when undertaken with engagement over a period of time and are mutual in nature.

In terms of next steps, the session called for "results-focused capacity development as the explicit focus of country led compacts" and noted a need for a more organized and explicit approach to capturing and sharing donor knowledge on capacity development. "Capacity development is not just an add-on, an afterthought, but requires an engaged political leadership to put capacity development at the centre of country-led development priorities" (OECD 2011, 105–6). Here we see a call for further institutionalization of capacity development within the very architecture of donor spaces. I do not expand further on forms of institutionalization to share capacity development knowledge among donor institutions as it is outside the confines of this already expansive project, but an analysis of the offices and positions created and established by the various donor institutions is a topic for analysis that would further reveal the institutionalization of global agendas for practice.

Notably, calls for capacity are also littered across human rights-based strategies for development, even though there is no comprehensive donor framework for HRBA to development. Institutions and agencies of development such as the USAID began to develop strategic frameworks for HRBA to development following the 2003 UN Common Understanding framework, which called for all development cooperation to "contribute to the development of the *capacities* of duty-bearers to meet their obligations and … towards strengthening the *capacities* of rights-holders to make their claims" (UNSDG 2003, 2–3). While there has been forward movement on the part of development agencies and institutions to establish institutional arms and strategic frameworks to advance HRBA within development programming, this implementation is haphazard and relatively uncoordinated (Evans 2009). I elaborate upon this issue in Chapter 4.

In this section, I provide an introduction to capacity development in the global agendas for aid. I also highlight a few examples of ways in which the various regional or international task forces and working groups comprised of representatives from states, donor institutions, and the like have taken agendas that call for capacity development and sought to define them further. The important point to take away from tracing this process is that the international agendas resulting from the MDGs, the High Level Fora on Aid Effectiveness, and the subsequent conferences, meetings, and workshops are *reinforced* by donor state institutional policy frameworks. In this way, capacity development has become integrated into the architecture of development governance at national, regional, and global levels. In the next chapter, I break down this integration further in strategic frameworks, tracing the transformation of capacity development methodologies from OECD and UNDP to USAID.

Summary and Conclusion

Donors, practitioners, and recipients working toward the objective of development operate within a diversity of spaces with varying scales of operation and reach. In order to understand the challenges to the development of Afghanistan and Pakistan, or any state for that matter, it is important to consider the influences that have shaped these spaces within which actors and organizations operate as well as the dynamics that define the processes of that space. In this chapter I have focused on the space within which donors operate, tracing the influence of modernization framework for development and highlighting the institutionalization of global inequality within the donor institutions that set the architecture for ODA. While this project primarily contends with the manifest-ation of capacity in practice, we see that important notions surrounding the concept—its relation to *performance* and *systemization* processes as an element of the development of political institutions—emerged from within the scholarship that shaped the founding of the development space. These lurking notions of *performance* and *systemization* processes behind capacity also carried forth subrequisites for modernization—an agenda for the universal protection of human rights amidst growing concerns over global security in the bipolar reality of a Cold War world.

As there is an increasing diversity of actors operating within the development spaces of practice, tensions from the wide range of epistemological and professional frameworks impact processes of knowledge production and what is considered to be legitimate knowledge. The professionalization of development has in some ways led to the "trained incapacity" of those who dominate the field of practice. With the example of the field of IDS, we see how this has resulted in the marginalization of critical scholarship and traditional scholars. Furthermore, these tensions obscure dis-cursive constructions of designations and classifications surrounding recipients of aid within the defining narratives of donor discourses and obfuscate the influences behind concepts such as capacity.

Among those actors, organizations, and institutions operating within the development space, the OECD/DAC traditional system of donors hold the most weight in deter-mining the international agenda on aid, producing a discourse within which capacity development has been defined and identified as integral to the achievement of develop-ment goals. Further, as these *supranational* governing bodies have facilitated international spaces for collaboration, they produce agendas that call for institutions and agencies of development to establish frameworks, tool kits, and resources in order to integrate capacity development into their work. As this project seeks clarity on these institutional frameworks and methodologies of practice, the following chapter examines more closely the example of USAID's framework for capacity in policy and practice.

Chapter Three

CAPACITY IN DEVELOPMENT POLICY AND PRACTICE: *THE QUEST FOR PERFORMANCE EXCELLENCE IN THE GOVERNANCE OF DISABLING ENVIRONMENTS*

This project examines the transformation of the concept of capacity from roughly the last decade of the Cold War until the present (1977–2017)—a span of 40 years. In unpacking this transformation of capacity within the policies and practices of donors, perhaps the most striking aspect upon review of these frameworks is that one might not have any idea of where we are in history *or* of the context surrounding the relationships between donors and recipients or "beneficiaries" when reading them. There are, of course, references to containing the Soviet threat, developing the emerging markets of post-Soviet countries, and now references to violent extremism and terror—but we do not see these references in capacity development methodology or the conceptual design of projects. This very methodology for change—*to build capacity*—is seemingly devoid of any deeper engagement with the societies targeted for transformation. Capacity development both as a method and in practice is distinct from the identification of capacity (or lack thereof) as a source of state stability and fragility.

The *processes* and *sites* of capacity development are largely abstract even as there are significant shifts in the macro-historical context as well as in project design to assess, monitor, and evaluate programs. As Roxborough (2012) remarks upon review of the US Field Army Manual FM 3-07 on stabilization, in spite of calls for the necessity of the analysis of local social and cultural environments in design and execution to cultivate local ownership, there is little actual instruction on how to do so. I argue that this is in part due to a "trained incapacity" of the donor, inhibiting the donor's ability to recognize the distance between agenda-setting elites and kinship-based groups in subnational spaces. Instead, donors conceptualize capacity in discrete units—usually skills based (e.g., management, entrepreneurship, technical, or vocational-based skills) and designed to build relationships to expand the operational reach of the state. These so-called beneficiaries of capacity development are hoped to be the carriers of networks into subnational spaces, cultivating local linkages with the state and, by extension, with the broader system of state, regional, and global markets.

Thorstein Veblen (1914) coined the term "trained incapacity" in the context of the problems in modern industrial organizations, problematizing the housing of business schools within universities and their training of individuals as resulting in the *widening of fields of ignorance* as they become increasingly "effective within their speciality" (Veblen

1918, 152). He argues that humans are inherently "goal oriented" and, when combined with the narrowing pecuniary interests of business education training, lead to an actual trained incapacity in the individual to consider the broader impact of business practices. Kenneth Burke (1935) argues that Veblen's concept of trained incapacity actually "properly applies to all men" and not just those in business, relating it to John Dewey's concept of "occupational psychosis" or, as Dewey put it, "pronounced character of the mind" (Wais 2005).

I extend this argument as applying to those within donor spaces whose training, work (*and "occupational psychosis"*), and dialogues lead to the production of agendas for the capacity development of so-called fragile states. Development specialists, state managers, human rights activists, and military strategists all suffer from this trained incapacity. The cadres of international elites from both the Global North and South, educated within Western institutions in professionalized disciplines and then socialized within the professional environments of international institutions, fundamentally fail to recognize the inadequacies of their own trainings.[1] The same applies to the military strategists grappling with how to incorporate capacity development into counterinsurgency strategy to achieve the goal of governance. Roxborough (2012) identifies this gap in understanding and highlights the need for sociological analysis in conceiving of cultivating the local ownership of projects. I expand upon the substance of this conceptual gap in this chapter on capacity in policy in practice and in the following chapter through an examination of capacity development as *statecraft*.

As noted in the previous chapter, the idea of capacity emerged from within a nexus of political scholarship that propelled nineteenth-century Western notions of progress and institutionalized an infrastructure that enabled a cadre of professionals and specialists to drive forward a development machine of modernization. As the strength of the modernization theorist's rally cry gave way to the disoriented and fragmented discourses of globalization, capacity only became more salient in the dialogues among scholars, policy makers, and practitioners and the frameworks of donor institutions. It is notable that this salience took place during a time when the grand plans of modernization were being challenged, activities of security and military were increasingly becoming integrated with development, and those theorizing on development—from scholars to practitioners—sought to identify and propose alternative sites of development aside from the state.

In the previous chapter, I examined agenda-setting processes within the donor space that led to the depoliticization of development and salience of capacity. In considering this salience, I examine institutional frameworks on capacity development throughout this chapter, with a focus on USAID. Institutional frameworks on capacity development are outlined and furthered in many forms: working papers, concept notes, reports and evaluations, tool kits and resource libraries, as well as policy and strategy documents.

---

1. Also true for academics, whose critical scholarship on models of growth and progress falls on deaf ears within the distance worlds of practice. It is merely a reality of positioning and vocation.

I begin this chapter with a review of OECD, UNDP, and the European Commission (EC) strategic frameworks on capacity. I include these frameworks here because they: (1) are the most developed among donors, (2) actually address the distinction between capacity building and development, and (3) are heavily cited by other institutions, such as the USAID (many of which do not provide basic definitions). The OECD, UNDP, and EC frameworks thus provide a basis from which to contextualize the frameworks developed by the other institutions and agencies of development, such as USAID.

Capacity: Basic Definitions and Attributes

In order to conceptualize any form of policy from which to develop methodological frameworks for the actual practice of building capacity, it is obviously necessary to start with the issue of definitions. I highlight those provided by the OECD, UNDP, and the EC in more recent years to provide the context of the present before turning to USAID's usage and methodologies of capacity. I focus in particular on the distinctions between capacity building and capacity development as well as the framing of the "enabling environment" as a *site* of donor capacity initiatives. Throughout this project I do not personally distinguish between capacity development and capacity building, using them somewhat interchangeably throughout as I broadly contend with usage and definitions covering the span of over half a century. Presently, there is no actual consensus in practice or among donors between the usages of capacity development and capacity building. That said, since the turn of the twenty-first century, the usage of capacity *development* is far more pervasive in international donor agendas than capacity *building*. I address this slight discursive shift moving forward, but first I present the definitions from the EC, OECD, and UNDP in Figure 3.1.

There are two important components to the distinction between capacity building and capacity development and these are reinforced in the methodologies on capacity development in other donor frameworks. Most donors converge toward a general consensus in frameworks on capacity development in recognizing that:[2] (1) determinants of capacity development are *not merely technical* and are *explicitly related to politics and governance* (e.g., strong political commitment, favorable incentive systems, government-wide reform); (2) capacity development is *multidimensional* and goes *beyond knowledge and skill transfer* at the individual level to consider organizations, institutions, networks, and the systems in which they are embedded[3] (OECD 2010b, 4). Upon addressing the matter of definitions and themes in the shift in usage to capacity development, I highlight a few important attributes surrounding the concept of capacity itself as they are defined in institutional frameworks:

---

2. Italics are my own.
3. Some donors place strategic focus on capacity at the organizational level and an open systems approach (United States, UK, Japan, EU, Denmark, Switzerland) recognizing organizations, networks, and institutions as the main unit of analysis, viewing organizations as open systems that interrelate through networks and influenced by external context.

Definitions of Capacity, Capacity Building, and Capacity Development

- **EC definition of "capacity"**—*Refers to OECD 2006b definition*, followed by "Capacity is an attribute of people, individual organisations and groups of organisations. Capacity is shaped by, adapting to and reacting to external factors and actors, but it is not something external—it is internal to people, organisations and groups or systems of organisations" (EC 2010).

- **EC definition of "capacity development"**—*Refers to OECD 2006b definition*; CD can entail change of knowledge, skills, work processes, tools, systems, authority patterns, management style, etc. Like learning, *CD takes place in people or organisations*, and, *like learning, it cannot be forced upon them*. People and organisations can have strong or weak incentives to change, develop and learn. It can come from the environment or from internal factors—but eventually the change is an internal process that has to happen in the people or organisations changing.

- **OECD definition of "capacity"**—*the ability of people, organizations and society as a whole to manage their affairs successfully* (OECD 2006b).

- **OECD definition of "capacity building"**—a process starting with a plain surface and involving the step-by-step erection of a new structure, based on preconceived design (OECD 2006b).

- **OECD definition of "capacity development"**—the process whereby people, organizations and society as a whole unleash, strengthens, creates, adapts and maintain capacity over time (OECD 2006b).

- **UNDP definition of "capacity"**—"ability of individuals, institutions and societies to perform functions, solve problems, and set and achieve objectives in a sustainable manner (UNDP 2009a:53–4).

- **UNDP definition of "capacity building"**—a process that supports only the initial stages of building or creating capacities and alludes to an assumption that there are no existing capacities to start from ... It is therefore less comprehensive than capacity development. Capacity building can be relevant to crisis or immediate post-conflict situations where existing capacity has largely been lost due to capacity destruction or capacity flight (UNDP 2008:5).

- **UNDP definition of "capacity development"**—the process of creating and building capacities and their (subsequent) use, management and retention. This process is driven from the inside and starts from existing national capacity assets (UNDP 2008:5); "the process through which individuals, organizations and societies obtain, strengthen and maintain the capabilities to set and achieve their own development objectives over time" (UNDP 2009a:53–4).

Figure 3.1 Definitions of Capacity, Capacity Building, and Capacity Development.

1. The *Sites* of Capacity—the site or target of capacity development processes (three levels: individual, organization, and "enabling" environment);

2. The *Processes* of Capacity—donor processes of programming and recipient processes of implementation;

3. *Ownership (of the processes)* to cultivate Capacity (for Performance)—by donors and beneficiaries; and finally

4. The *Context* of Capacity—largely to do with the varying scales of the "enabling" environment and especially relevant in so-called fragile states.

Consider these four key attributes within the context of the function of strategic frameworks. It is an important function of strategic frameworks to provide models for implementation that consider relational and contextual aspects of potential outcomes. Yet, it is critical to consider that notions of these attributes of capacity I identify—*sites, processes, ownership,* and even of *context* in donor models—actually *do not* and *cannot* transcend beyond the boundaries of the donor's positioning and political framework. That is, capacity development models (while taking into account the experience and findings of donors) are designed to achieve optimal outcomes on donor investments. Donor *processes* of programming are geared toward a systemization of networks to capitalize on for further development projects, and *ownership* of these processes is integral to building the sustainability of this systemization, excluding (and in "fragile states," explicitly challenging) opponents of this process. The sites of capacity development are selectively determined by donors—to ensure the highest likelihood for optimal outcomes and return on investment. When an environment is disabling and becomes a site of capacity development programming, this results in an integration of security and development activities (to be further examined in the following chapter).

Sites of Capacity Development

The *sites* of capacity development models represent a multiplicity of layers of society. Individuals, organizations, institutions, networks, systems, societies, and "enabling" environments are cited as the entities within which capacity resides and is to be transformed. It is widely recognized in institutional frameworks and practitioner literature that there are three scales at which capacity development takes place: the individual, organization, and "enabling" environment. The UNDP Capacity Development Primer lists out these three points where "capacity is grown and nurtured" (UNDP 2009a, 11):

1. *The enabling environment*—the broad social system within which people and organizations function ... includes all the rules, laws, policies, power relations and social norms that govern civic engagement.[4]
2. The organizational level—the internal structure, policies and procedures that determine an organization's effectiveness. It is here that the benefits of the enabling environment are put into action and a collection of individuals come together.
3. The individual level—the skills, experience and knowledge that allow each person to perform. Some of these are acquired formally, through education and training, while others come informally, through doing and observing. Access to resources and experiences that can develop individual capacity are largely shaped by the organizational and environmental factors described above, which in turn are influenced by the degree of capacity development in each individual (e.g. human capital).

At these three scales, the contextual factors of "enabling" environments contain the greatest challenge to capacity development strategy, especially in so-called fragile states such as Afghanistan (and Pakistan). In the terminology used by donor institutions, "enabling" is used as a qualifier for the environment—in the sense that an environment is either enabling of the development of capacity or it is not. In an attempt to address these environmental factors, donors employ an *open-systems approach* in the design of models for capacity development programming, targeting individual organizations in an attempt to impact the context of the environment. The OECD framework elaborates on how the open-systems approach applies specifically to organizations and organizational behavior:

> Organisations, as the unit of analysis, are seen as open systems that are interrelated through networks and are influenced by the external context (OECD 2010b, 4) ... Organisations or

---

4. The OECD Capacity Development Note (2006) defines the enabling environment as "the structures of power and influence and the institutions—in which they are embedded," ending with, "Capacity is not only about skills and procedures; it is also about incentives and governance" (7).

networks of organisations can be viewed as "open systems," which are in constant interaction with elements of their context (the enabling environment). The context provides incentives to the organisation(s), stimulating them to act in certain manners. Some incentives foster productivity, growth and capacity development, others foster passivity, decline or even closure". In turn, organisational and institutional rules influence individuals' capacities by creating incentive structures that either give or deny them opportunities to make good use of their abilities and skills. (OECD 2006b, 13)

This basic framework for understanding organizations and organizational behavior is pervasive in donor models for capacity development programming. The EC also highlights a few (rather basic) key points of the relationship between organizations and the context within which they operate as it relates to capacity development efforts: (1) that organizations operate in a context, (2) that performance leads to outputs—some intended, others unintended, (3) outputs leads to outcomes and impact—though this chain is influenced by a multitude of other factors, and (4) capacity resides and develops internally, but whether or how capacity develops is largely determined by the "demand-side" or external factors (EC 2010, 10). The idea is that *while the context within which organizations exist plays a significant role* in their agency and performance abilities, *organizations themselves are vessels for change* and can lead to positive outcomes for donors. Thus, donors should seek out points of entry for capacity development activity, even in the most dire of contexts such as in "fragile" states. In determining these points of entry, donors have developed matrices and assessment checklists to guide the donor calculus on investment.

The EC's Toolkit for Capacity Development is one such example that provides insight into this donor calculus in selecting recipient organizations. The publication first highlights that organizations have both *functional* and *political* dimensions, and that striking a balance between the two is crucial for capacity development. This involves an approach that targets both internal elements (deemed as the supply side) and external stakeholders (the demand side). The *functional* dimension pertains to the task-and-work system related to the outputs of an organization, whereas the *political* dimension largely deals with external factors such as power-and-loyalty systems using incentives (sanctions and rewards) to entice favorable outcomes (EC 2010, 10). Building upon this framework of understanding, the EC has developed a multitude of assessments to assist donors in capacity development planning, including one to determine the balance between the functional and political dimensions of organizations. A full review of these assessments and matrices is outside the realm of this book, but may be an area for future research on variation and transformation in capacity development methodologies. That said, the design of these various matrices and assessment tools demonstrates donor attempts to develop methodologies to transform organizations and environments as sites of capacity development. They enable donors to determine the viability of their investments in capacity development programs and also to predict outcomes to guide their investments.

Contexts and the Tensions between Processes and Ownership

This leads to the second and third aspects of capacity development programming: *process and ownership*. Process and ownership are linked in the contemporary framing of capacity development in the donor-conceived notion that development processes should be driven by the recipient and not the donor. This focus on capacity as "internal to people, organizations and systems"[5] and on change as "being driven from the inside" is pervasive throughout the institutional literature on capacity development. This exposes a unique tension in the relationships of development where foreign donors must selectively determine organizations to invest in and apply models of growth for capacity development that should either *intrinsically* or *eventually* assume ownership of capacity development processes. This tension is not wholly ignored in the institutional literature. The OECD's Working toward Good Practice publication encourages donor patience regarding the ownership component of capacity development:

> Country ownership of capacity development (is) to be treated as a process—as it is not the sort of feature that either exists, in a fully-fledged form, or does not exist at all, and donors sometimes have the tendency to assume leadership of capacity development efforts when they perceive bad results as confirming weak capacity or commitment on the recipient side. (OECD 2006b, 24)

That said, patience as a strategy is hard to digest when donor institutions operate on budgets and timelines. The notion of ownership is particularly problematic when considering the situation of so-called fragile states.[6] The state of *fragility* is actually a form of enabling environment (or perhaps in this case a *disabling* environment). Consider the following definitions of the enabling environment from the UNDP, OECD, and USAID:

> The *enabling environment* is the term used to describe *the broader system within which individuals and organizations function and one that facilitates or hampers their existence and performance.* This level of capacity is not easy to grasp tangibly, but it is central to the understanding of capacity issues (5). *They determine the 'rules of the game' for interaction between and among organizations. Capacities at the level of the enabling environment* include *policies, legislation, power relations and social norms, all of which govern the mandates, priorities, modes of operation and civic engagement* across different parts of society. (UNDP 2008, 6)
>
> The *enabling environment influences the behaviour of organisations and individuals in large part by means of the incentives it creates.* For example, whether or not an organisation is able to achieve its purposes depends not just on whether it is adequately resourced but on the incentives generated by the way it is resourced under prevailing rules ... *Successful efforts to promote capacity development therefore require attention not only to skills and organisational procedures, but also to issues of incentives and governance.* Capacity development initiatives almost always take place in a particular organisational setting, where there will be a particular incentive structure deserving attention. However, the broader process of institutional transformation or stagnation in a

---

5. See Figure 3.1 for citation.
6. I discuss this concept further in the following chapter, but highlight the OECD definition here: "... countries recovering from conflict as well as regimes that are chronically weak or in decline for reasons unrelated to conflict ..." (OECD 2006b, 35). OECD provides guidance for capacity building in fragile states, integrating tool kits from the World Bank (Transitional Results Matrix—TRM) and the UN.

country may be no less important as a source of the behavioural incentives and disincentives that affect capacity. (OECD 2006b, 13)

The *enabling environment* includes the overall macroeconomic, political, and social context as well as specific policies and regulations that affect local organizations and the local private sector. Some important examples include the existence and enforcement of laws on NGO and business registration, charitable contributions and non-profits, and licensing of commercial activities and media operations. However, informal practices and social norms also affect the space for local organizations, the types of activities they can undertake, and their cost structures and effectiveness. Examples can include identity roles in politics, degree of corruption, government decision making, and treatment of critical viewpoints. Relevant aspects of the enabling environment should be identified or analyzed in planning, implementing, and monitoring and evaluation of capacity development activities. (USAID 2017d, 9)

In order to become familiar with the context of the enabling environment, donors collect various types of assessments to determine the development context and points of entry for projects. They vary in title. An assessment may be called an *institutional analysis, power analysis, feasibility study, drivers of change analysis, conflict analysis or assessments,* and now *capacity assessments.* These assessments "provide a more sophisticated understanding of political and social systems, incentive structures, and sources of leadership … to incorporate … into operational work (on capacity development)" (OECD 2006b, 21). This is especially important in so-called fragile states,[7] such as Afghanistan and Pakistan.[8]

In these so-called fragile states, *capacities* at the level of the enabling environment, such as policies, legislation, power relations, and social norms that define the broader system of operation, are often disrupted. OECD suggests "… a useful rule-of-thumb (for donors doing capacity development in fragile states) is: understand the country context and work towards an approach that seems likely to work in those specific circumstances" (OECD 2006b, 35). This is obviously a very vague recommendation, but traditionally in practice, state environments deemed too "fragile," or that put development workers at high-security risk, can translate into a cessation of assistance or a combining of assistance with military operations.

There are two important aspects to note about the enabling environment that are poorly articulated in strategic frameworks. The first is that the enabling environment has *multiple scales of operation.* This is because an enabling (or disabling) environment exists at all levels of authority and scales of governance where incentives and coercion impact individual and organizational behavior. In the context of development, the enabling environment operates at a subnational, district, provincial, national, regional, transnational,

---

7. This term is often adopted by donors in formulating strategy and metrics for development in conflict and postconflict situations.
8. The Fragile States Index, a ranking established by the Fund for Peace (a nonprofit based in DC and Abuja, Nigeria), determines state fragility based upon 12 indicators. Afghanistan and Pakistan are ranked the 9th and 17th most fragile states, respectively, out of 178 countries (Fund for Peace 2017).

international, and global scales. Furthermore, forms of governance and incentives to influence behavior at each level of authority and scale of governance have influence on the other levels and scales as well.

This leads to the second important aspect that goes relatively unacknowledged in institutional frameworks: donors are also a part of the environment and influence whether an environment can be enabling or disabling, both in overt and strategic (e.g., targeting areas of insurgency for development) and passive ways (e.g., ignoring areas of high need in favor of targeting areas of insurgency for aid). These frameworks for capacity development target processes largely at the *state* and *substate* scales, but it is important to recognize that donors operate on just about every other scale. Donors are able to provide incentives for cooperation and centralized governance through the carrot of assistance, selectivity in partner choice, and the promise of greater economic opportunity through trade. Donors also maintain influence on global and regional environmental scales and seek to further extend the globalization processes of the capitalist system. By providing incentives through development, donors increasingly become part of the enabling environment at the state (and sometimes subnational) scale.

In the following chapter, I outline transnational networks of resistance in Afghanistan and Pakistan. These networks also operate as part of this context on subnational and transnational scales, and thus the donor's battle for governance and their efforts to provide incentives for capacity development to create an enabling environment largely take place at the subnational and transnational scales. A 2012 USAID background paper on *country systems strengthening* shows that recognizing the donor role in the environment is still fresh in the donor mind-set:

> A radical implication is that donors also acknowledge that they are part of the system and not just talking from the outside. This also implies that the donor accepts the need to be part of the change and to relinquish control. Both of these elements are part of the rhetorical commitment to the Paris Declaration; neither is clearly evident in practice. This political-institutional context for USAID, and its impact on decision-making is a factor that must be taken into account in understanding how these issues might be made operational. (Gillies and Alvarado 2012, 19)

The transformation environments from disabling into enabling, particularly in so-called fragile states contending with transnational militancy, represent an area in which global security-oriented foreign policies and global development objectives overlap in a security–development nexus. I contend that a significant method by which donor institutions have sought to address the capacity development of the enabling environment in fragile states is through this nexus. Within institutional frameworks, the ability of a country (or organizations within a country) to develop capacity is identified as an issue of governance. While capacity development is not framed (or used) as interchangeable with state building, the OECD acknowledges that the processes are closely related, noting that "capacity development can be an entry point into countries with weak governance" (OECD 2006a,b, 13–14). OECD provides a list of recommendations and lessons donors have learned from working on capacity development in fragile states (ibid., 37):

Targeting Core State Functions—Where state capacity is weak but political will is present, capacity development efforts need to focus selectively on core state functions with a few to making the state at least minimally effective in providing for its people. (36)

    Using planning tools for post-conflict environment—such as the World Bank's Transitional Results Matrix, could be useful in embedding support for capacity development by drawing together security, diplomatic, and development efforts;[9]

    Avoid duplicating existing capacity and work with existing local institutions—It is important that new capacity development initiatives do not erode or duplicate existing capacity—watch out for parallel systems of delivery and accountability;

    "Sectoral selectivity" or "partial alignment" can deliver pay-offs—e.g. investments in capacity development in the health sector during the Taliban regime.

A few major themes emerge from these frameworks: (1) as capacity building shifted to capacity development, the focus of efforts shifted from the individual as a change agent to an open-systems framework of explaining organizational behavior within the context of an enabling environment, (2) capacity development programming of the enabling environment inherently overlaps with state-building efforts, especially so in so-called fragile states, (3) the shift in definition of capacity development in donor strategic frameworks mirrors a shift in the military–development nexus. I devote much of this next section to uncovering the ways in which USAID, the focal donor of this project, engages in capacity development in the context of these lessons learned about operating in so-called fragile enabling environments, particularly on (1) how USAID translates its capacity development framework into projects, (2) whether or not this translation is actually distinct as a donor tactic, and (3) whether or not capacity development strategies can be successful at altering the enabling environment at the state scale.

USAID Frameworks and Methodologies on Capacity

While references to capacity building are littered throughout the theory of change and strategy documents since the 1990s, USAID did not develop an official or formal capacity development strategy until 2010 with the publication of the Human and Institutional Capacity Development (HICD) framework. This framework is cross-cutting and was developed to be implemented in all USAID programming. While this framework was published long after the earliest High Level Fora meetings called for international focus on capacity development in the early 2000s, USAID has established approaches to capacity building from experiences at project level. In the five decades of USAID operation leading up to the creation of the HICD, I take stock of how some of these approaches to capacity have been conceptualized from USAID program experiences to trace the evolution and shifts in strategy and methodology.

    References to capacity exist in USAID literature on projects and policy dating back to the agency's founding. From the very beginning, USAID's usage of capacity has been inherently linked to (1) *capital* and (2) *systemization*. In this early literature, capacity

---

9. This lesson learned casually suggests an integration of military and development activities.

is defined and conceptualized in the context of *capital*. Publications in 1965 touch on "absorptive capacity" and "capacity expansion planning factors," which are conceived of through a capital-centric framework (Adler 1965, Norton et al. 1965). In a discussion on the expansion of "industrial capacity," donors are advised to consider "two types of factors" (capital output ratios and input capital ratios) in determining how to expand industrial capacity to produce products and services in developing countries (Adler 1965). "Absorptive capacity" is again referred to as the "total amount of capital, or the amount of foreign capital, or the amount of foreign aid (capital plus technical assistance) that a developing country can use productively ..." (Adler 1965, iii). A 1990 USAID study employs a similar definition of "absorptive capacity"[10] as referring to "the ability of an economy to use capital productively regardless of its source (whether local or foreign) based on some standard of productivity" (Reyes 1990, 14). Notably, these studies are produced by economists commissioned to determine the usefulness of such concepts for policy purposes (ibid.).

In the previous chapter, I engaged in a review of capacity in sociological notions of progress and of the political scientists who pushed forth a vision of development as modernization, but from the early years of USAID operations, capacity was largely conceptualized by economists and engineers. The engineering framework referred to the technical aspects of capacity, for example, the physical nature of facilities, machines, and production processes. A 1975 USAID-supported study by Evelyn L. Ripps differentiates between the "engineering" and "economic" definitions of capacity, the latter defining capacity as the "value of capital goods and structures available" (Ripps 1975, 12). As the engineering references to capacity refer to discrete measurements, we see that during this period the actual concept of capacity is born primarily from the theoretical framework of economists, which reduces notions of development to capital and production. As Lawrence Klein, a University of Pennsylvania economist testifying at Hearings on Measures of Productive Capacity, declared, "Capacity is an *economic* concept" [op. cit., p. 56] (Ripps 1975, 19).

A cursory review of projects specifically on capacity during this period shows donors preoccupied with the application of economic models and attempts to measure the productivity of manufacturing and agricultural industries (as well as strengthening government institutions in order to assist in the implementation of development programs). Projects of capacity also sought to systematize processes that would assist in donor

---

10. Absorptive capacity is again referred to by the 1969 Pearson Commission Report, produced as a result of collaboration among the president of the World Bank and political leaders from donor countries. The purpose of the report was to provide a new strategy for global development and references capacity in numerous ways: (1) in regard to education and research—in increasing the capacity of developing countries to "absorb, adapt, and develop scientific and technical knowledge (17)"; (2) in the economic and administrative capacity of *colonies* to cope with change and transition from traditional law and order into modernity and statehood (20, 22); (3) in individual capacity and underemployment, as well as the need to increase capacity to absorb labor (28, 30); and (4) in regarding the capacity to develop the environment in order to cultivate resources (30).

planning and schemes for more projects.[11] One such example of developing capacity for *systemization* involved knowledge collection for donors to enable state planning for agricultural and industrial development. In a 1977 USAID-commissioned study on building and institutionalizing an "investigative capacity" as a way to take a systems approach to agricultural sector development, the concept of "institutionalization" is considered as necessary to building a sustainable capacity:

> *Institutionalization*, as conceptualized here, *is the process through which the investigative capacity*, in this case including simulation models and their attendant trained manpower, *is focused through an investigative unit positioned in the agricultural decision-making structure* in such a way and at such a location *that optimum interaction with, and utilization by, decision-makers will take place*, thus *guaranteeing functional continuity of this capacity* ... It deals with the *organization, interactions*, and *linkages* necessary for continuing optimum usage of an investigative capacity by decision-makers in the form of an investigative unit institutionalized in the decision-making structure. It also deals with establishing the capacity of indigenous researchers, analysts, and policy-makers to use the models in designing, analyzing, and evaluating policies, programs, and projects ... The overall process of institutionalizing an investigative capacity in which organizational, technical, and human change are require, is an extremely complicated venture at best. *The process must begin within the context of a given political ideology, human resource base, technological level, and configuration of institutions and their linkages with each other.* (Rossmiller 1977, 127–28)

These notions of establishing a *system* and institutionalizing a *capacity for planning* evolve, as I will demonstrate further in Chapter 6, in a deconstruction of USAID's statecraft in Afghanistan and Pakistan. The publication also identifies certain prerequisites for the institutionalization of "investigative capacity": (1) recognition by key decision-makers that objectives are not being fully realized, (2) demonstrated intent and will to improve the decision-making process, (3) demonstrated will and ability to commit the manpower and resources necessary, and (4) appropriate decision-makers must be willing and able to make necessary organizational changes (ibid., 128). Similar variables are identified in present-day capacity development methodologies in considering partner selection criteria, yet in practice they have proved extremely difficult to realize, especially within the context of war when most partners cannot escape convoluted associations and incentives for action.

Reaching the end of the 1970s, we see some attempts to develop a methodology for determining "current capacities" and also "development needs." In a 1978 USAID Baseline Studies Field Manual on Least Developed Country (LDC) agricultural research, education, and extension systems, the authors first noted the "widespread agreement" among agricultural specialists that there is a need for an effective institutional structure to provide research, educational, and extension services to the agricultural sectors of LDCs

---

11. For example, Norton et al.'s (1965) study on capacity expansion planning factors, a 1971–76 project for developing beneficiary analytical capacity for planning agricultural sector development (USAID 1976), a 1977 study on institutional capacity needed to expand programming for rural development (USAID 1977), and so on.

(USAID 1978, 1). However, it is further recognized that there is wide variation in "institutional *form*," as well as coordination and integration in the *provision* of necessary services, and also little agreement on approaches to increasing the capacities of LDC institutions (ibid.). The manual treats "capacity" again as a reductionist form of capital—as *services* LDC institutions should provide in order to expand agricultural research, education, and extension capabilities (ibid.). As a recommendation, the authors suggest a "baseline methodology," essentially an assessment conducted by donors as part of the planning process in projects involving the production of quantitative and qualitative estimates, evaluations of existing capacity, and providing "detailed and current data," as well as recommendations for USAID, host countries, and other interested parties (ibid., 2). While it would be years until conducting base assessments became standard practice for USAID projects, we see an emerging understanding on the part of the donor that in conceptualizing how to build capacity, it is necessary to first consider what capacities already exist.

At the turn of the decade into the 1980s, USAID released several publications on private and voluntary organizations (PVOs), the role of "local social organizations," and local participation in building capacity, particularly in the context of "community" and "indigenous" and "rural" development. While the focus on various forms of nonstate, nonindustry organizations as a target for capacity-building efforts did not really gain traction until the 1990s, these publications demonstrate their emerging role in development efforts. This subtle shift toward community development is representative of a shift among the OECD/DAC donors away from the state as the sole and primary site of donor investment to build national markets and infrastructure to a greater focus on building communities to carry out these functions. That said, as I elaborate upon further in Chapter 5, section b: i and ii, most infrastructure and market building development projects involve components of state building, even if they were not labeled as such.

In one of the earliest USAID-funded studies on local social organizations and local project capacity, Barbara Miller (1980) explores the role of "indigenous voluntary associations in Third World countries, (in) contributing to project capacity in rural areas," highlighting the incredible variation of local social organizations in terms of their ability to carry out government programs. Miller's study suggests that voluntary associations could be tapped by development agencies to "contribute to project capacity in rural areas" in both tangibles (cash contribution and cost-sharing) and intangibles (labor, commodities, organizational linkages, para-administrative functions, and service delivery) (5). Her study ultimately concludes that policy makers should view these organizations as alternate and viable sources of development support to contribute to project capacity, only when the organization is "formalized and hierarchically organized, with recognized headquarters, officials and regulations" (ibid., 57). A 1980 USAID agreement for a program to build capacity for Ecuador's PVOs further displays the agency's concern over PVO capacity, lamenting PVO inability to "assess community needs, articulate local interest, identify opportunities, formulate viable development alternatives, design investment strategies and local plans, and implement and manage projects" (TELACU 1980, 1).

As donors explored community organizations as alternative sites for investment, rural development continued to present a challenge. Questions of capacity also emerged within this context in the USAID publications of the time as the agency grappled with the challenges of rural development. While donors explored and examined the role of "local" involvement and ownership of projects, building capacity to *manage* programs remained top of mind. A 1981 publication produced by DAI for USAID's Office of Rural Development and Development Administration entitled, "Management Performance for Rural Development: Packaged Training or Capacity Building?" identifies the objectives of development project management training as both to "improve organizational performance [and to] enhance the organization's ability to *effectively function* within a *changing environment*" (Honadle and Hannah 1982, 2). The publication goes on to cite the limitations of traditional training approaches emphasizing mere *knowledge transfer* and suggests a "capacity-building approach," which views training as having a two-fold purpose: "improving an organization or project's performance [and also in] enhanc[ing] the organization's capacity to cope creatively with a changing and uncertain environment [to meet the] long-term objective of developmental change [and] short-term objective of more efficient and effective organizational action" (ibid.).

This is strikingly similar to objectives for organizational performance seen in present-day strategic frameworks and implies a donor need for recipient ownership of organizational development in order to function within the enabling environment. Further, it implies that capacity equates to maintaining *resiliency* to shifts in contexts. What does cultivating resilience require? Is it possible for an organization to continue carrying out development projects or delivering services in the context of conflict? Can an organization be expected to act and make decisions to respond to rapid and sudden shifts or prolonged and sustained shifts in their environment when their mission and function is tied to the slow-moving administrative apparatus of the state? This is all very abstract and there are obviously limitations not only to the extent to which an organization can maintain resilience but also to consider this objective in relation to the issue of cultivating local *ownership* of development projects.

On this topic, another USAID-supported study in the same year (1981) explores questions of *participation, decentralization,* and *capacity building* for rural development. The paper is unique among USAID literature in that it actually addresses the issue of the divide between central government bureaucrats or technocrats and local actors or so-called villagers in project implementation at the field level. The study notes that

> The blueprint approach to rural development carries *an implicit aura of authoritarianism with it.* Such an approach is typified by certainty on the part of planners and managers that predetermined technologies and intervention techniques will work **in** *any given situation.* It assumes solutions to problems are known and that projects are vehicles for the application of these solutions. In its purest form, such an approach means little or no participation by either beneficiaries or project staff, who are expected to obediently follow instructions from headquarters. Policy is set above and administered below. (Honadle and Gow 1981, 3)

Ultimately while the study emphasizes the empowerment of local villagers through decentralization and the encouragement of local participation in the implementation of development projects, the authors ultimately revert to a reinforcement of notions of centralized structures of authority. In the conclusion, the authors mention that the central government bureaucrat should be "put back on the center stage—not as a hero or as a villain—but as a *key supporting actor*. Villagers need the bureaucrats perhaps more than the bureaucrats need the villagers … without the bureaucrats there is little chance that self-sustaining development will take place" (ibid., 15). The study ultimately focuses on the agency of the bureaucrat in central government/subnational relationships and concludes with suggesting three "mutually supportive strategies to improve the perform-ance of bureaucrats":

1. Participatory management—characterized by:
    a. Access to power—specifically the capacity to mobilize resources to accomplish tasks
    b. Opportunity—specifically chances for advancement, input into important decisions, and increase in skills and rewards.
2. Controlled decentralization—in which the center gives field personnel the autonomy and resources to demonstrate their capabilities while at the same time retaining a modicum of symbolic control … retaining the best features of centralization and decentralization:
    a. By stimulating officials to be more responsive to local population,
    b. By increasing efficiency
    c. By achieving both economic and political goals
3. Capacity building—which to a certain extent, subsumes the first two and is characterized by the following process dimensions (15): risk sharing, involvement of multiple organizational levels, collaborative implementation styles, demonstration of success, and emphasis on learning, but also incentives for behavior, and organ-izational resources. (Honadle and Gow 1981, 16)

The authors conclude that all three of these strategies emerge from the belief that "alterations in the existing authoritarian, centralized bureaucratic setting can be accomplished, and in doing so provide bureaucrats with incentives and skills to play a lead role in development" (16). The usage of language in this publication is particularly interesting, because while the authors argue for "controlled decentralization" for "par-ticipation," what they really mean is "decentralization" to increase the scale of operation of centralized institutions to reach and encompass subnational spaces to accomplish the objective of managing rural development. What does *ownership* of development truly mean here and whose *ownership* matters? Does mere participation qualify as ownership? Do USAID and other development agencies conduct projects to really cultivate local ownership of development in subnational spaces, or are they more interested in culti-vating linkages that support a state-centric vision of national (and vertical) ownership of subnational spaces?

   This emphasis in USAID publications on *participation* for building capacity is furthered throughout the 1980s. A 1986 publication on participatory evaluation as a methodology for measuring and monitoring local capacity in a USAID irrigation management and agricultural production project in Sri Lanka also highlights the advantages of *beneficiary ownership*, but in the *evaluation processes* in building capacity. The publication notes that the "participatory evaluation" approach involving self-evaluation by the project bene-ficiaries "strengthens local capabilities for self-learning and joint problem-solving" and "has the advantage of measuring and monitoring the capacity of local organizations for self-management in a self-strengthening way" (Uphoff 1986, 2–3). In suggesting partici-pant self-evaluations as a methodological tactic for measuring local capacity, the concept of beneficiary ownership of development processes is further institutionalized, notably during a time when conducting evaluations for projects was not standardized practice.

In conceptualizing how to cultivate local ownership of development processes, donors also turned to building the capacity of *individuals* to take on projects. In empowering com-munity organizations to take on development projects, individual capacity would also be needed for project success. A 1994 publication for USAID, entitled *Human Capacity Development: People as Change Agents*, reinforces this notion, arguing that people must be thought of as "change agents ... [to] ensure the success of sustainability of USAID devel-opment projects" (USAID 1994, 1). In addition to the standard focus on training and selection, a nod is given to the organizational and "enabling" environment components of individual success, "an individual can seldom be successful without the support of others in the workplace or the community." Addressing the failures of previous trainings for "change agents" in El Salvador, the publication provides important recommendations for the future sustainability of USAID projects. *Ownership* or the necessity of active par-ticipation in development processes by all stakeholders is noted. A "human capacity needs assessment" is also cited as the "cornerstone of a results-oriented human capacity development program," as well as the inclusion of "a monitoring and evaluation effort to assure that human capacity development goals are being met" (ibid., 6).

In considering the publications of the 1980s and the 1990s, it is important to keep in mind a few things. First, conducting assessments preaward, as well as the inclusion of monitoring and evaluation mechanisms, while encouraged, was not standard prac-tice for all projects. As capacity was increasingly identified as requiring monitoring and measurement in order to determine if projects were sustainable and had impact, this led to a furthering of the institutionalization of assessment and M&E processes in develop-ment practice. Furthermore, it is evident from even the early 1980s that the two obvious and major issues surrounding the monitoring and measurement of the capacity compo-nent are (1) stakeholder engagement and participation—at the individual and organiza-tional level (which is an issue of process ownership) and (2) sustainability of development programs (again, an issue of ownership, absorption, and implementation).

In the post-Washington Consensus development policy world, the OECD/DAC donor attention turned to developing the capacity of former Soviet countries in transi-tion to market economies and representative government. These former Soviet countries marked an area of experimentation for donors in the expansion of global capitalism. In a 1993 study on building capacity for local government training in the Czech Republic and Slovakia, the authors assess the impact of the donor effort to strengthen leadership training for representatives of political institutions, focused on the management of muni-cipal government to create "sustainable capacity in existing institutions" (IPA 1993, 1). The authors note that there is an enormous amount of work to do in this area of capacity-building. What makes it both interesting and challenging is that neither the American, British, French or Scandinavian models were exact "fits" as they are … (and that addressing stability of government on a local level … and the complexity of problems faced) … requires a more flexible, hybrid model probably developed by an international team of human resource specialists who can work within the context of central Europe. (ibid., 439)

A few years later in 1996, the USAID commissioned a nontechnical study on capacity building in these "emerging market economies" to address the "deficiencies" faced by "transitional countries" struggling with the "inability of central planning to sustain economic development" (Rondinelli 1994, 2). The study provides a laundry list of "capacities" that are "essential for creating and sustaining market-oriented economic systems" (ibid., 157). The capacities are as follows:

1. Capacity to implement macroeconomic policies that support market systems (157)
2. Capacity to develop liberal trade and investment policies (158)
3. Capacity to establish and sustain decentralized systems of government (159)
4. Capacity to transfer ownership and control of state enterprises to the private sector (159)
5. Capacity to develop social institutions that facilitate market transactions (160)
6. Capacity to expand and strengthen private enterprise (160)
7. Capacity to develop human resources for participation in market systems (161)
8. Capacity to develop an "Entrepreneurial Milieu" and a value system that supports democratic market economies (162)

The author presents the "Capacity Requirements for Emerging Market Economies" in Figure 3.2 (ibid., 157):

As evident from the list and the figure, capacities required for market development are all-encompassing and reflect the neoliberal ideologies of the time. The development of market economies required the development of political, economic, and social institutions, wide-scale reforms, and a complete reorienting of policy toward privatization of the state and an embrace of trade and foreign investment.

The schemes of building capacity for development called for total systemic transformation. In a 1996 USAID study produced by the MSI on enhancing capacity for the strategic management of policy implementation in developing countries, author David Brinkerhoff identifies three key capacities for managing reform: (1) looking outward, (2) looking inward, and (3) looking ahead (Brinkerhoff 1996: 1). Brinkerhoff also provides a spectrum for how capacity is conceived:

At the narrow end of the spectrum, capacity is conceived of as what individuals are able to do, and thus capacity- building refers to education and training in particular skills. In its broadest conception, capacity is treated as synonymous with development at the national level, and capacity-building refers to any and all efforts targeted toward promoting socio-economic advancement. Between these two poles lies a middle range of perspectives that focus upon organizations/institutions and the people who function within them. (ibid., 7)

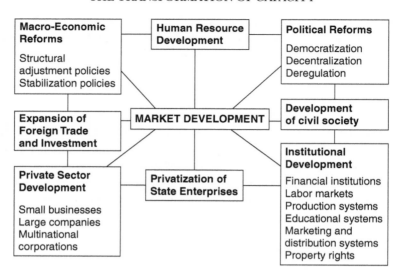

Figure 3.2 Capacity Requirements for Emerging Market Economies.

In the study, Brinkerhoff distinguishes between factors that influence the impacts of strategic management capacity-building efforts in the public sector versus the private sector (30), as well as defining four basic roles for "technical assistance" and draws attention to the issue of "context" in understanding incentives for change and "interorganizational strengthening" (ibid., 8). I touch on issues of context throughout this project, particularly in regard to donor understanding of relationships and concerns over recipient ownership of development projects in countries dealing with war and insurgency. Brinkerhoff portrays this issue aptly:

> Unless someone or some group in the country where policy reform is being pursued *feels that the changes are something that they want to see happen, externally initiated change efforts* whether at the local or national level *are likely to fail. This internalized desire for change is a precondition for sustainable capacity-building;* otherwise the capacities that are developed or strengthened will either wither from lack of support, or migrate to where they are appreciated and applied. (30) The *more successful capacity-building interventions* responded to what the host country counterparts thought was most important, moved at their pace, and accommodated their changes in direction and emphasis. *The less successful activities* were locked into a variety of predetermined choices: policy areas, organizational partners, timetables, etc. Despite its pluses, however, *the flexibility needed for building ownership and participation is beset by a number of countervailing forces.* These include: donor agency procedures and accountability requirements, weak financial and reporting systems in countries that allow misuse of donor and national resources, lack of understanding of process and facilitative TA (technical assistance) approaches, and short-term politico- bureaucratic time horizons. (ibid., 31)

This issue of recipient-driven agendas for development is at the core of the capacity-building challenge for foreign donors. As my review of the USAID literature shows, the method by which this issue is approached is by focusing on attempts to cultivate ownership of development projects through attempts to build the capacity of various entities: state ministries, local community organizations, individuals, and so on. Throughout the literature produced in USAID's first few decades of operation, there are allusions to issues related to context or environmental factors that inhibit or deter capacity-building processes and cultivating recipient ownership of development projects, but these references do not start to become more explicit until the mid-1990s. It is then that we start to see more explicitly references to an "enabling environment" as a component of capacity building, particularly in relation to the sustainability of donor investment. Notably, this also parallels designations of "fragility" by in-country classification tools by OECD/DAC donors (Nay 2013, 217–19).

We start to see references to the "enabling environment" in the 1990s during the shift in capacity-building approaches from a focusing on the individual to the organization as the target of development efforts. A 1996 monograph based on a USAID PVO/NGO support project in Senegal suggests an approach to capacity building for organizations at the community and intermediary-NGO level. This publication directly calls for the "creation of an enabling environment" by donors through facilitating communication among relevant institutions and sectors, including representatives from the donor community, national and local government, and NGOs active in development activities (USAID 1996, 2–3). Echoing findings from "Human Capacity Development (1994)," the monograph finds that capacity-building programs are more successful with active participation from all project stakeholders and that "in addition to strengthening the capacity of NGO grantees through direct interventions such as training programs and technical and financial assistance, project managers must work with government, donors, and other support organizations to build a system that can function after funding is completed" (13). The monograph concludes that "capacity building is an essential ingredient for sustainable development" (13). The question of sustainability of development efforts has actually always been an issue of development projects. It has only been given a name as the major issue of development in the context of the transformation of capacity.

This linkage between capacity building and sustainability is further entrenched in the institutional literature of the 1990s. A 1996 USAID assessment carried out by World Learning, CARE, and the World Wildlife Fund on capacity-building issues surrounding NGOs and natural resources management (NRM) found that NGO capacity building was *necessary* but *insufficient* to promote sustainable NRM. The assessment highlighted the difference between "sustainable" and "improved" NRM, noting that most who use the term "sustainable" are actually referring to "improvement," which "under the right conditions (could) become sustainable" (i). The authors noted in their findings (1) that the *terms and qualities* of the initial relationships between Northern and Southern NGOs should entail negotiation of mutual objectives and consider all assumptions and constraints, (2) that North–South NGO relationships should be conceived and developed on a continuum: from working relationships, to collaborative relationships, to partnerships (a process involving increasing quality and depth in relationships), and lastly (3) that donors needed to be more realistic in general about what collaboration and partnership *should* and *could* accomplish (Brown 1996, ii). While this sort of donor reflexivity regarding donor–recipient relationships appears in some USAID assessments and evaluations, it does not find its way from project lessons into institutional policy.

In further considering the linkage between capacity building and sustainability, a 1999 technical report entitled "Capacity Building in Training: A Framework and Tool for Measuring Progress" builds on experiences from USAID's PRIME project,[12] which provided training and support for primary providers of reproductive health services in 20 different countries. The report theorizes the linkage between "capacity building," "institutionalization," and "sustainability," as distinct phases (capacity building → institutionalization → sustainability) and assumes that

> Assessing various dimensions and indicators of capacity building can help to explain when an organization is passing from *building capacity* to *institutionalizing* of training … Likewise, once training is legitimized by policymakers and/or the community, and the resources "financial, physical, etc.) are in place <u>and</u> there is a track record of independent activity, then and only then can the training efforts (and the institution) be said to be reaching **sustainability** of operation. In that sense, the three terms describe a *continuum* of development, overlapping among them. (Fort 1999, 20)

This distinction of phases from *building capacity* to *institutionalization* to *sustainability* in today's terms might simply be called the process of capacity development. It is a matter of semantics, but in the literature detailing capacity approaches, much of the conceptual evolution is masked by discursive shifts in terminology. Achieving sustainability involves multiple scales of ownership—at the individual and organizational scales, as well as ownership surrounding cooperation and coordination at varying scales of the "enabling" environment within which individuals and organizations operate. The sustainability of the development project continuum is inherently linked to a demonstration of ownership of development processes through individual and organizational performance.

This link between recipient ownership of development processes and the sustainability of capacity initiatives is furthered and also reframed as issues of *performance* in a discussion on methodological issues surrounding how to measure capacity in a 2001 report, "Measuring Capacity Building." This report was specifically on supporting health systems in developing countries and draws attention to an important element of how donors measure capacity in the present day. While acknowledging that capacity is said to be linked to improved performance, the report notes that there is little consensus (among donors) on the role capacity plays in *actually improving* performance. This is due to a number of reasons (Figure 3.3): (1) a lack of understanding (by donors) about the relationship between capacity and performance, (2) variation in what constitutes "adequate" performance, and (3) the influence of the external environment on capacity and performance (Brown et al. 2001, iii).

The report traces these issues in large part to the shortcomings of *capacity assessment tools* employed by donors, noting that half of the tools available are self-assessments, with only

---

12. PRIME was a project for training and supporting primary providers of reproductive health services around the world implemented by INTRAH at UNC, Chapel Hill in collaboration with ACNM, Ipas, PATH, TRG, Inc., OMG Booksource and AMZCO, Inc.

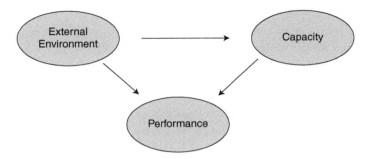

Figure 3.3 Factors of Performance (ibid., 11).

a few that were a combination of self- and external assessments (iv). The authors argue that methodological techniques that depend heavily on assessments are unreliable if used over time for monitoring and evaluation purposes because assessments measure *perceptions* of capacity and not actual capacity (iv). The report ends with the methodological challenges of measuring the linkages between capacity and performance remaining unresolved and calling for "experimental" approaches.

Moving from the 1990s into the early 2000s, USAID's literature rebrands *issues of capacity more explicitly as issues of "performance."* While the issue of performance was highlighted in the context of developing the capacity of political institutions by modernization theorists decades prior, this notion did gain salience in the discourse of practice until decades later. This slight reframing also indicates a discursive shift in the development literature toward the language, techniques, and methodologies of private sector models of organizational growth applied to the development context. This shift has also led to a general conflation in how donors conceptualize the change processes of private sector and public sector organizations, including the objectives and outcomes outlined in project methodologies.

The issue of *performance*, at the individual and organizational level, is at the center of USAID's 2010 HICD framework: A USAID Model for Sustainable Performance Improvement (PI). The framework defines HICD as "a model of structured and integrated processes *designed to identify root causes of performance gaps* in host country partner institutions, *address those gaps through a wide array of performance solutions in the context of all human performance*[13] factors, and enable cyclical processes of continuous PI through the establishment of performance monitoring systems" (USAID 2010, 7). The authors claim that the HICD approach "can be successfully applied to *any type of organization* including government organizations, non-profit organizations and professional associations … (and) will enable these organizations to responsibly meet the needs of their countries and their citizens" (USAID 2010, 5). The HICD framework provides several figures to visually conceptualize the model. I include two here.

The first is much more detailed, including subvariables affecting every stage of the model. The more detailed model also incorporates a PI model that "provides a systematic

---

13. Italics are my own.

process for analyzing and improving performance" (USAID 2010, 8). The stages from "considering institutional context" to the near conclusion "implement performance solutions" stage are all considered part of the HICD's PI (Figure 3.4).

One of the most important aspects of the HICD handbook is that it provides guidelines for donors to engage with partner organizations to identify needs and create plans to improve performance for capacity development. It also lists prerequisites for partner selection to theoretically improve the odds of success: (1) the commitment of the organization, (2) ability to change, (3) stable leadership, (4) alignment between the partner organization's objectives and those of the USAID, and (5) sustainability of the organization after USAID assistance. The PI model is embedded within the HICD model. This second figure simplifies the previous model but better demonstrates how monitoring and evaluation components occur throughout the process of PI (Figure 3.5).

The HICD handbook is results oriented. It houses numerous tools—assessments, matrices, metrics—to be employed in USAID projects. It also relies upon an adaptation of the Balanced Scorecard (BSC), a methodological concept first published in a 1992 *Harvard Business Review* article and eventually as a book in 1996. The BSC is a "management system tool" developed for company executives to "guide current performance and target future performance." This is notable for several reasons. First, BSC is a methodology developed by and for the elite private sector leaders of developed nations for organizational transformation, yet is supposed to serve as the basis for USAID's framework for capacity development in developing countries, which operate in a wide range of contexts with unique challenges. Second, the BSC was created in the early/mid-1990s, yet is the methodological framework of choice for USAID's capacity development framework nearly twenty years later in 2010. I do not claim that this model is necessarily inapplicable in all development contexts, but it is telling that USAID's framework for capacity development entering its sixth decade of operation is not one developed in conjunction with other development agencies, partners from the Global South, or from knowledge gained from assessments and evaluations from the previous decades (much of which is outlined in this section), but instead relies upon a methodology created for private sector companies operating in an already "developed" country context.

That said, the BSC targets measurements in four different categories: financial performance, customer knowledge, internal business processes, and learning and growth "to align *individual, organizational,* and *cross-departmental* initiatives to meet *customer* and *shareholder* objectives." Figure 3.6 displays (A) the four categories of measurement of the BSC juxtaposed against (B) the BSC model in the HICD (USAID 2010c) manual (Figure 3.6) adapted for the public sector (10), as well as (C) a figure on "Domains of Performance" from a 2017 USAID publication on "Organizational Capacity Development Measurement" (USAID 2017d, 5).

As I've noted, the BSC was designed for private sector companies. As the language surrounding capacity building shifted to frame issues of capacity as performance issues, a new development strategy emerged that applied performance-based methodologies of organizational growth for private sector organizations in the markets of the Global North to the capacity development of public sector organizations of war-ravaged countries to build barely existent, and sometimes duplicate, systems of state and market.

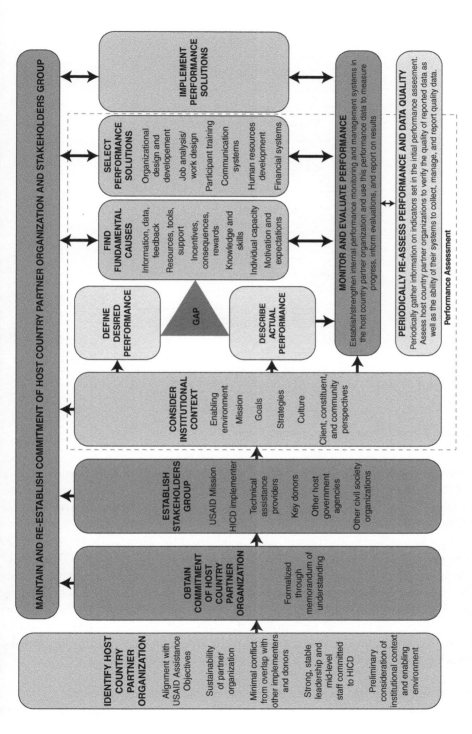

Figure 3.4 HICD Model (Expanded) (USAID 2010, 7).

HICD Model

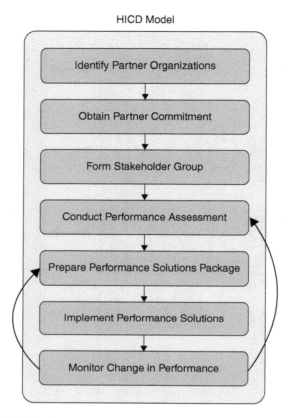

Figure 3.5 HICD Model (Condensed) (USAID 2010, 7).

The differences between the HICD scorecard (B) and the BSC (A) are minimal. The HICD "customer" also includes constituents and stakeholders. "Learning and Growth" is rebranded as "employees & organizational capacity," and "business processes" become "internal processes."

Fast-forwarding to the present day, the marriage of capacity development as *PI* has become fully cemented into USAID's development strategy. The "Domains of Performance" (C) differs from the 2010 HICD public sector scorecard (B), in part because the scorecard was intended to be used as an assessment tool and guideline to set organizational strategy for performance, whereas the "Domains of Performance" figure defines the pillars of performance. Unsurprisingly, the incorporation of all four components of strategy is inherent within the four domains. The 2017 publication also provides recommendations for measuring organizational capacity:

- *Measurements* for organizations *should be based on* organizational *performance*;
- *Performance should be measured across multiple domains* (including adaptive functions) to reflect capacity development investments in short-term and long-term aspects of performance;

USAID HICD Framework: Capacity Development as Performance Management

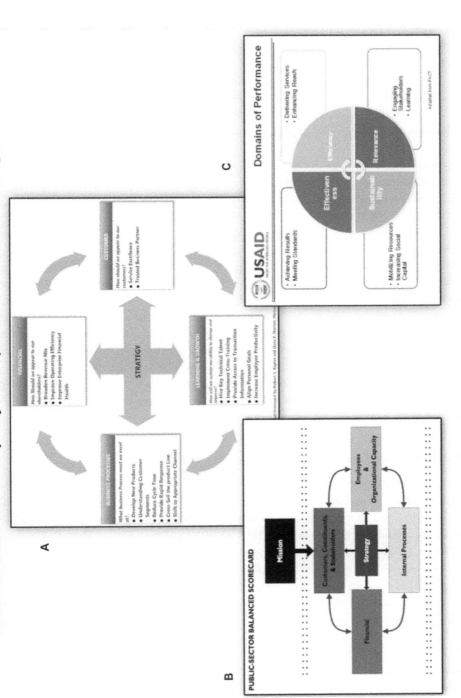

Figure 3.6 USAID HICD Framework: Capacity Development as Performance Management.

- *Organization's performance depends on fit* in wider local system with actors and interrelationships;[14]
- *Organizational performance change is pursued in order to affect wider, systemic changes,...* [but] attribution for change is hard to prove ... [so] we should trace the credible contribution from organizational to system change with rigor;
- *Some ways organizational capacity development will affect future performance cannot be anticipated* from the start. Therefore, attend to multiple pathways of change and to the unpredicted in order to perceive the full spectrum of results.

One main theme that stands out here is how issues of performance are tied into environmental factors (e.g., focus on the adaptive functions of domains of performance, on "fit in wider local system ...," and "change pursued to affect wider, systemic changes"). We see that there is an acknowledgment of the contextual factors impacting the ability of USAID to build capacity for performance. Yet, in these methodologies the task of addressing performance issues is formulaic and seems relatively simple and straightforward. Further, these frameworks are designed for project-level planning. There is not much given in USAID's institutional framework in terms of assessing and determining the contextual factors that impact projects and exist beyond the project level, particularly in considering USAID's role or the role of other foreign actors, stakeholders, and particularly military or security forces as they impact capacity development. While the performance-based methodologies *do* actually acknowledge the systemic aspects that impact the ability of an individual or organization to perform tasks and functions, they do not actually address the variation and diversity of contexts that enable or prevent performance outside of a framework that mildly encourages systemic change through individual and organizational transformation.

Summary and Conclusion

In this chapter, I presented contemporary definitions of capacity development used by donor institutions and agencies in present-day frameworks. I did not conduct a comprehensive review of the various frameworks of development agencies on capacity, but rather highlighted the frameworks of OECD, UNDP, and the EC since these frameworks established the foundation of definitions and methodologies employed by other agencies, such as the USAID. I explained that, within this literature, we see that the discursive shift from capacity building to capacity development signifies a change in donor frameworks from an emphasis on the individual and organization to an emphasis on the "enabling" environment as a target for development processes. I identified four defining aspects of the concept of capacity in institutional frameworks: (1) site, (2) ownership, (3) processes, and (4) context. Analyzing how donors interpret these aspects, I examined how USAID methodologies define, conceptualize, measure, monitor, and evaluate these aspects of capacity. Donor capacity development targets three sites: the individual, the

---

14. This is a nod to the enabling environment level.

organization, and the "enabling" environment. This last site is the most difficult for donors to impact because, within the context of war and insurgency, the *environment*, particularly in subnational spaces of militant activity, represents a site where the legibility of the state is openly contested. This is an important point and theme throughout my research examining USAID's capacity-building efforts in Afghanistan and Pakistan.

This examination of capacity in USAID project and policy reports, studies, assessments, and agreements reveals capacity within the development framework to be a primarily *economic* concept steeped in notions of *capital*. Pushing forth capacity in the context of modernization involved the *systemization of planning processes* and *centralization* of states to ultimately enable the conditions conducive to establishing market systems and increasing production. In USAID literature on rural development, building the capacity of local or subnational forms of nonstate organizations (PVOs, local social organizations, NGOs, etc.) is prioritized in order to encourage participation and ownership of development projects and processes for donors. As the sustainability of development projects and donor investment increasingly became a concern, the calls for capacity building increased throughout the literature. Investing in "change agents," to take ownership of capacity-building processes, as well as conducting preaward assessments to measure existing capacity and provide a basis for planning, monitoring, and evaluation became increasingly institutionalized.

In the post-Washington Consensus world where capitalism triumphed over the threat of Communist expansion, capacity building emerged as a cornerstone of donor tactics to create sustainable market-oriented economic systems in post-Soviet countries. Ironically, as I detail in the following chapter, this donor focus on post-Soviet countries was a contributing factor to the withdrawal of international assistance to Afghanistan and Pakistan in the early 1990s. During this decade, capacity building gained salience within the development discourse as donors sought to increase the capacity (1) of organizations and the enabling environment (instead of merely the individual), (2) to enhance recipient ownership of development projects, and (3) to establish conditions for market development in post-Soviet countries.

Leading into the 2000s, donor frameworks for capacity development rebranded the issue as one of "performance," adapting private sector-based methods for organizational growth and performance developed in the 1990s intended for companies in the Western world to USAID development projects and public sector institutions in the developing non-Western countries. Finally, the most recent turn of "capacity" in the discourse is in the context of the growing concern of Western donors over the rise of global Islamic militancy, turning the issue of global security into a development priority, particularly with regard to counterinsurgency in fragile states. More urgently than ever, the need to build the capacity of so-called fragile states—as well as government at the local level— is the heavy task of the development agency. I discuss this topic more at length in the following chapter, as well as the centrality of the state to the cultivation of capacity within the context of a sociological framework for the capacity project.

Chapter Four

CAPACITY AND FRAGILITY: *THE SOCIOLOGICAL FRAMEWORK FOR THE CAPACITY PROJECT AND DEVELOPING "FRAGILE" STATES*

The previous chapter examined how capacity as a concept gained salience within donor spaces, moving from agendas to institutional frameworks to finally be implemented within projects. A concept gains salience by becoming a common theme or underlying thread within varying discourses, primary areas of stakeholder collaboration, and when it becomes subsumed within overarching narratives that drive forth the reality of the spaces within which actors operate. As a concept of practice, capacity lives everywhere and across all issue areas. It is in many ways an all-consuming concept that only gains substance when within the context of other concepts. As we work toward a conceptual framework of understanding for capacity, this teasing out major discursive relationships is tedious, but necessary. This chapter is about the relationship of "capacity" to another pervasive, descriptive concept that has implications for development strategy, global security concerns, and the prevention of mass human rights violations: "fragility."

As this term is generally used as a descriptor for the status of states, and much of capacity building has to do with the building of the state, this chapter approaches the relationship between these two concepts first through an examination of sociological frameworks for understanding projects of capacity and later through the lens of USAID's involvement in counterinsurgency operations, which is particularly relevant as we consider fragility. The scholarly frameworks I examine explain capacity building as a community-building project and identify major themes of capacity building as *state power*, *community*, and *social capital*, using examples from the Global North to conceive of the construction of capacity through the lens of frames and habitus. These frameworks are both illuminating and limiting for an analysis of donor-driven capacity-building efforts in states deemed "fragile," such as Afghanistan and Pakistan. I juxtapose these examples against the context of the case this book examines, examining these limitations and exploring the ramifications of them when considering the question of *capacity* as it relates to *fragility* within the context of statebuilding. This leads into a discussion on the role of security within development agendas and *fragility* as a designation for states deemed lacking in *capacity*, as well as how rights-based approaches to development fit into this framework for statebuilding.

Beyond the task of defining and conceptualizing capacity building, this project examines how donors, specifically USAID, conduct capacity-building projects as a *tactic* to achieve broader donor objectives. The literature examining capacity building, as a method to achieve certain outcomes and objectives, is varied and produced by authors from a wide range of disciplinary and professional backgrounds and frameworks. Throughout this project, I contend with academic, institutional, and practitioner literature on capacity building. In the first part of the chapter, I explore some particularly relevant sociological and anthropological literature on capacity building to tease out the conceptual framework of capacity projects, as well as the limitations surrounding the pertinence of these studies to the situation of development in so-called fragile states.

"Capacity building" as a term was born from community-building programs in the 1950s (Smillie 2001). As capacity building is a term of practice, born from spaces of practice, there are few scholarly works that provide theoretical frameworks to explain this topic, likely because the concept itself is so shallow and ambiguous outside of the contexts of practice. I present two cases of community-building programs as capacity building that work toward a theoretical framing of capacity building here: one a study of neighborhood regeneration programs in the UK and Denmark (Fallov 2010) and the second coastal zone management (CZM) in Louisiana (Norris-Raynbird 2008). These examples are some of the only scholarship that applies sociological frameworks (Foucauldian notions of *governmentality* and *social capital*, Bourdieu's *habitus*, or Goffman and Berger and Luckmann's *frame analysis*) to examine capacity-building programs and to conceptualize the meaning of capacity.

The question to keep in mind with the presentation of these cases is whether models of community development in so-called developed, Western countries can apply to situations of international development in the global South. This is not a new or novel question, but relevant in considering how these examples inform scholarly frameworks that attempt to explain capacity, and the application of this framing in explaining capacity building in so-called fragile, non-Western states. I argue that the frameworks that these authors present illuminate the core conundrum of building states—or *statecraft*—and the critical role of spatiality and scales of operation for donors attempting to build state capacity (within a presumed capitalist framework) to manage transnational militancy. Keeping this in mind, it is helpful to examine the context of community capacity-building programs in developed, Western contexts to highlight these distinctions between building state capacity in developed and undeveloped contexts.

Fallov (2010) explores the concept of community capacity building and its relation to social capital, arguing that community capacity building depends on *particular forms of social capital* involving the *naturalization of particular capacities*. Fallov (2010) draws upon a Foucauldian framework for governmentality "as a grid of intelligibility," for understanding the *role of capacity* under the Third Way's "governance of exclusion" (797). In both the British and Danish cases, neighborhood regeneration programs were to prevent the social exclusion of "risk groups" through capacity development and targeted intervention (790). Adopting Foucauldian notions of governmental power as the "management of possibilities," Fallov argues that capacity building occurs through "imposing particular capacities as the *path to inclusion*, that is, the *capacities of employability* and *active citizenship* ... (797) (otherwise designated) ... *legitimate capacities*" (798). Development agencies such as the USAID use these same tactics of donor statecraft in Afghanistan and Pakistan, which

I detail further in Chapter 6. Consider that spaces where capacity building is to take place are far more complex—where projects as *paths to inclusion* involve matters of tribal conflict exacerbated by transnational Islamic militancy, pervasive disputed notions of autonomy, and the legacy of waves of foreign invasion and occupation.

My examination of capacity building also departs from examples of community building in developed, Western countries when considering notions of *community*. "Community" within Fallov's framework "becomes the central territory between state, market, and individual ... as both object and target of government" (797). This is also central to the foreign donor framework for projects, except that those targeting the communities typically involve a conglomeration of stakeholders. The projects are *not of* the government, nor of the people. Fallov describes this relationship between donors and recipients as the "governors" and the "governed," and as a "spacialization of exclusion," at the community level, with capacity building as an attempt to "govern inclusion" (801). Invoking Bourdieu's notion of *habitus*, Fallov conceptualizes capacity building as "the collective orchestrating of a habitus ... in a specific direction by inculcating a curriculum to which the excluded might aspire" (798). Fallov highlights an important point about the design, curriculum, and objectives of such capacity development programs:

> *Capacity development* becomes *a process that legitimizes the curriculum itself,* and the *processes of acquirement result* in the *legitimization of the privileged* access obtained by some groups *and the improbability of acquirement of other* groups. At the same time, negative sanctions are imposed on those unable to acquire the necessary capacities. (799)
>
> *Capacity building* becomes a question of *moulding the habitus towards new possibilities* and *of realizing and legitimizing particular governmental practices and institutions* ... the realization, legitimization and success of the area-based approach to the neighbourhood regeneration depend on the moulding of the collective habitus of the governors to be able to engage in the process of capacity building, concomitantly with the moulding of the habitus of residents. (799)

Here, Fallov conceptualizes neighborhood regeneration programs to build capacity as a governing tactic to manage community inclusion and molding of a habitus. Fallov finds that in both the British and Danish cases, building *formal networks* that took on a *recognizable form* (from the perspective of the governing bodies) opened doors to residents gaining influence and government funds, thus creating *legitimate types* of *network demands* for *specific capacities* (800). This building of networks and bridges between organizations was considered to be essential to the "regeneration process" (799). This point is crucial to understanding the scale of the challenge of capacity development in Afghanistan and Pakistan. The establishing of formal networks to increase state capacity to govern community inclusion is a much more complex task when the "risk groups" targeted have already been manipulated and violated by decades of conflict, and either have no desire for *inclusion* with a government they have had little relationship with and are openly hostile to those attempting to manage them—particularly from the outside.

While Fallov (2010) conceptualizes capacity-building projects as *paths to inclusion* and the construction of a habitus, Norris-Raynbird (2008) conceptualizes the process of capacity-building projects as a *shifting of frames*. Drawing largely from Berger and Luckmann (1967) and Goffman (1974), Norris-Raynbird (2008) uses frame analysis to evaluate capacity building in local coastal programs in Louisiana. Historically, there has been much contention among stakeholders over the use and regulation of land and other resources in Louisiana (Krogman 1995). Norris-Raynbird identifies those with the *regulator* framework as believing that regulation is necessary to protect resources in the market economy, while the *regulated* find regulations to be obstructionist, permitting processes unnecessarily complicated, and value solutions to conflict over understanding the complexities surrounding environmental issues (Krogman 1995, 28). Norris-Raynbird (2008) explains these distinctions between *regulator*, *regulated*, and *environmentalist* frames, ultimately defining capacity as the presence of the *regulator* frame.

Notably, Norris-Raynbird (2008) also highlights the role of social capital in capacity building as the imbuing of the *regulator* frame in CZM programs. Her findings showed that project activities that provided additional exposure to the CZM ideology or the *regulator* framework, such as "trainings, conferences, reading CZM related journal articles, technical reports, etc. were part of the educational and socialization (social capital) processes that work toward the building of institutional and human capacities in CZM" (Norris-Raynbird 2008, 38). This is similar to capacity-building project activities in foreign donor-led development projects in so-called fragile states.

Further, Norris-Raynbird goes on to note that "the *facilitating environment* created by the program structure and process, relate to the 'character of the individual' and the frames that are built as individuals and groups" (38). This is an important point that is critical to the success of capacity-building programs and helps to explain the failure of such programs in the international development of so-called fragile states. The realities of a warzone are generally not the most facilitating in which to build capacity.

Using frame analysis to explain how capacity building takes form, Norris-Raynbird associates the accumulation of social capital between the *regulators* and *regulated* with the shifting of individual and group frames:

> Framing is a repeating process with a shifting dynamic that constantly takes in new information and carries past information forward into new frames (Goffman 1974; Snow et al. 1986). *Repeated interaction is crucial to building cooperation and trust. Cooperation is facilitated by social networks and norms, through and around which interaction occurs, and trust is built.* Putnam (1993) refers to these organizational features and the mutual benefits that follow from them as *social capital*. Flora and Flora (2005) similarly link lateral community learning to networks and social capital. (Norris-Raynbird 2008, 27)

This *social capital* framework is pervasive in the literature on community capacity-building projects in developed countries. However, this emphasis on the important factor of *repeated interaction* as being crucial to building cooperation and trust, together with the idea that this interaction must be facilitated by social networks and norms, is particularly relevant when it comes to the challenges of capacity building at subnational scales within fragile states. I detail further these challenges in particular in Chapter 5 by examining the rise of transnational militancy in sub- and transnational spaces alongside the transformation of the security–development nexus on the donor end, and in Chapter 6 by detailing the struggle of donor statecraft in the context of USAID's attempts to build capacity in Afghanistan and Pakistan.

However, it is equally important to understand the deficiencies of Fallov's (2010) and Norris-Raynbird's (2008) studies of community capacity-building programs in the UK, Denmark, and the state of Louisiana, when applied to international capacity development programs in the "developing" world. We must ask why these community capacity-building programs were effective in imbuing the "regulator" frame or in the molding of habitus. For one, the scale of donor operation—USAID's networks and operation—does not encompass subnational spaces in either Afghanistan or Pakistan. This is a significant point.

Consider the dynamic between the *regulator* and *regulated* frames of the donors and recipients of capacity-building programs in the international development of fragile states. In the context of Afghanistan and Pakistan, the *regulator* frame encompasses a wide range of both foreign and state actors. Foreign actors include a variety of donors—such as USAID—as well as military forces. Recipients—local populations and even government officials—generally lack access to and influence within the spaces foreign actors operate and collaborate to create agendas and frameworks for development. The USAID consultant traveling to Afghanistan for a one-year tour to complete a project is too far removed from the everyday realities and narratives of those living in Helmand Province to be able to define the needs of those communities. S/he is concerned with carrying out the project and meeting deadlines.

Alternatively, Afghan and Pakistani state actors are generally not able to influence US foreign policy toward their countries. Considering this spatial distance between foreign and recipient networks (and the belief systems that govern the legitimacy of these networks), one could hardly call the environment within which these diverging frameworks interact for projects as "facilitating" or "enabling." The spaces within which projects take place are affected by the dynamics surrounding relationships of invasion, occupation, tribal autonomy, and transnational militancy, usually requiring foreigners (and even state actors) to maintain a security or military presence to conduct project activities. Consider the impact these dynamics have on the relationship between those who are imbued as the "duty-bearers" and the "rights-holders." This also relates to why capacity-building projects in this context cannot lead to the construction of a habitus.

As we see from these analyses of community development programs in developed countries, processes of building social capital through capacity development programs are only effective when participants establish working relationships based on a collective understanding of the *regulator* or, in Fallov's case, the "governor" framework. It is then that the communities which are targets of capacity building *organically* (and not through force or coercion) adopt the regulator or "governor" frames and take ownership of projects to expand this framework. This process of ownership is not organic in the international development of other countries, particularly those housing transnational Islamic militant groups that target donor states as their enemies, involving frameworks far more complex than in the case of the UK, Denmark, or the state of Louisiana. I detail the epistemological and professional convergences and tensions of the donor framework in greater detail in Chapters 2 and 3; and then, in Chapter 5, I analyze the tensions and transformations that emerge within a context fraught with endless waves of invasion, fresh trauma, and conflict among warlords.

Ultimately, both the concepts of habitus and frames are illuminating and useful for understanding capacity-building programs. I would contend that USAID projects are, in some sense, working toward the construction of a habitus and that an understanding of divergent frames is integral not only to conceptualizing capacity but also to successful capacity building. Further, Foucauldian concepts of governmentality and the "management of possibilities" are applicable to tactics employed by donors in the development of so-called fragile states. However, none of these concepts are the most useful for this particular analysis because they do not sufficiently capture the transformation of capacity building in discourse, policy, and projects over the past four decades in Afghanistan and Pakistan. Furthermore, they do not help to explain the rise of transnational militancy or the reasons behind the various forms of international integration of military and development activities. Thus, a major limitation of these frameworks for understanding capacity building is that they do not factor in the dynamics of *power* and *norms* that constitute the *relationships* and *networks* that either enable or inhibit development. I expand upon this in the following paragraphs.

Throughout this project, I deal with concepts of *spaces* within and *scales* at which various actors and institutions operate. I argue that the scale of the space at which any given donor operates may reach, but does not encompass, the spaces within which transnational Islamic militant groups operate, and vice versa. For this reason, capacity-building programs in "developed nations" are distinct from foreign donor capacity-building programs in "developing," but particularly "fragile," states. They are distinct in their ability to have capacity take root and contribute to the construction of a donor-envisaged habitus, which is largely due to the complex nature of the relationship between foreign donors and recipients and the spaces within which they interact. There is no organically occurring space for interaction between these two groups outside of the context of development projects and countering the spread of militancy. This is a significant point that those who work in development must contemplate in considering how to build capacity for sustainability.

In Norris-Raynbird's (2008) analysis of capacity building, she discusses how to bridge the *distance between spaces* within which individuals and networks of diverging frameworks operate, which is identified as an *aspect* of capacity building. The local coastal programs in Louisiana brought together federal, state, and local parish governments, as well as resource managers and concerned citizen stakeholders (e.g., big business, landowners, resource users) to coordinate planning for coastal management and were fraught with difficulty in coming to agreement on common goals and on shared governance. Norris-Raynbird (2008) highlights that the *facilitation of relationships* through *dynamic and adaptive reciprocal learning processes* helps to converge diverse framing perspectives and aid in the construction of a regulator frame among disputing stakeholders. The structure and process of the local coastal programs both provided participants with greater exposure to CZM ideology and also interaction with regulators. This created a facilitating environment from which to build sustainable relationships and imbue the regulator framework. In another sense, one could say that this program built relationships and trust between those who were the "regulators" and those who were the "regulated."

This would not apply to development projects in a "fragile" state context. Capacity building in subnational environments—villages and cities such as Khost, Afghanistan or Miranshah, Pakistan—generally does not involve *adaptive reciprocal learning processes* between locals, administrators, state officials, and donors. Development projects involve knowledge transfer and a distribution of resources to select recipients to carry out projects and facilitate official linkages with the state, ideally imbuing a recognition of the centralized authority of the state.

Let us consider the *regulated* frame within the context of tribal Pashtuns living in the border regions of Afghanistan or Pakistan. It is not merely a case of regulations being obstructionist or that permitting processes are complex—this is but a base level of attempting to shift *modes* of operation. Rather, it is that those who are the "regulators" and who operate from a "regulator" framework comprise a vast, complicated, and corrupt array of individuals and official and covert networks of states, militants, and donors (both state based and private). The barriers to shifting from the "regulated" frame of those in positions of authority in subnational and transnational tribal networks to the "regulator" frame of the state are far greater and more significant than simply transcending the roles of those involved, as Norris-Raybird suggests occurred in local coastal programs in Louisiana. Furthermore, those in Afghanistan and Pakistan who comply and participate in projects sometimes put themselves at risk. This feeds into a donor–recipient dynamic where the donor must incentivize cooperation in order to complete projects, and these projects are rarely initiated or directed by locals. This serves to further politicize projects to build capacity, undermining the sustainability of capacity development efforts.

Furthermore, capacity building for the construction of a habitus would likely have very different outcomes if the governors and regulators in Fallov's cases in Denmark had maintained relationships with donor institutions and agencies funded by foreign governments. It is unlikely we will ever see India or China working with the Danish government to invest in neighborhood regeneration to construct a habitus that legitimizes the practices and institutions of the state of Denmark. If this hypothetical situation were ever to be realized, consider what these community development projects might look like. The facilitation of networks and linkages carried out through projects, as well as the structural framework within which they are being constructed, would be impacted by the added dynamics of the relationship between the Chinese government and the Danish state, as well as the Chinese framework for development, governance, and trade (which would influence all aspects of the projects).

Further, it is likely that this framework for capacity development would reinforce and legitimize the structures and relations of power, enabling the existence of whatever global or international "habitus" places China in a position of dominance in relation to other states (in which the Chinese government has the interest and ability to invest and influence the construction of boundaries and governing structures of other societies). While China is, in reality, increasing investment in the global development space, I present the hypothetical of Chinese investment in the capacity building of subnational communities in "developed" states such as Denmark to highlight how the dynamics between foreign donors and the central government of a recipient state differ fundamentally and influence capacity-building projects in a way that Danish investment in the capacity of its own neighborhoods would not.

Additionally, the construction of a habitus requires a shared common framework for approaching interactions, relationships, and institutions. It also requires a sustained convergence of the spaces and scales to which the *donor, regulator, governor* or *duty-bearer* and the *beneficiary, regulated, governed,* or *rights-holders* operates. In both Fallov's and Norris-Raynbird's studies, participants and stakeholders share spaces of operation during the projects, and the general framework regarding the legitimacy of institutions of the state are shared by both the *regulator* and the *regulated,* though they may in some instances still disagree on issues and management tactics. While in Fallov's (2010) work, community development projects are to *regenerate* neighborhood capacity, capacity building in fragile states is both for the *generation* and (in some cases) *regeneration* of networks and structures. In order for there to be a habitus, actors and organizations must exercise agency and be engaged in relationships and networks based upon shared notions of positioning, beliefs, and rules for interaction and operation. Donors build projects that fit into donor-defined frameworks for interaction and operation—market-based economies, centralized state structures, fixed national boundaries, and of relationships and networks as social capital.

Another important aspect of community capacity building in these "developed" country examples that makes them intrinsically distinct from the situation of "fragile" states has to do with *the concept of community at subnational scales.* The Danish and English "neighborhoods" Fallov refers to are fundamentally different from tribes operating subnationally and transnationally in Afghanistan and Pakistan. Neighborhoods are spatially situated; tribes are not totally, and include non-spatially situated forms of community (e.g., nomads, refugees). The situated-ness of neighborhoods limits their scales of operation. Additionally, neighborhoods typically do not maintain autonomous systems of authority that sometimes challenge the legitimacy, as well as the relevance, of centralized institutions or the state system. While individual and community capacity building in the UK and Denmark may become a process that realizes and legitimizes governmental practices and institutions through making capacity building about *processes of inclusion*—this same model simply does not apply in the case of Afghanistan and Pakistan.

In attempting to imbue the donor's framework into the sociopolitical fabric of fragile state contexts, I contend that donors engage in capacity building through *statecraft,* a notion I borrow from James C. Scott's (1999) work on the failure of grand state planning schemes and management tactics, which I expand upon further in Chapter 6. In my conceptualizing of USAID capacity-building projects as a form of *statecraft,* I argue that donors attempt to construct networks and relationships (or what some scholars and practitioners reduce to, problematically as I explain, "social capital"[1]) through projects surrounding the cultivation of legitimate markets and centralized state structures. These donor projects reinforce the Western donor state's broader framework for the expansion of global capitalism and attempt to regulate the spaces of exclusion (from which

---

1. I argue that this is a reductionist and donor-conceived frame for relationship and network building.

militancy stems), ascribing legitimacy to situated ways of being and networks of social relations within the spatial confines of the state. Through my analysis of USAID projects in Afghanistan and Pakistan, I highlight how the meaning of "capacity" has been transformed throughout the donor literature *in conjunction with* and *influenced by* transformations in geopolitical dynamics, as well as within and among the epistemological and professional frameworks of the foreign policies and operations of donor states.

Finally, there is some anthropological literature that touches on the narratives, themes, and functions of capacity building within the context of international development and projects within developing countries, which is relevant to my project. Douglas-Jones and Shaffner (2017) conducted a study of capacity building comparing various ethnographies on the topic in an attempt to develop a disciplinary approach to the study of a topic that "operates across quite distinct settings" and "re-describes the world in its own terms" (10). The authors argue that the capacity narrative emerged from within the development agenda and has evolved and become pervasive within, "a bewildering range of sites … the lexicons of *government* (Hughes et al. 2010), *third sector* (Linnell 2003, O'Reilly 2011), *religious* (McDougall 2013), *medical* (Kelly 2011, Geissler et al. 2014), *environmental* (United Nations Environmental Programme [UNEP] 2002) and even familiar *academic agendas* (Danaher et al. 2012, Pfotenhauer et al. 2013, 2016)" (Douglas-Jones and Shaffner 2017, 4–5). In this project, I find that the capacity narrative has also become salient in the discourses surrounding human rights, statebuilding, and global security, particularly within foreign policy agendas.

In examining how capacity building "re-describes" the world in its own terms, the authors find that narratives of capacity are framed around tones of *hope, insufficiency*, and *potential*, justifying a *need* for *intervention* and *development*. They argue that capacity building works through "comparative transformation." As they explain, capacity building "… *must generate* (preferably measurable) *insufficiencies* that need to be made apparent—*an absence* that *becomes a potential*" (Douglas-Jones and Shaffner 2017, 7). Further, the combination of "capacity" with "building" means we must attend to how (and which) capacities can become sites of *cultivation* or *intervention* (ibid., 6). Douglas-Jones and Shaffner note how the very term itself encourages intervention and invents particular sufficiencies within which donors lay claim to expertise. This sort of language also inculcates a tone of condescension and superiority within the foundation of donor–beneficiary relationships. In Chapter 2, I further explored and addressed these justifications for intervention and expertise in regard to the growing salience and institutionalization of capacity within donor systems and the development space.

Themes of Capacity: State Power, Community, and Social Capital

In reviewing this literature, I identify three major themes of capacity-building projects that emerge: (1) *state power and control*, (2) *community* (varying notions of: community building, development, national communities, neighborhoods, etc.), and (3) *social capital*, specifically the framing of relationships around the concept. Numerous scholars, including some reviewed here, relate capacity building to various aspects of state power and control (Mowbray 2005, Bryson and Mowbray 1981, Adams and Hess 2001, Norris-Raynbird

2008, Fallov 2010). In explaining the ability of the state to exercise power, many studies link capacity building to effective policy implementation (Bardach 1977, Burby and May 1997, Gargan 1981, Hershmann et al. 1999, King and Olson 1988, May and Williams 1986). Further, the language employed by Norris-Raynbird (2008) and Fallov (2010) on the *regulators* and *regulated* (also see Dietz and Rycroft 1987, 1989, Krogman 1995) as well as the *governors* and the *governed*, reinforces notions of power and control over resources and institutional support for community capacity-building initiatives (also see Flora and Flora 2005, Hershmann et al. 1999, Olsen et al. 1997).

The other two themes I identify as major elements of the capacity-building discourse—that of *community* and of *social capital*—are linked. Communities take many forms and operate on a variety of scales, and there is extensive literature that ties building the capacity of communities (and of civic engagement) to *social capital* (Holtgrave et al. 2014, Bhuiyan 2011, Mandarano 2015, Morton and Lurie 2013, Smith 2015, Jung and Viswanath 2013, Simmons 2011). West[2] (2016) notes that capacity development schemes are "thought" to be appropriate for all scales, though like much of the institutional literature produced by donors, instead of *communities*, she identifies individuals, organizations, and "whole societies" as the primary objects of capacity development efforts (71). This is an interesting distinction between community capacity-building programs in developed nations and capacity building as a broader donor project of development. Development agencies conduct many different types of capacity-building projects, their targets being individuals, organizations, societies, and environments—but not primarily or explicitly *communities*. Thus, foreign donor-led projects of capacity are often divorced from notions and projects of community building. This is not to say that the cultivation of broader community is not an objective of the variety of projects that fall under the umbrella of capacity building, but it is usually not made explicit.

In addition to community building and civic engagement, there are many studies linking social capital to capacity building within *health and medicine* (Gnaedinger and Robinson 2011, Mantopoulos et al. 2010, Morton and Lurie 2013, Smith 2015, Zea and Belgrave 2009, Jung and Viswanath 2013, Putland et al. 2013, Kim et al. 2016, Simmons 2011) and *education and research* (Wong 2018, Zea and Belgrave 2009, Haslam et al. 2013). In addition to Norris-Raynbird (2008), Amir Zal (2016) also links social capital to coastal management in his study on capacity building among Malaysian fishermen. A full review of these works is outside the realm of this project, but I highlight these three themes of state power and control, community, and social capital, as they are themes that are relevant and also emerge in my study of USAID capacity building in Afghanistan and Pakistan.

These three major themes of capacity are all fundamentally about *relationships* and *networks* of power—the context of the spaces within which they exist and the scales at

---

2. West (2016) also argues that capacity building's ideology is steeped in narratives of European and Western superiority with assumptions that "there is an inherent lack in non-European persons, institutions, and social systems," which necessitates the need for intervention and technical solutions such as training, structures, and audit cultures (72).

which they operate. In this regard, I examine USAID's efforts at capacity building, the reasons for donor failures to facilitate and expand the capacity of the Afghan state, as well as explain the rise of transnational Islamic militancy and the increasing integration of development and military activities in a security–development nexus. This project explores the (donor) "spaces" within which notions of capacity have transformed, as well as the context of the (recipient) spaces within which donors' attempts to imbue capacity have failed to take root.

Of the three major themes of capacity, my analysis of USAID projects highlights the limitations of the donor framework for relationships and networks as *social capital*, particularly in regard to the cultivation of the other themes: the cultivation of *state power and control*, and *community* (in the broadest sense of the term). USAID's frameworks for capacity have historically been steeped in notions of *capital* (economic, institutional, human, etc.), which I expanded upon in Chapter 3 in my examination of donor methodologies on capacity development. From the donor framework, donor–recipient relationships are largely transactional, treating networks and relationships as resources that should have exchange value. This framework is inherently reductionist and does not by any justifiable measure factor in the complexity of relationships and networks steeped in generations of conflict (which I expand upon in the following chapter). Donors merely hope that their investments yield commitment and cooperation by the recipient—to the central government and to the donor.

In building this argument, I expand upon James C. Scott's (1999) notion of *statecraft* as a project of *legibility* requiring *state simplifications*, carried out through projects. Scott defines "legibility" as a "condition of manipulation" required for state planning schemes (Scott 1999, 183). Scott gives examples of the adoption of surnames, cadastral mapping, forest management, impositions of official language, land tenure practices, taxation techniques, and even traffic centralization as examples of projects of legibility. As subnational insurgencies and transnational militant networks have evolved into global threats, strengthening the capacity of the state to implement schemes to manage the subnational spaces within which these militants operate has become imperative. I detail this donor *statecraft* through my analysis of USAID projects in Afghanistan and Pakistan in Chapter 6. I argue that donor institutions, such as USAID, integrate particular methods of capacity development into projects as a tactic, involving *state simplifications*, treating networks and relationships as transactional and exchange-based *social capital*, in an attempt to gain what is actually *social power and influence* to expand the scale of state legibility and enable the centralized planning of development of subnational spaces that house transnational threats.

My project also expands upon the work of Monika Krause (2014). Krause adopts Bourdieu's notion of *fields* in an examination of humanitarianism and the production of projects by NGOs. Krause argues that "*relief* is a form of production" with "one primary output or product, which is the project" (Krause 2014, 4). In pursuit of "good projects," managers produce projects in a market where donors and not beneficiaries are consumers, resulting in the commodification of the beneficiary. While the Bourdieusian framework of *fields* adopted by Krause is relevant to humanitarian relief aid, I argue that this is a limited framework for understanding development aid in the context of counterinsurgency in Afghanistan and Pakistan. This is because the production of projects to build state capacity is not primarily for humanitarian relief but to expand the reach of the state and to manage threats. Beneficiaries are still in some ways commodified in this production of development projects, but the projects often fail to create the linkages donors desire in subnational spaces.

Bourdieu conceptualized fields on the scale of the nation-state, though he notes that the boundaries of fields do not typically correspond with geographic or political boundaries (Krause and Go 2016, 11). In *Fielding Transnationalism*, Krause and Julian Go (2016) note, "For Bourdieu, the ideal-typical national state is a state with the capacity to regulate and define other forms of capital in its territorial domain. This is the state's 'meta-capital': a form of power which, by regulating and defining what counts as capital, also carries the ability to regulate relations between fields" (17). This is an objective of donors. Donors conceptualize development on the scale of the state, as this is the scale of operation within which donors are able to penetrate. A state with the aforementioned capacity is one that manages threats so that they do not spill over boundaries and also one that actively facilitates trade and capitalist growth. This is a limited framework for understanding the issues of state capacity development, but it is one that is consistent with donor strategy to build capacity through projects.

Actors and organizations operating at subnational and transnational scales do not agree on the "rules of the game" or hierarchies of power inherent within the development field of practice, nor is their objective of "development" of societies in any context similar to the OECD/DAC-mandated agendas for global aid. In fact, transnational networks of resistance actively work to disrupt these agendas! This disruption represents a fundamental clash of frameworks and narratives surrounding relationships and networks of power: that of global capitalist development and global militant Islam. I contend that the Western donor framework, exemplified through USAID in this study, reduces the very notion of capacity by approaching relationships and networks of actors at the subnational scales as *social capital* to be gained to expand the legibility of the state. While capacity development methodologies include mechanisms that get at the integration of already existing forms of capacity into the design of projects, in practice they tend to fail both in implementation and in understandings of process ownership. Furthermore, these processes in design are not actually inclusive of actors or groups considered to be threats or merely resistors to the objectives of the broader donor project of statecraft.

I find that donors largely ignore and misunderstand cultural context and the way in which social power is conceived at various scales of operation, attempting to win it as a consolation as they try to transform the *objects*[3] of development projects by building capacity. While I provide some of this context in Chapter 6, in expanding upon the work of Monika Krause (2014) and James C. Scott (1999), I reveal how donors (USAID) produce projects as a tactic to gain social capital, as an incomplete and simplified conception

---

3. I expand upon the notion of *objects* of capacity building and development projects in the previous chapter.

of *social power*, to extend the legibility of the state of subnational spaces. This tactic demonstrates donor strategies to contain the act and project of "development" (of societies) to a national framework, in large part to manage and contain political threats in so-called fragile states and expand global capitalism.

Fragility and the Role of the State, in Theory and in Practice

> Fragile states are losing their capacity to govern (1) ... USAID's fragile states strategy and program priorities embody a different relationship between governance and aid. Namely, that more, not less, aid will be used in these countries to improve their governance. We will have more of both governance and aid. Fragile states will get more aid because they are losing their capacity to govern, not because their governance performance is strong, or even satisfactory. Our strategy and program priorities are thus pressed to succeed—to improve governance and thus change key patterns of fragility or bolster patterns of resilience—even though we will be at work in some of the globe's weakest "development" environments. The challenge is, in our analysis of fragility and shaping of program responses, to know enough and do enough to improve governance sharply in these fragile settings"—USAID Fragile States Assessment Framework. (USAID 2005b, 35)
>
> For countries transitioning toward democracy, building state capacity and promoting institutions that create checks and balances, *such as the legislature, judiciary, media, local governance, and civil society*, are critical, if longer-term, steps for fostering stability and reducing the ascendancy of criminal networks—Organized Crime, Conflict and Fragility: Assessing Relationships Through a Review of USAID Programs. (USAID 2015a, 13)

Throughout this project, the issue of the state is at the core of how donors portray the "capacity" problem. In Chapter 2, I highlight the dominance of the traditional system of DAC-donors in determining international agendas for development practice, underscoring an ascription of legitimacy to the state system. In the previous chapter, I traced the evolution of capacity methodologies within donor frameworks, within which the state has remained central despite major macro-historical, ideological, and political shifts. The following chapter highlights the transnational struggles of statehood within the contexts and heritage of colonialism, as well as the history of bilateral assistance in Afghanistan and Pakistan. Finally, Chapter 6 turns to an examination of USAID's attempts to craft the state in Afghanistan and Pakistan through capacity building, highlighting how USAID and other donors struggle to navigate the complex power dynamics of Afghanistan and Pakistan.

In my discussion of capacity building in Afghanistan and Pakistan, the discursive designation of "fragility" is often applied to these two states in the literature by donor institutions and donor state policies. In this section, I address and problematize this designation. Before I delve further into this discursive tactic and the metrics ascribed to them, we must ask what role the state is *supposed to* perform to not be considered "fragile." What actually makes for a "successful" state? In part to legitimate their investments, donors have developed criteria by which they measure stability, affiliated with measures of economic performance and political representation of national societies. Every project to build the capacity of individuals and organizations—private sector actors and state managers—seeks to construct an environment of political stability to attract investors. In our sociological understanding of the *state* and theories surrounding the movement, flow, form, and operation of *power, resistance, profit,* and *production,* we must not ignore how development (and capacity development) fits into this discussion on the state.

My project examines how USAID attempts to build capacity—ultimately that of the state—and more broadly how a US-led donor community engages in statebuilding processes. The transformation of capacity over the past four decades has occurred over monumental shifts within macro-historical and epistemological frameworks, which have reconfigured how relationships and networks of power operate in relation to the state. I find through my examination of USAID projects that the state remains a central vessel in donor attempts to build capacity, regardless of neoliberalist attempts to redistribute the functions of state governance to private actors. I elaborate further upon these governance functions of the state, and how USAID projects attempt to construct them, in my discussion of donor *statecraft* in Chapter 6.

I argue that regardless of macro-historical or epistemological shifts and major reconfigurations in the networks and political forms of power, in the practice of international development, *the state remains central* (especially in cases of designated fragility). Transformations in donor methodologies have thus far failed to lead to the cultivation of sustainable relationships and networks required to build the capacity of the state. In the chapters that follow, I expand upon these shifts in frameworks (both donor and "recipient") over historical periods, highlighting the social context of the spaces within which these shifts occur. I do this in order to demonstrate the challenge donors face in attempting to extend the arm of the state into subnational spaces—where the territoriality of state boundaries is often barely paid lip service by locals. The sociological literature on the state and processes of statebuilding is vast, and the focus on the state as a unit of social analysis is hotly disputed within certain scholarly circles. In order to situate our understanding of (1) the transformation of capacity, (2) the narratives and ideologies that linger behind this transformation, (3) the role of the development agency in processes of statebuilding in so-called fragile states, and (4) the rise of new forms of the development–security nexus, we must consider how the movement of power and the operation of the state are theoretically conceived.

I start by highlighting the work of Michael Mann and Charles Tilly. Both scholars examined and conceptualized the state and state formation processes of European states as the bipolar world of the Cold War gave way to a post-Washington Consensus world. Mann (1993) argues that the state form emerged and took shape as European states transitioned from feudalism to capitalism and consolidated national markets and productive structures. Tilly (1992) highlights that the state formation processes of European states were lengthy—occurring over centuries and marked by conflict and complex struggles, which yielded a diversity of different state form outcomes. State forms were not the products of deliberate planning and calculation, but rather occurred as the result of one of three primary patterns Tilly identifies in his analysis of European state formation: coercion-intensive, capital-intensive, and capitalized-coercion. Tilly ultimately asserts that *warmaking* has become a specialized, professional enterprise that has driven *statemaking*, leading to varying outcomes in state trajectories across different settings. This is an important notion to consider, particularly as we examine forms of the development–security nexus and consider the place of human rights approaches to capacity development.

This conceptualization of *capital* and *coercion* as the driving patterns behind the interaction of societal groups leading to the creation of the state form is significant, particularly as we conceive of how these two drivers lead to the creation of other forms and networks of power. Fred Block (1987) takes a Marxist approach to explaining how the operation of capitalist power flows within the state form. Block argues that it is not a class-conscious ruling class but rather a "capitalist rationality"—propelled by relationships between capitalists, workers, and state managers—that defines the management of the state apparatus. He claims two "subsidiary mechanisms" explain why the state rationalizes capitalism: the lobbying of business people and the more general "bourgeois cultural hegemony" designating the "proper role" of the state to maintain political stability for investors (Block 1987, 15). Notably, Block identifies several factors, which he argues impact the state's role in maintaining *stability*: control of the working class, taxation, and government involvement in the market and determining the price of labor (ibid., 16). These are important considerations within the context of development in understanding the role and also expectations donors have of the state with regard to capitalist development. I argue that this framework is consistent with how donors (unconsciously) frame the state in their strategies for developing capacity and also in their attempt to construct it in practice.

Mann, Tilly, and Block all conceptualized the state coming off the end of a bipolar global context, where states were the site of political contests between the USSR and the United States as a strategy of containment and to practice Soviet communist and Western neoliberal capitalist models of development. As the Soviet Union fell, and this bipolar context gave way to a post-Washington Consensus era of unbridled economic globalization, capitalist production was no longer state-centric and new transnational forms defined the flow of capital. William Robinson asserts that we are in a new stage in global capitalism, characterized by the rise of transnational capital, a transnational capitalist class (TCC), a transnational state (TNS), and subsequent global rebellion marked by popular, working-class, and leftist struggles (Robinson 2017, 172). In Chapter 5, I examine the construction of the transnational infrastructure for resistance—that of insurgency and ultimately global terror. My findings to an extent challenge Robinson's portrayal of the global rebellion as popular, working class, and leftist.

Robinson asserts that the material basis for the *nation-state*, as a "political form of correspondence" between production, social classes, and territoriality, has been superseded by *globalization*—an interwoven process of global capitalist production and transition away from national linkages to integrated international markets (Robinson 1998, 563–65). This change in the material basis of political form is why Robinson argues for a "return to the theoretical conceptualization of the state, not as a 'thing' but as a specific social relation inserted into larger social structures that may take different, and historically determined, institutional forms, only one of which is the nation-state" (565). Mann (1986) also claims that nation-states are *historically bound* and argues that the analysis of society should be within the parameters of historical periods, focusing on four basic networks of social interaction, which constitute *social power*: economic, political, ideological, and coercive. Through my examination of capacity development in policy and practice, we are able to see in what ways donors conceive of the material basis of the state and also how donors exercise networks to extend the reach of the state (and ultimately and ideally that of the donor) into subnational spaces.

Robinson's work is particularly relevant to mine as the international invasion of Afghanistan presents new forms of international and transnational organizing—both for intervention and resistance. My research adds an interesting empirical component to Robinson's promotion of global capitalist theory and the emergence of transnational elites. Robinson sees globalization as a qualitatively new epoch in the evolution of global capitalism, with the institutions of development and global trade characterizing the transnationalization of capital and integration of countries in the interstate system into a new global production and financial system (Robinson 2011, 352). Robinson also argues that globalization offered a viable strategy for capitalists and state managers searching for new modes of accumulation, "shak(ing) off the constraints that the nation-state capitalism had placed on accumulation …" (Robinson 2011, 352) and that since the 1970s, the emergence of "globally mobile transnational capital increasingly divorced from specific countries has facilitated the *globalization of production.*"

In Robinson's theorizing of globalization, the TNS, and the rise of transnational elites and the global financial system, *relationships are organized around capital and production.* Robinson notes that under this global structure of accumulation, "socioeconomic exclusion is immanent … The very drive by local elites to create conditions to attract transnational capital has been what thrusts majorities into poverty and inequality" (2011, 361). My research explores this very conceptualizing of relationships and networks around capital and production as a tactic of development institutions (and, by extension, donor states) to penetrate subnational spaces harboring transnational insurgency through development projects to build state capacity. This conceptual framework for cultivating relationships around development projects to strengthen the capacity of the state is at the root of the fundamental failure of donor efforts in combating transnational militancy and so-called state fragility. I expanded upon these frameworks and the ideological roots of how donors conceive of relationships and networks through a discursive examination of USAID's usage of capacity in policy and projects in Chapter 3, the construction of a transnational infrastructure for militancy through bilateral, military, and humanitarian networks in Chapter 5, and detailing of donor statebuilding efforts through USAID's *statecraft* in Chapter 6.

In the examination of how USAID crafts the state in the coming chapters, I expose how international and transnational coalitions of state, private sector, humanitarian, and military actors have operated in relation to the state primarily during two significant and very different "global" conflicts: the Cold War and the War on Terror. Robinson calls for the framing of states "as *historically changing constellations* of social forces operating through multiple institutions, including state apparatuses that are themselves in a process of transformation as a consequence of collective agencies" (Robinson 2017, 183). Yet, he asserts that this persistent focus and reification of the nation-state paradigm within development studies and international relations that analyzes nations as "discrete units within a larger system," limit our understanding and explanation of social phenomena (Robinson 2017, 175). He goes on to claim, "If we are to understand global capitalism and the nature of the ruling class we must train our focus on configurations of social forces existing in constant contradiction, struggle, and transformation, analytically prior to focusing on the ways in which they become institutionalized and expressed in political (including state), cultural and ideological processes" (183).

In this study of USAID's work in Afghanistan and Pakistan, I present an empirical example of modern state formation processes in practice. This reveals the way in which the development agency (USAID), as an institution of a powerful donor state (the United States), facilitates the construction of state infrastructure and systems for social management both to contain threats and to expand global capitalism in the name of capacity. I also highlight new forms of subnational, international, and transnational cooperation that occur during the transformation of the capacity project under the globalization of security. I affirm Robinson's call for moving away from state-centric social analysis toward transnational studies, but I assert that a significant component of this transnational study should examine how international and supranational institutions, state actors, the TCC, transnational militants, and criminal networks all interact and engage in various projects through the vessel of the state—in the construction, circumvention, and deconstruction of the state.

While Robinson demonstrates how economic globalization led to the formation of transnational networks and infrastructure for capital accumulation, an examination of the discursive designation of fragility requires greater explanation when considering contexts like Afghanistan where we see development overtly becoming a part of military strategy for counterinsurgency, stability operations, and statebuilding—and not merely the expansion of global capitalism. Hughes (2001) brings to our attention what he calls the "globalization–security nexus." Here, he portrays the "essence" and territoriality of globalization as a *security problem* that transcends "barriers to interaction across social space" and thus challenges the state as "the existing basis for the global security order" (418). Hughes credits decolonization and "bipolarization" as creating states defined by internal contradictions relating to the territoriality of its societies. He argues that these states are fundamentally unprepared to cope with and respond to the economic processes of globalization, and they also exploit the benefits of liberal capitalism to "paper over" political and security cracks (419).

Instead of focusing on the states' role in the facilitation of markets, Hughes draws attention to the role of states in managing conflict. Hughes points out how states rooted in territorial notions of social space *facilitate, impede,* and *mediate* interaction between various groups, organizations, citizens, and other categories of collective and individual societal units within their borders (409). His defining of globalization is not inconsistent with Robinson's—as a "process … driven by political choice in favour of liberal economics … result(ing) in forms of social interaction which transcend territorial borders and state sovereignty" (5). He identifies three interrelated dimensions of threat—issues of global security—caused by the processes of globalization: *economic* (through the production of spaces of economic exclusion, which can feed into military tension and internal unrest), *environmental* (degradation and extraction of natural resources—which threatens the health of groups in various regions through the pollution of soil, water, and air), and *military* (trans-sovereign crime, expansion of markets for illicit products—e.g., narcotics or arms) (Hughes 2001, 414–18). All of these dimensions of global security threats cause instability or "fragility" and challenge the state's ability to manage conflict and social interaction among groups within its borders.

Statebuilding is one way in which donors have attempted to define and address security threats. Ian Roxborough (2012) attempts to flesh out a sociology of statebuilding in which he draws attention to the relevance (and lack) of sociological analysis in statebuilding processes. He argues that ultimately, the epistemological shifts from modernization to globalization did not actually lead to a substantive rethinking of the processes and difficulties of statebuilding *in practice*, noting that the Washington Beltway elite are not necessarily receptive to the debates of social scientists (199). In this analysis of the state, state formation, and statebuilding, discursive designations within policy and strategic frameworks of donor states and development institutions play an important part in the conceptualization and production of interventionist processes by donor states. The US FM 3-07 Army Field Manual that Roxborough examines, proclaims "... the greatest threat to our (the United States) national security comes ... from fragile states ... we will work through and with the community of nations to defeat insurgency, assist fragile states, and provide vital humanitarian aid to the suffering ..." (U.S. Army 2008). These are the justifications provided for statebuilding. Roxborough's focus is not discursive, but it's worth noting the labeling used alongside interventionist language in a US Army Manual concerned with the task of building states.

Roxborough's analysis of the FM 3-07 Army Field Manual and international stability operations reveals three main issues within military frameworks for statebuilding, as follows (Roxborough 2012, 194–96). First, he highlights how there is no real acknowledgment of the contradiction in how statebuilding involves a highly centralized external attempt to facilitate diffuse local participation and ownership of statebuilding processes. This is an issue of donors not fully acknowledging their role and positioning in the macro-level context of relationships surrounding development. I touch upon this issue in my discussion of capacity development in donor (USAID) project methodology in Chapters 3 and 6. The second issue is with regard to the sequencing and prioritization of the multiple and interacting tasks of statebuilding, of which there is little to no direction provided aside from an acknowledgment that coordination and cooperation are necessary. The third issue Roxborough identifies is a general and shallow framing of state failure and internal war, again without general acknowledgment of the role external actors play. Ultimately, Roxborough's highlighting of these shortcomings reveals the relevance of sociological analysis in the integration of local knowledge and appreciation of macro-historical processes as they relate to statebuilding.

Yet this question of how external transnational and international networks engage in the practice of building states and the question Tilly and Mann are concerned with—how states actually form—are two distinct processes about which there is much debate. Bliesemann de Guevara (2010) frames the distinction as a matter of time. Statebuilding is a short-term process, whereas state formation is a long-term process. Heathershaw (2012) identifies and summarizes three major interpretations of how international statebuilding and state formation have thus far been intertwined in modern global politics. First, there is framing of statebuilding as a neocolonial imposition of internationalized states, postulated in both policy-prescriptive and critical literatures (Zaum 2007, Chesterman 2004, Chandler 2006, and Paris and Sisk 2009). The second frames international statebuilding within the context of it being superseded by the parallel processes of either state formation or state collapse, which preexisted and outlasts the period of international intervention (Herring and Rangwala 2006, Bliesemann de Geuvara 2008, Kuhn 2012, Isachenko 2008). Finally, there are those whose focal point on statebuilding is to call into question the national, territorial, and hierarchically organized elements of the state concept (Sassen 2006, Ong and Collier 2005, Veit and Schlichte 2012, Mitchell 1999,) 246–47). My work combines aspects of the first and last of these interpretations in my examination of USAID not only as an extension of the US-led interventions but also as an institutional node within the international architecture for statebuilding whose efforts to craft the state demonstrates important empirical evidence on the international framing and practice of constructing the elements of the state.

Consistent with Robinson's call for a turn away from state-centric social analysis, Heathershaw suggests that the "unity and exclusivity of the state ... posited as an objective standard against which both statebuilding and state formation is judged is, in fact, a subjective effect of power" (2012, 257). Heathershaw concludes:

> If we recognize that the state is not just phantom or contested but as an empirical and normative entity is transformed, then we must also attend to the constitutive power of globality and performativity in the emergence of states out of violent political conflict. We must study *the globality of the state*: how its problems are not exclusively national but partially global. We must study the *performativity of the state*: how taking part in the state involves not merely the capture of resources, but publicly playing a part to multiple, often divergent audiences from the local to the global. (257)

Thus, in our theoretical study of the state, I argue it is imperative to consider development and development institutions in processes of statebuilding and state formation. There are a whole slew of ways in which we must examine development and development institutions in this regard. We must consider the ways in which they organize themselves in order to conduct practices of statebuilding, the way in which they assume and portray local problems as global problems requiring intervention, how their intervention and external facilitation impact or become a part of the form of the states they are building, how they conceptualize and put into practice the capture and use of resources within so-called fragile states they argue require intervention, how they "perform" development alongside military intervention and occupation, and how they expect states to "perform" in order to not be designated threats by the broader community of states, international coalitions, and transnational elites. My work offers but a glimpse into these areas.

An important situation to turn toward in examining the role of development in processes of statebuilding and state formation in practice is counterinsurgency. When considering development in cases of foreign military intervention, such as Afghanistan and Pakistan, the role of the development institution in counterinsurgency operations to build the capacity of states designated as "fragile" is particularly critical to understanding the transformation of capacity and how it has been impacted by security-based frameworks for development. Before turning specifically to the cases of Afghanistan and Pakistan in the following two chapters, the later parts of this chapter outline USAID's discursive framing of its historical involvement with counterinsurgency operations, in part to highlight the discursive relationship between *capacity* and *fragility*. This chapter concludes by outlining USAID's strategic approach to fragility.

USAID and Counterinsurgency Operations in Fragile States

> Uncertainty about the nature and potential of the insurgency makes development programming a hazardous task, but even if the knowledge of the Thai insurgency were complete, an even greater uncertainty remains: What is the impact of any development program on a country's ability to resist or repel an insurrectionary assault? Any hope that a development program might be planned to achieve a specific security strategy may well remain illusory. (Heymann 1969, 3)—*from a Seminar on Development and Security in Thailand attended by USAID, CIA, State Department officials as well as academics (political scientists and anthropologists) from elite US universities and economists from Rand Corporation*

Earlier in this chapter, I reviewed some of the debates surrounding how to define and conceive the role of the state in development, as well as statebuilding and state formation processes in order to situate the task ahead—one of examining USAID's capacity-building efforts in Afghanistan and Pakistan. I argue that since 9/11, we have entered a new macro-historical period defined by concerns surrounding global security. A defining feature of this period is the overt and public framing of development as essential to achieving military objectives—with little discussion or debate among practitioners or policy makers acknowledging that this shift even happened and whether or not it is actually contributing to greater progress for human society.

While this integration of activities is not actually new—particularly with USAID we can trace the development agency's role in counterinsurgency operations going back to the US invasion of Vietnam—it was not commonplace nor was it a defining feature of military or development mandates. We must ask what the implications are of this normalization of security objectives as an explicit aim of development agendas and also the framing of development as essential to military strategy. How can we evolve a HRBA when a major objective of development is to establish security and stability in areas with ongoing violence? Finally, we must ask, what role does the transformation of capacity play in this normalization and what does it mean more broadly for the meaning of "development" itself? In placing our focus on the usage of key concepts (e.g., "capacity") within discourse and institutional literature, as well as the function of discursive labeling (e.g., "fragility"), we can better understand these transformations and tease out the intersection of human rights and security in both the narratives and approaches of development.

It is significant that both "capacity" and "fragility" gained salience across multiple donor-end discourses after 9/11, paralleling the public militarization of development activity and growing donor concern with issues of security. Why did these terms gain salience at a time when the international interventions of states has become the norm and framing development activity as a component of military strategy and counterinsurgency goes relatively unquestioned within Western policy circles? As processes of globalization have impacted notions of the state, as discussed in the previous section, the transformations in networks and structures of power also impact the processes by which concepts and discursive labels gain salience within transforming spaces of discourse. I elaborated on these donor spaces in which capacity has gained salience in Chapter 2. But first, it is necessary to examine exactly how issues of security are portrayed and addressed within USAID's development agenda when these issues were initially *not* part of USAID's core mandate.

From the earliest years of its operation, USAID was involved in US counterinsurgency efforts in southeast Asia—most notably not only Vietnam but also Thailand and the Philippines. Roughly from 1964 until the early 1970s, USAID publications demonstrate a grappling with questions surrounding counterinsurgency and "nation building," "resource control," and conducting proper analyses of insurgencies for effective development programming. A 1964 report on *Police and Resources Control in Counter-Insurgency* in Vietnam defines insurgency as "an uprising using force and illegalities against political or governmental authority; a state of rebelliousness" (Adkins 1964, 4) and an insurgent as "an individual or group of individuals who enter or infiltrate an area for the purpose of overthrowing the governing authority of that area by subversive, guerrilla or other illegal activities" (5). The report calls for the National Police, along with other Vietnamese government agencies, to fight "for a system of free democracy … (noting that) officers must not treat their prisoners as totalitarian dictators do, sending them to prison without trial or executing them as the result of a kangaroo court decision" (50). But at this point, the United States was not in the business of building states—let alone democratic ones. While not explicitly referenced within this literature, US concern over the spread of Soviet influence obviously underlies the calls for democracy and modernization that drove the development agendas of the day.

In 1967, USAID supported a study on *Counter-Insurgency and Nation Building*, focusing specifically on Southeast Asia. In this study, the author portrays the struggle of "*traditional societies* striving for modernization … committed to democracy without the attributes and mechanisms to render this possible" (Silver 1967, 115). In considering how to modernize these "primitive societies … (where) the channels between government and people are largely unorganized" (114), the author highlights the critical importance of "political development" alongside "economic development" to address "problems of political instability (noting that) programs of economic development alone will not meet US objectives" (94).

This language reveals two key points. First, it carries with it a tone of objective altruism and condescension placing the donor (USAID) in a position of knowledge and authority—these "primitive" societies are "striving" for modernization and "committed to democracy," but need help getting there. In fact, another USAID report frames counterinsurgency and stabilization strategy as separate but key elements of modernization (Darling 1973, 66–72). Second, the language frames local problems of political instability in other countries as impediments to US objectives, thus justifying intervention. This sort of language is typical both today (in new discursive forms such as "fragility") as it was during the period of modernization (further discussed in the first section of Chapter 2). That said, the important takeaway here is the way in which discursive designations are used to justify intervention. This is not a new tactic of the development agency, yet at this point in time the institutional architecture for aid was not as established (USAID was one of the first bilateral development agencies to exist) or globalized, and the context for operation was within a bipolar world order.

Now, in these cases counterinsurgency was largely to contain the expansion of Communism in Southeast Asia. When the Soviets invaded Afghanistan, the United States did not have a counterinsurgency strategy because it was actually supporting the "insurgents" or the Mujahideen through Pakistan. However, this was not called counter-insurgency and was broadly under the umbrella of US bilateral assistance packages to Pakistan in the 1980s (see the following chapter for an in-depth examination of these packages). During the 1980s and after the fall of the Soviet Union, US resources and thus USAID was preoccupied with assisting the development of the emerging market economies of the former Soviet countries. Countering insurgencies and other military objectives did not take priority within the development agendas, but it was not entirely on the backburner either.

In 1990, USAID commissioned a study (of which only a draft is available) on "Insurgency and Development." The study makes a number of important claims in the introduction, which I outline here.

1.   The spread of insurgency is a symptom of failed development and *not* fundamentally a clash of ideologies;
2.   Countering insurgency is a challenge to the development profession;
3.   The military is the first line in countering insurgency, but the establishment of physical security is merely the initial objective, and must be closely coordinated with economic and political development to complete the process;
4.   Defense strategists and foreign aid specialists must stop viewing each other with skepticism and view their work as part of the same process. (Schaefer 1990, 3–4)

The report highlights the Philippines, El Salvador, Sri Lanka, Sudan, Colombia, and Peru as examples of AID-assisted countries that face insurgency and also contain a section on LDC (least-developed country) "Perceptions of American Values," identifying obstacles in addressing the sources of counterinsurgency.

The language in this section romanticizes the American model: "It is hard for Americans who live in the heart of the greatest democratic capitalist nation to understand skepticism about either our intentions or what our system offers" (10). Schaefer then outlines three critical points of explanation—that the United States has a history of supporting corrupt dictators, that while the United States "speaks warmly of the private sector," it has few allies that are actually capitalists, and that Americans mistake elections in LDCs for democracy.

The study then prescribes a list of principles (based off of Lord Robert Thompson's formulation) for a counterinsurgency program. Perhaps not surprisingly, some of the principles on this list could very well describe the US counterinsurgency approach today: political and economic opportunity, rule of law for all citizens, establishing a clear approach and plan, attacking the political cadre and wooing guerrillas, securing base areas, and expanding security zones through economic activities (27). Notably, lingering within the suggested principles for counterinsurgency we see the identification of various forms of rights as pillars for a security strategy: ensuring political and economic opportunity as well as rule of law. These are identified as security-related objectives that require development and not military force, in order to achieve.

Outside of this study's call for a greater cooperation and integration of military activities in counterinsurgency activities—countering insurgencies, extremism, and terrorism—was not a primary objective of USAID's policy framework or operation during the 1990s. As the United States settled into triumph following the fall of the Soviet Union and no longer faced grand threats to the expansion of liberal democracy and the capitalist system, USAID and other donors turned their attention to building the capacity of former Soviet states and new language emerged to classify the development status of states. "Fragility" was one of these discursive designations. As both Afghanistan and Pakistan are presently labeled as "fragile" states by Western donors, and there is no shortage of discussion within practitioner spaces and policy circles on how to remedy the plight of state "fragility," it is particularly relevant to our understanding of capacity to examine this designation.

Capacity: The Remedy for Fragility

Somewhat like *capacity*, the concept of *fragility* gained salience in policy discourses after 9/11 (Gisselquist 2014, Barakat and Larson 2014, Duffield 2001, Engberg-Pedersen et al. 2008). As I demonstrate throughout Chapters 2 and 3, capacity has a far deeper discursive history than fragility, though arguably the underlying concepts behind both discursive labels run deep. Afghanistan and Pakistan are considered fragile states by DAC-donor states, international organizations, and development agencies throughout the development discourse. There are other designations surrounding the so-called status of states such as "weak" or "failed," which are similar to "fragile" states, but a discussion of the full discursive variation of these designations does not contribute much value to my argument and is outside the scope of this project.

The designation of states as *fragile* emerged from country classification tools employed by the World Bank, DFID, the OECD/DAC member states' institutions and agencies in general as a part of processes to determine feasibility and plans for donor investments (Nay 2013b, 217–19). Notably, the concept of fragility does not apply to countries with advanced market economies, highly institutionalized states, and democratic systems (ibid., 219). The concept has also been advanced by think tanks and academic institutions exploring the nature of state fragility and questions of how development aid can be of assistance in the path toward *stability*. Nay (2013b) concludes that the concept of "fragility" is merely a perpetuation of international hegemony by DAC-donors.

The Fund for Peace (a nonprofit based in Washington, DC and Abuja, Nigeria) has established a "Fragile States Index," which is heavily referenced in the literature on fragile states. It determines state fragility based on 12 indicators, ranking Afghanistan and Pakistan the 9th and 17th most fragile states, respectively, out of 178 countries (Fund for Peace 2018). Nojumi (2012) argues that the methodology behind this index determines fragility to be based upon two broad assumptions: the (1) administrative capability and (2) coercive capacity of states (64) and, ultimately, that the international perspectives of security and justice surrounding failed states, as argued in the literature and enshrined in US national security policy, demonstrate a gap in local perceptions of the security situation. Nojumi, thus, concludes that these broad assumptions, by failing to include local perceptions of the security situation, provided insufficient guidance for US intervention in Afghanistan.

I highlight three overarching points from the literature on fragile states. First, "fragility," like capacity, is a poorly defined concept without an agreed-upon concrete definition (Fabra Mata and Ziaja 2009, Barakat and Larson 2014). Some scholars link fragility to institutional dysfunction (Kaplan 2008), issues relating to sovereignty, legitimacy, and security (Andersen et al. 2007, 89, Siegle 2011), or as rights based (Stewart and Brown 2009). However, as a term it has become a catchall designation for a variety of donor-perceived "failures" of developing countries. Bhambra (2016) claims that this discursive labeling of "fragility" by the donors of the Global North is generally only afforded to non-Western postcolonial states. Bhambra posits three explanations for the designation of this status upon these states: (1) coming into being through movements of national self-determination against colonial domination, thus not conforming to standard definitions of the nation, or (2) not being capable of self-governance given dependent status as colonial territories (347). Bhambra suggests a third possibility: that "*supposedly successful nation-states* were actually *imperial states*[4] ... [and that] subsequent states seeking nationhood are unable to reproduce the (problematic) conditions of that 'success' ... [and] many former imperial states ... have difficulties when required to reproduce themselves as 'mere' nation-states" (Bhambra 2016, 347).

Second, as noted in the beginning of this section, designations of fragility are related to donor concerns over terrorism, regional militancy, and global security (Walt 2002, Gisselquist 2014, Barakat and Larson 2014, Monten 2014, Siegle 2011, Buzan and Waever 2003). Furthermore, construing threats to global security as issues of state weakness or fragility serves to justify intervention and counterinsurgency in some cases, which has led to an abundance of literature on the methods by which to resolve issues of fragility. As donors identify the drivers of instability to be "institutional in nature," efforts at stabilizing fragile states become an exercise in statebuilding. In the case of Afghanistan, it also becomes an exercise in counterinsurgency (Siegle 2011, 4). These may seem like obvious facts to policy makers, but we must critically examine the impact of allowing this language to define our global reality.

Third, there is a general conflation of terms and concepts surrounding *statebuilding, institution building*, and *stabilization* among the practitioner and academic literature (Jochem et al. 2016, Monten 2014, Gisselquist 2014, Siegle 2011, Hameiri 2009), and this conflation is

---

4. Italics my own.

tied to an integration of military and development activity and strengthening of a security–development nexus. In my examination of the literature on donor processes of stabilization and state and institution building, I find that this literature largely does not contend with the *political aspects* of the very designation of fragility, in favor of examining cases to determine best practices. That said, in understanding the political nature of this discursive designation, it is necessary to look at the donor processes of *statebuilding*, *institution building*, and *stabilization* that attempt to address sources of fragility. Below, I include a very brief discussion of these processes as well as the ways in which they are tied to notions of capacity and a general obfuscation of military and development activity.

In an examination of donors' tactics for establishing local government in fragile states, Jochem, Murtazashvili and Murtazashvili (2016) review the case of elections in Afghanistan. The authors note that statebuilding in fragile states is not merely for the improvement of government capacity but represents a concerted effort by the donor community to establish democracy (Barnett and Zurcher 2009, Zurcher 2012). They highlight two broad factors that are said to influence the successful *transplantation* of new institutions in fragile states: (1) the presence of customary systems of governance and "bureaucratic capacity" (Berkowitz et al. 2003; Fukuyama 2013) and (2) social norms, which explain the consequences and "institutional stickiness" (Boettke et al. 2008) of new institutions, where norms "consistent with democracy influence how well (new institutions) transplant" (Jochem et al. 2016, 293) and "penetrate society" (Acemoglu et al. 2014, 362). The authors found that in a "*crowded institutional environment* populated by customary councils and development councils (like Afghanistan), elections are not the only ... (or) best option to establish *representative institutions* at the local level" (307). Rampant election fraud, as well as the questionability of whether the government could financially support new local units of government, made it so that the full establishment of village-level governance was unlikely (307).

This discussion of institutional *transplantation* and statebuilding is very much tied up with notions of state capacity for improved governance and security. Shaher Hameiri, a political scientist at the University of Queensland, writes extensively about donor processes of building state capacity in the context of statebuilding and global governance. He argues that statebuilding and capacity are actually one and the same, in terms of how the concepts are deployed and in their ultimate objectives, but that the distinction lies in the practice of statebuilding interventions, since they tend to combine activities that are defined as "capacity building"[5] with activities aimed at achieving more immediate security and governance objectives (Hameiri 2009, 66). He makes several additional important claims (2009):

1. State capacity is not an objective and technical measure of performance that can be "built," as many involved in processes of capacity-building claim.

---

5. Furthering notions of development as a process contingent to military activity, Fukuyama (2004a,b) defines the donor process of "nationbuilding" as involving two parts: (1) stabilization (addressing immediate post conflict needs) and (2) capacity building (the creation of self-sustaining political and economic institutions).

2. State capacity is an inherently political and ideological mechanism for "operation-alizing projects of state transnationalisation," and that the building of capacity is an inherently political project (58).

3. State capacity is actually a contingent of broader social and political relationships rooted in historical patterns of economic development and associated state forms, and that the building of capacity exemplifies external attempts to transform the ways in which power is produced and reproduced within targeted weak states (ibid.). These external attempts at transforming the production of political power in so-called weak states reveal attempts to shift and rearrange the purpose, location, and actors that employ state power (69).

The designation of fragility and the conflation of capacity building in the statebuilding activities of so-called fragile states display the increasing militarization of development. It also reflects shifts in the donor literature during the twenty-first century to *security* as an objective of development. Other scholars note how contemporary statebuilding interventions are influenced by a neoliberal institutionalist notion of state capacity (Craig and Porter 2006, Leys 2001, Richmond 2013). This perspective conflates the perceived security risks associated with fragile states with economic depravity, which has the effect of distancing capitalist development from political and social conflict (Berger and Weber 2006). Interventions then become justified for the human-security needs of citizens within weak states and international security needs of other states. Barbara (2008) argues that the donor community has recognized and approached statebuilding as a security and development challenge (308). Often, resources are redirected, in the name of statebuilding, toward building security institutions, instead of economic and political institutional development (Carment et al. 2007, 51).

Barakat and Larson (2014) argue that "fragility" is a donor-serving concept in that (1) "it *facilitates identification* of *supposedly bounded geographical areas* that might pose a threat to domestic and international security, and … (2) allows a *certain cataloguing* and *categor-ization* of otherwise unwieldy and complex political scenarios, lending to an *oversimpli-fied* and *bureaucratic* response" (26). The authors highlight the example of "Af-Pak" as a region and also relate the application and designation of so-called fragility by donors to James C. Scott's analysis of processes of state formation and planning schemes (or as I expand on in Chapter 6, *statecraft*). Barakat and Larson (2014) argue that present models of fragility "lack the capacity to analyse sub-state sources of fragility … [and in the Afghan example] do not take into account the way in which a considerable pro-portion of (the) population has very limited contact with the state, preferring to solve disputes and address community concerns within the community itself" (30). This issue of donor models failing to conceptualize and actualize development at subnational scales is a major theme of this project, which I further elaborate in Chapters 3, 5, and 6 of this book.

Barakat and Larson (2014) also draw attention to the *role the donor plays* in state fragility, in that for one, *the role of the donor* is generally not recognized, but also by highlighting sta-bilization operations and the military–development nexus in Afghanistan as an example of how donors actually contribute to insecurity (33–35). Further, the dissemination of aid is a politically volatile decision. Communities in conflict zones that donors perceive as potential threats to broader donor objectives often receive aid priority over the communities that actually have the greatest amount of need (Boutton and Carter 2014; Nielsen 2010). As Goodhand and Sedra (2010) reveal, strategies for the dispersion of aid "signal … that support for the government and the maintenance of state stability is not in the best interests of communities" (505). As I will argue throughout this project, this tunnel-visioned calculus of determining need and ascribing recognition to local actors to ensure the sustainability of donor efforts is usually also short-sighted and ignores important social and cultural dynamics that determine the long-term outcomes of projects.

While capacity building is prescribed as the salve to prevent the state from falling apart after conflict, projects to build the capacity of countries with continuous conflict and weak central governments tend to lead to aid dependence and not nation "formation" (Verkoren and Kamphuis 2013, 521). Gisselquist (2014) identifies four major lessons among the literature on state institution building: (1) there are limits to aid and external influence, (2) there is a distinction between *building* and *rebuilding*, and knowledge of historical state institutions matters, (3) weak preconditions do not necessitate failure, and (4) incentive structures vary and so do their outcomes (17–18). Talentino (2009) also highlights issues surrounding the general weakness and inefficiency of "emerging institutions"—

> Citizens are not confident in the ability of new institutions, dissociate with a new government unable to make fast and significant changes … (contributing) to fragmentation and the maintenance of separate networks as a matter of practicality … (which prevents the) government (from) establishing legitimacy and control … the very focus of nation-building's focus on participation perpetuates the dispersion of authority. (82)

Christoph Zuercher (2012) suggests additional explanations for reasons why aid is often ineffective in so-called fragile states:

1. Interests of donor-peace-builders and recipient governments rarely align; recipients lack political will to implement reform and donors lack leverage to promote fundamental change.
2. Lack of basic security in fragile states impedes aid effectiveness, while projects designed to increase security have little impact.
3. Aid is more likely to fuel patronage and corruption in countries with unstable governments due to the difficulty in tracking resource flows and international actors ignorance regarding basic information about the host society. (466–67)

These issues of impact or, in development lingo, "aid effectiveness" in fragile states—lack of aligned interests, lack of basic security, and corruption—are inherently related to how societies resolve (or rather, challenge) notions of statehood and the cultivation of a political framework that supersedes subnational rivalries. Developing state "capacity" within the fragmented contexts of "fragile" states is a complex endeavor. Donor projects of capacity thus far have focused on training individuals and organizations, strengthening infrastructure, and building institutions to support markets. However, the process of cultivating a centralized system of state institutions that is both legitimate and resilient is another matter entirely, particularly in the countries of focus in this project. Finally, as designations of fragility serve to justify intervention and counterinsurgency activities and ascribe an urgency to development practice, they also *obscure* yet at the same time *normalize* the creation of new forms of security–development integration. I explore this obfuscation more fully in the following two chapters, but first turn to an examination of USAID's approach to "fragility," particularly within a context of counterinsurgency and how human rights-based frameworks do or do not guide this approach.

Taking a HRBA? Counterinsurgency and USAID's Approach to Fragility

With the United States leading the charge against transnational Islamic militancy in a Global War on Terror, the global security concerns of donor states have reached the forefront of development agendas. At the same time, at the turn of the twenty-first century we also see within the global development agenda renewed proclamations of donor commitment to uphold a universal legal framework on human rights, as outlined in the UNDHR and subsequent conventions, and explicit calls for the implementation of HRBAs to development programming. These objectives—the addressing of global security concerns and upholding of universal human rights—are conflated, obscured, and subsumed by the discursive umbrella of capacity, and this is especially so upon an examination of USAID's engagement in fragile states and role in counterinsurgency operations. This section contends with two interrelated issues: (1) highlighting the tension between USAID's strategic frameworks on (a) fragility and insurgency and (b) integrating HRBAs in programming, as well as (2) how both these approaches conceptualize capacity.

Development institutions and agencies have identified both Afghanistan and Pakistan as so-called fragile states that house violent insurgencies and militant groups with global objectives. As USAID began working in Afghanistan and Pakistan, particularly after the US-led invasion of Afghanistan, cultivating an understanding of environmental context became incredibly pertinent to development success. USAID developed several policy frameworks to respond to this geopolitical climate: Fragile States Assessment Framework (2005), Fragile States Strategy (2005), and a publication on the "Development Response to Violent Extremism and Insurgency" (USAID 2011a). Underscored by a sense of urgency, capacity is identified as both an *issue* and a *need*.

The Fragile States Assessment Framework opens with a proclamation, "Fragile states are those losing their capacity to govern" (USAID 2005b, 1). The framework notes that in fragile states, "*social capital* is thin and society is likely to have little capacity to reconstitute missing state functions … (and that) conditions in these countries are not amenable to traditional development programming (ibid.)." Here we again see a reduction of the needs of society and relationships for development (in rather complex, volatile contexts) to a capital-based framework. The framework suggests identifying "bridge builders" or "actors and groups that reach across divisions in society … and have capacity to work formally and informally in society" (ibid., 10). This sounds simple enough, but consider that the only actors and groups with the ability to "reach across divisions" in society in a place such as Afghanistan are strongmen and warlords with a history of violence and conflict, many with covert connections and backdoor involvement in the opium industry. Identifying those with strong formal and informal networks in society fundamentally means working with those who have the ability or connections to either subdue or coerce militant groups into cooperation.

The Fragile States Strategy (2005) identifies four interrelated strategic priorities of USAID in fragile states: (1) enhancing stability, (2) improving security, (3) encouraging reform, and (4) developing the capacity of institutions. These strategic priorities "are fundamental to lasting recovering and transformational development … (especially in) institutions that serve key social and economic sectors (healthcare, education, financial services)" (USAID 2005c, 5). The publication goes into further detail around some of the nuances surrounding each objective, but it is worth pointing out that these strategic priorities are a rather tall order for a development agency to accomplish—both alone or in a coordinated effort with other development agencies or security forces, such as with counterinsurgency operations.

One aspect that is notable in the USAID publication on the "development response" to violent extremism and insurgency is that while it provides recommendations to consider whether or not conditions are even suitable for development activity, it does not seriously engage with the question of the appropriateness of the development agency's role. That question has been superseded by donor government concern over global security. The development of USAID's strategy

> is to provide a policy framework that USAID can use to improve the effectiveness of its development tools in responding to violent extremism and insurgency, as well as its capacity to interact constructively with its interagency and other partners in these challenging environments. The policy (was) also to help USAID focus more tightly on *capacity building* and *sustainability*, which are critical to our long–term security and development goals. (USAID 2011a, iv)

The strategy emphasizes again the need for program *sustainability* and the need to "build capacity and systems to strengthen resilience to violent extremism and insurgency" (ibid., 6), providing the example of provincial reconstruction teams (PRTs)[6] to improve stability in building "host nation capacity to govern" (7), developing "local capacity related to service delivery and good governance principles" (1), and cited cash-for-work programs[7] as a tactic in building capacity for sustainability against extremism (11).

Counterinsurgency is not a new area of operation for USAID as the agency has been involved in such operations since Vietnam. That said, the extent to which USAID has become involved in counterinsurgency operations in the twenty-first century is unprecedented, particularly in the US invasions and occupations of Iraq and Afghanistan. Development agencies are less a part of counterinsurgency operations in Pakistan as the government of Pakistan does not allow foreign governments to conduct their own

---

6. I discuss the PRT as a form of the development–security nexus in the following chapter.
7. Cash-for-work programs as they were carried in Afghanistan proved to be epic failures in design and implementation, discussed further in Chapter 4.

counterinsurgency operations in their country (Paczynska 2009). Counterinsurgency in Pakistan is conducted by the Pakistani government and military, not development agencies or foreign military forces (ibid.). This is not to say that military and development activities are not integrated in Pakistan. Carrying out development projects in parts of Khyber Pakhtunkhwa or Baluchistan may still require Pakistani military or security forces for project implementation and the objectives of projects may include aspects of discouraging extremism (e.g., through educational or vocational training programs) or building linkages to establish state authority in subnational insurgent spaces. However, this integration of security and development activities and objectives is a different form and of a less integrated nature than, for example, the establishment of over twenty-five PRTs with a variation of foreign military forces, foreign governments, and development agencies throughout Afghanistan. I discuss PRTs and this integration more at length in the following chapter, but the important point here is that in the context of combating insurgency and transnational militancy in "fragile" states, development cannot be separated from military or security operations *and* capacity has continued to gain traction in the discourses surrounding the integration of these activities (particularly with counterinsurgency strategy, fragile states strategy, and in conceptualizing HRBAs).

It is only in this most recent period of the twenty-first century that we see a conflation of capacity with issues of global security, particularly in the literature surrounding counterinsurgency strategies. This conflation represents a significant transformation in the role of USAID, of development agencies, and more broadly of development, as a foreign policy tool of donor governments. What is the purpose of capacity development in the context of active insurgency and transnational militancy? What capacities are most crucial to counterinsurgency and whose capacity should donors invest in? How can capacity be cultivated in the context of war when donors are also considered by much of the local population as invaders and unwanted occupiers?

Seth Jones, who has written extensively on US counterinsurgency, writes, "Counterinsurgency requires not only the capability of the United States to conduct unconventional war, but, most importantly the ability to shape the capacity of indigenous governments and its security forces. US military and civilian efforts should focus on leveraging indigenous capacities and building capacity" (Jones 2008a, xiv). Governance capacity is identified as critical to counterinsurgency outcomes, with "stronger more competent governments" that are able to provide services as having greater legitimacy and central control (18; see also Paczynska 2009). In an attempt to "build indigenous capacity," the United States embarked on a "light footprint" approach in Afghanistan, attempting to establish security and avoid nation-building with few foreign troops on the ground and through the use of "indigenous forces" during operations (ibid., 88). This approach worked during the overthrow of the Taliban, but not well when the country was in the stabilization phase (ibid., 90). Jones argues that in order for counterinsurgency to be successful, the United States must work toward improving eight areas to assist in establishing security and building governance capacity: police, border security, ground combat, air strike and mobility, intelligence, command and control, information operations, and civil–military activities (ibid., 111).

Developing governance capacity was also a major cornerstone of US stabilization and counterinsurgency strategy in Iraq. In an evaluation of USAID's Community Stabilization Program (CSP) in Iraq as a *nonlethal model* for counterinsurgency, the authors highlight USAID's three-year transition strategy that included first, stabilization of areas affected by insurgent violence; second, "supporting capacity building and governance of local and national government," and lastly, "increasing economic opportunity" (Glenn et al. 2009, 16). While designed to complement broader counterinsurgency efforts, CSP was "unique and non-traditional for USAID ... constituting the largest cooperative agreement worldwide" (ibid.). USAID adapted the CSP model from the US Marine Corps Counterinsurgency manual concept of "Clear-Hold-Build phases," which calls for "assisting with the building of governance and social capacity, respect for rule of law, delivery of essential services, and economic recovery, all of which are key to transitioning to a sustainable, safe and secure environment" (ibid.). Here we see that capacity even in the context of a military counterinsurgency manual is about governance and, interestingly, "social" capacity, which the manual relates to various aspects of development.

This last example follows suit, identifying building *government capacity* as an essential component of counterinsurgency operations conducted by PRTs.[8] In a 2008 technical evaluation on a US PRT[9] in Jalalabad, Afghanistan poses the question of how to best program development funds in order to support counterinsurgency at subnational levels as a strategy for stability. The main issue highlighted in this report is the lack of governance capacity on the part of the Government of Afghanistan (GoA), as it is against the PRT mandate for it to act as an alternative to the GoA, but rather the PRT must function to help build the capacity of the GoA to govern itself (Parker 2008, 3). The Jalalabad PRT chose to meet program deadlines instead of building the capacity of the GoA, and the evaluation notes that this was a mistake as it did little to actually cultivate local ownership of the program, ultimately inhibiting its impact on insurgency (ibid., 13).

We see in this brief review that the cultivation of "governance capacity" is an area of overlap between the objectives of counterinsurgency and of development. However, the conceptualizations of this concept within a military–security–counterinsurgency framework are vastly different from that of development. Governance capacity from a military framework refers to developing infrastructure for security and stability, sometimes "civil–military activities" such as reconstruction. Obviously, development cannot take place in unstable environments with active insurgency without security, and a military framework would conceptualize the role of government within the context of security. That said, the debate continues whether it is more important to establish security for the development of areas that are of strategic interest to donors or to focus on building a comprehensive foundation of local capacity to ensure ownership of systems to maintain security and for development. This tension has played out in a variety of ways in how donor states have

---

8. I discuss the role of PRTs as an innovation of the military–development nexus in Chapter Four, Section C.
9. Consisting of representatives from USAID, the US Department of State, US Department of Agriculture, and the US Army Civil Affairs.

put into practice this integration of military and development activity, particularly when looking at the differences among PRTs run by NATO partners, which I briefly examine in the following chapter. This variation exposes tensions among donor states as to what extent the military should play a role in reconstruction and stabilization activities.

That said, as USAID and other donors consider the role of development in responding to extremism and insurgency, as well as how to evolve HRBA to development in fragile states, it is important to make note of the ways in which the language of development becomes transformed in other discursive spaces. As the literature on counterinsurgency highlights the importance of governance capacity, we must ask how this affects the narratives on notions of governance capacity within the context of development, particularly as these spaces of operation become further integrated. Do the objectives of global security supersede the objectives of development, and if so, what are the implications for how USAID and other donor agencies define capacity development and evolve HRBA in "fragile" states? In looking at USAID's capacity development efforts in Afghanistan and Pakistan, I engage in a broader discussion of USAID's statecraft in Chapter 6, including a discussion on the role of security and rule of law, which I discuss as one of *four* major components of governance that USAID targets for capacity-building efforts.

Keeping these approaches and objectives in mind, let us now turn toward USAID's frameworks for advancing HRBA to development. USAID actually did not establish an explicit human rights-based strategic framework for development until fairly recently. In 2012 USAID established a Center of Excellence on Democracy, Human Rights and Governance (DRG) and a year later published a DRG strategic framework for programming—almost a decade after the UN Common Understanding calls for a broad-scale integration of HRBA in 2003. The Center's work is organized around three central objectives: (1) *Learn*—increasing knowledge on the global advancement of DRG, (2) *Service*—improving the quality and impact of DRG technical assistance in the field, and finally (3) *Influence*—to elevate the role of DRG in key USAID, USG, and multilateral strategies, policies, and budgets (USAID 2019a, 1). The DRG Center's task is heavy, but its establishment demonstrates an important turn in the direction of building out institutional learning infrastructure, which is more effective as a centralized effort to consider lessons learned and coordinate improvements for future programming than reliance on individual program or country assessments and evaluations.

USAID's (2013) "Strategy on DRG" provides a framework for advancing HRBA to development. Prior to this strategy, USAID did not have any explicit framework in place for taking HRBA to development programming, although since then has published a "Human Rights Landscape Analysis Tool" (USAID 2016a), a literature review on "Human Rights Struggles by Domestic Actors" (USAID 2017h), as well as a "User's Guide" to USAID's DRG programming (2019a), among other non-HRBA-specific technical research publications intended to inform and guide future approaches. The 2013 strategic framework highlights the importance and challenges of both state and nonstate institutions attaining certain types of capacity—specifically democratic capacity, adaptive capacity, advocacy capacity, capacity of local and national government institutions, judiciaries, public financial management, and CSOs, among others—as prerequisites for effective, accountable governance and sustainable development (USAID 2013d). It claims the advancement of DRG as central to US foreign policy, national security, global prosperity, is generally in the US national interest, and "is a reflection of American values and identity" (ibid., 6, 9).

Notably, there is no framework specifically on the matter of HRBA to development programming in fragile states,[10] though as of this writing USAID's website offers resource page that consists of a compilation of technical publications on DRG.[11] However, USAID's publications on HRBA do implicitly acknowledge and provide guidelines for programming in cases of "fragility," even without using the term. As part of a Research and Innovation Grants Working Paper Series, in 2017 USAID published a literature review on "Human Rights Struggles by Domestic Actors." The publication identifies seven "enabling environment" variables critical to human rights struggles by domestic actors: regime type, economic development, rule of law, armed conflict, civil society capacity, international environment, and points of entry in the enabling environment.

The review classifies the different types of rights (political, civil, social, cultural, and economic) and provides three general principles to predict difficulty actors may face in fighting certain types of rights: (1) if the rights claim is not generally recognized as a right in domestic or international society (e.g., LGBTQ rights), (2) if granting the rights claim would fundamentally change the current political system, or (3) if the rights claim threatens major economic interests (USAID 2017h, 11). The review also identifies various points of entry in the "enabling environment," in difficult contexts—advising focusing on promoting economic development when direct assistance to human rights institutions or civil society is difficult, or focusing rights support on basic rights of expression and association, as well as reminding states of their obligations under international agreements as an attempt to help shape normative discourse and assist domestic organizations in reframing the rights discussion (ibid., 18).

The way that capacity is mentioned within this literature review is entirely related to the cultivation of civil society—civil society capacity, mobilizing capacity, HRD capacity, transactional capacity (in developing vertical ties), capacity of domestic rights groups, NGO capacity, as well as the capacity of local actors. USAID's Human Rights Landscape

---

10. In USAID's DRG Strategic Framework, there is a section on stakeholder analysis with a description of "security services" as a stakeholder, and in this section there is a paragraph on the situation of fragile states or states emerging from conflict with half a page of bullets listing basic assessment questions on security situations and services intended for assessment teams. This is the extent of USAID's explicit guidelines for taking a HRBA to fragile states.

11. This resource compilation includes four "DRG Program Resources" frameworks—a user's guide to DRG (2019), a handbook on democracy and governance indicators (1998), the DRG Strategic Assessment Framework (2014), and a document on Gender Integration in DRG (2016). It also includes Capacity Development Guidance—consisting of a general capacity development measurement guide, recommended approaches to local capacity development, and links to DRG-Funded Research studies. There are no reports or guidelines for engagement in fragile states on the DRG Technical Publications resource page.

Analysis Tool references capacity in relation to national human rights institutions (NHRIs) and also HRDs or other nonstate actors, providing "environment building," "response," and "remedy" activities to specific situations. In situations where NHRIs are weak, but accredited as being "fully compliant" with the Paris Principles, the Tool advises environment building activities—capacity-building support such as management audits of the institution, exchanges with other effective NHRIs, as well as support for the development and implementation of HR training, or other programs for government institutions to improve approaches and tools for monitoring, documentation, and investigation (USAID 2016a, 18). For individual nonstate actors fighting for human rights, the tool kit advises building the capacity of key individuals and organizations—including capacity to respond to various contingencies and imminent dangers (ibid., 17).

Now, it is relevant to note that both USAID's HRBA and approaches to fragility reaffirm the centrality of state institutions and the protection of society as well as the targeting of varying levels of environment as an object of development approaches. There is nothing outright within USAID's frameworks for fragility or HRBA that are in conflict, but their objectives present a tension within USAID's institutional approach to programming. The objectives for development programming in fragile states lean toward security and stability, ultimately working toward strengthening the capacity of institutions that uphold the rule of law. HRBA approaches to development programming are also concerned with security and the protection of rights—though HRBA frameworks elaborate on the forms of rights and distinguishes between rights that are more difficult to protect. That said, USAID's HRBA approach focuses on building the capacity of institutions upholding the rule of law, but even more so there is a focus on political process and institutions—specifically building the capacity of civil society and independent rights bodies. While USAID's HRBA provides a fairly comprehensive assessment framework for determining context-specific country-based strategies for development programming, and arguably these assessment frameworks provide guidelines for considering "fragility" and situations of counterinsurgency, it is notable that they are not explicit. The following two chapters situate the tensions of this discussion within the cases of Afghanistan and Pakistan.

Summary and Conclusion

This chapter highlights the important discursive relationship between "capacity" and "fragility." In evolving a sociological framework for capacity projects, it is necessary to consider community development programs—as capacity building was born from these programs within the Global North. The chapter opens with an examination of two cases of capacity building as community development programs in order to present potential sociological frameworks to explain the capacity project. Both cases present community-building programs in the Global North as examples and put forth two different, though complementary, frameworks—that capacity-building programs are ultimately for the construction of a habitus (Fallov 2010) and the shifting of frames (Norris-Raynbird 2008). From these examples emerge three primary themes of capacity projects: state power, community, and social capital. Local communities serve as the contested grounds for capacity-building projects, requiring the cultivation of social capital in order to build community and strengthen ties with the state.

Among the themes of capacity, the donor framing of social capital, especially in regard to cultivating state power and building community, reduces relationships and networks of power to projects surrounding markets and centralized state structures. This is in order to facilitate the centralization of remote or contested *subnational* spaces with the state. I argue this framework is limiting and inhibits donor understanding of the complex realities surrounding the flow and movement of power among relationships and networks within communities and across borders, particularly in the case of Afghanistan and Pakistan.

Considering the central role of the state to capacity building is extremely critical in understanding donor approaches to international development, after the fall of the Soviet Union, the literature surrounding state formation processes was largely influenced by the context of the realities of life in a post-bipolar world. Statebuilding and designations of the status of states, such as "fragility," served to further the influence of military frameworks in development programming as well as the integration of military and development programming (this is a major area of focus of the following chapter). As problems of capacity are inherently linked with fragility, building state capacity evolved as a remedy to fragility.

As we are now in an era defined by complex global threats, I argue that we should consider nonstate-centric forms of relationships and networks as particularly relevant, especially in considering transnational architectures and infrastructure for resistance (another major area of focus in the following chapter). In this sense, the case of USAID's work to build the capacity of Afghanistan and Pakistan presents an important empirical example of modern state formation processes in practice, particularly in examining how military frameworks for development influence statebuilding processes.

USAID is not a stranger to statebuilding and has historically been involved in counterinsurgency operations. This involvement sheds light on how USAID began framing issues of security, decades before there was an explicit relationship between issues of capacity and the designation of state fragility. Since countering insurgency has never been a primary or explicit objective of USAID's policy framework up until post-9/11, the emergence of language to classify states after the fall of the Soviet Union and the designation of fragility mark an important discursive shift that further ingrained capacity within development frameworks, particularly on the topic of statebuilding.

Finally, the chapter concludes with a brief examination of USAID's frameworks for responding to fragility and insurgency, as well as how USAID has worked to evolve a HRBA to development programming. Through a cursory review of these frameworks we find a reaffirmation of the centrality of the state and protection of society from differing programmatic angles. The following two chapters give substance to the theory and discursive tensions raised in this chapter. Chapter 5 provides a backdrop for the complexity of the development situation in Afghanistan and Pakistan as it relates to the building of state capacity especially in the subnational spaces USAID and other donors attempt to reach. Chapter 6 details USAID's attempts at *statecraft* (comprised of projects falling under four interrelated programmatic areas that make up the material basis of the state) and what these attempts reveal about actual donor approaches to building capacity beyond the frameworks examined in the previous chapters.

In the following chapter, I unpack this development–security nexus further and contend with the question of agendas and methodologies in practice, focusing on the example of USAID in Afghanistan and Pakistan to contextualize the emergence of capacity within the broader discourse on development. The formation of these states, as well as the subsequent shifting roles of superpowers in each country as donors, invaders, and architects of national schemes for development, exposes nuances in the discourse as well as political context within which capacity has emerged as a defining feature of the development discourse and masks the deeply political projects of development work in Afghanistan and Pakistan.

Chapter Five

THE CAPACITY PROJECT IN "AFPAK": *DEVELOPMENT EXPERIMENTS, SUBNATIONAL SPACES, AND TRANSNATIONAL NETWORKS*

The Tribal Areas Development Project (TADP) has the opportunity to assist in the development of an area of the world relatively untouched for centuries. The tribals abide by a law of their own. They have resisted the advances of other cultures, from the Greeks (under Alexander the Great) to the British. Only in the last three decades has the geographically inaccessible area of the tribal areas reduced ... If USAID is successful in TADP, it will be a "first of its kind." ... The problem, then, is how to overcome the constraints of working in FATA while respecting the centuries-old tribal culture and established political autonomy.—USAID evaluation (Williams and Rudel 1988, 142)

What does it actually mean to build capacity in Afghanistan or Pakistan? This question is at the heart of the work of development. There are few cases in the world where a global collision of capitalist and communist projects coalesced with the struggles of postcolonial statehood to create a perfect storm of transnational infrastructure enabling the globalization of terrorism. The situation(s) of Afghanistan and Pakistan reveal an epicenter of *global, transnational,* and *national* religious, political, and economic intersection that challenges the very notions of governance that the international system is dependent upon.

Development does not exist in a vacuum. Attempts to consider contextual factors in project design and to make development initiatives locally owned processes, while laudable, are dwarfed by the reality of how development assistance coexists alongside military aid, political alliances, and foreign occupation. These greater macro-relationships between nations engaged in global conflict impact the meso- and micro-level institutional and organizational relationships that make up the so-called partnerships of development. They impact who can be considered a partner, a beneficiary, and where capacity needs to be built.

Projects of development cannot actually be divorced from the transnational tribal conflicts that challenge the structures of market and statehood. Both states have toiled through these struggles of statehood as recipients of development aid. The objective of this chapter is to situate the capacity project within this complexity in order to parse out its meaning and function as a project of development. This chapter is divided into five sections in an attempt to coherently consolidate the complexity of the challenges facing the development of capacity in Afghanistan and Pakistan. Each section represents a component of the situation and relationships of development that are inherent to the challenges of capacity development.

Territorial Vagabonds and the System of States

An important theme in the development challenges of Afghanistan and Pakistan is the lack of a cohesive national identity. Much literature is devoted to the ethnic and tribal conflicts that define central governance in Afghanistan and Pakistan. I do not intend to engage in a dissection of military Punjab dominance in Pakistan, the conflict dynamics among shifting Pashtun or Tajik rule in Afghanistan, or the religious ideological disparities among the various factions of government and insurgency. While critical components of the development situation, this section focuses more broadly on the ways in which these dynamics have played off one another in the context of the production of state and boundary as they relate to the work of development. Particular attention is paid to the manifestation and convergence of these dynamics among the Pashtun population, who operate extensive networks as territorial vagabonds of Afghanistan and Pakistan.

The actual reality of building stable and resilient centralized institutions and infrastructure is not achievable without addressing issues of boundary and identity embedded within societies that have been consistently subjected to and manipulated by waves of global conflict. Perhaps the greatest territorial inhibitor to building capacity in Afghanistan and Pakistan is the actual border, which is more like a "geopolitical fault line" (Brown and Rassler 2013, 4) between the two countries. It is questionable whether it is actually possible to build the capacity of a state or market that institutionally reinforces a border that splits centuries-old networks of major populations in half. From inception, both Afghanistan and Pakistan have faced difficult questions regarding notions of governance, sovereignty, and borders.

The issues plaguing Afghanistan and Pakistan today can in large part be traced back to the demarcation of the border between Afghanistan and British India at the end of the nineteenth century. The border was drawn by Sir Mortimer Durand, a colonial Brit, using maps local tribes refused to acknowledge, that determined the boundary between the two countries—placing half of the Pashtun population in British India and the other half in Afghanistan. The partitioning of Pakistan further exposed this long-standing, repressed border issue and triggered, within this new context, a fresh round of open political contention. To this day, Afghanistan does not recognize the border between the two countries. Only in 2017 did both countries agree to dispatch technical teams to conduct a geological survey using GPS and Google Maps in an attempt to settle this border dispute and reduce the violent conflict "once and for all" (Agence France-Presse Kandahar 2017).

In the mid-eighteenth century, Pashtun tribes that had strategically pitted Mughal and Persian powers against each other established what is now the modern state of Afghanistan (Romano 2003, 29). In 1747, Ahmad Khan Abdali Durrani, a Pashtun who had gained the cooperation of previously warring tribal leaders, became the Shah of Afghanistan (ibid., 31). The conflicts of the "Great Game" between the British and the

Russians vying for influence over Afghanistan marred nineteenth-century Afghanistan. After three Anglo-Afghan wars, the British invited Emir Abdur Rahman to take the throne of Afghanistan in 1880, his reign lasting until his death in 1901 (Janjua 2009, 16).

The demarcation of the Durand Line occurred during Rahman's reign. The decision to designate a boundary came about as a result of skirmishes between Abdur Rahman, the British, and the Russians over two territories in Badakhshan—land that was technically under Russian influence but loyal to Rahman (even paying revenues to the leader) (Gulzad 1991, 298). Rahman requested a map to show the official boundaries in order to clarify the disputes, unaware of an unmapped boundary agreement that had been drawn up between the British and Russians in 1873 over the very disputed lands (Janjua 2009, 18). Rahman claimed the territories as part of Afghanistan, while the Russians claimed that he was violating the 1873 agreement (Janjua 2009, 18) and the British looking to avoid a potential conflict with the Russians (Gulzad 1991, 298). Eventually, a commission was organized to decide on the border.

The demarcation process took place between 1892 and 1896 and concluded without an agreed-upon map. Mortimer Durand had provided a map; however, Rahman never approved it (Gulzad 1991, 334). The Durand Line agreement was eventually implemented but with virtually no contribution by Afghan representatives—the very population it split in half: the Pashtuns. This was a profound period in Pashtun history that has direct implications upon the viability of the state model in both Afghanistan and Pakistan, as well as the legitimacy of the top-down model of central governance. The conflicts of the past century can largely be attributed to disputes along this border.

This prophetic passage of what was to come was written in a letter from Emir Abdur Rahman to the British following the signing of the Durand Line agreement:

> As to these frontier tribes … if they were included in my domains I should be able to make them fight against any enemy of England and myself, by the name of a religious war, under the flag of their co-religious Muslim ruler (myself). And these people being brave warriors and staunch Mahomedans, would make a very strong force to fight against any power (that) might invade India or Afghanistan. I will gradually make them peaceful subjects and good friends of Great Britain. But if you should cut them out of any domains, they will neither be of any use to you nor to me: you will always be engaged in fighting in troubles with them, and they will always go on plundering. As long as your Government is strong and in peace, you will be able to keep them quiet by a strong hand, but if at any time a foreign enemy appears on the borders of India, these frontier tribes will be your worst enemy. You must remember that they are like a weak enemy who can be held under the feet of a strong enemy, as long as he is strong; and the moment he ceases to be strong enough to hold him, the weak one gets out of his hold and attacks him in return. In your cutting away from me these frontier tribes who are people of my nationality and my religion, you will injure my prestige of my subjects, and will make me weak and my weakness is injurious for your Government. (Gulzad 1991, 337)

The Durand Line agreement itself does not actually identify an international boundary because it was not clear where the territory of Afghanistan ended and British India began, leading to British-created buffer zones between the tribal areas and the Indian empire (Gulzad 1991, 336). The tribal belt was neither stable nor safe. In 1897, the year after the demarcation process had concluded, Pashtun mullahs organized a tribal uprising, in the same areas that are still hotbeds of conflict between both countries today (Khan 1999, 5). Below, I present several figures to show the boundary transformation of Afghanistan from 1849 until the present, along with a geographical display of the present-day conflict (Figure 5.1).

This first map displays the boundaries of Afghanistan in 1849. Here we see that Afghanistan's territory extends deep into present-day Pakistan (then British India). In the middle map, I have highlighted the Durand Line as well as disputed areas, insurgency hotbeds where the Taliban maintains influence. In the last map on the right, we see that these same disputed areas are outlined as the main fronts of state insurrection, with the red lines showing NATO supply routes leading into Afghanistan from Pakistan and black lines demonstrating streams of foreign fighters pouring into Haqqani Network (HN) territory where Tehrik-i-Taliban and al Qaeda operate from. I provide these maps to visually demonstrate the extremely fundamental issue of the Durand Line boundary. This issue was only exacerbated by the partitioning of Pakistan.

At the turn of the century, in British India the seeds for the movement that would advocate for the creation of Pakistan began taking root. The idea of creating a political organization in order to protect Muslim political rights in India came to fruition in 1906 with the establishment of an All India Muslim League (Ahsan 2003, 353). In the first few decades of the twentieth century, India began to push for independence from Britain, provoking protests among Muslims in India who feared that an independent India would be detrimental to the rights of the population.

During this period of struggle for independence, Abdul Ghaffar Khan aka "Frontier Gandhi" led a nonviolent Pashtun army (the Khudai Khidmatgars, or "Servants of God") against the British. Khan was opposed to the partitioning of India, and at its peak the Khudai Khidmatgar was 100,000 members strong (Rowell 2009, 599). Volunteers from the army engaged in work with objectives that were similar to those of development projects today: promoting the advancement of their communities, working on local development projects, promoting hygiene and sanitation, and maintaining order at public meetings (Johansen 1997, 59). Meanwhile, Afghanistan was providing support to the National Awami Party, a Pashtun nationalist political faction in British India, to battle the Muslim League in the Indian National Congress in the hopes of abolishing the Durand Line and establishing a greater Pashtunistan (Liebl 2007, 495).

These efforts did not yield success and by 1946, Muhammad Ali Jinnah, leader of the Muslim League, had successfully campaigned for the creation of the Muslim state of Pakistan. Subsequently, the British administered a referendum to determine whether those living along the border were in support of the partitioning of Pakistan. Pashtun nationalists dispute this referendum, which had a 99 percent approval of an independent Pakistan, as the survey did not provide an option to join Afghanistan (Minority Rights Group International 2017). This forced Pashtuns to choose only between India and Pakistan or to abstain from the vote (which about 50 percent did) (ibid.). Adding insult to injury, the international community acknowledged and supported the creation of an independent Pakistan even though Kabul rejected the referendum. Since this partitioning, the threat of Pashtunistan has dominated Afghan–Pakistani relations.

Afghanistan Boundary Transformation and Conflict Map (1849 - Present)

FIGURE 1: ***Boundary between Afghanistan and British India (1849)***

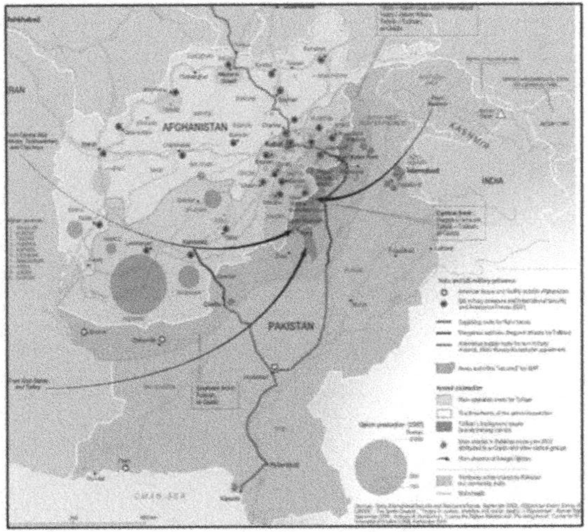

FIGURE 2: ***Present-day boundary between Afghanistan and Pakistan***

FIGURE 3: ***Post US-Invasion Conflict Map of Afghanistan and Pakistan***

Sources:

- Figures 1 and 2: World Future Fund. 2018. "Afghanistan and Pakistan Historical Maps." Accessed online 11 March 2018. (http://www.worldfuturefund.org/wffmaster/Reading/Maps/afghan.map.htm) (Figure 2 adaptations my own)
- Figure 3: Fisher, Max. 2015. "40 maps that explain the Middle East." *Vox*. Accessed online 11 March 2018. (https://www.vox.com/a/maps-explain-the-middle-east).

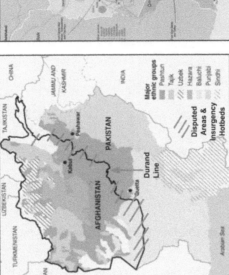

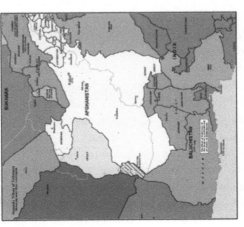

Figure 5.1 Afghanistan Boundary Transformation and Conflict Map (1849–Present).

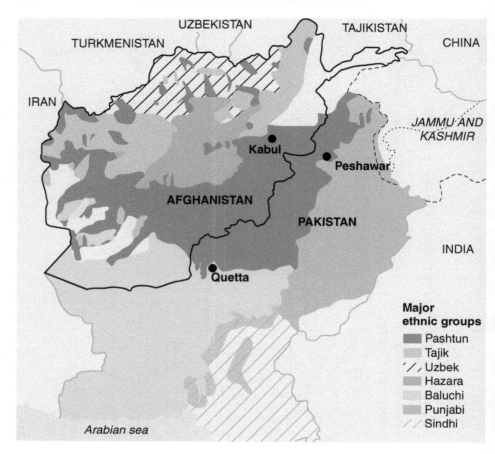

Figure 5.2 Ethnic Population Distribution Map of Afghanistan and Pakistan.

From the Afghan perspective, the demarcation of the Durand Line and the partitioning of Pakistan mark two instances in which colonial Britain determined the boundaries of Pashtun land without local consent. The partitioning of both Afghanistan and Pakistan is a disastrous example of colonial attempts to ascribe the state model to territorialities that do not logically constitute nations. Given the porous and mountainous nature of the border, the Pashtun tribes who live there have largely enjoyed a politically autonomous existence from the central governments of both Kabul and Islamabad. It is in part for this reason that this area is a hotbed fostering national, regional, and global conflict.

The Pashtun population is one of two major populations that straddles the border of Afghan and Pakistan. The following map (Figure 5.2) shows a partial purview of the ethnic composition of both countries (World Future Fund 2018).

The Pashtun lands of Central Asia have served as the battlegrounds of global conflicts for centuries. The population follows a code of social conduct known as *Pashtunwali*, which values honor, revenge, equality, and hospitality (Rzehak 2011, 2). It is not merely a code of social etiquette. It is a system that determines fundamental social and legal

Figure 5.3 Pashtun Tribal Population Map.

relations on interpersonal, community, and intercommunity levels. The Pashtun legal system is centered around the *jirga* and employs law enforcement bodies (*lashkars, chigas,* and *arbakais*) to resolve individual and tribal conflicts and uphold the tenets of Pashtunwali (Khan 1999, 40, 55, Tariq 2009, 27). Presently, areas in which there is poor infrastructure rely on jirgas. In cases where both tribal jirgas and the state system are prevalent, the option between both systems creates competition for whichever can provide quick as well as favorable "justice," raising questions of legitimacy (Tariq 2009, 24).

There are five major overarching Pashtun tribal confederacies: Durrani, Ghilzai, Karlanri, Sarbani, and Ghurghust (Afsar et al. 2008, 62). The Durrani, Ghilzai, and Karlanri are the largest of the five, and while there are some independent Pashtun tribes they do not constitute significant populations (Liebl 2007, 497). Pashtun loyalty is bottom-up, but individual and family loyalties are constantly changing. In the context of global conflict, loyalty can shift based upon which side appears more likely to win (Green 2010, 26). Despite ever-present tribal infighting, Pashtun tribes tend to unite in the face of a foreign invader. The following map (Figure 5.3) displays the territorial jurisdictions of the major Pashtun tribal confederacies (Afsar et al. 2008, 62):

Pashtun politics have played an important role in shaping the development of Afghanistan and Pakistan. In Afghanistan, control of the central government has primarily shifted among warring Pashtun and Tajik leaders. In Pakistan, fears of a greater Pashtunistan have been the main frame of Pakistan's regional policy toward both Afghanistan and India. Among the five overarching tribal confederacies, the Durrani and Ghilzai are the most influential and are also rivals. Most conflicts in Afghanistan in the past century, whether intertribal or against a foreign invader, have played upon tribal loyalties and rivalries. Most of the Taliban is from the Ghilzai confederation with some support from the Kakar tribe of the Ghurghust confederation, and the senior leadership almost solely consists of members of the Hotaki tribe (which is in the Ghilzai confederation) (Johnson and Mason 2007, 78).

Historically, Pashtuns unite under the banner of Islam when confronted with a foreign enemy. The heritage of Pashtunwali predates Islam among the Pashtuns, but most are devout Sunnis who follow the Hanafi school of thought and are heavily influenced by the Naqshbandiya Sufi orders (Liebl 2007, 504). The Soviet invasion and with it a migration of Arab-funded madrassas and fighters brought new forms of Islam[1] that have ideologically influenced Pashtun-based insurgent groups active today, most notably the Taliban. The integration of imported forms of Islam and subsequent adoption by insurgent groups has changed the governing structures of Pashtun society. Traditional systems of tribal governance and authority have been damaged by insurgent groups such as the HN, leaving leadership vacuums to be filled by extremists after campaigns of targeted assassinations against community religious and tribal leaders. In the context of development, this creates challenges when extending the arm of the state system.

Over the past several decades, Mujahideen infighting, strategic assassination campaigns, and Taliban governance have resulted in a simultaneous destruction and duplication of systems in local governance and security. Furthermore, decades of foreign occupation, conflict, and refugee migration have further entrenched the intermingling of Afghan and Pakistani Pashtuns and the flourishing of cross-border relationships. It is within this multilayered realm of conflict, systemic disruption, and transient migration across borders that development must take place.

Battle for Hegemony: The Early Decades of Development (1950–1980)

After World War II, the donor architecture and the field of international development began taking form. The Cold War shaped global geopolitical relationships, and the United States made unprecedented investments in the development of countries around the world. Development assistance became a new aspect of the bilateral relationship that exists between countries, alongside trade and military alliances and agreements. To truly understand the transformation of the capacity project requires a situating of development assistance within the full context of bilateral relationships, alongside these other forms of engagements. The international development of Afghanistan and Pakistan began in the early 1950s via bilateral government-to-government assistance from development agencies and lending institutions. US bilateral assistance to Afghanistan and Pakistan can be divided into several periods:

---

1. Islamic influences among the Pashtuns: Sufi orders (Naqshbandiya, Christyya, and Qadiriya— indigenous to population); Deobandi Islam (origin: India), Salafism (Egypt), Wahhabism (origin: Saudi Arabia), Ahl-e Hadith (origins: India and Saudi Arabia).

1.   Cold War prior to the Soviet occupation of Afghanistan (1950–1979)
2.   From Soviet occupation to Taliban rule of Afghanistan (1980–1994)
3.   Post-9/11

In these first two periods, a Cold War-inspired battle of development between the Soviets and the Americans was played out over Afghanistan. This 30-year marathon of investment began with the partitioning of Pakistan in 1947. As Pakistan gained independence as a state in 1947, the United States welcomed Pakistan's "emergence into the family of nations" (DOS 2017). As de facto Cold War allies, the United States began providing assistance to the newly independent state to help Pakistan overcome the economic consequences of partition from India (USAID May 2006a). This refreshed the "Pashtunistan" issue and reality that colonial boundaries would continue to divide the Pashtun population on the border of Afghanistan.

In this section I rely heavily on three special evaluations USAID contracted out to DEVRES, Inc. and Jeffalyn Johnson & Associates to review USAID programming during the Cold War period in Afghanistan and Pakistan between 1950 and 1988. Both contracting firms are no longer active, and the special evaluations I reference are henceforth cited as Williams et al. (1988) (DEVRES, Inc.), Williams and Rudel (1988) (DEVRES, Inc.), and Jeffalyn Johnson & Associates (1981) (no authors listed). The latter conducted a review of US development assistance to Pakistan between 1952 and 1980, which was "urgently recommended" by the US ambassador to Pakistan and the acting director of USAID Pakistan (Jeffalyn Johnson & Associates 1981, 7). Williams and Rudel's (1988) evaluation was on US economic assistance to Pakistan between 1982 and 1987. This particular evaluation is called for because the economic assistance program during that period is "unique," in that: (1) a large level of economic aid was committed before discussion or agreement on the content of the program, (2) the large-scale assistance at the time represented a sharp reversal of US assistance policy toward Pakistan, and (3) "while the rationale … was primarily political and strategic, the program … was in large measure, directed toward longer term economic reforms and development objectives" (4). Lastly, in "A Retrospective Review of US Assistance to Afghanistan (1950–1979)," published in the context of the Soviet withdrawal from Afghanistan, Williams et al. (1988) note the objective of the review is to "gain insights from the record of past US development assistance to Afghanistan as a possible guide to future US policies and programs … (noting that) Afghanistan provides a valuable case study in the application of development theory and practice" (1). These three special evaluations contain the bulk of the programming I review in order to set the Cold War context of development assistance in Afghanistan and Pakistan.

The United States initially did not intend to invest much in Afghanistan. When President Truman announced his Point Four program, signing an agreement in Kabul in 1951 for a US program of technical cooperation, the United States allotted only $1.5 million per year for five years. However, when Khrushchev visited Kabul in 1956, promising $100 million line of credit to orient the economy and trade of Afghanistan toward the Soviet Union, the United States decided to up its commitment (Williams et al. 1988, 11–12). Among USAID country programs between 1950 and 1979, Afghanistan became "unique," given the intensity of the Cold War dynamics and "seriousness of the economic development efforts" (ibid., 41). US development assistance jumped from $1.5 million per year for a five-year commitment to an average level of $28 million per year, starting with a huge capital-led infrastructure project in the Helmand Valley (ibid.).

US assistance to Afghanistan prior to the Soviet invasion reflected popular modernization theories of economic growth typical of the time period. From the 1950s until the early 1960s, programs were designed around the assumption that productivity could be lifted through applying "advanced" US knowledge and technical assistance and that building infrastructure was the best way to stimulate a stagnant economy toward growth and poverty reduction. In an attempt to integrate Afghanistan in regional trade, the United States initiated a program to strengthen transit for trade between Afghanistan and Pakistan, investing $26 million for roads, vehicles, and airports (ibid., 11–12). In the 1960s, the focus of the development agenda in the donor discourse shifted to "human capital and institutional development," directing investment toward infrastructure—constructing schools and government agencies, improving financial management and tax systems, as well as general budget and planning processes (ibid., 17). While the Russians continued to maintain high levels of investment in Afghanistan's physical infrastructure, the Kennedy administration sought to reduce US investment in large capital projects, instead focusing on training people to manage and expand the "institutional capacity for development" (ibid.).

The first decade of US bilateral assistance to Pakistan was oriented toward helping the country to overcome the economic impact of partition from British India. The United States invested in technical assistance and disaster relief, rehabilitating and expanding infrastructure, programming to modernize public service, and industrialization (Jeffalyn Johnson and Associates 1981, 9–10). In order to coordinate the massive levels of development assistance among donors, the World Bank formed the Pakistan Consortium in 1960. USAID established "goal plans" to rapidly expand the industrial sector and boost agriculture. Investments were made for major projects to expand power, transportation, and communications networks (in order to facilitate plans for the expansion of industry and agriculture) (ibid., 11–12). That said, in these early years of assistance evaluations note the instability of political conditions and seeming lack of commitment to development from Pakistanis (48). Regardless, the United States made an annual commitment of $400 million (around $3 billion total between 1960 and 1965) to Pakistan, accounting for more than half of Pakistan's foreign aid, 35 percent of the government's development expenditures, and 45 percent of its import bill (ibid., 89).

These aid plans were disrupted in 1965 due to the Indo-Pakistan war, leading to a temporary cessation of new commitments and the cancellation of the sixth and seventh meetings of the Pakistan Aid Consortium (ibid., 12). While aid resumed briefly in the late 1960s, resource commitments were sharply reduced and after the rising tension and subsequent civil war between East and West Pakistan, the aid program again closed out in 1971 (Williams and Rudel 1988, 10). This was the second disruption of bilateral assistance to Pakistan in under ten years. Even in USAID special evaluations, it is noted that this uneven distribution of aid likely contributed to tensions between East and West Pakistan, leading up to the civil war (ibid., 10).

In 1973, the US Foreign Assistance Act changed the development agenda. The legislation stressed the importance of assistance not merely for growth, but for growth *with equity* to meet basic human needs (Jeffalyn Johnson and Associates 1981, 17). US assistance to Afghanistan during this time focused on "people-oriented development and equity," operating under the assumption that meeting basic human needs through agricultural and rural development was a more effective route to economic growth than central planning (Williams et al. 1988, 16–17). US assistance to Pakistan during this time was marred by disputes about how to spend money; the GOP had little interest in investing in human capital and the "social sector," preferring instead actual income-producing investments in the agricultural and industrial sectors (Williams and Rudel 1988, 20–21).

The aid to both countries was short-lived. In 1977, General Zia ul-Haq returned to power in Pakistan. In response to Pakistani attempts to develop nuclear capability, the United States terminated the bilateral aid program in 1978 (ibid., 92). While some ongoing projects surrounding basic health services and agriculture continued, all other aid ceased, and following an attack on the USAID mission in Pakistan in 1979, staff was also greatly reduced (ibid., 11). In Afghanistan, the overthrow of President Daoud in 1978 and subsequent infighting among PDPA led to a Soviet invasion and a halting of US bilateral assistance to Afghanistan.

Prior to the Soviet invasion, this first period of US bilateral assistance to Afghanistan and Pakistan was defined by attempts to contain the Soviet threat in the region. Broadly speaking, the development goals of this period are not terribly out of line with the objectives of development today: sustainable growth, the alleviation of poverty, meeting basic human needs, improving systems of governance, and so on. Since the Soviet package of assistance to Afghanistan was so much more generous than that of the United States, US strategy focused on offering an alternative to overreliance and dependency on the Soviet Union in order to maintain some semblance of Afghan nonalignment. Additionally, US investment in Pakistan prevented allyship with the USSR. While relations were not outright hostile, Pakistan's security alliance with the United States (SEATO) and refusal to join the Soviet-led Asian Collective Security System meant there existed a baseline of tension between the two countries. Pakistan's Soviet policy was largely influenced by American policy, plus the Soviet presence in neighboring Afghanistan and India also created strain (Shah and Parveen 2016, 188).

These bipolar political tensions played out locally in development projects. As a result of the US–Soviet competition, the US overcommitment of resources strained Afghan resources and manpower (Williams et al. 1988, 34; 47). Donors competed with one another and coordination was weak (ibid., 47). In Afghanistan, development advisors became frustrated that central government officials were actually elites who knew little of local concerns and were overconfident in applying Western techniques and technical solutions to local problems (ibid., 46). In Pakistan, the United States was finding that there were limits to the political leverage of assistance, and traditional attitudes often stubbornly prevailed in the aggressive attempts of government reorganization programs (Jeffalyn Johnson & Associates 1981, 14). Government officials sought generalized/commodity aid that was untied to projects, which led to increased manipulation on both the donor and the recipient end (ibid., 26–28). Furthermore, the fact that the bilateral program to Pakistan was interrupted three times between 1951 and 1980 (1965, 1971, 1978) had a high cost, negating potential impacts of assistance and complicating attempts at planning (ibid., 24; 94).

The Cold War battle of development ended when the Soviets invaded Afghanistan. Furthermore, this failure is perceived in the evaluations, from a development perspective, as largely a failure of Afghan state capacity. While "capacity building" was not part of the lexicon of the Cold War era, notions of capacity are pervasive in program methodology and objectives. The US bilateral assistance "policy toward Afghanistan was based on the premise that the country's capacity to resist communist inroads was directly related to its economic development and progress" (Williams et al. 1988, 3, 13). Ultimately, it was issues of capacity that prevented progress. "Absorptive capacity," or the ability of Afghan institutions to implement programs, is regularly cited as a constraint (ibid., 13). In an attempt to address this issue, resources went toward programs to strengthen human capital and institutional development. Consequently, lack of "institutional," "managerial," and "technical capacity" was cited as shortcomings that constrained "effective development" (ibid., 57) as well as "inadequate planning, management, and administrative capacity" to mobilize resources and manage programs (ibid., 131).

Efforts were made in programming from the 1950s through the 1970s to enhance the technical capabilities of the bureaucracy, to train individuals in modern management techniques (ibid., 47), and to increase managerial and technical capacity (ibid., 57). Yet, by the time of the Soviet invasion, it was unclear what impact US bilateral assistance had.

> Programs to improve administration and management continued into the 1970s for basically the same reasons that had impelled their initiation in the 1950s, namely that weak capacity to manage and implement in virtually all Afghan institutions was a critical constraint to the achievement of economic growth and social advancement.(ibid., 136)

Similar issues regarding limited capacity and the "capabilities" of the GOP are also noted (Jeffalyn Johnson & Associates 1981, 29; 31), but the scale and scope of investments in programming were far greater[2] and did yield some results so the failure of development was not as complete as in Afghanistan. In an evaluation on the assistance program between 1950 and 1980, the question of programmatic success in Pakistan is debated extensively, but ultimately gains are noted primarily in agriculture and infrastructure development and failures (particularly of commodity assistance programs) are attributed primarily to the regular disruptions in aid and not exclusively to issues of capacity (though they are noted) (ibid., 91).

With the Soviet invasion, an era of development had ended. US development strategy was no longer merely for containment and economic growth. The 1980s saw a shift in which objectives and activities of development became intertwined with military sales agreements. The overarching objective was to manage the regional and global threat

---

2. Between roughly 1951/52 and 1979, the United States invested $525.7 million in Afghanistan (Williams, Kean, et al. 1988: C-1) and $5,082.95 million in Pakistan (Jeffalyn Johnson & Associates 1981, 111).

of a Soviet-occupied Afghanistan. This process set about an evolution of new forms of transnational networks set up explicitly to bifurcate state boundaries in order to manage threats, blurring the line between donor and invader. In the next section, I address this dual status and implications for the work of development.

Donors or Invaders? Development Under Occupation and the Architecture of Civilian–Military Development

After years of Soviet and American investment in Afghanistan, the Soviet invasion of Afghanistan and subsequent attempt to apply the Soviet model to Afghanistan called into question the role of development in military conflict. This section focuses primarily on development strategy and projects during the two periods in which Afghanistan has been under military occupation by a foreign power: the Soviet occupation in the 1980s and the invasion of US and coalition forces following 9/11. I open up the notion of invader for examination in the context of both military occupation and development.

I do not review the Soviet style of occupation or frameworks for development extensively here. That is outside the realm of this project. However, the Soviet example and the subsequent transnational networks that emerged during this period highlight important considerations about the nature of development work. Military occupation is one form of invasion. Development agendas implemented in conjunction with military occupation politicizes projects and conflates supposedly apolitical objectives of development with the political priorities and strategy of war. The same holds true for development projects that aim to contain political threats. This conflation presents a particular challenge to the ability of a state to build capacity, as projects to build infrastructure or extend the governing arm of the state become aligned with parties to conflict.

The supposed neutrality of donors comes into question when those same donors are also directly (or indirectly) funding violence that targets and impacts civilians. Additionally, many development projects are often locally unpopular, either because of their affiliation to the central government and, by extension, foreign powers or due to blatant ignorance and oversight in project planning in applying development strategy to local reality. Carrying out projects often requires hiring local militias and security in order to be carried out and when locals view projects of development (i.e., building a road through or to their village, constructing a government building, etc.) as an imposition, projects become a form of state and foreign invasion.

Soviet-occupied Afghanistan presented an opportunity for the USSR. The country served as a laboratory to practice the grand communist experiment. Building upon investments since the 1950s, the Soviets attempted to transform Afghanistan by applying a vision of state control and made moves to centralize industry. The Soviets embarked on a campaign of total systemic upheaval. Advisors were sent into ministries, the country's legal system was rewritten, and resources were funneled into massive infrastructure projects: gas pipelines between Afghanistan and the Soviet Union, copper smelting plants, bridges, antilandslide infrastructure along the Salang Pass, and hospitals (Nunan 2016, 130–31). Cargo exchange between the Soviet Union and Afghanistan grew to the point that the USSR accounted for 40 percent of Afghanistan's total trade turnover (ibid.). However, the challenge (and ultimate downfall) of Soviet-style development was translating the Soviet system to a country with essentially no national industries that employed workers on a mass scale, expansive private agriculture, and a rural, illiterate population (Nunan 2016, 153, 161).

While the development–security nexus had yet to become commonplace in the policy or academic lexicon, the seeds for this nexus took root in Pakistan during the Soviet occupation. Within a year prior to the Soviet invasion, the United States cut off bilateral assistance to Pakistan due to concern over the country's ambitions to develop nuclear capability. However, with the Soviet invasion of Afghanistan, the United States subsequently waived legislative restrictions on the prohibition of aid to countries seeking nuclear capability and rehabilitated the US bilateral assistance program to Pakistan (William and Rudel 1988, 3). As a result of the invasion, Pakistan played host to the largest refugee population anywhere in the world at the time—around three million Afghan refugees[3] (representing about a fifth of the total Afghan population)[4] (Williams and Rudel 1988, 281). USAID documents frame Pakistan as a worthy beneficiary; Pakistan was "working diligently with (the US & international community) for the restoration of an independent and non-aligned Afghanistan, [and] … was host to Afghan leaders and refugees working for these objectives." There is no mention of the Mujahideen, but that is undoubtedly what this refers to.

In addition to the Soviet occupation of Afghanistan, there was also a general concern on the part of the US government about the geopolitical direction of the Persian Gulf and Central Asia.[5] Pakistan was seen as a potential "force for stability in the region … [and] playing a pivotal role with the moderate Islamic nations" (Williams and Rudel 1988, 12). These concerns provided justification not only for economic assistance but also for "strengthening and modernizing Pakistan's defense capabilities," with the assumption that investment in the growing economy would "sustain the defense burden, and meet the social and economic needs of its poor population" (ibid., 13). Further justification is provided for the renewal of the US–Pakistan relationship and bilateral aid. In a review of US assistance in the 1980s, Pakistan is portrayed as a ready and deserving ally:

> After the internal political turbulence of the 1970s, Pakistan found renewed political stability and a return to policies favoring a more solid basis for longer-term economic development … signalling *pro-market* and *private sector orientation*,[6] … declaring intention to denationalize a number of industrial and service enterprises and to introduce incentives for

---

3. 75 percent of Afghan refugees were in NWFP, 20 percent in Baluchistan, and 5 percent in Punjab.
4. US bilateral assistance was purposefully kept separate from international efforts (including the US) toward refugee relief. The United States provided over $500 million between 1980 and 1987 toward Afghan refugee relief (accounting for 30 percent of United Nations High Commissioner for Refugees' program budget in Pakistan).
5. Keeping in mind that the Islamic Revolution also occurred in Iran in 1979.
6. Italics my own.

private investment, including guarantees against further nationalisation ... these policy and structural reforms (were the result of) cooperating closely with the IMF and World Bank. (Ibid., 12)

Thus, in spite of the martial law and execution of political opponents occurring under the military state established under General Zia ul-Haq only a few years prior, Pakistan's embrace of the open market, privatization of national industry, and authoritarian stability made the country an ideal candidate for one of the largest US bilateral assistance programs in history.

In a State Department statement on US Assistance to Pakistan in 1981, it is noted that "both sides (US & Pakistan) agreed that a strong and independent Pakistan was in the mutual interest of the United States and Pakistan, as well as the rest of the world" (ibid., 219). This translated into the first of two massive assistance programs between the United States and Pakistan in the 1980s. The first aid package was from 1982 to 1987 and contained two components. The first was $1.625 billion for *economic assistance* with the principal objective of strengthening Pakistan's balance of payments to better service foreign debts and make purchases of defense equipment from the United States (ibid., 13). The second component involved foreign military sales (FMS) totaling $1.575 billion for military equipment. The total proposed package of US assistance was $3.2 billion, though repayment for the FMS was scheduled over a longer term period of 12 years (ibid., 13).

While the motivations for this assistance package were in no unclear terms to manage the Soviet threat in Afghanistan, the fact that economic assistance and military sales are nearly equal raises important questions about the actual *role* and *nature* of economic assistance in the context of a military sales agreement. How exactly was economic assistance being used to strengthen Pakistan to enable the repayment of foreign debts and military sales agreements? Out of the programmatic areas of focus, the largest portions of economic assistance were set aside for Balance of Payments programs (specifically commodity import and export[7]) and building up the agricultural[8] and energy[9] sectors. Smaller, though not insignificant,[10] amounts were allocated to social and human resources development[11] as well as area development programs.[12] Programming was by and large national in scope, with the exception of the area development programs, a special request on behalf of the GOP, targeting Baluchistan, the Federally Administered

---

7. Facilitating trade of agricultural products between the US and Pakistan—for example, edible oils.
8. Research and education, improving productivity in dry areas, irrigation, and so on.
9. Water, coal, industrial research laboratories, oil and gas, energy planning and conservation.
10. Between $75 and $100 million.
11. Health, malaria control, population planning, human resource development (training), and women in development programs. (No education programs under this category between 1982 and 1987, but the 1988–93 program included a primary education project.)
12. Mostly small rural infrastructure projects—roads, schools, village electrification, skills training, water supply, and irrigation.

Tribal Areas (FATA), and the Northwest Frontier Province (NWFP) (which all border Afghanistan and Baluchistan parts of Iran) (ibid., 27–29).

USAID faced significant challenges with the area development programs. These provinces border Afghanistan and are areas the GOP has little reign over, with large Pashtun and Baluchi populations,[13] which were still operating on the Frontier Crimes Regulation law established by the British in 1901. The stated intentions for the area development programs were entirely political—to integrate areas which were bases for separatist political movements and high levels of refugees into the mainstream national economy, accelerate socioeconomic development, and combat the cultivation of opium poppies (ibid., 135–43). The activities of the area development programs were fairly basic—mostly road construction, water sector improvements with some related agricultural assistance, as well as a few programs for human resource development focusing on technical skills and vocational training.

However, the programs were fraught with complications and were deemed largely unsuccessful. Security remained a constant concern, with USAID staff requiring militia escorts (ibid., 138). Popular perception of the projects was not only low but generally skeptical and at times turned violent, with some groups even organizing to protest against project activity. Political permission by "tribals" had to be granted for development work to be carried out, often requiring USAID staff to go through third-party political agents instead of working directly with the population (ibid., 147). USAID policies and procedures did not take into account all of these constraints. An evaluation of the area development programs reveals exasperation (ibid., 140–42):

> If the Mission was looking for a challenge, it certainly found it. It would be difficult to find a more inhospitable environment in which to operate … One wonders why the most remote reaches of Baluchistan, offering limited potential for development, were selected for this experiment. In the case of the Tribal Areas, the uncertainty of receptivity by the beneficiaries for the proposed improvements gives one pause to wonder whether the US has placed itself in too vulnerable a position … one would expect the utmost cooperation and support from the GOP. This is an activity in which the GOP should take the lead. USAID's role should be in support. The evaluations do not indicate this is the case … (and) puts into question the sustainability of these efforts. At some point, USAID assistance will have to terminate. (Ibid., 147)

USAID was one of the three largest donors in Pakistan in the 1980s, the World Bank and Asian Development Bank being the two others, and had the largest technical staff of any donor in the country (ibid., G-6). These donors coordinated extensively on projects, applying conditionalities to projects to maintain adherence to economic and political policies such as the privatization of industry. For example, in a joint World Bank/USAID Agricultural Sector project, a loan requirement was that at least 60 percent of fertilizer distribution needed to be carried out by the private sector (in order to help reduce government subsidies for fertilizer) (ibid., 243–44).

---

13. See Figures 5.2 and 5.3 to reference the geographic distribution of these populations.

From the sheer resource allocation to programs for economic assistance, it is clear that the underlying hopes of aid were to: (1) strengthen the reach of the central government and (2) economically integrate parts of the country that operated under local law. Additionally, the expansion of private sector industries would further enable Pakistan to engage in trade in the global marketplace, particularly with the United States, and to increase accessibility and connectability (through energy and infrastructure projects) to more remote parts of the country. There was an obvious political purpose behind this, and looking at the area development programs in particular sheds light. The GOP specifically requested for assistance in the development of areas in which the central government was unpopular—the border regions.

Bilateral economic and military assistance to Pakistan was renewed with a second package between 1988 and 1993 for $4.02 billion (military sales accounting for $1.750 billion matched by economic aid of $2.280 billion (Williams and Rudel 1988, 5)). Discussions for the continuation of aid beyond 1987 started in 1984 and concluded in 1986, with President Reagan verbally reassuring President Zia there would be continued assistance (ibid., 53). The GOP was explicitly interested in maintaining the link between military and economic assistance, and post-1987 economic assistance level was heavily influenced by GOP repayment obligations of 1982–87 FMS agreements (ibid.). New components to the program included funding for large-scale programs on child survival, population and malaria control, primary education, women's development, and NGO development[14] to support the presence of decentralized entities (ibid., 56). While the agreement for US assistance to Pakistan had been authorized through 1994, the passing of the Pressler Agreement in the US Congress shifted priorities. Given concerns over Pakistan's growing nuclear weapons capability, the Pressler Amendment called for curtailing and phasing out US assistance to Pakistan (USAID 1995a, 1; Blackton 1994, 1).

While USAID did not operate economic development programs in Afghanistan during the Soviet occupation, Congressional funding was eventually approved for humanitarian assistance in 1985 at around $8 million. When the Soviets withdrew, this amount increased to $121 million to include funding for health, educational, agricultural, as well as reconstruction programs (MacDonald 1994, 2). As the Mujahideen captured Khost, the area became a hub for transnational humanitarianism—with European state agencies, UNDP, UNICEF, as well as 60 other NGOs funded by European governments and donations from wealthy European groups (Nunan 2016, 265). Most programs were implemented with the assistance of contractors and PVOs/NGOs. Afghan NGOs were seen as assisting in the reconstruction process, enabling rehabilitation and contributing to the demilitarization of Afghan society, generating employment, and predicted as helping the new government "develop sensible policies on accepting and using foreign aid" (Carter 1991, 5, 7). Unfortunately, many Afghan NGOs were established merely to take advantage of the stream of funds and turned out to be fraudulent (ibid.; Nunan 2016, 267).

---

14. Consistent with the international development focus on strengthening NGOs and civil society as a part of healthy, functioning governments.

The humanitarian–development machine, for all its good intentions, waned in activity during the 1990s. Humanitarian organizations and development agencies were dependent upon Mujahideen groups and local tribes (and not a centralized state) in order for operations to continue. With the Soviet threat eliminated, donor attention turned to Eastern European countries transitioning from the Soviet model, and foreign expenditures in Afghanistan and Pakistan were subject to scrutiny by the donor governments, especially given the security situation on the ground. The same year USAID produced an assessment for the International Rescue Committee (IRC); on the promise of Afghan NGOs (Carter 1991), USAID enacted a cross-border assistance ban between July 1991 and January 1992 due to security incidents involving the kidnapping of a French national, two Americans, and stolen vehicles and equipment (USAID 1993).

Anticipating transition, the USAID laid out three stages for the pullout of the Afghan Mission starting in 1991: "the Survival Phase, the Renewal Phase and the Reconstruction Phase. The Survival Phase was concluded with the collapse of the communist regime in Kabul in April, 1992, which introduced the Renewal Phase ... (the Reconstruction Phase) focuses on urgent social and physical needs" (USAID 1993, 1). It is noted that "Until a stable, functioning government emerges in Kabul and the security situation measurably improves, the program will continue to be implemented on a cross-border basis from Pakistan" (USAID 1993, 2). A year later, a close-out plan details factors contributing to the decision to terminate the Afghan program, including the Clinton Administration seeking a new direction for USAID, the failure of Afghanistan to demonstrate significant progress toward "stability, reconstruction, and rehabilitation of infrastructure" (MacDonald 1994, 34), broken down rule of law, no constitution, no national judicial system, absence of effective central authority and ongoing civil war, large-scale human rights violations, and failure to stem narcotics production and trafficking (MacDonald 1994, 35). Additionally, in a rather condescending tone, "Afghans, for many years, have not had the ability to change their government through peaceful, democratic means" (MacDonald 1994, 34–35).

In spite of laying out rather optimistic phases for withdrawal, Afghanistan was unable to make it through the "survival, renewal, and reconstruction" phases following the Soviet collapse within a matter of four years. Seeking an exit, the international community pulled its resources and left Afghanistan in the midst of violence among Mujahideen groups the Americans had armed. Citing the Pressler Amendment, concerns over Pakistan's nuclear agenda that had been waived for the massive bilateral military sales/ economic aid program during the Soviet occupation again became justification for the cessation of bilateral assistance. The pullout was complete by the mid-1990s, save for a few "meaningful units of assistance which will contribute to the long-term development of Pakistan" (Blackton 1994, 3).

The issue of security had always been relevant, but the security–development nexus was still in the nascent stages during the 1980s and 1990s. At this point, the nexus meant combining FMS with economic assistance to strengthen the state apparatus to manage the Soviet threat through enabling covert transnational resistance. Today, the nexus has been fully integrated with military forces, development agencies, and governments working together as teams on specific projects in a combined counterinsurgency effort, as opposed to combining military and economic assistance to the central government to disburse as necessary. Between 1987 and 1990, while the United States allotted roughly $1 billion in FMS to Pakistan, less than $300 million went to Afghanistan in bilateral nonmilitary assistance[15] (DOD 2015, 233–38, 330–3). This raises important questions. What is development in the context of strategic bilateral military relationships? When economic assistance is framed "a (valuable) instrument of foreign policy" (Williams and Rudel 1988, 31), how does the dual status of donor and invader impact overarching goals of development and the authenticity of capacity-building initiatives? Why do we see these shifts in how the development–security nexus is conceptualized?

After 9/11, the United States spearheaded an international invasion of Afghanistan and embarked on a strategy to contain the threat of global terrorism and stabilize the security of the region. The Taliban fell shortly after the US invasion in 2001 and retreated into the hinterlands and border areas of Pakistan. The task then became the reconstruction and reintegration of Afghanistan into the global community of states, which required cooperation from Pakistan and donor coordination of development and military activity on a scale never before seen. The question of development had become a question of global security.

The dual donor/invader status was less complex during the Soviet occupation than it is today. While development workers in 1980s Pakistan may have required the protection of state or local militias to carry out their work, the situation and work of development was wholly divorced from full-scale state or foreign military occupation. The line between donor and invader is called into question during this period primarily due to the tension between the central government and the communities selected for and subjected to projects of development. In Afghanistan, part of the Soviet occupation was to invest and remake Afghanistan in the image of the Soviet model. While the USSR had been investing in Afghanistan for decades prior to the occupation, the Soviet Union transcended fully into an invader.

Since the al Qaeda attacks of 9/11, the United States has led two major international military campaigns in Afghanistan. Operation Enduring Freedom (OEF) was launched by the United States in conjunction with UK forces and joined by the Northern Alliance (which had evolved from Massoud's United Front against the Taliban in the 1990s). When the Taliban fell in 2001, the UN mediated the Bonn Agreement. The agreement (1) put in place an interim government to be led by Hamid Karzai (a Pashtun from the Northern Alliance); (2) required Afghan cooperation with the international community on countering narcotics, crime, and terrorism; and (3) established the International Security Assistance Force (ISAF), an international peacekeeping force intended to assist with the securing of Kabul (Bonn Agreement 2001). Tasked with "building capacity and transitioning to Afghan lead," the ISAF was originally deployed only to provide security in Kabul and train the Afghan National Security Forces (ANSF), but in 2006, NATO

---

15. Includes funds allotted for development assistance, economic support funds (ESF), P.L. 480 (Title I & II).

endorsed expanding ISAF's presence to cover the entire country[16] (NATO 2015). As a result, ISAF engaged in combat while also assisting with reconstruction.

The international effort in Afghanistan required great coordination. In order to increase independent oversight of US assistance to Afghanistan, the US Congress established a Special Inspector General for Afghanistan reconstruction (SIGAR), modeled after Iraq (Katzman 2008, 44). The UN also established the UN Assistance Mission to Afghanistan (UNAMA) in order to coordinate the work of donors and strengthen the cooperation between ISAF and the Afghan government (Katzman 2008, 11; UNAMA 2017). A series of donor conferences[17] established priorities for development, laid plans for coordination, and established policy and program frameworks for action.

The general nature of the plans for the transformation of Afghanistan were all-encompassing. I claim that the way in which donors collaborated and set benchmarks for Afghanistan (and Pakistan) in international agendas is defined by naivete and deluded optimism toward the reality of the political and economic situation of the countries. The objectives and concerns do not vary much from conference to conference, agenda, or framework. "Promoting good governance," "accelerating economic growth and development," and "strengthening security" are the top three pervasive umbrella objectives,[18] broken down into program areas with time lines for projects to achieve these objectives. At the 2014 conference in London, Afghanistan is encouraged to "realize self-reliance," justifying further support from the international community in order for Afghanistan to "become a full partner to the community of democratic nations," laying out further plans for transformation (Afghan Ministry of Foreign Affairs 2014). As donor agendas continue presenting justifications for intervention, time lines to achieve these objectives almost seem arbitrary.

While there is some variation in the methods of development in the 1980s and present day, the objectives and agendas are not so different, instead placing the responsibility and impetus for change more on the recipient than on the donor. In USAID's Afghanistan 2015 Plan for Transition, "the transition is based on the premise that private sector-led economic growth will become the main source of increases in government revenue to replace donor assistance and provide resources for quality delivery" (USAID 2014c, 3). This was essentially US strategy toward Pakistan in the 1980s in that the justification for economic support development programs was that they would facilitate the private sector revenue Pakistan would need in order to repay the United States for FMS. Ironically, when USAID returned to Pakistan in 2002, a large portion of nonproject ESFs[19] were

---

16. At its height, the ISAF had 130,000 peacekeeping troops on the ground from 51 countries (26 NATO members and 14 partner nations).

17. Bonn (2001), Berlin (2004), Kabul (2005), London (2006), Rome (2007), Paris (2008), Moscow (2009), The Hague (2009), London (2010), Bonn (2011), London (2014), Brussels (2016).

18. Afghanistan Compact from the London Conference on Afghanistan (2006); International Conference on Afghanistan at the Hague Declaration (2009); London Conference on Afghanistan (2014).

19. Nonproject assistance provides cash to support "mutually agreed upon objectives" such as social sector programs, with no conditionality tied to the disbursement (Kunder 2007, 3).

set aside for the purpose of paying off debt Pakistan owed to the United States, the World Bank, and the Asian Development Bank (USAID 2003b, 22).

After 9/11, USAID's mission upon rekindling assistance to Pakistan was clearly defined: "to tangibly improve the lives of the poor in Pakistan and to build support for Pakistan's decision to join the international war on terrorism and thwart further terrorist recruiting" (ibid., 2). This translated into funding for projects on four major areas: education, democracy and governance,[20] economic growth,[21] and health. "Capacity building" is fundamental to the design of each USAID program to ensure the sustainability of each project:[22]

> USAID builds sustainability into the design of each program. The major role of USAID technical assistance is to undertake the training and capacity-building that will ensure we leave behind teams and institutions in place that have the skills and systems needed to keep programs operating after USAID projects end. (Kunder 2007, 6)

Parts of FATA and Waziristan, where militant groups such as the HN hold authority, received special attention as part of the USAID strategy. Reports to Congress make note of the security situation in the FATA region, highlighting the agency's accomplishments in constructing infrastructure projects to meet "community-identified needs" (Bever 2010, 4). While citing the back-and-forth of civil and military rule in Pakistan as the major cause for the erosion of democratic institutions, the reconstruction projects in FATA are implemented by the Pakistani military and FATA Secretariat (ibid., 4–5). More than ever before, after 9/11 the operations of those whose task it was to maintain law and order became increasingly integrated with the implementation of development projects.

Funding to Pakistan sharply increased, with military assistance surpassing development assistance between 2001 and 2010 (Center for Global Development 2017). However, US disgruntlement with the terror threat harbored in Pakistan led to Congressional attempts to disassociate military and development assistance with the passage of the Enhanced Partnership for Pakistan Act.[23] Over the past few years, the United States has attempted to decrease its reliance on Pakistan, with US defense companies increasing sales to India, much to Pakistan's disgruntlement (Ali 2016). In August 2017, US President Trump allotted $255 million in military assistance to Pakistan, accessible only if Islamabad demonstrates increased crackdowns on the internal terror threat (Harris 2017). Theoretically, the carrot of US military assistance is expected to incentivize the disentanglement of Pakistan's military and Inter-Services Intelligence Agency (ISI) with the scores of militant groups operating within the country. That said, despite legislative

---

20. For example, programs intended to build civil society, independent media, political party reform, legislative "strengthening," and accountable and responsive local governance.
21. Measured by GDP growth rate, for example, programs whose purpose was to increase access to micro-credit/micro-finance in rural economies, market-based opportunities, and quality education in business and agriculture.
22. Discussed further in Chapter 3.
23. Also known as the Kerry–Lugar–Berman bill.

attempts to separate military and economic support spending, security and development operations are still significantly integrated. In Pakistan, this integration has taken the form of assistance as incentive for bilateral cooperation. In Afghanistan, the integration involves foreign military presence.

Figure 5.4 presents the architecture of the integration of bilateral and international military and economic support that makes up the development–security nexus in Afghanistan.

This figure is not meant to be specific to Afghanistan or Pakistan, but is broadly based on the development–security nexus in Afghanistan with the United States serving as the model for the donor state. To understand the development–security nexus it is necessary to see some totality of these donor–recipient relationships. I did not include the private firms, particularly security contractors, in this figure because these firms exist as exogenous beneficiaries[24] to the development industry facilitated by donors. In this way, I consider their activities as encompassed by donor–recipient relationships.

On the far right are various government entities involved in development and security activities of the donor state (ministries, departments, development agency/ office, military forces). The United States is unique in that among the many donors it has a special oversight body for the coordination of US reconstruction efforts in Afghanistan, the SIGAR. This donor state oversight body is part of military development integration on the policy end, as opposed to on the ground, which is where we see military development integration in activities. The middle column represents various forms of donor networks engaged with recipient states. Bilateral military assistance and international military networks display the military/security aspect of donor– recipient relationships. The donor political processes that determine bilateral military assistance and the coordination of an international military invasion are wholly separate from the coordination processes of development, but processes of development are inherently tied to donor military activities, particularly in reconstruction efforts and counterinsurgency.

An example of this architecture in practice is the innovation of "Provincial Reconstruction Teams" (PRTs). Civilian–military cooperation reached a new level with the establishment of PRTs, or "enclaves of US or partner forces and civilian officials that provide safe havens for international aid workers to help with reconstruction and to extend the writ of the Kabul government" (Katzman 2008, 31). Since 2002, PRTs have been integral to USAID operations in Afghanistan, enabling monitoring and evaluation of programs throughout Afghanistan (Johnson 2014, 9). PRT composition was a mixture of military personnel, Department of Defense officers, representatives from USAID, the State Department, and other relevant agencies, as well as Afghan government personnel (Katzman 2008, 31). Largely criticized, these "integrated civilian-military organizations" were tasked with improving security, extending the reach of the Afghan government, and facilitating reconstruction in priority provinces (USAID 2006b, 8) (Figure 5.5).

---

24. I discussed the notion of "exogenous beneficiaries" in Chapter 2 in the section *Traditional Donor Systems and the Development Space.*

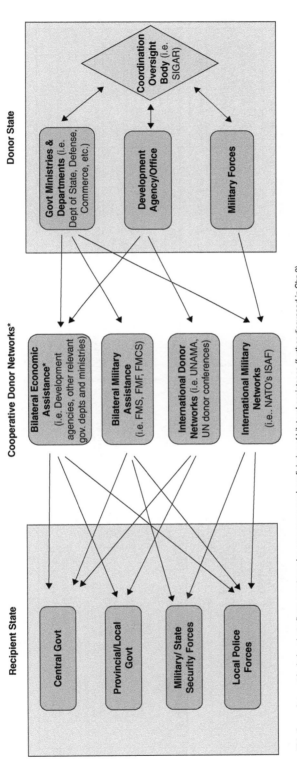

• This figure does not include private firms or actors who are exogenous beneficiaries of bilateral assistance (further discussed in Chp 3).

Figure 5.4 Post-9/11 Development–Security Nexus.

US and German PRT Models

	US-PRT	German PRT
Institutional set-up	Department of Defense in lead agency	Separate branches of government: Ministry of Foreign Affairs, Ministry of Defense, Ministry for Economic Cooperation and Development, and Ministry of the Interior
Size	Approx. 100 soldiers, 3–5 civilians	300–400 soldiers, about 10–20 civilians
Objectives	Combat (global war on terror) and stabilization, Quick impact Projects	Stabilization, reconstruction and emphasis on long-term development
Command structure	Military command and subordinated development agencies	Civil-military double command (Ministry of Foreign Affairs and Ministry of Defense)
Funding	Department of Defense is main donor	Each ministry is funding its activities
Interaction with development agencies	Development advisors are 'embedded' in the PRTs	Development advisors are not 'embedded' NGOs are independent of the PRTs

US PRT Structure

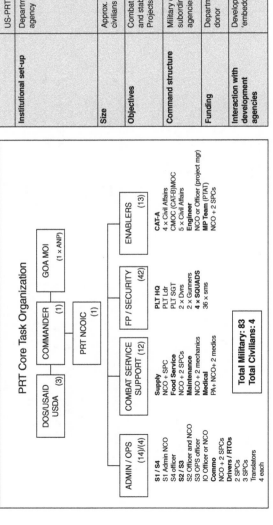

PRT Core Task Organization

DOS/USAID USDA (3) — COMMANDER (1) — GOA MOI (1 x ANP)

PRT NCOIC (1)

ENABLERS (13)

CAT-A
4 x Civil Affairs
CMOC (CAT-B)MOC
5 x Civil Affairs
Engineer
NCO or Officer (project mgr)
MP Team (PTAT)
NCO + 2 SPCs

FP / SECURITY (42)

PLT HQ
PLT Ldr
PLT SGT
2 x Dvrs
2 x Gunners
4 x SQUADS
36 x sms

COMBAT SERVICE SUPPORT (12)

Supply
NCO + SPC
Food Service
NCO + 2 SPCs
Maintenance
NCO + 2 mechanics
Medical
PA+ NCO+ 2 medics

ADMIN / OPS (14)/(4)

S1 / S4
S1 Admin NCO
S4 officer
S2 / S3
S2 Officer and NCO
S3 OPS officer
IO Officer or NCO
Commo
NCO + 2 SPCs
Drivers / RTOs
2 SPCs
3 SPCs
Translators
4 each

Total Military: 83
Total Civilians: 4

Figure 5.5 PRT Models.

PRTs are a manifestation of civilian–military cooperation of the security–development nexus. Their implementation has displayed important inconsistencies in how national obligations to international alliances (NATO) and subnational discourses (at the ministry/ departmental and military levels) interact to manage conflict and engage in development activities. Horký-Hlucháň and Szent-Iványi (2015) describe Czech and Hungarian PRTs as a failure of the security–development nexus, noting that both countries' obligation to NATO outweighed both security and development interests in the national policy discourse justifying PRTs. In looking at UK PRTs, Jackson and Gordon (2007) argue that PRT priorities of "stabilization" were distinct from the priorities of military-led and developmental frameworks espoused by PRT elements, resulting in planning that was not comprehensive or integrated (660).

The dynamics of PRTs were affected by a conflict of roles among actors, which was confounded by incompatibilities between various sectors of government on how to implement state-building programs. The security-minded interests of the military meant that US-led PRTs often functioned as insular military strongholds rather than as hubs for development and diplomacy. Personnel of the State Department, USAID, and the DoA echoed respective departmental policy and methods. This resulted in divisive policies, contradictory goals, and incoherent objectives (Keane and Wood 2016, 112). As an example, Colonel Augustine who was commander of the US PRT in Helmand wheedled USAID contractors into operating in areas they determined unsafe and unfeasible for operations (Hafvenstein 2007). While widely controversial, PRTs demonstrate the variation in subnational interpretations of civilian–military integration and also the emergence of tensions among subnational entities (civilian departments and military forces) implementing tasks set out by global governing institutions (such as the UN and NATO).

In this section, I highlighted how the convergence of military and development strategy and activities has become integrated in Afghanistan and Pakistan. The story of this integration is tied with the evolution of transnational networks of resistance and the rise of global militancy. As development projects along the border became imperative to contain global threats, the state had to be strengthened in areas operating under local tribal law. In the next section, I address how the convergence of security and development activities contributed to the legitimation of militant groups and building of infrastructure that has strengthened transnational militant networks opposed to the state system and expansion of global capitalism.

Transnational Networks of Resistance and Building Local Capacity

Networks of resistance take many forms, and often the organizations and actors active within the network have different and sometimes competing objectives. While the Taliban resists US and coalition forces' occupation of Afghanistan, al Qaeda resists the spread of Western ideology and seeks to establish a global Islamic caliphate. The web of transnational operations of resistance out of the region are extremely complex, and I do not set out to define them in totality. Rather, in the context of this project, I identify primary transnational networks of resistance active during the Cold War, tracing their evolution to the present day. These networks have played important roles in (re)defining the trajectory and internal political dynamics of both countries, and their transform-ation is integral to understanding the donor's challenge in developing state capacity in subnational spaces in Afghanistan and Pakistan.

Cold War transnational networks saw a convergence of state actors, intelligence agencies (US and Pakistani), humanitarian organizations (mostly European), bilateral development agencies, as well as Islamic militant groups organizing in the fight for Afghanistan. After 9/11, relationships born from Cold War transnational networks evolved, with some of the same actors operating across the same swaths of land and strongholds across Afghanistan and Pakistan. The objectives of the various post-9/11 networks vary, but most have some relation to or involvement with the situation of con-flict in Afghanistan. These twenty-first-century networks are much more complex than during the Cold War, but so is their enemy. While the Mujahideen enabled transnational resistance against a lone Soviet presence, post-9/11 networks are battling a US-led inter-national security–development apparatus.

The Cold War transnational networks of resistance centered around the organiza-tion of the Mujahideen and Pakistan's ISI, which served as an intermediary for for-eign governments to finance the Afghan Mujahideen through Pakistan. All international support to the Mujahideen flowed through Pakistan. The cause of Afghan liberation from the godless Soviets attracted Arab fighters from the broader Islamic world to migrate and fight alongside Mujahideen groups. French and Swedish humanitarians drawn by the plight of the Afghan refugee rallied and sought out avenues to provide assistance to those affected by conflict. The United States and Pakistan, fearing the Soviet presence, needed Afghan allies in the fight for regional dominance against the communists. The Mujahideen groups knew the terrain, enabled access to Afghanistan, and led the fight against the Soviets—they represented an ideal investment opportunity for anti-Soviet donors. The leaders of the Mujahideen groups began mobilizing through subnational Islamic networks in Afghanistan. While some of the Mujahideen leaders, such as Mohammadi and Mojaddedi, had been involved in anti-Communist activity since the 1950s, the other leaders adopted strong anti-Communist political stances as Soviet influ-ence grew and ultimately subsumed Afghanistan in the 1970s.

There were four primary subnational Islamic networks active in Afghanistan during the 1970s, a few of which evolved in organized Mujahideen factions fighting against the Soviet occupation: the Kabul University network, the Mullah (Mawlawi) network, the Sufi network, and the Pashtun tribal leaders of the royalist elite (Siddique 2014, 151–52). The Kabul University network was pan-Islamic in ideology, with transnational influences from the Egyptian Muslim Brotherhood (MB) and Pakistan's Jammat-e Islami. In the 1970s, Jalaluddin Haqqani, Younis Khalis, and Burhanuddin Rabbani[25] were all part of Gulbuddin Hekmatyar's anti-Soviet, anti-Daud, Hizb-i Islami (Islamic Party). Rabbani

---

25. Both Hekmatyar and Rabbani (along with several other Mujahideen leaders) studied at Egypt's preeminent school of Islamic jurisprudence, al-Azhar University in Cairo (Abbas 2014, 57). Interestingly, the school still holds significance for Afghan Islamic scholars. The USAID's 2010–12 Afghan judicial training component of the Rule of Law Stabilization Program involved international study tours in both Turkey and Egypt, including setting up an exchange

and Khalis eventually split from Hekmatyar's party, creating their own factions which were active during the Soviet occupation (Dressler 2010, 7). Haqqani went on to fight the Soviets as a commander under Khalis's faction and his group, which eventually evolved into the HN and ran madrassas and mosque congregations in Pashtun regions. The HN is still active today as one of the most sophisticated insurgent groups in the world, operating essentially as a transnational state in Afghanistan and Pakistan.

The Sufi network consisted of parties and organizations of Pashtun royalists, intelligentsia, and tribal leaders. The Mahaz-e Milli Islami (National Islamic Front) and Jabha-e Nijat-e Milli (National Liberation Front) came from this network and were also active funneling Central Intelligence Agency (CIA)-supplied weapons from the ISI during the Soviet occupation (Siddique 2014, 151). The final group consisted primarily of exiled Pashtun tribal leaders who wound up allying themselves with the Sufi network parties. These individuals were openly detested by Pakistan due to their nationalism and loyalty to the Afghan monarchy, representing the threat of Pashtunistan the Pakistanis feared (though they often quarreled with the Kabul University and Mullah networks) (Siddique 2014, 152). Prominent members included Durrani, Karlani, and Ghilzai tribal chiefs, intellectuals, and officials—Pashtun clan networks that continue to play an important role in the dynamics of conflict today. The Mawlawi Mullah network was the precursor to the Taliban (Siddique 2014, 151).

The Afghan Mujahideen that was active and somewhat coordinated during the Soviet occupation consisted of seven major factions. They were known as the "Peshawar Seven (*tanzim*)," the "Alliance of Seven (*haftgana*)," and the "Islamic Unity of Afghanistan Mujahideen" (Ruttig 2006, 10–11). In Figure 5.6, I highlight the leaders of the "Peshawar Seven," including information about ethnic/tribal backgrounds, network affiliations (ideological and political), as well as notable alliances and feuds.

The Peshawar Seven were far from the only Mujahideen groups fighting against the Soviets. The date of the actual formation of their alliance is disputed, though it is argued that their officiation is primarily nominal in nature and was determined in 1979 by the United States, Saudi Arabia, and Pakistani ISI's decision to exclusively fund these seven groups (Coll 2004, 344). A significant factor in this determination was Pakistan's inclination to support Sunni Afghan Islamic groups that were perceived to be disinterested in establishing a broader Pushtunistan (Emadi 1990, 1516; Napoleoni 2003, 79–83). As a group, the Peshawar Seven operated as more of a conglomerate, laying claim and fighting battles on different fronts with frequent infighting between the groups. The most dominant factions were Hekmatyar's Hizb-i Islami (HIG) party and Rabbani's and General Massoud's Jamiat-i Islami (Gardezi 2003).

While the ambitions drastically varied among those active in Cold War transnational networks—be it in the struggle to assist refugees, reclaiming homeland, fighting jihad, or containing the spread of communism—networks of cooperation emerged and some even have evolved to survive today. An understanding of these networks is important

---

program with al-Azhar University and Dogus University, given their tradition of Islamic jurisprudence with Sufi roots (USAID 2012f, 19).

Ethnic/Tribal Background: Pashtun
Ideological Influences: Qadiriyah Sufi; rejected Islamism & Communism, pro-democracy & nationalism.
Political Affiliations:
• Represented Pashtun royalists;
• Received limited foreign funding (Committee for a Free Afghanistan, Heritage Foundation, Freedom House, and Radio Free Kabul; but not Arab funding);
• Ceased major activity in 1990s.

Ethnic/Tribal Background: Pashtun
Ideological Influences: Naqshbandi Sufi; politically moderate
Political Affiliations:
• Kabul University network
• Founding member of Ikhwan-ai-Muslimun
• Served as President of Afghanistan briefly in 1992;
• Extensive political activity after the fall of the Taliban in 2001 (Chairman of Loya Jirga (2001), Member of Parliament (2007), ran for President (2014).)

Ethnic/Tribal Background: Both Tajik
Political Affiliations/Rivalries:
• Rabbani (led the Jamiat-i Islami party)
  ○ Founding member of Ikhwan-al-Muslimun;
  ○ Close ties to Jamaat Islami Pakistan (JIP);
  ○ Served as President of Afghanistan (1992-96);
  ○ Relations with Hekmatyar: Both supported by ISI in attempts to overthrow Daoud regime in 1970s, but had a checkered relationship during the post-Soviet, pre-Taliban period with Hekmatyar serving as PM under Rabbani's presidency during two brief periods.;
  ○ Joined Northern Alliance during Taliban years;
  ○ Assassinated by Taliban In 2001.
• Massoud (was a General under Rabbani)
  ○ Involved in failed overthrow of Daud's govt with Hekmatyar & Rabbani in 1975, resulting in a split with Hekmatyar who subsequently attempted multiple assassinations against Massoud;
  ○ Created the United Front to oppose Taliban rule in 1996 (United Front became the Northern Alliance) composed mostly of Afghan non-Pashtuns;
  ○ Bin Laden openly opposed Massoud; was assassinated two days before 9/11, purportedly planned by al Qaeda operatives.

Ethnic/Tribal Background: Pashtun
Ideological Influences: Afghan Wahhabist
Political Affiliations:
• Kabul University network;
• Founding member of Ikhwan al Muslimun;
• Saudi favorite during Soviet occupation;
• Affiliated with Massoud's United Front, but also closely affiliated with Bin Laden/al Qaeda;
• Post fall of Taliban (2001): part of Loya Jirga (2003); converted Islamic Union group to political party (2005).

Ethnic/Tribal Background: Pashtun
Political Affiliations:
• Party separated from Hekmatyar's Hezb-i Islami in 1979;
• Pro-Taliban in 1990s;
• Notable Commanders: Jalaluddin Haqqani (Haqqani Network), Abdul Haq, Amin Wardak;
• No longer active.

Ethnic/Tribal Background: Pashtun
Political Affiliations:
• Kabul University network;
• Ikhwan-al-Muslimun (one of founding members), and PDPA in 1970s;
• Heavily funded by Saudi Arabia and received greatest amount of aid from Pakistani ISI during Soviet occupation;
• Close ties to Muslim Brotherhood (Egypt) & Jamaat Islami Pakistan (JIP);
• Relations with Rabbani: Both supported by ISI in attempts to overthrow Daoud regime in 1970s; Hekmatyar was PM for two brief spells under Rabbani during post-Soviet, pre-Taliban period; Many Hezb supporters joined the Taliban in 1990s, but Hekmatyar fled to Iran during Taliban rule;
• Post-Taliban, the Hezb party experienced splits, with the party supporting the Karzai government and Hekmatyar critical of American collusion with Karzai;
• 2016 - Hekmatyar and Hezb-i Islami agreed to cease hostilities & were officially pardoned by Afghan President Ghani in a peace deal.

Ethnic/Tribal Background: Pashtun
Political Affiliations:
• Served as VP of Afghanistan under Rabbani (1993-96)
• Pro-Taliban (many of Mohammadi's followers supported Taliban)

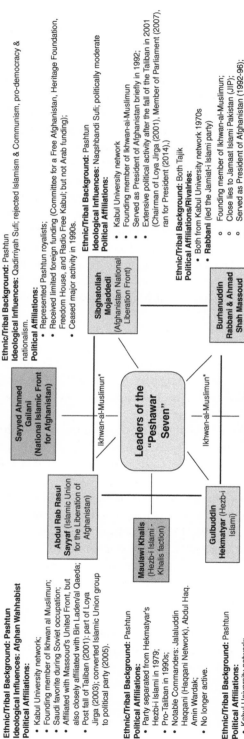

Sayed Ahmed Gailani (National Islamic Front for Afghanistan)

Abdul Rab Rasul Sayyaf (Islamic Union for the Liberation of Afghanistan)

Maulawi Khalis (Hezb-i Islami - Khalis faction)

Gulbuddin Hekmatyar (Hezb-i Islami)

Leaders of the "Peshawar Seven"

Ikhwan-al-Muslimun*

Ikhwan-al-Muslimun*

Sibghatollah Mojaddedi (Afghanistan National Liberation Front)

Burhanuddin Rabbani & Ahmad Shah Massoud (Jamiat-i Islami)

Mohammad Nabi Mohammadi (Revolutionary Islamic Movement)

*Rabbani, Hekmatyar, Sayyaf, and Mojaddedi studied together at al-Azhar University in Egypt and founded the Afghan Muslim Brotherhood (Ikhwan-al-Muslimun) in the 1970s; Massoud was also a member in the 1970s.

Figure 5.6 Leaders of the "Peshawar Seven."

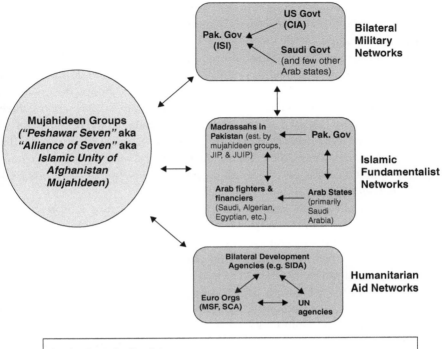

Figure 5.7 Cold War Transnational Networks of Resistance.

to realizing the present-day challenges of building state capacity, particularly in the subnational spaces housing transnational militant networks. In Figure 5.7, I display a breakdown of the major transnational networks active during the Cold War.

These military, humanitarian, and Islamist transnational networks would not exist were it not for the Mujahideen groups. The Mujahideen groups enabled access in and out of Afghanistan, knew the lay of the land, and as "freedom fighters" represented the West's only option against a Soviet-occupied Afghanistan.

Bilateral military networks supplied the ammunition and supplies the Mujahideen needed to fight the Soviets. A major component of the US assistance package to Pakistan, as noted in the previous section, was an FMS agreement with Pakistan. This agreement was made under the assumption that in conjunction with an economic assistance package to stimulate Pakistan's economy, the country would be able to repay the United States for the FMS. Throughout the conflict in the 1980s, the US CIA discreetly provided $600 billion and around 900 Stinger missiles to Pakistan's military intelligence agency, the ISI, who made decisions, completely independent of the United States, on how to distribute the money and weapons to the Mujahideen groups (Bergen 2002, 67–8, 71, 77). The Mujahideen leaders, in turn, then determined to which warlords to distribute weapons (Gardezi 2003). Even though there were hundreds of resistance groups, the ISI chose the Peshawar Seven by which to establish offices and from which to channel support: three of the seven chosen were Ghilzai Pashtun groups[26] that constituted the beginning of what is now the Taliban—none were Durrani Pashtuns, Karzai's tribal affiliation, and Ghilzai enemies (Johnson and Mason 2007, 75). By the end of the war, 200 Stingers remained unused and found their way into the hands of, among others, Iranians, the Taliban, and al Qaeda (Bergen 2002, 77).

Notably, the United States was not the only country facilitating a bilateral military relationship with Pakistan to fund the Mujahideen. Saudi Arabia also provided major support to Pakistan's ISI. General Zia ul-Haq requested Saudi assistance to strengthen the Mujahideen, to which King Khalid immediately agreed to supply resources to the ISI and encouraged private Saudi citizens to donate money and join the jihad (Riedel 2014, 61). Perhaps lesser known is that to strengthen this partnership, Zia dispatched Pakistani troops to Saudi Arabia near the border with Israel between 1982 and 1988 to help the Saudi defense against regional enemies (ibid.). Saudi military funding to the ISI for the Mujahideen strengthened their relationship not only with Pakistan but also with the Americans. From 1979 under President Carter through the Bush administration (1992), the Saudis agreed to match US support for the Mujahideen (Riedel 2014, 93, 98–99). The weapons and resources supplied by bilateral military networks were the bread and butter of the battle fought by the Mujahideen against the Soviets. It is questionable whether the Mujahideen would have been able to defeat the Soviets without the sheer amount of financing and weapons provided by foreign governments and enabled by these bilateral military networks.

The Islamic fundamentalist networks of the Cold War were largely facilitated by Pakistan. The Soviet occupation attracted a migration of radical Islamist fighters— Arabs who established bases and madrassas mostly in Pakistan and fought alongside the Mujahideen. This flock of Arabs and systemic promotion of Islamist organizations was enabled by Pakistan, which sought to promote the cause of jihad to further legitimize Pakistani military rule, prevent India from gaining a foothold in Afghanistan, and ideally support an eventual Mujahideen client regime in Afghanistan (Siddique 2014, 41). The religious schools or madrassas operating on the border were an important site of social-ization that further entrenched transnational connections among Afghans, Pakistanis, and Arabs. For many Afghan refugees in Peshawar and Baluchistan, sending their sons to madrassas was the most attractive option for securing their futures. The schools provided

---

26. (1) Mohammadi's Revolutionary Islamic Movement, (2) Khalis's Hezb-i Islami (Khalis faction), and (3) portions of Hekmatyar's Hezbi-i Islami (though Hekmatyar did not support the Taliban himself).

free room and board as well as a monthly stipend many students sent to support their families in the refugee camps (Nojumi 2002, 119). These religious schools were by and large controlled by two powerful Islamic parties in Pakistan: Jamaat Islami Pakistan (JIP) and Jamaat-e-Ulema-Islami Pakistan (JUIP).

The JIP was one of the strong political forces behind General Zia ul-Haq and had much influence within the Pakistani Army. Under US influence and funding, the Pakistani army grew significantly, giving the Pakistani army political legitimacy (in spite of it being one of the primary obstacles to democracy in Pakistan) (Ravi 2006, 143). One consequence of this was a steep increase in the number of madrassas designed specifically to indoctrinate not only young Muslims from the Pashtun areas but also Arabs who flocked to fight against the communists (Gilani 2006, 87). The JIP also had strong ties to the Egyptian MB, even funding MB leaders Hassan al Bana and Sayyid Qutb, and the party even had a Wahhabist segment (Nojumi 2002, 119). Mujahideen leaders Hekmatyar and Rabbani both had ties to the JIP and were involved with the JIP-funded madrassas in Pakistan. Hekmatyar had the strongest relationship with JIP's leader, Qazi Hussein Ahmed, which enabled him significant access to the ISI; he received the most significant amount of funding from the ISI throughout the resistance (Nojumi 2002, 120).

The JUIP was more ideologically traditionalist—with the Deobandi influences and funding from the Saudis. The party was originally sponsored by the GOP for the purpose of combating the Awami National Party (a Pashtun nationalistic separatist party) in the NWFP of Pakistan (Nojumi 2002, 119). While the madrassas were not providing military training to students for battle, it was very common for students and also teachers to participate in the war against the Soviets. The Mujahideen groups were active in the refugee camps and the madrassas—most Afghans could not escape the proximity to which their situation of displacement had bound them to the conflict of their homeland.

The migration of Arab fighters and financiers to the madrassas and the battlefront was also facilitated by elements within the GOP. As the bilateral military relationship between Pakistan and Saudi Arabia strengthened, transnational private–diplomatic relationships enabled Arab fundamentalists to infiltrate Afghan resistance networks. In addition to Saudi bilateral assistance to the ISI, the Saudi ambassador in Pakistan also provided money and aid directly to Jalaluddin Haqqani, who was the first Mujahideen commander to invite foreign forces (mostly Arabs, including bin Laden) to join his Pashtun forces in the war (Riedel 2014, 54). As previously mentioned during the Soviet occupation, Haqqani operated as a commander under Khalis's Hezb faction of the Peshawar Seven. Osama bin Laden, as the son of an extremely wealthy Saudi builder, enjoyed a close relationship to Haqqani, leading Arab volunteers to fight under his command (Riedel 2014, 54). bin Laden was also contracted by the ISI to engineer humanitarian and infrastructure projects, including the construction of an elaborate cave complex in Haqqani territory used to train Arab fighters (Dressler 2010, 7–8).

This intermixing of radicalized Arabs with the Afghan Mujahideen and Pakistani officials is what resulted in the most feared global Islamic terrorist groups of today. The Egyptian "volunteers" sent to fight alongside the Mujahideen were actually political prisoners such as Ayman al-Zawahiri (bin Laden's number two) and Khalid Islambouli (the militant Islamist who assassinated Egyptian President Anwar Sadat in 1981) (Farivar

2009, 177). The concept of al Qaeda was born during this time—formed in Peshawar in the late 1980s with the objective of waging jihad against the state of Israel and the West (Siddique 2014, 61). That said, the Arabs also remained dependent on the Mujahideen for access to Afghanistan. There was only one semi-independent Arab unit that fought the Soviets in Paktia Province close to the border; most had to attach themselves to Mujahideen groups in order to fight and were generally regarded as poor fighters with deep pockets (Farivar 2009, 177).

While war attracted ideologically motivated Arabs to Afghanistan, a record number of Afghans were displaced and became refugees. Over a million Pashtuns were killed and approximately 80 percent of those remaining became IDPs or refugees that fled to Pakistan (Liebl 2007, 502). The refugee situation drew the interest of the Europeans. While the United States sought to strengthen Pakistan both economically and militarily in the early 1980s, Médecins Sans Frontières (MSF) and the Swedish Committee for Afghanistan (SCA) forged networks with both the Pakistani state and anti-Soviet Mujahideen groups in order to operate clinics and dispensaries in both Pakistani refugee camps and in Afghanistan. While the Americans funneled billions into Pakistan to support the Mujahideen, the Europeans scrambled to organize a response to what was, at the time, the second-largest refugee crisis in history.

The Afghan refugee situation created unlikely networks of cooperation. "On the one side stood the Afghan communist state, the Soviet Union, and territorial sovereignty … On the other side was the humanitarian project of transnational morality, embedded into the mujahideen groups based out of the territory once imagined as 'Pashtunistan'" (Nunan 2016, 148–49). SCA operated mostly from Pakistan, supplying MSF doctors in Afghanistan with medicine, while MSF could ensure that the Afghan-run clinics where the SCA supplies were headed actually existed. SCA developed a thriving operation, but mistakes were made in determining which groups to disburse funds to. For example, SCA funded the Society of Afghan Doctors (SAD), a group that ran only one clinic inside Afghanistan and discriminated among patients, favoring Pashtuns over non-Pashtuns. Receiving the bulk of SCA medical shipments were Jam'iat-i Islami (Rabbani's party), Hezb-i-Islami (Hekmatyar's party), and Harakat-i Inqalabi (Mohammadi's party) (Nunan 2016, 225). SCA eventually developed their own intelligence arm that sent surveyors into refugee camps to inquire into the trustworthiness of applicants of SIDA aid and developed a reputation for being difficult to cheat and awarding aid on the basis of technical qualifications (Nunan 2016, 145).

Eventually, the Americans and UN agencies (UNICEF and UNDP) increased involvement as the French and Swedes lobbied on behalf of the "Afghan social emergency" (Nunan 2016, 138) at the UN. Soviet-run Kabul even accepted UNDP and UN Disaster Relief assistance due to the 1984 earthquake (Nunan 2016, 138), and in 1985 Congress opened the floodgates for humanitarian aid in approving $60 million for humanitarian relief for Afghanistan (Nunan 2016, 224). Suddenly, Peshawar became the gateway to Afghanistan and home base for a flood of NGOs, the largest concentration of any single place in the world and completely overwhelmed aid workers and Mujahideen groups alike (Nunan 2016, 224):

Interaction between United Nations Office Complex in Afghanistan (UNOCA) and established NGOs was complex ... a slew of NGOs that had never worked with Afghans or even in any refugee camp in the world flooded Peshawar. Bolstered by far larger sums of cash than MSF could muster, such groups swarmed mujahidin offices to discuss how to disburse their millions of dollars ... UNOCA engaged almost exclusively with Geneva-based NGOs in the post-withdrawal Afghan theater, prompting established organizations to found an Agency Coordinating Body for Afghan Relief and Development (ACBAR) as an umbrella organization for the groups that actually had experience in Afghanistan. Conversely, however, while UNOCA and UN agencies had limited room for action in those territories under mujahidin control—like Panjshir—UNOCA also cooperated with Peshawar-based NGOs to coordinate aid activity to rebel held areas in Afghanistan. (Nunan 2016, 259)

Humanitarian activity ultimately had to be linked to transnational Mujahideen groups because outside of the 1984 earthquake relief, the Soviet Union had blocked assistance through UN arms like UNDP, UNICEF, or the WHO (Nunan 2016, 263). While Mujahideen groups were treated as functionally equivalent to the Kabul government by UNICEF, they lacked international recognition and had been essentially ignoring the border of the central government in order to obtain international resources to provide services within the national territory of Afghanistan (Nunan 2016, 260).

This created a dilemma after the Geneva Accords and Soviet withdrawal. Suddenly as the Soviet Union fell, Afghanistan lost international attention. The Soviets had been defeated and the wellspring of international funding began to dry up. Additionally, the security situation became too dangerous for the European humanitarian NGOs once the "alliance" of Mujahideen groups proved unable to rise above infighting, centralize, and take the reigns of the Afghan state. Militant infighting resulted in threats to aid workers, and when a French doctor was murdered in 1990 all MSF doctors were withdrawn from Afghanistan (though they returned in 1992) (Nunan 2016, 263–64).

Through their sheer existence and operation, these transnational humanitarian, military, and Islamist networks that existed during the Soviet occupation challenged and further damaged the legitimacy and territoriality of the Afghan (and ultimately Pakistani) state. The networks that were created and operated out of the broader "Pashtunistan" cemented relationships and paths traversing Afghan and Pakistani land. They built the legitimacy and strengthened the potential capacity for future resistance groups to establish local (and transnational) authority that disputes the extension of the state into its territory. International as well as state attempts to "build capacity" are fundamentally challenged by the transnational territoriality of these networks.

Network Transformation During the 1990s

The Soviets withdrew in 1989 following the Geneva Accords, as the conflict was proving to be a huge strain on their dwindling resources (Klass 1988). Reminiscent of the British and Russian 1873 negotiation of Afghan boundaries that subsequently influenced the establishment of the Durand Line, the Mujahideen was not party to the negotiations and rejected the accord. This resulted in civil war between Najibullah's government and Mujahideen forces, which promptly began fighting among each other for power (Katzman 2008, 2). The fall of Najibullah's government led to a succession of short-term governments led by the Mujahideen leaders. Mojadeddi, who led one of the smaller factions of the Peshawar Seven, was president between April and May 1992. An agreement among the major parties led to Rabbani becoming president in June 1992 with the understanding that he would serve until December 1994, at which point he refused to step down due to concerns that the political situation was too volatile for transition without a clear successor (ibid., 3). Kabul was continually under attack, including by "Prime Minister" Hekmatyar's Hizb-i Islami faction, who accused Rabbani of refusing to give up power (ibid.).

However, as infighting among the Mujahideen groups threatened aid groups, donor foreign policy priorities shifted, and concern over Pakistan's nuclear program heightened, the donor community withdrew most assistance from Afghanistan and Pakistan by the mid-1990s. Regardless, the infrastructure to enable the flourishing of transnational activity was firmly cemented. The inability of the Mujahideen leaders to establish a stable government eventually gave way to the Taliban, who gained legitimacy through winning against and protecting communities from the harassment and corruption of the Mujahideen, thus preventing the complete collapse of the state at the hands of infighting (Siddique 2014, 47, 52). Under the Taliban, humanitarian aid continued to function at a minimum. UN agencies delivered aid to NGOs, but the Taliban's attitude toward them was inconsistent and they monitored international activity closely (Nunan 2016, 274–75).

As the donor community largely abandoned both countries, the GOP saw an ally in the rise of the Taliban.[27] The emergence of the Taliban was largely facilitated by the transnational Islamic networks cultivated by the GOP. Figure 5.8 displays the various sources of Taliban fighters.

Of the Mujahideen groups, Khalis and Mohammadi's factions supported the Taliban (Marsden 1998, 32; BBC 2006), while Massoud created the United Front (also known as the Northern Alliance) to oppose Taliban rule also supported by Rabbani and Sayyaf (Abbas 2014, 65). Hekmatyar fled to Iran, returning only after the fall of the Taliban in 2001, although many HIG supporters joined the Taliban in the 1990s (Nojumi 2002, 127; Abbas 2014, 69).

Most of the Taliban came from the Pakistani madrassas of the 1980s. The leaders of the Taliban emerged from a JUIP-run madrassa based in Karachi during the Soviet occupation, while many other future Talib were educated at other JUIP madrassas in Peshawar and surrounding areas (Nojumi 2002, 220). Mullah Omar in particular enjoyed a close relationship with JUIP leader Maulana Fazl-ul-Rahman, enabling the Taliban generous support from Pakistan in the 1990s (Nojumi 2002, 221). Many of these madrassas still operate today, producing insurgents affiliated with present-day transnational militant groups such as the HN (Dressler 2010, 4).

---

27. Distinction between Taliban, Tehrik-i Taliban, and QST (Quetta Shura Taliban).

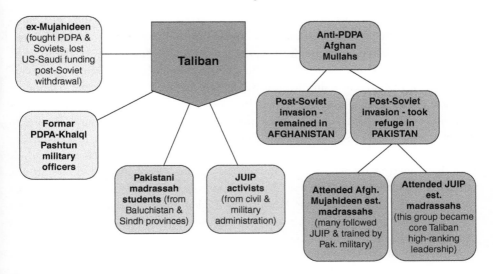

Figure 5.8 Sources of the Taliban Network.
Source: *Figure adapted from text in *The Rise of the Taliban in Afghanistan* (2002) by Neamatollah Nojumi (pp. 125–27).

Noting the inability of the Mujahideen leaders to form a stable centralized government and losing faith in Hekmatyar, the GOP saw an opportunity in supporting the Taliban. The Taliban were predominantly Pashtun, but not pro-Pashtunistan; they would enable Pakistan to expand trade links throughout Central Asia and provided a sanctuary from which to launch covert attacks against Indian targets (Abbas 2014, 64). Thus, the Taliban received heavy support[28] from the ISI to enable the group to take control of Kabul (Aziz 2014). The ISI supplied resources, weapons, and training to the Taliban to ensure a close relationship with Pakistan (Coll 2004, 293). The ISI even paid the medical bills of wounded Taliban fighters (Jones 2009, 31). With this backing, Mullah Omar's Taliban actually managed to create relative law and order—disarming many Pashtun warlords—but the Taliban did not focus on building state capacity and infrastructure, and specifically excluded non-Pashtuns from participating in high-level positions (Mishali-Ram 2008, 482).

In order to maintain a hold on Afghanistan, the Taliban established relationships with other militant networks operating across the border. Shortly after capturing Kabul in 1996, Mullah Omar formally created alliances with the HN and al Qaeda, as well as with Osama bin Laden (CFR 2015). The HN connection was crucial, as the Haqqanis controlled swaths of territory in Loya-Paktia where the Taliban had never been able to gain a foothold (Kagan 2009). However, the relationships were uneasy. Jalaluddin Haqqani remained nominally loyal to the Taliban but maintained an autonomous power base over his territory in Afghanistan and Pakistan (Dressler 2010, 9).

---

28. The Taliban also received funding from Saudi charities and religious ministries, funneled through Pakistan (Coll 2004, 296).

The Taliban and al Qaeda also maintained a terse relationship during the 1990s, especially given Osama bin Laden's designated fugitive status by the states and organizations within the international community (e.g., the United States, Saudi Arabia, the UN, the Organization of Islamic States [OIS]). In exchange for hospitality, bin Laden made promises to Taliban leadership to fund what were basically development activities—to build infrastructure, advance agricultural development, and to fund reconstruction projects (Siddique 2014, 65). These promises did not come to fruition, leading to disagreements among the Taliban leadership about the protection being afforded to bin Laden and whether or not he should be turned over to other entities such as the OIS or even the United States (who refused to recognize Taliban leadership) (ibid., 66). It was ultimately decided, to the detriment of the Taliban's global standing in the international community of states, to continue housing bin Laden given the role of Arab fighters during the Soviet occupation and also due to Pashtun codes of honor surrounding rules of hospitality toward guests (ibid.).

The failure of the Mujahideen to centralize and rise above factional infighting speaks to the challenges of centralized governance in Afghanistan. The Mujahideen groups, while operating transnationally, maintained control and loyalty over different parts of the country. Furthermore, it is important to note the very transnational nature of the rise of the Taliban. Leaders and fighters emerging from Saudi-funded, Pakistani-run madrassas provided a religious education and indoctrination that merged fundamentalist Islamic ideology from the Arab world to Central Asia and provided a site for the international intermingling of Afghan refugees, Arabs, and Pakistanis.

By the end of the 1990s, the Taliban had established control over most of the country with the exception of a sliver of land in the Panshjir Valley, where Ahmad Shah Massoud and the Northern Alliance forces had retreated (Jones 2009, 19). The networks established during the Soviet occupation transformed the challenges of central governance in Afghanistan. Mujahideen leaders whose groups initially operated primarily within Afghanistan, subnationally became well-oiled transnational operations in the 1980s and 1990s, laying the infrastructure for the operations of a wide range of militant groups whose aims are to disrupt global and state systems of trade and governance.

The Globalization of Transnational Networks Post-9/11

The networks of resistance active after 9/11 are significantly more complex than those of the Cold War. They represent a nexus of international terrorism, regional and global insecurity, and crisis of state. Furthermore, while their aims and objectives may differ, their cooperation has increased and their operations integrated. In this section, I do not seek to provide an exhaustive explanation of the complex nature by which these networks of resistance transcend all manner of boundaries of authority and governance, but rather to highlight the interconnected nature of groups operating at many levels. The linkages and complexity of these networks are significant because they challenge attempts by the donor community and the state to build capacity on every scale. The legitimacy, stability, and resilience of state and international systems of governance, industry, and

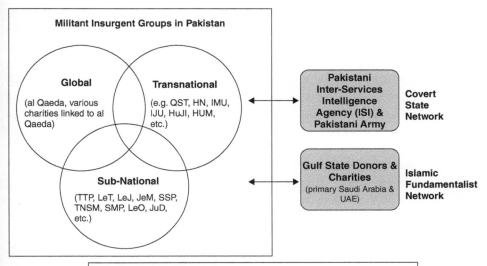

Figure 5.9 Post-9/11 Networks of Resistance.

infrastructure are challenged by subnational, transnational, and global networks resisting the authority of states and expansion of global capitalism.

The network infrastructure that was established during the Cold War continued to evolve as Afghan refugees and the Taliban (QST[29]) moved back into Afghanistan. While the QST controlled Afghanistan, it maintained roots and support in Pakistan. In response to the attacks on the twin towers, the United States launched an attack that reignited the very cross-border network infrastructure that enabled Mujahideen resistance against the Soviets. When the US-led coalition forces defeated the QST in December 2001, the QST leadership retreated to Pakistan, operating out of three cities: Quetta (the head-quarters[30]), Peshawar (the propaganda and media base[31]), and Karachi (the financial base) (Jones 2009, 31). Pakistan again became the home base for the Afghan insurgency and a hub for international terrorism (Figure 5.9).

29. As a point of clarification, after 9/11, "Taliban" has been used as somewhat of a catch-all term for various groups of militants. Moving forward, in this section I refer to the Taliban as "QST" or Quetta Shura Taliban.
30. Quetta also enabled easy access to Afghanistan's southern provinces, particularly Kandahar (where Mullah Omar grew up) (Jones 2009, 31).
31. Peshawar is home to a Sunni jihadist support network, which has existed since the Mujahideen war against the Soviets. The Taliban also uses al Qaeda's production company, as-Sahab Media, which is based in Peshawar (ibid.).

The dominant insurgent networks in the region operate transnationally with home bases largely in Pakistan, many operating out of Pashtun regions. Their targets are the central governments of Afghanistan and Pakistan, Indian officials, Western entities, and other ideological opponents. The primary active groups are: QST, the HN, al Qaeda, Hezb-i-Islami,[32] Tehrik-i-Taliban Pakistan (TTP),[33] Tehrik-i-Nifaz-i-Shariat-i-Muhummadi (TNSM), Swat and Baujaur Taliban, as well as unaffiliated sectarian and criminal groups (Stanford Mapping Militant Organizations Project 2017). Figure 5.10 shows a partial breakdown and scope of four major insurgent networks currently active: QST (the Taliban), al Qaeda, Tehrik-i-Taliban (TTP), and the HN.

These relationship maps (Figure 5.10) provide merely a glimpse into the extent of the relationships between militant groups. Most groups operate transnationally, meaning that the reach of their presence and/or objectives spans more than one country. Most of the transnational groups highlighted operate across Pakistan and Afghanistan and are connected to other organizations of resistance not noted.

This is well exemplified by the transformation of the HN. The HN is notoriously violent and were the first to adopt suicide bombing as a tactic for attacks in Afghanistan (Gopal 2009). The HN has been around since the 1970s, when leader Jalaluddin Haqqani trained in Pakistan to combat Daoud's regime (Brown and Rassler 2013, 46). Haqqani fought as a commander during the Soviet occupation under Hezb-i-Islami (Khalis faction) and was the only Afghan Islamist known to have actively recruited Arab foreign fighters into his ranks (Brown and Rassler 2013, 7). Haqqani maintained an alliance with the Taliban during the 1990s, although his allegiance to Mullah Omar is more strategic than genuine (Kagan 2009), but given the level of control and influence the group has in Loya-Paktia, Mullah Omar has respected Haqqani's autonomy, even naming him regional commander for East Afghanistan (Dressler 2010, 20).

After 2001, the leadership of the HN transitioned from father to son, though Jalaluddin still maintains much influence (Roggio 2009). Many of the current Afghan fighters under HN are actually the sons of those who fought against the Soviets (Gopal 2009). While the Haqqanis control Loya-Paktia in Afghanistan (which includes the provinces of Khost, Paktya, and Paktika), the group is headquartered in Miram Shah, Pakistan, and they control the surrounding areas as well as parts of South Waziristan (Dressler 2010, 14). Miram Shah is a breeding ground for insurgent groups operating on a transnational and global scale and is home to al Qaeda and other anti-US/coalition forces (Flynn 2009).

HN funding comes from numerous sources—Arab and Gulf states, al Qaeda, taxation both in Miram Shah and Loya-Paktia, and payments from Afghan and foreign construction and contracting firms in Loya-Paktia (JTSM 2009). This includes money from development agencies such as USAID for projects. Contractors and district elders pay protection money to Haqqani affiliates, sometimes as much as half the money received

---

32. As of 2016, Hekmatyar made a peace agreement with President Ghani of Afghanistan to pardon Hekmatyar in exchange for ceasing hostile activity against the government of Afghanistan (Rasmussen 2016).
33. Not to be confused with QST or the "Taliban" (as referenced elsewhere in this chapter).

Major Transnational Insurgent Networks in Pakistan

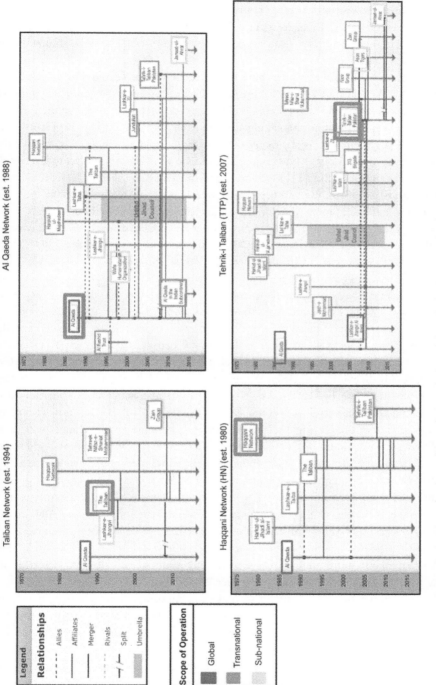

Source: Stanford University, Mapping Militants Project: http://web.stanford.edu/group/mappingmilitants/cgi-bin/

© Mayville 2018

Figure 5.10 Major Transnational Insurgent Networks in Pakistan.

for reconstruction and development projects (Toosi 2009). The HN runs a parallel shadow administration that includes courts, recruiting centers, tax offices, and security forces (Dressler 2010, 11). Elders of Haqqani's own tribe (the Pashtun Zadrans) who have challenged HN authority have been assassinated, leaving tribal elements vulnerable in the absence of leadership (Dressler 2010, 17).

Development efforts in HN areas have been relatively unsuccessful. Part of a USAID project formulated in mid-2005, Zadran Arc Stabilization Initiative (MITSI) promised the Zadran (and other areas) increased security and development in exchange for their support and engagement in stabilizing the area (Dressler 2010, 18). Residents were promised employment and pay by the Afghan government and coalition forces, but it did not materialize, which isolated and angered locals who were already subject to large-scale intimidation by the HN (ibid.). These sorts of instances, where the Afghan government and Coalition Forces promise and then disappoint locals, only further damage the legitimacy of the state and potential to build trust and linkages on subnational scales.

The HN also enables foreign fighters to operate in the region—Arabs, Pakistanis (non-Pashtuns), Uzbeks, Chechens, and Turks affiliated with groups like al Qaeda, IMU, TTP, and LeT—who require local guides, facilitators and protection (ibid., 14). Most foreign fighters are unfamiliar with their surroundings and require local assistance for just about everything—transportation, weapons, supplies, shelter, as well as access to other groups. The HN facilitates these operations, and groups like al Qaeda would not be able to operate in the Loya-Paktia or North Waziristan without the protection of the Haqqanis (Brown and Rassler 2013, 4–9). Punjabi extremist groups (Sipah-e-Sahaba and Lashkar-e-Jhangvi) also operate out of Haqqani territory in North Waziristan, united through their intent to strike Western targets in Afghanistan, the United States, and Europe (including Indian targets). Hekmatyar was also active in HN territory and has brokered alliances with HN and the Taliban (McGirk 2010), but it is now split given Hekmatyar's interest in playing a role in the actual Kabul government (Jones 2009, 234). The Pakistani government turns a blind eye to these activities, in large part because the Haqqanis also carry out covert ISI agendas and strike Indian targets (Dressler 2010, 32).

The HN strategy is to wait for coalition forces to leave and to contribute to general insecurity through harassment and persistent attacks (Dressler 2010, 20). As seasoned militants, the HN believes that the international military commitment to Afghanistan is only short term and they must merely wait out the invader/donor presence. Since security is the primary requirement for any governance or development progress, they believe that maintaining an unstable security environment will prevent effective and lasting progress on any and all fronts (Dressler 2010, 20).

By highlighting the HN, I intend to make an important point about networks of resistance in Afghanistan and Pakistan. The HN is an embodiment of the transformation of networks of resistance from the Cold War until the present day. The HN, as a well-positioned group with territorial and historical ties on both sides of the border, maintains relationships with local, regional, national, and global clients. The HN has access to, control of, and has contributed to the construction of infrastructure along the border. Building local and state capacity in Haqqani territory would translate into challenging their authority, creating duplicate systems, or overthrowing them. These networks exist both due to and in opposition to the national and global networks that created the security–development nexus, and subsequent manifestations of it such as the PRTs.

My intention in defining and tracing the evolution of these networks is to raise important questions about processes of building capacity and the international development of Afghanistan and Pakistan. The transnational networks that evolved from the Cold War were the result of collusion between nonstate revolutionaries with international actors and state officials. Agents within the apparatus of the Pakistani military–intelligence state, in conjunction with the governments of the US, European, and Arab nations, awarded international recognition to transnational actors developing systems of authority in opposition to the legitimacy of the Afghan and Pakistani states.

Networks of resistance do not operate within a binary and are a function of the global context within which they are conceived. During the Cold War, transnational networks formed not in explicit opposition of the Afghan state or the state system but to the threat of Soviet occupation, its potential implications for the expansion of the Communist project, and Pakistani regional insecurity. The bilateral military pipeline legitimized the transnational nature of militant groups, who built upon and established systems and mechanisms of intertribal and intergroup governance and trade, and handled local and intertribal disputes and justice. Furthermore, while their success has in part been facilitated covertly by states (Pakistan, Gulf states), operators such as the Haqqanis have established such an extent of power and influence that their operations do not *depend* on the state. This begs the following question about capacity: How does the donor community intend to build the capacity of states when they are competing with transnational networks of resistance that are firmly rooted in local and transnational planes that transcend the boundaries of states?

Summary and Conclusion: The Problem of Existing Networks and State Capacity

Development efforts during these first three decades of investment in Afghanistan and Pakistan were largely blind to the issues of boundary and national identity stemming from the colonial partitioning of both states. These transnational tensions and internal dynamics among tribes and ethnic groups, while referenced in USAID evaluations as challenges and inhibitors to projects, are not actually taken into consideration in development strategy or project design. In this chapter, I have pointed out the dual nature of donor identity, given the initially concurrent and progressively integrated nature of security and development activities. From issues of security in the implementation of projects to the conflation of military sales with development assistance to the official integration of military and development activities in PRTs, development assistance has largely taken a backseat to military priorities.

The first few decades of US development in Afghanistan and Pakistan were defined by Cold War politics. The American containment strategy translated into overwhelming Afghan systems with resources and demands in an attempt to build state and develop industrial and agricultural infrastructure receptive to trade with capitalist countries and resilient to Soviet influence, in spite of far greater Soviet investment in the country. US investments in Pakistan provided further insulation of US interests in the wake of the Soviet threat, but disruptions to aid due to the internal political dynamics and uncooperative nature of Pakistan as a beneficiary neutralized much of the potential impacts.

The function of bilateral assistance to Afghanistan and Pakistan has been to a significant degree for the foreign policy purposes of containing global, regional, and subnational threats as well as to offset costs of military sales through projects designed to build state and facilitate trade and revenue. This strategy and the subsequent overt and covert relationships it spawned with militant groups undermined the authority of the state system and gave rise to transnational militant networks firmly rooted on the border of Afghanistan and Pakistan. This infrastructure of resistance not only challenges Western systems of state and the expansion of global capitalism but also attempts to build the capacity of the state and local populations to combat militant networks.

Chapter Six

THE BATTLE FOR POWER IN DISABLING ENVIRONMENTS: *STATECRAFT AND DEVELOPING CAPACITY IN AFGHANISTAN AND PAKISTAN*

The success of the Marshall Plan in reconstructing the war-ravaged infrastructure of Europe gave birth to an optimism about the ability of such programs to develop the untamed and unproductive areas of Africa, Asia, and Latin America. This optimism also provided a new challenge for (development) institutions... Worldwide frontiers offered these institutions both a chance to flex and build their technical muscles as well as a rationale for institutional survival. Thus, the development industry was born.—A DAI evaluation on the role of capacity building in development administration for integrated rural development projects (Honadle 1981, 2)

The history of international development of Afghanistan and Pakistan yields important lessons for the future of aid. Development assistance to both countries has been defined by geopolitical dynamics and Western attempts to contain global and transnational threats. This foreign policy strategy has yielded forms of bilateral assistance that integrates military strategy with development strategy, culminating in the emergence of new forms of *multilateral military –development planning schemes* to build the state. At the same time, the global agenda for aid calls for the integration of human rights into development agendas, prompting development agencies and institutions to establish strategies to advance human rights as a development objective. Within this context, capacity development has emerged as a cornerstone of global development strategy. In the previous chapter, I placed the progression of international development within the context of the political and economic reality of insurgency and transnational militancy in Afghanistan and Pakistan, tracing the evolution of transnational networks of resistance alongside the integration of development and military strategy.

I trace the transformation of the security–development nexus from a conflation of economic assistance and military aid as a single bilateral assistance package to Pakistan in the 1980s to contain the Soviet threat from Afghanistan and maintain a US presence in the region to the present-day integration of military and development assistance through counterinsurgency strategy and the innovation of PRTs in Afghanistan. I distinguish between the various forms of the security–development nexus as combining military and development aid as:

1. *Bilateral assistance packages.*
2. *Engaging state military, police, or local militias* in order to provide security for the implementation of development projects in remote (subnational) territory.
3. *The strategic integration of foreign/international military forces and development objectives,* in particular through the US post-2001 counterinsurgency strategy and the emergence of PRTs.

This evolution of various forms of the development–security nexus has occurred alongside rising calls for human rights frameworks in development and has unwittingly facilitated the expansion of transnational networks of resistance that ultimately seek to damage and challenge the territoriality of the Afghan and Pakistani states and that of former colonial powers. International and state attempts to "build capacity" of the state are fundamentally challenged by the transnational territoriality of these networks. Both from within and outside this context, capacity development has emerged as a key element of global development strategy.

In Chapter 2, I examined the space within which donors operate and capacity has gained salience, followed by a review of the transformation of capacity in policy and practice in Chapter 3. I highlight how the development space is constituted by an epistemological and vocational diversity of actors and institutions who make claims of ownership on development knowledge. Both *underlying* and *as a consequence of* this diversity of actors is an unquestioning and unyielding commitment to capitalist progress within the field of practice.

As the spaces within which ownership of development knowledge is produced have become increasingly privatized within elite Western spaces, capitalist models of organizational transformation that decontextualize environmental factors have pervaded the capacity development frameworks on how to build public sector institutions. Donors have adapted these strategies to be then translated into projects intended to strengthen the structures of developing states to theoretically expand markets, reduce poverty, advance human rights, and contain global and transnational threats. In Chapters 2 and 3, my examination of global development agenda-setting processes and USAID frameworks for capacity reveals that the environmental or situational factors of development have emerged as issues of *sustainability* and *security* inhibiting the impact of projects and also as contributing to the failure of states to counter the rise of global terrorism. Cultivating capacity in order to promote *democracy, human rights,* and (good) *governance* is considered integral to US national security and global prosperity (USAID 2013d).

Capacity development has emerged as a linchpin of global development strategy, embedded in agenda-setting processes dominated by OECD/DAC member states and donor institutions. These agendas are then tasked to development institutions to develop frameworks for practice and implementation through projects. Example of this are UNDP's, OECD's, and USAID's Human and Institutional Capacity Development frameworks (2011), highlighted in Chapter 3. A weakness in the donor strategy is in the understanding of environmental context, which is either enabling or disabling of the capacity development of the state. Another major weakness is in the donor framing of relationships surrounding power and influence, which are reduced to notions of social capital to be gained in the context of projects.

In Chapter 4, I highlight the major themes of capacity as state power, community, and social capital, underscoring this weakness in how the donors frame relationships and networks of power, particularly in attempting to facilitate the centralization of remote or contested subnational spaces. This illuminates the centrality of the state to projects of capacity, which is advanced through the discursive emergence of "fragility" as a designation for the status of states, within the literature on statebuilding, and evidenced through the example of USAID's involvement as a development agency in counterinsurgency operations. I introduce James C. Scott's notion of *statecraft* as a framework for conceptualizing the production of development projects and donor (USAID) approaches to building state capacity in fragile contexts, which I expand upon within this chapter.

As the turn of the twenty-first century saw calls for institutionalized HRBAs to development alongside a Global War on Terror, the discursive framing of capacity within frameworks for fragility and HRBAs exposes a tension and inconsistency in donor strategy. While this project examines this transformation of capacity in regard to the rise of transnational militancy over a period of four decades, it also witnesses the transformation of donor—*in its positioning* as contingent upon the foreign policy frameworks of the donor's state *and as an actor and active participant* involved in the construction of relationships to continue the production of projects and promulgation of narratives to frame the activities of development.

The task of this present chapter is as follows. This chapter explores (1) the application of these methodologies to USAID projects, particularly within the context of building state to counter insurgency and advance democratic governance, as well as (2) the way in which this application displays the USAID experience in conceptualizing the attributes inherent to the development of capacity (*sites, processes, ownership,* and *context*). Moving from global agendas and institutional frameworks to projects, I evolve a framework based upon the implementation of donor notions of capital and statecraft to explain the tasks of development in Afghanistan and Pakistan, the production of "capacity" within projects, and more broadly donor attempts to build states to combat transnational militancy.

Donor Statecraft and State Planning Schemes: Building Social Capital in Disabling Environments

Both in scholarship and in practice, frameworks for capacity have historically been based upon notions of capital (economic, institutional, human, social, etc.). The cultivation of various forms of capital within the context of development is sometimes explicitly but mostly implicitly tied to the promotion of rights—political, economic, cultural, social—and democratic governance. In framing the relationships surrounding development projects—between foreign donor and recipient *or* subnational communities and the central government—donors aim to cultivate relationships framed as social capital to build governance capacity to sustain development projects.

What donors and donor networks truly lack is *social power and influence* in subnational spaces. Building and maintaining state capacity require durable relationships, which must be built upon relationships of power that are embedded within networks that can operate at varying scales. This is particularly relevant in the context of donor efforts to build relationships between communities and leaders operating within the subnational spaces of Khyber–Pakhtunkhwa or Lashkar Gah and the national spaces of the central government in Kabul or Islamabad. Development agencies attempt to build these relationships around state and market infrastructure in what I go on to describe in this chapter as statecraft or building components of state, while (sometimes) paying lip service to relationships based upon indigenous or already existing forms of religious and tribal governance. Further, how does a development agency like USAID go about building relationships for social capital through projects when the International Security Assistance Force (ISAF) also funded by the US government recently invaded and also seek to build relationships to establish security and state control as part of a counterinsurgency campaign? Building relationships for social capital becomes about ascribing legitimacy and determining the beneficiaries of various forms of rights.

In this sense, the development agency (or, more broadly, the donor) reduces and often ignores already existing relationships and networks of power, attempting to redirect power at subnational scales to surround market and state infrastructure, which are donor conceived, and not recipient defined. While development strategy may frame projects and the role of the donor as *supportive*, in practice this is rarely the case as recipients either lack the capacity or the will (or both) to take ownership of development initiatives. Through projects, donors try to build relationships through an exchange of donor-provided knowledge and resources to gain loyalty and build infrastructure to strengthen state and subnational linkages to ultimately extend the arm of the state. However, these projects usually fail for a multitude of reasons, sometimes in fantastic fashion, at the subnational scale. Fairweather (2014) provides some notable examples of USAID projects gone awry. I highlight two here:

> In 2004, USAID has extended a program called Alternative Livelihoods to Helmand to encourage farmers to grow other crops (instead of opium) … The project boiled down to creating the equivalent of 2.5 million workdays in Helmand in 2004–2005, with locals receiving roughly $3 an hour. The problems in executing the program were manifold. For starters, the company had no idea where to apply so much manpower. In their desperation to find projects, the Chemonics team hit upon repairing drainage ditches, known locally as *karezs*. It subsequently transpired that Afghanistan had a long-standing tradition of doing just that for free, and by introducing money Chemonics was turning a shared community endeavor into a system of patronage that inevitably favored one clan over another. (Fairweather 2014, 131)
>
> The Afghanistan Vouchers for Increased Productive Agriculture (AVIPA) program … (was) designed to pay day laborers an hourly rate for odd jobs around the district. Without the staff to assess the work or a good grasp of the local community's needs, the only measure of success USAID could come up with was "burn rate," … how much money they could get out of the gates of military bases. A high burn rate equaled success. In towns like Nawa, population 89,000, almost $30 million was spent in one year, $18 million of that through AVIPA and a sister program that handed out tractors and bags of wheat to Afghans the aid workers

hoped were farmers. USAID's skewed metrics profoundly distorted the local economy. Nawa residents soon ran out of cleanup jobs around the town and were left to unclog irrigation canals. Yet because the AVIPA rate represented more than even doctors and teachers could earn on their own accord, Afghans of all professions turned out in droves to toil away at the ditches. Schools and clinics were shuttered, and fields went untended. In fact the only sector the AVIPA program didn't affect was the opium industry, which like any good market merely raised its prices to ensure that enough manpower was available to work the harvest. As for the tractors and sacks of wheat, there were traffic jams at the Afghan border crossings as the supplies were driven to Pakistan to be sold or exchanged, in some cases for sacks of fertilizer to make roadside bombs. (ibid., 301)

It is important to note here that USAID projects, particularly during the Global War on Terror, are largely conducted in conjunction with US counterinsurgency operations. Now, in my examination of projects, I consider projects over a span of 40 years, between 1977 and 2017. However, a large portion of the institutional literature and projects I examine are from this post-2001 period. For this reason, it is necessary to context-ualize the crafting of the state by the development agency within international efforts to counter insurgency—as development projects during this period, particularly in the context of US strategy, are part of a broader military strategy and political project to construct relationships and networks of power that extend the legibility of the state into subnational spaces.

A full discussion of US counterinsurgency is outside the realm of this project, but in order to contextualize the capacity development tactics of USAID projects I provide some necessary background here on this integration of civilian and military activities. After the US-led international invasion, the US military embarked on a counter-insurgency campaign that targeted the eastern and southern parts of Afghanistan to prevent a Taliban resurgence and also to garner local support for the new central gov-ernment of Afghanistan. USAID projects during these years up till 2005 were largely conducted through PRTs in order to strengthen local government in these insecure and unstable areas. This civilian–military (civ-mil) campaign was organized at district, pro-vincial, and regional levels in order to integrate counterinsurgency measures, which included investment in infrastructure and service delivery systems (USAID 2015c, 6). I examine some of these projects (particularly as they are framed to develop capacity) later on in this chapter.

That said, the attempted integration of military and development activity exposed tensions in priorities, objectives, and institutional frameworks, with military priorities often taking precedence over civilian agencies (for a breakdown of PRT composition and example of diversity in composition, command, and objectives, see Figure 5.5). This often resulted in poor coordination on the ground between military and civilian agencies such as USAID, with USAID implementing a few stabilization programs in isolation of military involvement (SIGAR 2018). It is important to recognize here how USAID programming is entirely conceptualized within the donor (US government) framework as the civilian component of a broader political project to craft the state and counter militancy.

Following a deterioration in security in 2008, in 2009 the Obama administration called for a surge of (50,000) troops to clear insurgents in "key" areas, tasking civilian agencies such as USAID to implement programming to "hold and build" these areas (SIGAR 2018). This involved assistance programs to "increase" and "build" the "capacity" of the Afghan government, focusing on five key ministries to provide "critical services," with the idea that this would further legitimize the Afghan government (USAID 2015c, 3). Obama's strategy, as laid out in his historic 2009 West Point address, called for a combination of an aggressive military strategy, enhanced international coordination in pursuit of civilian assistance to strengthen Afghan government capacity, and also the US government's relationship with Pakistan, which was identified as being "inextricably linked" to success in the defeat of al Qaeda, the Taliban, and other violent extremists (USAID 2015c, 3–4). Yet, the US government's Afghanistan and Pakistan regional stabilization strategy primarily focuses on Afghanistan, largely designating Pakistan's role as a cooperative and supportive ally in order to prevent militants from utilizing transnational networks to enjoy safe haven on the Pakistani side of the border.[1]

In the most recent years (2012–2017), the focus of counterinsurgency has been to move from stabilization activities to transitioning key territories to Afghan control. According to SIGAR's own 2018 reporting, these tactics have largely failed for several reasons. First, the districts that US Department of Defense prioritized for counterinsurgency operations were the most unstable and also perpetually insecure (SIGAR 2018). They required consistent and continual presence of military forces to clear insurgent activity. It is important to note that these are spaces (e.g., Helmand, Kandahar, Paktika, and Nuristan, among others) that the central government of Afghanistan has never truly exercised control over, particularly if we consider the exercise of control and perception of legitimacy as tied to aspects of governance in which USAID attempts to craft the state. I detail these aspects (see Figures 6.1 and 6.2) and examine them at length below and throughout this chapter. As a related issue, civilian agencies such as USAID were compelled to prematurely embark on stabilization programs in areas fiercely contested and simply not ready for them. These mistakes of donor ambition to counter insurgency and manage militant threats coming from subnational spaces led to Afghans losing faith that districts would remain in government control, preventing locals from participating in local government and also enabling power brokers and predatory government officials with access to projects to fuel patronage and conflict within and between communities (SIGAR 2018). This has a direct effect on the ability of development agencies to cultivate relationships and networks to build capacity at any scale.

While donors have strong networks, donor networks and relationships are not operational at a scale that reaches subnational spaces. The networks and relationships that

---

1. Afghanistan and Pakistan Regional Stabilization Strategy—six assistance objectives: (1) rebuilding Afghanistan's agricultural sector, (2) strengthening Afghan governance, (3) enhancing Afghan rule of law, (4) supporting Afghan-led reintegration, (5) combating the Afghan narcotics trade, and (6) building an economic foundation for Afghanistan's future (USAID 2015c, 4–5).

are operational both transnationally and within subnational spaces of Afghanistan and Pakistan, as well as their frameworks for operation, stem from sources of social power and influence that have been built over the years and are characterized by shared fellowship, trust, respect, reciprocity, information, and cooperation. It is not merely language and dialect or familiarity with tribal composition that dictates these networks of social power, which is basic knowledge donors often still lack about communities. Furthermore, the networks operating within these subnational and transnational spaces of Baluch and Pashtun land were formed by communities in the context of waves of war, occupation, displacement and forced migration, and struggle to reclaim homeland. In considering the rise of transnational militancy, some of these relationships are in part steeped in the social code of *Pashtunwali* (valuing honor, revenge, equality, and hospitality), which impacts relationships of basic "social intercourse"—structures of authority and governance, relationships of business, trade, and war, which tie into shared overarching narratives surrounding the donor/invader.

To give the example of the Haqqani Network, the Haqqani family network has roots across both Afghanistan and Pakistan. As a prominent military commander, Jalaluddin Haqqani invited Arab fighters and financiers to Afghanistan and facilitated covert military networks among Arabs, local Pashtun tribes, and Pakistani military and government officials. The Haqqani Network assisted in the integration of these Arab militants and financiers, such as bin Laden, into networks operating within subnational spaces at transnational scales, facilitating relationships built around business, the construction of local infrastructure and cave systems, and transfer of weapons and fighters, strengthening the transnational infrastructure for militancy. These are relationships steeped in shared understandings of cultural legitimacy and alliances over common enemies. This is one scale of operation where the networks of (particularly Western) donors do not have power and are unable to penetrate with their own existing networks. Furthermore, state actors such as Pakistan's ISI or military who do have access to subnational spaces and the Haqqani Network, for instance, depend on these networks to carry out covert state agendas, disrupting civilian attempts by the state and foreign donors to strengthen linkages between the central government and networks in subnational spaces.

From my analysis of hundreds of USAID program-related documents, I clumped projects into four emerging and overarching areas of *donor statecraft*, where donors, government officials, and often security forces engage in projects to build state capacity:

1. Provision of services,
2. Facilitating and enabling trade and economic opportunity,
3. Keeping rule of law and security, and
4. Maintaining transparent and democratic political processes and institutions.

I contend that this donor "statecraft" encounters the most struggle at the *subnational* and *transnational* scales of society. This is where state, military, and private actors employed by donors struggle to build relationships and networks through exchange-based projects with local communities to extend donor and state scales of operation and fail to penetrate and compete with transnational networks of resistance.

Throughout this project, I have detailed the multitude of actors operating within the field of international development, from Mujahideen leaders to security contractors to NGOs, government ministries, international security forces, development agencies, and international institutions. In the task of development, national and international institutions (donor institutions as well as state institutions) compete with individual and organizational actors on subnational and transnational scales (e.g., the Taliban, QST, Haqqani Network, TTP, etc., their organizations and networks). Within these subnational contexts, relationships of power and cultural legitimacy are not steeped in capital-centric notions of relationships as transactional and exchange based. This impacts whether or not an environment will be enabling or disabling of development projects. Social power is imperative to cultivating local "ownership" of political and economic relationships. Understandings of language, dialects, codes of conduct (e.g., Pashtunwali and the way in which it has assumed new forms under militant Islamic groups), tribal feuds and other forms of entrenched conflict (including religious and ideological), gendered relations, local forms of dispute resolution, barter and trade, and so on characterize an environment where donors are at a disadvantage in attempts to build political and also trade-based relationships that legitimize the state and extension of centralized governance.

In this chapter, I advance Krause's (2014) examination of how humanitarian relief NGOs translate values and interests into projects to justify and continue their existence, except I examine USAID as a development agency. I argue that the way in which development agencies such as USAID go about this production is through *statecraft*, executing state planning schemes through the production of projects that aim to build relationships and networks that support (1) the continued production of development projects (ideally with state and local ownership), as well as the expansion of (2) the reach of the central government (and donor) to govern spaces of insurgency within the territoriality of the state, and of (3) global capitalist networks. In this chapter, I define components of *statecraft* including a discussion of USAID efforts to construct each component through projects.

In James C. Scott's (1999) seminal work, "Seeing Like a State," he poses a case against state planning schemes, which he argues disregards the values, desires, and objections of its subjects. Scott defines four conditions common to all such "planning disasters": (1) an administrative ordering of nature and society by the state, (2) a "high-modernist ideology" that places confidence in the ability of science to improve every aspect of human life, (3) a willingness to use authoritarian state power to affect large-scale interventions, and (4) a prostrate civil society that cannot effectively resist such plans. Scott applies this to development theory, and it is in this spirit that I contextualize development strategy and the application of capacity development methodologies to USAID projects. He describes these large-scale projects of state planning as projects of legibility requiring state simplifications, which are "never fully realized" (Scott 1999, 80).

Scott's notion of *state simplifications* is an important concept in the context of capacity, particularly with regard to donor attempts to systematize markets and governing institutions. To build capacity, institutions require metrics from which to measure capacity. Development projects that target building the capacity of institutions involve building capacity to collect and keep track of data and statistics about society from which to enable government planning for more development projects. State simplifications have five main characteristics: (1) they are *interested, utilitarian* facts, which are (2) nearly always *written* (verbal or numerical) (and) *documentary*, (3) *static*, (4) *aggregate* (and often impersonal—e.g., density of transportation networks, employment rates, literacy rates, residence patterns), and (5) must be *standardized*, "... along a scale or continuum that are of interest (to the state)" (Scott 1999, 80). State simplifications are essentially a process of systemization.

State simplifications assist with building and maintaining state *legibility*. According to Scott, *legibility* "implies a view whose place is central and whose vision is synoptic. State simplifications ... are designed to provide authorities with a schematic view of their society, a view not afforded to those without authority" (Scott 1999, 79). The *legibility* of a state essentially translates to the strength of its ability to centralize authority within its territorial boundaries. The centralization of authority is required for the sustainability of development projects, especially after donors leave, and thus is an implicit objective of capacity development.

Legibility is a condition of manipulation. *Any substantial state intervention in society—to vaccinate a population, produce goods, mobilize labor, tax people and their property, conduct literacy campaigns, conscript soldiers, enforce sanitation standards, catch criminals, state universal schooling—requires the intervention of units that are visible.* The units in question might be *citizens, villages, trees, fields, houses, or people grouped according to age,* depending on the type of intervention. Whatever the units being manipulated, *they must organized in a manner that permits them to be identified, observed, recorded, counted, aggregated, and monitored.* (Scott 1999, 183, emphasis mine)

He goes on to argue that legibility is the central problem of statecraft: "... immanent in any statecraft aimed at manipulating society ... undermined by the intrastate rivalries, technical obstacles, and above all, the resistance of its subjects" (Scott 1999, 80). Statecraft is how donors assist states in planning schemes of centralization to create states complicit in the expansion of global capitalist networks and that will contain donor-identified risks. The issues of performance I identify in capacity development methodologies in Chapter 3 are inherently tied into the key aspects of capacity, as objects of capacity, ownership of processes and context, and ultimately conditions of legibility. Scott decries large-scale capitalism as just as much of an "agency of homogenization, uniformity, grids, and state simplification as the state is, with the difference being that, for capitalists simplification must pay" (Scott 1999, 8).

The role of statecraft becomes that of maximizing the productive, settled population in ... state spaces *while at the same time* drawing tribute from, or at least neutralizing, the nonstate spaces. These stateless zones have always played a potentially subversive role, both symbolically and practically ... such spaces and their inhabitants were the exemplars of rudeness, disorder, and barbarity against which the civility, order, and *sophistification* of the center could be gauged. Such spaces ... have served as refuges for fleeing peasants, rebels, bandits, and the pretenders who have often threatened kingdoms. (187, emphasis mine)

The instruments of statecraft are state simplifications, which are required for the *whole-sale transformation* of society including things like: censuses, cadastral maps, identity cards,

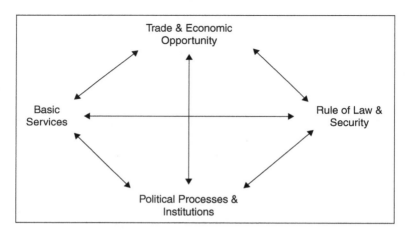

Figure 6.1 Web of Donor Statecraft.

statistical bureaus, schools, mass media, and internal security apparatuses (Scott 1999, 343). In my deconstruction of donor statecraft through the example of USAID in Afghanistan and Pakistan, I took an inventory of and subsequently clumped projects into four emerging components of governance that comprise donor statecraft efforts: (1) provision of basic services, (2) rule of law and security, (3) political processes and institutions, as well as (4) trade and economic opportunity. Figure 6.1 displays the *relational* aspects of these four functions:

These four components are interdependent. Without rule of law and security, access to economic opportunity, and the ability for business to operate without threat of theft and violence, the subsequent potential for the expansion of trade is limited. Without transparent political processes and accountable institutions, basic services may only be provided to those already privileged, working within the government or private sector businesses affiliated with or supporting the government. Building these functions of governance is the primary task of donor statecraft and development projects, and each function is difficult to measure and define. In my review of projects, I tracked objectives, design and methodology, activities, as well as findings and outcomes of development projects and programs in order to (1) parse out the way in which donors pursue the construction of each function, (2) reveal how each function relates to the others in donor statecraft, (3) demonstrate the shortcomings of capacity development methodologies in statecraft and (4) expose how the "capacity" concept plays a role in continuing development narratives surrounding the construction of the state.

Statecraft in Practice: USAID and the Donor Community in Afghanistan and Pakistan

Capacity building to do capacity building may be needed—Analysis of USAID's Capacity Development Program (USAID 2008a, 10)

In considering the question of donor statecraft, it is necessary to consider the role of the development agency in the crafting of the state within the context of bilateral relationships, as noted in the previous chapter. While counterinsurgency strategy provides a framework for contextualizing the role of USAID in capacity development in the crafting of the state in Afghanistan and Pakistan post-2001, this counterinsurgency framework was not the basis for USAID programming in either of these countries prior to 2001. That said, as a development agency, USAID's role since its inception in implementing civilian assistance programs has historically been within a context of counterinsurgency, particularly in considering the case of Vietnam. Under President Johnson, the United States attempted to improve counterinsurgency operations in Vietnam through coordinating civilian assistance programs with military operations with the landmark establishment of an interagency organization known as CORDS (Civil Operations and Revolutionary Development Support), which was continued under President Nixon (NARA 2016).

Counterinsurgency strategy in Vietnam led to the implementation of a range of civilian assistance programming by USAID: civilian assistance, community development, land reform, migration and resettlement, public health, and public safety (ibid.). Similar types of projects continue as part of counterinsurgency operations in Afghanistan, particularly in subnational environments, such as Local Governance and Community Development (LGCD)—discussed later in this chapter. In this chapter, I focus largely on USAID projects post-2001 but do also include examples of projects from the 1980s and 1990s. We see in post-2001 USAID projects in Afghanistan and Pakistan a new scale of development—military integration in US counterinsurgency operations and also a broader range of projects included under this umbrella of counterinsurgency. USAID (and more generally, development) projects are conceptualized within counterinsurgency frameworks as playing an essential role in the cultivation of government capacity, and ultimately in donor crafting of the state. That said, while post-2001 USAID development strategy in Afghanistan and Pakistan is conceived within the context of counterinsurgency frameworks, not all projects explicitly cite this as an objective even if they are used or framed as a tactic within counterinsurgency strategy. It is within this broader examination of the types of projects to develop the capacity of these four areas of governance that donor statecraft is revealed.

From the sample of documents I detailed in the introductory chapter, I examine how USAID has implemented capacity development into projects of statecraft that attempt to expand the reach of the state and of donors. The donor project of statecraft is ultimately a project of building state capacity to implement development projects. Every project is significant—both defining and producing discrete components, which theoretically are designed by the architects of development knowledge discussed in Chapter 2, to build state infrastructure. Each project attempts to extend the objective of systemization into the remotest spaces of human society. Systemization requires and enables tracking, oversight, and regulation. It demands the construction of social, political, and economic infrastructure to support the legitimacy of centralized governing institutions and to ensure compliance and accountability at multiple levels of authority. It is in this way that the arms of the state attempt to reach spaces of insurgent activity. Every individual project supports this development strategy to build the components of state and

Objects & Processes Targeted (for and by projects) to enhance	Functions of Governance (national and sub-national {provincial/district/municipal})
– Public Sector Institutions & Facilities (power, energy, water, transportation, health and education) – Social Infrastructure (NGOs) for service delivery (mostly health & education) – Fiscal policy planning (tax/revenue collection, budget planning)	Provision of Services (sub-national, national)
– Private Sector (esp. agriculture and manufacturing sectors, public-private partnerships, private enterprise/SMEs) – Banking and Financial Sector Institutions – Transportation System Infrastructure – Fiscal & Trade Policy Planning, Customs – Regional & Global economic integration (e.g. WTO accession) – Media & Public outreach (on economy & financial literacy	Facilitating and Enabling Trade and Economic Opportunity (sub-national, regional, international)
– Legal System & Institutions (Judicial and Police) – Legislative Processes (e.g. law making, legislative/parliamentary "strengthening") – Legal Education System – Public outreach (media & education)	Rule of Law & Security
– Political Party Development/Reform – Electoral processes – Civil society infrastructure (NGOs/CSOs/CBOs) – Government Monitoring Systems – Civil Service Sector – Public outreach (media, civic engagement)	Democratic Political Processes & Institutions

Figure 6.2 Statecraft: Developing State Infrastructure.

industry that assist with (1) the integration of states into the global capitalist system[2] and to (2) better contain subnational and transnational threats to this system. In Figure 6.2, I have expanded upon Figure 6.1 and broken down the processes targeted by projects to enhance each of the functions of governance and develop state infrastructure. I follow with a discussion on each function.

I approach a deconstruction of how donors target these four components of statecraft, with USAID as my example, starting with a discussion on the provision of services and trade and economic opportunity. Both require state infrastructure to enable activities. In particular, when looking at projects geared toward improving business or encouraging the expansion of trade, we see a conflation of these activities with that of building state infrastructure. With this conflation, there is also an emphasis on "performance-based"

---

2. Not only through trade—import/export activities—but also through participation in regional and international trade alliances and associations, which only recognizes the authority of the state (for membership purposes) and thus is dependent on the legitimacy of the state system to function.

methodologies consistent with USAID's Capacity Development Framework and the treatment of public institutions like private entities by donors. I provide some examples from USAID projects that present donors' framing of these functions of governance, and the donor definition of functionalist "needs" that the state has in order to facilitate services and economic activity. In this language, it is easy to see how donor projects attempt to extend the legibility of the state through a systemization of services and economic activity with project activities that seek to institutionalize simplifications for state planning purposes.

I then turn to the rule of law and security as well as political processes and institutions. These two components are a bit more complex, as development and military activities increasingly coalesce and legitimize forms of organized violence and state control explicitly targeting transnational insurgent networks of resistance, usually only referred to as "terrorists" or "insurgents" (which actually serves to decontextualize the *environment* within which they flourish). From a development perspective, the situation of building rule of law in Pakistan is much different than in Afghanistan. I assert that the actual task of this sort of development activity at the subnational scale, however, is not that different, but that the minimum existence of a functioning central government not destroyed by war obviously places Pakistani state institutions at a greater advantage in any form of institutional strengthening projects. While projects to build state infrastructure to enable the provision of services or increased economic activity may involve some elements of security in order to conduct project activities, the subject matter of law, the enforcement of law, as well as political process and institutions are entirely political activities conducted by donors implementing initiatives with military might. Furthermore, notions of law, political process, and institutions are culturally constructed, making the project of building capacity of these particular "functions" of the state a particularly challenging battle for donors over the political and social "capital" needed for their project of statecraft.

Provision of Services

Ensuring the provision of services by the state involves activities mostly concerned with building state infrastructure. State infrastructure involves and encompasses many *things*. Infrastructure includes buildings, roads, (trained) employees, office equipment, electricity, technology, and internet, to give a few examples. USAID goes about building state infrastructure through treating government institutions—line ministries and so forth—as organizations with weak capacity to perform donor-*defined* and -*mandated* functions of governance. A 2016 Annual Report on the SHAHAR (Strong Hubs for Afghan Hope and Resilience) project notes that "Governing institutions *should be able to*[3] consult citizens, assess needs, facilitate job creation, and respond to demands of the population" (USAID 2016b, 8). In the SHAHAR project, USAID identifies *municipalities* as *fiscally independent units of government*, capable of raising revenue and investing in urban services and

---

3. Italics my own.

infrastructure, and thus playing a unique and important role in Afghanistan's subnational governance (SNG) architecture (ibid.). Furthermore, a 2007 assessment of SNG in Afghanistan found that

> the development of local physical infrastructure and delivery of services has had more of an impact than any other factor on (a) subnational governance and (b) people's attitudes toward government ... but that the government levels and institutions ... do not at present have the capacity, authority, or mechanisms ... to ensure that this is occurring in an effective and responsive way. (Asia Foundation 2007, 11)

Programs such as the Kabul City Initiative were designed to strengthen the capacity of the municipality to provide services, represent the community, and also to be self-sustaining without donor funding. "KCI's overarching objective is to facilitate the development of Kabul Municipality's capacity to ensure that its citizens will experience consistently improving services provided by a steadily improving city workforce and modern management systems" (USAID 2012e, v). Further, report authors anticipated that "the public will credit the Kabul administration with the improvements, become more supportive of Kabul government, and, therefore, be more likely to take an active role in improving the urban environment and contributing to an expanded, locally derived revenue base" (ibid.). Ultimately, the purpose of building strong governing institutions is to be able to continue projects of development, which ideally are to be owned and carried out by beneficiaries (who theoretically will buy into the value of these projects) without the assistance of donors.

Yet, beneficiary dependence upon donors is common in projects to build state infrastructure. The LGCD program, which was designed to build the capacity of local governments, strengthen the legitimacy of the government of Afghanistan, increase constituent confidence in the government, and promote stability, also wound up perpetuating this cycle of donor dependence. In a 2009 evaluation on the program, it was noted that "The LGCD program itself hinders the Afghan Government's capacity by strengthening the government's capacity to work with international donors and the NGO community, rather than within the Afghan government structure itself. By providing assistance on proposal writing, English language classes and grants management, they are learning to perpetuate the donor assistance not their own system of governance" (USAID 2009, 11).

Donors such as USAID also invest in and enlist the involvement of NGOs and private sector actors in building state infrastructure. By investing in public–private partnerships, donors have sought not only to build support structures within the private sector and civil society for development projects but also to facilitate the privatization of public sector institutions. As far back as 1991, a development support training project focused on private enterprise sought to "expand the capacity to manage development projects in rural provinces, especially in health and education. Participation of private sector organizations is *aggressively sought* ... pioneering a workshop with a mix of senior officials of the GOP (Government of Pakistan) and influential senior executives from the private sector, in an effort to privatize select government organizations" (AED 1991,

4). While private-sector-adapted performance-based methodologies for public sector organizations were not as pervasive in donor frameworks for projects as they are presently, the emphasis on public–private partnerships as well as the privatization of select government organizations several decades ago already points toward a trend in this direction.

In the early 1990s during the period of Mujahideen infighting as donors were decreasing their activities in Afghanistan, investments in projects to strengthen the capacity of NGOs in particular were thought to minimize the impact of donor withdrawal and to ensure the sustainability of community projects. Furthermore, USAID sought to increase NGO capacity to work with local communities to access and deliver improved social sector services and to have "development advocacy capacity" at the national, provincial, and community level (USAID 1995b, 4,15). Interestingly, among the selection criteria for NGO partners was that "NGO independence such that it can resist increasing GOP involvement in NGO operations" (ibid., 16). This indicates that part of donor strategy in investing in NGOs for service delivery had to do with containing government corruption and misuse of funds.

During this period after the Soviet withdrawal from Afghanistan, NGOs were framed as the ideal target for development investment. A 1993 assessment notes that their "privateness" gives them comparative advantages as they tended to have more "programmatic flexibility," a greater "capacity for risk taking," and "would prove less sensitive to the ebb and flow of donor funds," thus ensuring programmatic sustainability (Smith, Shahjehan and Khalid 1993, 3). Their utility was to be judged on "their effectiveness in building institutional capacity at the grass roots" (ibid., ii). During this time, capacity-building programs were viewed as a way to protect donor investments in NGOs (ibid., 11), resulting in a flood of development resources and the evolution of a saturated NGO development community in the Northwest Frontier Province of Pakistan on the border with Afghanistan. Yet, while lauded as the answer to USAID's concerns about the sustainability of project investments, significant limitations of the NGO community are also noted: they were externally created, institutionally and financially dependent, had limited capacity, lacked trained personnel, and had a weak grasp of participatory theory and methodologies (ibid., 23). Additionally, since the emergence of the NGO development community was so new, it was relatively isolated from the Asian mainstream and most did not operate above the village level (ibid.).

Regardless, donor faith in NGOs has not waned. In a 2010 Audit Report on USAID programming in Pakistan and Afghanistan, NGOs are lauded as key to building the capacity of community and local organizations to establish quality programs in remote areas (USAID 2010d). Strengthening the capacity of NGOs, NGO networks, and NGO linkages with government not only for "social sector services" (such as girls' education, child survival, maternal health, family planning, and primary education) but also for advocacy is not a new objective and has been a focus of programming since the early 1990s (USAID 1995b). After 2000, the language to describe the varying types of organizations that would make up civil society infrastructure increased exponentially and the objectives for their role in democratic life as organizations of advocacy much more explicit. A 2005 assessment on civil society in Afghanistan notes that it is "often seen as an important means for self-determination and self-expression" (USAID 2005a, 18). USAID efforts to build civil society were largely focused on building management and technical capacity through trainings (ibid.).

In Afghanistan and Pakistan, donor investment in NGOs and programming to provide social services, cultivate civil society, build advocacy capacity, and ensure the rights of women and children is indicative of the growing pervasiveness of human rights approaches in the donor discourse. While identified as important fixtures in the development of democratic life in Afghanistan, focusing on the promotion of gender equality, culture, youth, and education, donor attempts to cultivate democratic societies are handicapped by the scale of donor influence. A 2005 assessment notes that CSO reach is generally limited to Kabul, where CSOs tend to be more active and well established (ibid., 10). This issue is further highlighted in a 2007 assessment of SNG in Afghanistan, which called for the need to build the capacity of CSOs in rural areas and for donors to provide them with funding to implement projects that meet the needs of rural populations (Asia Foundation 2007). A 2011 assessment of civil society in Afghanistan highlights these same constraints—most notably lack of funding, limited capacity, and major security concerns—challenging the very operations in the communities they work in (Counterpart International 2011, 6).

An additional concern with regard to investing in CSOs, particularly in Afghanistan, is the rampant corruption among CSOs vying for donor funds. USAID's 4A (Assistance for Afghanistan's Anti-Corruption Authority) Project was developed to combat this very issue—to build the capacity of the High Office of Oversight and Anti-Corruption (HOO) and CSOs to educate the public about corruption and highlight the government's anticorruption programs (USAID 2012c, 13). Unfortunately, public opinion surveys reported a significant degree of distrust of NGOs, some operating under the assumption that they gather intelligence on local populations. Respondents noted a lack of familiarity with NGOs as a concept, as well as general perceptions of corruption surrounding NGO financial processes and the selection of communities for project activities (USAID 2005a, 28):

- "No one knows the meaning of the letters 'N,' 'G,' 'O',"
- "They spend 70 percent for houses, car and big salary and 30 percent for the project"
- "NGOs represent second government in our country"
- "Most of the help has been done in the big cities but nothing in villages"

Partly exacerbating this issue of role and definition is that donor institutions have not explicitly defined what types of organizations constitute inclusion in civil society initiatives. From the USAID literature, we see the inclusion of community development councils (CDCs), village organizations (VOs), NGOs, and community-building organizations (CBOs)—all considered CSOs. A USAID assessment acknowledges that traditional groups of male elders (shuras and jirgas) have more "cultural legitimacy" (USAID 2005a, 13) than the CDC/VO organizations, "but in the urgency of reconstruction in Afghanistan, most distinctions, and definitions, blur" (19). It was estimated in 2005 that about 20,000 CDCs and VOs, and so on were formed in order to assist in the reconstruction efforts of the government's National Priority Plans (ibid.). These USAID assessments on civil society organizations have made several things clear. First, there is a general lack of clarity on what actually constitutes civil society organizations and their ability to effectively implement development projects is questionable due to their lack of capacity and legitimacy. That said, USAID has continued to embark upon the construction of civil society, particularly as it relates to the crafting of the state—helping to provide services, facilitate business, and support the legitimacy of the government due to their positioning within communities. This demonstrates how attempts to build civil society are in many ways a tactic by donors to gain the social power they desire and lack at the community level, and perhaps less so about imbuing a sense of engagement with the democratic process.

With these examples, we can see that the provision of services, while primarily framed as a responsibility of governance, also exists and is cultivated within the realms of private sector and civil society as well. This conflation of domains in an attempt to build infrastructure for the state (to provide the four functions of governance) continues from the early 1990s to the present day. As a final example, in the Building Integrated Capacity in Infrastructure (BICI) project in Afghanistan, both the government and the private sector are identified as lacking a greater capacity to finance, operate, and maintain infrastructure projects. "Capacity-building activities" are prescribed to create the conditions that encourage private participation and investment in public infrastructure services, investing in "building the capacity" of the private sector in addition to the state to build, own, and operate infrastructure (USAID 2008c).

This "integrated capacity" as the title of the project suggests along with the previous examples given in this section demonstrate how donor statecraft combines activities in projects to build the state while building other sectors to support it, and vice versa. In particular, with the BICI example, the donor method of statecraft is to invest in market infrastructure in order to build state infrastructure, in part through a distribution of resources to both private sector and state actors, simultaneously reinforcing market-friendly state infrastructure. This integration of activities contributes to an assimilation of political and economic systems at the national scale, designed to facilitate regional and global trade relationships with other states and with global governing institutions like the WTO. I expand upon this point further in the following section.

Facilitating Trade and Economic Opportunity

There are two notable features of donor statecraft to facilitate trade and economic opportunity in the USAID experience in Afghanistan and Pakistan:

1. Projects have targeted transnational operations at subnational scales both to extend the reach of the state and donor (during the Soviet occupation) and also to contain militancy (post-9/11).
2. Projects target the strengthening of markets from subnational to national scales, in part to facilitate the integration of national markets into regional and global trade relationships.

There are generally two primary vessels by which USAID has conducted projects to facilitate economic growth: through the state and through the private sector. On the state end, private sector activity and trade are inhibited through lack of sound state financial infrastructure. State regulations ascribe legitimacy to business activity and operation. Stable and uncorrupt financial institutions and banks are also necessary for the expansion of private sector operations, which involves the development of state infrastructure. Furthermore, state planning for industrial growth is inhibited when the state lacks data about industries and economic activity. Thus, development projects to build markets must also involve state building activities, in many ways highlighting how neoliberal ideology in practice is actually planned (Polyani 1944 [2001]), requiring the ongoing intervention of the state to steer and address conflicts often generated by the implementation of development projects.

For starters, state planning schemes (strategies and policies) to reduce poverty and target industries for economic growth require a *capacity* of governing institutions and officials to plan. Integrating state simplifications, or state simplification processes, into development projects helps the central government to systematize the planning schemes of the state and ultimately of the donor. Thus, systemization processes are built into many projects surrounding policy planning. For example, in order to increase the "analytical capacity of Pakistan's institutions involved in agricultural data analysis" and to assist the GOP in agricultural planning and policy analysis, USAID worked with the GOP of Pakistan between 1982 and 1987 to establish an *Economic Analysis Network (EAN)*, with various staff trained in areas such as economic analysis, econometric techniques, writing skills, and data management (Bever 1987, 9). The assumption being, as staff are trained they will be better able to establish systems to collect and house data, forecast projections, and plan in such a way that would enable development planners to manage production.

This systemization is also built into reconstruction activities. As the donor community embarked on the rebuilding of Afghanistan, USAID's FAIDA (Financial Access for Investing in the Development of Afghanistan) project sought to build meso-level financial infrastructure in Afghanistan (USAID 2012d, 17). Components of the program included focuses on enterprises, financial institutions, banking capacity, regulatory mobile money, branchless banking, agribusiness, and gender mainstreaming activities (USAID 2012d). This full-scale construction of national financial infrastructure is a part of the donor process to systematize financial activity on a national scale and attribute legibility by the donor community for Afghanistan's integration into global systems of trade (and WTO accession). Of course, this interest in propelling Afghanistan into broader systems of trade only came after 9/11, and presently the Trump administration is looking for ways to tap Afghanistan's vast mineral wealth for industrial manufacturing in order to recoup some of the investment the United States has made in the country (Amini 2017).

That said, there are numerous examples of this integration of concurrent state building and market building activities in projects. In order to "strengthen Afghanistan government capacity to sustain a market environment that supports *responsible economic management, private sector-driven growth, investment promotion, access to finance*, and *job creation*" (USAID 2011b, 3), the Economic Growth and Governance Initiative (EGGI) in Afghanistan embarked upon a myriad of training programs in topics such as inter-mediate statistics, audit fundamentals, developing an audit manual, on-the-job training, as well as presentation skills and business writing. The project also featured "interactive capacity building exercises" (ibid., 19), which entailed delivering group presentations and learning networking strategies. One must ask how specifically such trainings are to become embedded into government ministries and institutions and whether or not these trainings translate into an actual increased capacity to support legal market activities (the cultivation of which is another challenge donors face).

On the other end, projects designed to increase business usually also involve some com-ponent of building government infrastructure to facilitate business activities. For example, USAID's FIRMS project in Pakistan was designed to help small and medium enterprises (SMEs) in Pakistan improve their access to technology, domestic and export markets, and finance (USAID 2013b). The project had a "Business Enabling Environment (BEE) com-ponent" to "… improve the capabilities of the government at the district, provincial, and national levels to accelerate and facilitate economic opportunities" (USAID 2014e, vii). The FIRMS initiative also included a subproject for the institutional capacity develop-ment of the Khyber Pakhtunkwha Government Planning & Development Department with four strategic objectives: "(1) to build responsiveness and effectiveness of the state to restore citizen trust; (2) stimulate livelihood and employment opportunities; (3) ensuring delivery of basic services; and (4) countering radicalization" (ibid., 13), in large part by working with other state institutions to improve cooperation between public and private sectors (16). These projects attempt to extend the capacity of state and market systems to compete with transnational militant networks in the political and economic space of the relatively autonomous and remote tribal populations.

In fact, capacity-building efforts are largely for this purpose. USAID embarked on an ambitious cross-cutting Capacity Development Program between 2007 and 2012 to strengthen Afghanistan's "capacity-building institutions," to "become sustainable providers of capacity building services throughout the economy" (USAID 2008a, 101). There were five "components" of "capacity-building institutions" to target: (1) public sector, (2) private for-profit business, (3) NGOs, (4), higher education institutions, and (5) participant training and capacity-building technical assistance. The audit noted that "capacity building is needed on almost every sector in Afghanistan in order to rebuild and promote economic expansion" (ibid., 1). The program was intended to "build near-term capacity with target institutions … and develop a critical mass of Afghans trained in management and other basic skills … to support USAID/Afghanistan's mission strategic objectives: a thriving economy led by the private sector, a democratic government with broad citizen participation, and a better educated and healthier population" (ibid., 3).

There is only one publically available audit for this program, published in 2008—at the end of the first year of the program, though on the USAID's website there is a page for the program, with a three-sentence descriptor, and list of entities that received "training and support to build capacity" (USAID 2013a). The audit, however, details significant challenges faced in that first year. The contractors did not have detailed work plans in place, citing "mission staffing issues and broad and ambitious program objectives" (ibid., 6), and so the first 14 months of the program were largely spent "attempting to define the program's activities and priorities … (involving) ad hoc requests from the mission, the US Embassy, and benefiting ministries to implement tasks that did not always contribute directly to overall program objectives" (ibid., 5). Furthermore, contractors noted the program was "overambitious and very broad for workforce development because Afghanistan did not have skilled labor in any area". This labor issue for donors has not been an insignificant one.

In expanding projects (and government and market activities) to remote regions of Afghanistan and Pakistan, USAID has employed tactics of systemization to counter transnational extremist activity. A prime example of this is the Incentives Driving Economic Alternatives (IDEA) project, a USAID-funded initiative in Afghanistan to promote stabilization and support the transition of Afghanistan by expanding the Licit Economy in the North, East, and West of Afghanistan. The program is billed as "respond(ing) to community needs through Community Constructed Infrastructure (CCI)" projects that "foster trust" and infuse communities with cash by providing labor to local residents. The idea is to build upon and replicate economic relationships in agricultural and rural development sectors of those communities to further integrate them with the state. USAID has done this with a project emphasis on rural infrastructure, sustained agricultural production, enterprise development, and, of course, capacity building. The IDEA program's capacity-building activities are largely *activities of systemization*—trainings on agricultural and livestock topics, business and vocational skills, training relevant to the work of a government line staff, record keeping, business plan and strategy development, understanding local markets, marketing, demand estimation, association building workshops, financial training, and monthly coordination meetings (USAID 2011c, 45–46). All of these training topics intend to embed internationally standardized processes and practices to local scale of operation, which would theoretically enable greater integration into the economic activities and processes of the state.

Attempting to invest in a core community of laborers in rural areas is not a new donor tactic to integrate remote rural areas into state political and economic life. In rural areas where the majority of the population is illiterate, economic dynamism and opportunities for upward mobility are limited. In the 1980s, the way donors attempted to get at this issue was through skills training, although at that time donor governments maintained covert relationships with the transnational networks of resistance operating along the rural border regions. However, while the terrorist networks that exist today were merely budding during the time of the Soviet occupation, there was still the issue of state legibility in the border regions, where tribes operated relatively autonomously. During that time, the transnational operations enabled by the autonomous nature of governance on the border were ascribed international legitimacy by states providing weapons and humanitarian aid. While donor projects to invest in rural areas were initially to *support* the communities housing the transnational networks extending the activities of the state (and donors), this same tactic is now employed to combat the very same transnational social infrastructure enabling the operation of militant groups in an attempt to integrate autonomous communities with the state.

For example, in an attempt to address rural poverty in Pakistan in the 1980s, USAID funded the Agha Khan Rural Support Program (AKRSP), designed as a "private sector catalyst to promote development in selected rural areas of poverty, with the objective to "increase the capacity of local people ... to make use of opportunities to improve their welfare and overcome the problems facing them" (Aga Khan Foundation 1988, 32). The program invested in the creation of VOs primarily focused on skill development, improving agricultural techniques, livestock development, land management techniques, as well as computerizing and tracking project records. The program final report notes project success in improving yields and productivity, but notes that the primary concern is the "need to address the issue of longer-term and system-wide sustainability of the village level organization that the project helped to create" (ibid., 30). The VOs lacked legal status, which jeopardized their ability for "growth and continuity" and would need "evolving managerial skills at many levels ... that can take over most of the support functions currently being performed by AKRSP." Through attempts to build the skills and ascribe legal status to the activities of VOs, USAID attempted a systemization of traditional community organizations in remote areas.

While donor attempts at statecraft have traditionally involved this form of *pulling* the remote toward the center, post-9/11 donor activities have furthered this statecraft to more explicitly support the integration of the remote and the national into the global. The most notable attempt at this is in WTO trade accession. From the donor perspective, facilitating country accession to the WTO is a symbolic objective in the economic integration of neglected/remote spaces. It serves as an additional systemic relationship that should theoretically assist with the taming of the volatile aspects of the state. A 2003 USAID strategy document notes that USAID's trade capacity-building strategy supports the Doha Development Agenda, which advocates that continued multilateral trade liberalization is necessary to accelerate growth and reduce poverty in developing countries and that WTO member countries have a *moral obligation* to "developing" countries to help build their capacity to take advantage of trade liberalization (USAID 2003a, 3). USAID's trade capacity-building strategy supports country participation in trade negotiations, implementation of trade agreements, and economic responsiveness to opportunities for trade (ibid.).

Afghanistan, in particular, has been a target for WTO accession since the ISAF invasion. USAID's TAFA (Trade Accession and Facilitation for Afghanistan) project has been the vehicle for this effort. The purpose of TAFA was to help Afghanistan harness the trade and investment potential of its strategic location in the region so that increased investment, exports and market-based employment opportunities drive economic growth (USAID 2011d, 5). The 2011 Annual Report paints Afghanistan as a nation ready to harness its true place in the global marketplace,

> Afghanistan is reasserting itself as a global trading nation by renewing its long-standing spirit in which trade was both life blood and a way of life. At present, trade remains lopsided, with imports surpassing exports by a factor of ten. However, the fundamental underpinnings of a strong trading nation are developing and allowing Afghanistan to take advantage of its prime position on the famed Silk Road. (ibid., 9)

The rationalization for the program is to essentially improve Afghanistan's "capacity to develop and manage improved transport systems and to improve trade links with international partners" (ibid., 12). This involves removing trade barriers for both exports and imports, and creating space in the media for discussion of trade and economics (ibid., 12). These objectives were to be achieved through "on the job training, improved inter-institutional coordination, negotiation and implementation of bilateral, regional, and international trade and transit agreements …," which would enable "the Government of Afghanistan to improve economic opportunities for Afghan firms, create new jobs, and facilitate trade while laying the foundation for WTO accession" (USAID 2010e, 15).

Notably, the integration of countries into a global trading system was actually part of US National Security Strategy in 2002. Of eight goals listed, one is to ignite a new era of global economic growth through free markets and trade, while another is to "expand the circle of development (6)," goals USAID acknowledges as closely linked to its trade capacity-building strategy. The document goes on to note that developing countries will "reap the benefits of a rules-based global trading system … accelerating development progress … (and that) international trade agreements can act as an international anchor for critical national reforms *designed to combat corruption and promote democracy and good governance*" (USAID 2003a, 7). Inherent in this language is the perception by donors that international agreements can serve as a regulating force to keep states in line, as if the signature by a head of state will prevent Taliban operation and revenue stream coming from opium cultivation at subnational scales.

This link that is made in the donor literature—that state infrastructure and market infrastructure should be reinforcing and that the cultivation of this integration and assimilation with the international community of states in relationships based upon trade should subdue threats of "corruption" and encourage the promotion of democracy and "good governance"—brings us to the third function of governance and donor statecraft—the establishment of rule of law and security. Establishing rule of law and security is an integral component of statecraft and is vital to the operations of state and business. The scholarly debates surrounding this topic are extensive, going back to Weber's notion of the state as the community with the monopoly on violence. I do not intend to engage in a debate of what *rule of law* means, but rather to highlight in development projects what rule of law looks like as USAID engages in statecraft in Afghanistan and Pakistan.

Security and Rule of Law

A discussion of security, rule of law, political process, and institutions could be its own book. To contain this section, I provide a brief overview of the challenges to the establishing of rule of law, as well as democratic institutions and processes, while highlighting donor attempts to resolve this complex area of governance. In Afghanistan, establishing rule of law presents a vastly different challenge than in Pakistan, but in many ways the task of extending the legibility of the state into the relatively autonomous, hostile pockets of state territory is the same. Particularly in Afghanistan, continuous conflict and invasion have left gaping vacuums of governance. Many of the systems that did exist were destroyed or damaged, and the state system largely illegitimate and corrupt. Preventing a Taliban resurgence in Afghanistan became imperative for the donor community and US counterinsurgency campaign after the ISAF invasion. Given the context, any donor scheme to manage the security situation was ambitious to say the least. Nevertheless, after the invasion, a slew of reconstruction and development strategies were initiated to "stabilize" Afghanistan. USAID was one of many donors involved in rule of law and stabilization activities and so considering how USAID tackled these problems requires a situating of the broader scope of donor activities surrounding the military invasion of Afghanistan and general situation of security.

While the previous chapter traced the evolution of transnational networks of resistance, *it is outside the realm of this project to provide an extensive analysis of the security situation since the ISAF invasion*. This section focuses primarily on projects post-9/11, and the challenge of crafting the state is far greater in both Afghanistan and Pakistan during the past two decades, given the proliferation of transnational militant networks, than it was during the years of the Soviet occupation. That said, what is relevant and pertinent to a discussion on donor projects to build the governance functions of a state are a few components of the security situation, namely the impact of the invasion on: (1) already existing systems of governance, law, and law enforcement; (2) beneficiary receptivity to donors; and (3) the general integration of military and development activities and projects, particularly under counterinsurgency in the case of USAID. Astri Suhrke, a journalist-turned-scholar with decades of experience in Afghanistan, provides an excellent analysis of the "International Project" in Afghanistan (2011) and I borrow from her work, as well as Hassan Abbas's work on the Taliban Revival (2014), to provide some background of the security situation after the ISAF invasion and to help situate USAID's projects where the project literature decontextualizes findings.

Before discussing the security situation of development in Afghanistan, I should first clarify the difference between the integration of military/security and development activities. I use the terms "military" and "security" relatively interchangeably, but the reality is that "security" is provided by numerous types of actors, including militaries (foreign and Afghan), security contractors, militias, and so on. USAID projects post-2001 have largely been influenced by the demands of US military counterinsurgency strategy and resulted in integrative forms such as the PRT. Prior to 2001, USAID did not really engage in rule of law or security programs in either Afghanistan or Pakistan outside of programs to control the production of poppies in Afghanistan in the early 1990s. This demonstrates that investment in programs for rule of law and security, in particular, is a programmatic area that emerged within the context of counterinsurgency frameworks for development, effectively demonstrating the development activity in this post-2001 period.

That said, outside of PRTs, USAID relies on private security contractors (PSCs) in order for contractors and grantees to implement USAID-funded projects, based upon the logic that PSCs free up military forces to focus on their "core missions" (USAID 2010d,105). Upon allegations that USAID contractors were subcontracting to PSCs that were actually Taliban, USAID developed recommendations to "reduce the likelihood that subcontractors will misuse USAID funds to pay off Taliban insurgents or other criminal elements" (ibid., 106). These recommendations included risk and impact assessments of current and proposed locations, conducting audits of programs criticized of misusing funds, to implement cost analysis to detect fraud or inflated prices, and to develop an action plan to maintain oversight of subcontracting and purchasing systems by contractors (ibid., 106–7).

While laudable, the reality is that attempts to limit any collaboration or negotiation with insurgent elements inherently places limits on the reach of projects on subnational scales. Extending the reach of state governance is actually an imperialistic exercise requiring foreign or Afghan military intervention, as the task involves more than merely the provision of security and involves the coercion or subjugation of local tribal militias. Furthermore, there are examples of favoritism in contracts being awarded to those with ties to the central government, such as the granting of private security contracts to the Afghan defense minister's son in spite of formal regulations on family relationships that should have made him ineligible (Suhrke 2011, 135). These instances of corruption are peppered throughout donor attempts at statecraft and, whether intentional or honest mistakes, have an impact on local receptivity to donor and state engagement. Even prior to the ultimate integration of civilian-led USAID projects as a component of counter-insurgency military strategy, this problem of security to implement projects in subnational environments has been a persistent issue, requiring particularly in the case of Pakistan examples of military, militia escort, and the usage of PSCs.

A good example of the general instability of the security situation at the subnational scale is that of Marjah—a town in Helmand Province in southern Afghanistan largely held by the Taliban even after the initial 2001 ISAF invasion. The largest ISAF offensive, called Operation Moshatarak,[4] was launched in 2010 to take Marjah from the Taliban, which was the last Taliban stronghold in Helmand Province (Thompson 2010). To start, after the Taliban were chased out (and into Pakistan), the local Afghan police were dismissed en masse on suspicion of involvement in the drug trade or collaboration with the Taliban (Suhrke 2011, 64). Obviously, ISAF do not follow USAID capacity development methodologies, but, if they did, the decision of en masse dismissal without taking stock of baseline systemic capacities would have been an obvious mistake, as Suhrke also points out. Afghan National Police (ANP) replacements, mostly Tajiks who did not speak Pashto, were flown into Pashtun heartland to serve as the new police force, sparking such protests from elders in Marjah that the ANP had to be withdrawn (ibid., 64–65). This was not unusual as Western donors regularly intervened in appointments processes with civil service reform, police training programs, senior police officials, and governors (ibid., 137).

The security situation was so bad that some 15,000 troops were unable to provide security to a community of 60,000 (a ratio of 1:4, much higher than standard counter-insurgency density recommendations (Goode 2010). As an example of the context within which USAID and ISAF were attempting to operate, anyone found having installed water pumps distributed by USAID, or being in the possession of dollars, were actually vulnerable to retaliation. USAID's employment-creating projects had funding to hire 10,000 residents, but only 1,200 villagers even signed up, and only a quarter of 4,000 water pumps had been distributed (Chandrasekaran 2010). The "government in a box"

---

4. A Dari word meaning "together," even though in Marja they speak Pashto.

strategy of flooding Marjah with cash, equipment, and new (outside) leaders was largely a bust—as an example, General McChrystal's hand-picked Marjah district governor who had spent the last 15 years in Germany (4 of which in prison for stabbing his stepson who intervened while he was beating his wife) lasted all of six months, the majority of which were spent on a US military base (Druzin 2016).

> The invasion created a lot of local enemies. In addition to the Taliban, potential adversaries included local elders who had chosen or been forced to cooperate with the Taliban. Villagers who had lost relatives or property during the invasion, or whose families had been forced to flee, were hardly positively inclined. Then there were the drug smugglers. A survey conducted in Marjah soon after the offensive by an international NGO found that two-third of the villagers were more negative towards the NATO-ISAF forces after the offensive than before and did not want a strong international force presence in their area. Nor did they want the Taliban back. It was a means-ends problem, the analysts concluded; the coalition campaign was poorly conducted and badly communicated. (Suhrke 2011, 64, International Council on Security and Development 2010)

In spite of poor planning, this reception within the subnational context of a Taliban stronghold was to be expected. Poor donor coordination and planning, however, has been a persistent issue that in many ways sabotaged any donor efforts at statecraft, both with top-down and bottom-up efforts, throughout the history of USAID projects (both pre- and post-counterinsurgency). That said, this disconnection between donor strategy and recipient reality is a problem that is pervasive both within central government and subnational contexts. Immediately after the invasion, the American style of legal reform had USAID and US Department of Justice officials flown in to draft laws on the financing of terrorism, money laundering, and corruption that were based on foreign concepts existing outside the Afghan legal framework; made no serious attempt to explain or train jurists, police, or other stakeholders; and subsequently the laws were effectively ignored (Suhrke 2011, 192). The legal trainings that USAID did embark on were subcontracted out to a US-based consulting company and involved short two- to four-week courses where participants would receive certificates of completion (instead of assessments on what they had learned) (Suhrke 2011, 193). The trainings were further challenged by the fact that the vast majority of Afghan legal personnel were trained in Islamic law and were generally unfamiliar with the concepts and reasoning in Western law, which were the subject of the trainings (Suhrke 2011, 193).

This "crucial window of opportunity" after the initial 2001 invasion to construct an efficient rule of law infrastructure (functioning courts at both local and national scales) was missed by Western states involved in "statebuilding" (Abbas 2014, 178). Serious attempts by the donor community to tackle justice sector reform did not come until several years after the invasion (as part of broader counterinsurgency strategies). In 2004–2005, the Italians were put in charge of an international group to make a 10-year plan for justice sector reform, which was also plagued with problems. First off, the most important task was to create a new criminal procedure code, and the Italians excluded the Afghan Judicial Commission, paid little deference to Afghan laws and traditions, and when finalized in 2009, Karzai only acquiesced in signing it into law when the Italians threatened to withdraw funding (Abbas 2014, 179). In this same vein, US Department of Justice simply copied large chunks from the US Patriot Act in drafting a law on terrorism for Afghanistan, but in this case Afghan opponents won out and drafted a law prepared by Afghan experts (Abbas 2014, 179). These attempts at legal reform by the donor community do not all involve USAID, but these institutional actors often collaborate with USAID on projects and also represent the US government, thus serving as important examples for understanding the context within which USAID was conducting projects.

As the US counterinsurgency campaign was underway, USAID's role was largely that of running stabilization programs designed to facilitate national–subnational linkages and cultivate local support for the central government through a variety of programs. For example, in 2004, the international donor community embarked on the Afghanistan Stabilization Program (ASP), initially funded by numerous donors, including USAID, the Government of Canada, and DFID. The objective of ASP was to improve security and governance across the country and engender greater confidence in the capacity of the government to improve the lives of people around the country (USAID 2004, 9). The program was intended to build governing institutions and strengthen linkages between central, provincial, district, and village governance in Afghanistan (Miakhel 2012, 3). Seven National Priority Programs were launched by the Afghan government: the Afghan National Army, National Police, National Emergency Employment Program (NEEP), Disarmament, Demobilization and Reintegration (DDR), Justice Sector Reform, National Solidarity Program (NSP), and Civil Service Reform (ibid., 1).

In order for these reform programs to be successful, it was imperative to strengthen linkages between national and subnational entities, which involved building the capacity on the subnational end in part to prevent insurgent resurgence. Subprograms to support ASP were established, such as the Governance Advisory Services Program, to "accelerate reform, recruitment and training at the subnational (provincial and district) level and to provide a range of public administration based training … to strengthen the in-house capacity of the PMU (project management units) and departments of central government to provide sustained guidance and direction for long term training and human resources capacity development" (ibid., 20). Unfortunately, the program was plagued with planning and management issues between the Ministry of the Interior and President Karzai surrounding how to target provinces to build districts (the Ministry wanted to target border areas to secure them from insurgents) and also how to select districts for project evaluation, ultimately resulting in a withdrawal and reduction of donor funds (Miakhel 2012, 3).

In considering these issues of security and governance capacity, particularly in subnational environments in Afghanistan, it is critical to consider local perceptions of the very central government within which they were to be integrated. A 2017 USIP report on Stabilization in Afghanistan notes that a considerable proportion of Afghan citizens believe the main cause of insecurity to be their own government, which they perceive as massively corrupt, predatory, and unjust, and that "a stabilization theory that relies on using aid to win the population over to such a negatively perceived government would inherently face an uphill battle" (Kapstein 2017, 4). The report also cites the timeline of programming (short term—three to six months, medium term—six to eighteen months, long term—more than eighteen months) as making it difficult to actually know the effects of programming (ibid., 6). The role of the military was also significant in stabilization activities. Without military presence to provide basic security needs, development projects and stabilization activities would not have been able to take place. However, the military presence also caused complications in the decision-making process as differences in objectives, timelines, and cultures resulted in inefficiencies and sometimes limited the effectiveness of operations (ibid., 7).

In spite of these challenges, projects persisted. USAID has contracted out several Rule of Law Programs, both to Checchi Consulting and also DPK. The Afghanistan Rule of Law Stabilization (RLS) program, contracted to DPK, was tasked with supporting the development of a formal judicial structure in Afghanistan. The program targeted four elements for capacity building: the judiciary, court management, legal education, and public legal outreach (USAID 2012f, 6). In a 2012 program evaluation of the RLS program, interviews gave positive feedback on the judiciary capacity-building training, but noted that given that the "inspiration, the content, the techniques and the financing have been provided by international donors ... the sustainability of the program [is] in serious doubt. Unless the Afghan government provided financing as donors draw back, the efforts would not be sustainable" (ibid., 9). Other rule of law projects focused on strengthening or reestablishing community-based dispute resolution mechanisms. As part of the US government's 2011–2015 plan, the *principal focus* of US rule of law effort is to "reverse the public perception of GIRoA as weak or predatory by helping the Afghan government and local communities develop responsive and predictable dispute resolution mechanisms that offer an alternative to the Taliban shadow justice system" (ibid., 32).

The most recent USAID rule of law program is ADALAT (Assistance for the Development of Afghan Legal Access and Transparency), to be implemented by Checchi Consulting between 2016 and 2021. The objective of the ADALAT program is to improve the quality of legal services for all Afghan citizens by working with formal judicial institutions such as the Afghan Supreme Court, the Afghanistan Independent Bar Association to improve professional training and legal education for judges and lawyers, as well as building linkages between the formal and informal justice systems. The program also contains a public outreach and education component, utilizing CSOs to improve citizen awareness (and it may be useful here to consider issues identified in the previous section on the role of CSOs in provision of services). Given that the program is still ongoing, it is hard to measure outcomes, but it is easy to see how the components of this project do not differ much from previous projects with components involving (1) training and education, (2) strengthening institutions and linkages between institutions, and (3) raising public awareness to gain buy-in and ideally entice local ownership.

The most recently published quarterly report of the DEC from the first quarter of 2017 highlights the completion of the assessment phase, which involved reviews of the AIBA and Supreme Court mandates and bylaws, but notably also a USAID HICD assessment. That said, the program is already experiencing a number of challenges. Feedback received by the Afghan Supreme Court noted frustration at continued assessments and the potential redundancy of assessments being conducted by multiple donors. Furthermore, Supreme Court feedback was critical of the assignment of donor funds to developing managing capacity as outlined in the HICD (USAID 2017b, 1–2). An RFA (Request for Applications) to develop clinical legal education for law and Sharia students was cancelled upon the realization that potential applicants did not understand the concept of legal clinics. I do not intend to further unpack impediments noted in the Quarterly Report facing the program but highlight this one example to demonstrate the relative consistency of issues in donor projects of statecraft over time.

In the case of Pakistan, the central government has had to negotiate with the legal vestiges of British colonial rule, particularly in the border areas, and I highlight the example of the Federally Administered Tribal Areas (FATA) here. FATA has been administered by the Frontier Crimes Regulation (FCR), which was introduced under the British Government of India in 1901. While the tribal areas are represented in both the Senate and the National Assembly of Pakistan, the constitution prevents parliamentarians from legislating FATA (Idrees 2013, 5). In 2011, the President of Pakistan Asif Ali Zardari made major amendments to the FCR and in 2013, USAID commissioned a survey implemented by DTCE[5] among FATA residents regarding the implementation of these reforms. About half of the respondents reported never having heard about the FCR, and of those, over half were unaware of recent amendments. Those who were unaware reported that law was enforced by political agents, jirga leaders, maliks (tribal heads), or khasdars. Around three-quarters of respondents believed that there would be resistance from the old Jirga system (ibid., 20). Furthermore, large majorities believed that only people with political influence will receive the most benefits from any reform programs (ibid., 23). These findings are not surprising and in some ways are indicative of the failure of previous efforts by USAID to strengthen the capacity of state and local institutions to set and implement rule of law.

The tactics USAID has taken with Pakistan's rule of law program mirror some aspects of those in Afghanistan. USAID's Pakistan rule of law program (final report published in 2008) noted five broad objectives: improving the capacity of the judicial system to deliver more accessible and higher quality justice, strengthening citizen awareness and access to advisory and representational services, enhancing the quality of legal education and training, strengthening the capacity of law enforcement to function according to international standards, and clarify land titling and registration systems to reduce caseloads for provincial courts (Blue and Hoffman 2008, 44–45). The final report on the program notes that while there were modest successes, such as an increase in the number of judges and women judges, passage of consumer protection laws, and reduction of delays in subordinate courts in the provinces, numerous shortcomings are noted as well (e.g., subordinate courts were still in "primitive" condition, and a general failure to monitor CSO activities such as public safety and acting as police–citizen liaisons (ibid., 35–36)).

Another programmatic example of the challenges facing the GOP on subnational scales is the Capacity Building Program for FATA. The goals of the program were to "strengthen FATA governing bodies to support civilian/military cooperation, in terms

---

5. Devolution Trust for Community Empowerment, an organization commissioned and funded by UNDP, then USAID, Norwegians, and DFID (DTCE 2013).

of (1) the institutions' capacity to plan, implement, and manage funds for programs; (2) assist constituents and communities to communicate effectively, (3) ensure that development initiatives are aligned with local needs and expectations, and (4) to strengthen the capacity of CSOs in order to establish their ability to produce their own strategic plans …" (USAID 2010b, 1). The program faced numerous challenges throughout, such as ensuring the basic security and safety of the team, maintaining and ensuring the quality of USAID partners' data on village activity, and issues with qualified consultants demanding a pay grade higher than USAID's standard rates (ibid., 9). Insecurity prevented the setup of VSAT (satellite communications) system to work more closely with the GOP from being completed in Kuram and North Waziristan, and the GOP military noted that insecurity in these areas would continue to make it impossible for VSATs to be installed (ibid., 15). CSOs' lack of familiarity with grants compliance and monitoring mechanisms also impeded implementation processes (ibid., 18).

Additionally, there were challenges with the participants targeted to actually increase coordination for civilian and military activities in FATA. For instance, "key" participants in workshops had to be engaged separately in order to solicit their input, so there was no free-flow open exchange of ideas about content and design (ibid., 21). There was also generally low turnout, in part due to an "unanticipated" provincial cabinet meeting and high-level military conference, and also a general skepticism on behalf of participants who "needed to be constantly reminded that there are no exogenous agendas and the Capacity Building Program is facilitating the dialogue process among the stakeholders" (ibid., 21).

While most rule of law projects have components to strengthen national and subnational linkages or to build upon traditional systems of dispute resolution, they will nevertheless remain ineffective. The heritage of imperialism and war surrounding donor relationships undermines the legitimacy of the central government, most especially at subnational scales. Further, performance-based methodologies to increase organizational capacity will not take root when beneficiaries have to be convinced by donors about the merit of investment in various forms of management training or budgeting techniques over other areas of investment such as equipment and physical infrastructure. Ownership of processes and institutions requires social and cultural contexts—knowledge of local systems and relationships, of Islamic jurisprudence, and of basic traditional legal framework, which donors generally lack. The USAID example shows us that while donors make attempts to integrate this knowledge into planning, largely through assessments and feasibility studies, the attempts at systemization of knowledge for donor and state planning purposes are weak and usually fall short. This is the fundamental challenge of ownership in development projects and the ultimate failure of capacity development efforts.

Political Processes and Institutions

The period following the Bonn Agreement could be divided into two main historical periods. The first was the making and renewing of Afghan political institutions and infrastructure. This phase came to an end, and the second period began, with the introduction of the present democratic Constitution and the Presidential, Parliamentary and Provincial Council election. Political parties were legally recognized, and the political and cultural landscape was enriched by the emergence of a free press, hundreds of civil societies and free national debate. Thus the Afghanistan of today has a much more democratic and progressive system than that of the sixties. It has passed the phase of institution-making and has entered the phase of implementing plans for the democratization and economic and social development of the country through joint efforts of the Executive, Legislature and the people of Afghanistan. However, while the country is going through the phase of nation-building and democratization, two heinous enemies are threatening the very fabric of the social and political body and soul of the country: *These two enemies are terrorism* as the enemy of peace and security, *and corruption* that can result in the failure of any short-term and long-term plans and strategies for ensuring economic development and attracting foreign investment.—Support to the Establishment of the Afghan Legislature (SEAL) Project. (UNDP 2006, 1)

While attempting to construct a legal system is one task, constructing democratic political institutions that remain accountable to the public and transparent in transitions of power is another equally important task for donors. With the retreat of the Taliban, donors essentially went about the process of building Afghanistan's government from scratch. As donors facilitated the interim Karzai administration and set about the process of building institutions of democratic governance to enable economic development, it is necessary to touch on the point of inclusion in the construction of democratic institutions and processes. Without delving too far into a discussion on the nature of inclusivity in democratic processes, and the inherent volatility this already presents (especially in states where violent factions spar for control of centralized authority), it is necessary to acknowledge the impact that donors' designations of political and military actors have surrounding the authenticity of the very political processes and institutions that donors seek to build.

To give an example, at the end of 2001, Jalaluddin Haqqani actually sent a convoy of tribal elders from Khost to attend the inauguration of Hamid Karzai as president of the Interim Administration in a gesture of goodwill and to explore possibilities for peace (Suhrke 2011, 70). The US military were informed that the convoy were actually Taliban and dispatched a plane to bomb the convoy, resulting in 60 deaths (Suhrke 2011, 70). Whatever interest or consideration Haqqani might have had to strengthen linkages between the swaths of transnational territory his network encompasses, and specifically between Khost and Kabul, were thus effectively squashed, and the Haqqani Network has gone on to be one of the strongest militant groups working with the Taliban. I give this example to point out how any attempt by donors to build state infrastructure that is legitimate both at national and subnational scales must involve an integration and reconciliation with the populations loyal to and supporting groups such as the Haqqani Network. Properly addressing this topic—of the merit of including militant groups in the budding democratic processes of a state—is outside the realm of this project, but I raise it as an important factor to consider in constructing the legibility of political institutions as a project of donor statecraft.

I highlight a few examples of projects by the donor community and USAID that demonstrate donors' attempts to construct various components of political infrastructure, primarily, government ministries, legislative institutions, and subnational/national linkages. Civil society also plays a role in the construction of an enabling environment for political institutions, but as I review USAID's civil society initiatives in my discussion on the provision of services, I will not duplicate that section here. I highlight the instances of corruption in development projects, which is also peppered throughout a few previous examples given, since while corruption challenges the ability of statecraft to produce state legibility, it often also involves a manipulation of state simplifications except not on behalf of the state but of actors operating at scales above, within, and outside the state.

This first example I highlight of donor attempts to build central government infrastructure is the Afghanistan Reconstruction Trust Fund (ARTF)-designed "second civil service," executed through Civil Service Capacity-Building program. The ARTF is a multidonor trust fund supported by 34 donors and administered by the World Bank. The program involved two components: (1) recruiting qualified Afghan expatriates into positions as senior advisers in various ministries and agencies and (2) recruiting Afghans from the "domestic and regional labor markets into senior and middle management line positions in Ministries and agencies (called the Lateral Entry Program)" (ARTF 2010). Results are presented in numerical form: 143 lateral entrants recruited, 20 departments completed the PRR (Priority Reform and Reconstruction) process, and 35 departments completing stage 1 of PRR "enhancing capacity of existing civil servants to apply for PRR positions" (ibid.). These barebones results present the project as if building government ministries was like producing widgets, while the attempt to build a "second civil service" actually only reinforced Afghan dependence on donor money.

> With aid inflows exceeding Afghan state capacity, which was nearly nil, capacity in the form of international consultants was imported on a large scale ... In the USAID funded Ministry of Finance (considered the most restructured and reformed of all the ministries, ... the Ministry (went from) 30 international and 200 Afghan technical advisors (in 2003) to 70 international consultants and 300 Afghan technical advisors (in 2009), with all the Afghans on (full) salary support from donors ... Donor willingness to provide salary support was driven by the deteriorating security situation and attempts to turn things around before transitioning to full 'Afghanization'. But the scheme *reduced incentives* of the government to *take budgetary responsibility* for the Afghan advisers and integrate them with the regular civil service ... when a program was terminated, (so were) the technical advisors ... In the Ministry of Education, the appointments of 490 Afghan technical advisers funded by USAID were terminated when the program came to an end ... institutional capacity that could reduce long-term dependence was not being built. (Suhrke 2011, 130–31)

This is an important point to highlight. Since donor design of institution strengthening relies on donor expertise, the interwoven issues of *ownership* and *dependence* remained unresolved and the sustainability of donor investments becomes unlikely. After the first decade in Afghanistan after 9/11, USAID rated only 5 out of the 19 government agencies it supported as requiring only moderate or little external assistance (SIGAR 2010, Suhrke 2011, 132). Attempts to build institutional infrastructure were haphazard at best, and ensuring democratic and transparent political processes proved to be no less challenging.

Another major component of the political process is elections. Donors have played a much larger role in facilitating Afghan elections than in Pakistan, because in Afghanistan donors faced the task of *rebuilding* the structure of the government as opposed to *assisting already existing* electoral processes. SIGAR, along with USAID, UNDP, and other donors, conducted the ELECT (Enhancing Legal and Electoral Capacity for Tomorrow) project to strengthen the Independent Electoral Commission (IEC) in Afghanistan. The United States contributed $263 million (or about 54 percent) of the funds for the project through USAID (SIGAR 2009, 4). The project took a four-fold approach to support the IEC and election process:

(1) support the IEC Secretariat with international advisors working alongside IEC department directors to gradually transfer capacity through coaching, training, and mentoring, (2) coordinate international assistance through the UN to avoid conflicts, program overlaps, and gaps in international support, (3) create two key cross-cutting advisory roles—Capacity Development Advisor and Gender Advisor—to ensure capacity development remains at the forefront of the project and that gender equity and access issues are mainstreamed within the IEC, and (4) continue to advocate for relevant legislative changes consistent with the Afghanistan Compact and Afghanistan National Development Strategy. (ibid., 5)

During the four-phase registration process, there were cases of underage registration, multiple registrations by individuals and registration of absentees, particularly women registered by male relatives, and other violations potentially undermining the fairness and transparency of the election process. Further, there was a lack of IEC monitoring over field staff during registration (ibid., 5). The project continued to encounter issues, with the program audit noting that, "it had not established a long-term capacity building strategy to ensure Afghan electoral capacity building and transfer of skills" (ibid., 8). Issues such as staff retention, staff recruitment, training, and operational tasks limited the present capacity, and it was determined by donors that international advisors would have to cover for this inexperience (ibid., 8). Further, the Capacity Development Advisor position created was never filled as UNDP was unable to identify a "suitable candidate for the position" (ibid., 8). The IEC chief electoral advisor also expressed concern that the Afghan government would have little interest or capability to fund the IEC at sustainable levels between election cycles, leaving the sustainability of the project in further question (9). In describing the 2014 elections, a 2015 Grantee report by Democracy International on the International Election Observation program noted, "lack of political will" and "chronic deficiencies" have a "corrosive impact on the credibility of Afghan elections (and) ... the democratic legitimacy of the country" (USAID 2014a, 1).

USAID has not had projects for electoral strengthening in Pakistan, but did fund a grant to Democracy International to organize a US election observation mission for the February 2008 elections. The Democracy International report on the mission identifies a number of weaknesses and deficiencies in Pakistan's election system and processes, notably flaws in voter registration, obstacles to women's participation, and an electoral environment that restricts independent media and judiciary and limits the ability of parties, candidates, and civil society actors to criticize the government (Democracy International 2008, 5). The report found that these issues did not negate the legitimacy of the elections but draws attention to concern for the legitimacy of future elections. While the electoral observation was not so much a project, concern over the legitimacy of Pakistan's political processes has led to development projects, particularly at the legislative level.

Lastly, I touch on donor programs to strengthen legislative processes. Donors have conducted multiple programs to strengthen Afghanistan's Parliament. UNDP embarked on the SEAL (Support to the Establishment of the Afghan Legislature) project, launched in 2005 to *ensure the timely establishment of the Afghan Parliament and support to its functioning*. The intended overall outcome of the project was "the establishment of a fully operational and efficient parliament recognized by all the people of Afghanistan as their representative institution, accountable and transparent, and that will be the interface between the citizen and government" (UNDP 2006, 5). This undertaking was no small task and ambitious to say the least. This project commenced for a second round, dubbed SEAL II, which was supposed to run until 2012, but was cut short in 2010 due to lack of resources (UNDP 2010, 7). It is obvious that the undertaking of statecraft was also a test of donor capacity.

While other international donors provided support for SEAL, USAID began providing assistance in 2004 with its own program, Afghanistan Parliamentary Assistance Program (APAP). The program had four main objectives to improve Parliaments: (1) capacity to plan and implement institutional development policies, (2) capacity to represent, (3) oversight responsibilities, and (4) capacity to legislate (USAID 2012b, 31). The project evaluation reports that while the program was very successful in supporting Parliament to build its institutional capacity, sustaining growth would require "considerable additional support to achieve administrative and financial autonomy from the government" (ibid., 6). Again, the sustainability of modest gains for the central government is entirely dependent upon the donor funding pipeline.

Conversely, US interest in "parliamentary capacity building" in Pakistan over the years has been more tempered than in Afghanistan post-9/11, coming about as a result of "reacting to realities" (3), given levels of coercion, corruption, and vulnerability of the civilian government to the military influence. The first training and capacity-building assistance program for the country's parliamentary bodies came in 1991 (a full 37 years after the United States began providing assistance to Pakistan), and between 1995 and 2008 USAID conducted three parliamentary strengthening projects, which evaluators deemed to be "wise investments" in "... helping the country to steer itself on a new course toward construction of a solid foundation that could provide for a sustainable democratic future" (USAID 2008d, 3). Pakistan's Legislative Strengthening Project (PLSP)'s intent and goal was to provide training and assistance that complied with USAID's requirement that legislative capacity-building programs be implemented so that they can be sustained beyond the life of the program (ibid.). The PLSP program did encounter some difficulties but was overall deemed successful in the final evaluation. This is likely for the obvious reason that, in Pakistan, functioning legislative systems at the provincial and national levels have not been damaged by international invasion. Yet, despite these investments to strengthen Pakistan's political processes for democracy, the military–civilian tensions remain strong, with no less than two coups d'état occurring during the time frame of USAID's projects.

In this brief discussion on rule of law and political process and institutions as an area of donor statecraft, I highlight a few main points from this section. Notions of rule of law are contingent upon cultural notions of law and relationships and networks between individuals, communities, and whatever entity claims authority over governance. In spite of the problematic nature of donor tactics to construct legal and state infrastructure—and the general inconsistency in methodological approaches for implementation—attempts at systemization to extend the reach of state control (to ensure law and security, to integrate "democratic" processes in governance, to provide basic services, to enable trade, etc.) struggle in large part due to the integration of military/security and development activities as a tactic to win (as opposed to truly gain) social power and sustainability of official relationships required for state legitimacy.

Human Rights Approaches within Statecraft

The issue of human rights in Afghanistan and Pakistan is a topic far beyond the scope of this project, but each of the four areas of statecraft identified within this chapter touches on some aspect of human rights implicitly. The attempted inclusion of populations in remote or contested spaces through projects to *provide basic services, facilitate and enable trade and access to economic opportunity*, maintain *rule of law and security*, and promote *democratic political processes and institutions* relates to the recognition and legitimization of various forms of political, civil, social, cultural, and economic rights. Regardless of the various declarations and conventions recognizing the rights of various populations over the past 70 years, USAID only established its institutional home for the advancement of HRBAs (DRG center) as well as its strategic framework for advancing HRBAs over a decade after the US-led coalition invasion of Afghanistan.

As detailed in Chapter 4, this framework carries forth the language of capacity development methodologies, with heavy attention paid to assessing points of entry within the "enabling" environment within difficult contexts. Capacity is largely referenced within the context of cultivating civil society, national human rights institutions, and generally places focus on evolving forms of capacity related to the cultivation of political processes and institutions and the rule of law. While upholding international human rights standards are acknowledged nominally—by donor state governments and also implicitly (sometimes explicitly) within country strategies and project objectives—in practice, statecraft within the context of war and counterinsurgency fundamentally has failed not only to build the capacity of the state but also to uphold any consistent or meaningful HRBA to development.

Consider the task before coalition forces after pushing the Taliban out of power: to support the establishment of a legitimate government in a country impacted by successive generations of conflict and invasion. A valid question to pose here is how is a development agency—or more accurately, a coalition of international military forces, government officials, and development institutions and agencies—supposed to take a HRBA to the construction of a state whose previous government they just toppled? This is a question for those seeking to advance HRBAs to development programming to seriously consider—and one I expand upon in the final chapter of this book. As I explain through this chapter and the previous chapter, capacity development methodologies have also failed to develop a meaningful and substantive approach in this regard. In entertaining this question, I briefly turn to USAID's efforts to support human rights in the early years after the ousting of the Taliban. Part of the Bonn Agreement involved the establishment of an independent human rights institution in Afghanistan, as this was considered integral to the success and legitimacy of the new Afghan government.

Both Afghanistan and Pakistan have independent human rights institutions designed to promote, protect, and monitor human rights and human rights abuses throughout each country—a heavy task considering the toll generations of war, occupation, and repeated political upheaval carry on societies. The Afghanistan Independent Human Rights Commission (AIHRC) was founded in 2002 and the Human Rights Commission of Pakistan (HRCP) was founded in 1987. Both organizations are involved in advocacy campaigns, lobbying, providing redress to victims of human rights abuses, promoting democratic governance and the rule of law, training and mobilizing activists, and liaising with the UN system. USAID has not provided any support to the HRCP, but did support the establishment of the AIHRC since it was a result of the Bonn Agreement.

USAID's support to the AIHRC took place under the Office of Transition Initiatives (OTI) Afghanistan Program. Coined OTI's first ever "mega-program," the primary purpose of the OTI Afghanistan Program was to support the Bonn Agreement transition process—to promote the legitimacy of the new Afghan government and the democratic process. This was done through initiatives to increase the Afghan government's capacity and responsiveness, bottom-up initiatives to build connections between provincial departments and government ministries, and to educate on the electoral process and ensure women (especially rural woman) understood basic constitutional and rights issues under discussion.

The program's evaluation notes that USAID's funding to support the AIHRC did not appear to be "strategically anticipated" by the OTI. Only after "strong appeals" by the UN, the US State Department transferred $500,000 of Economic Support Funds (ESF) to OTI in order to help with the establishment of the AIHRC, focusing on building its capacities in the areas of: complaints and petitions procedures; advisory and institution-building activities; conflict resolution; gender; cultural, linguistic, and physical accessibility; human rights networking; and human rights data management (USAID 2005d, 34). The final evaluation notes mixed results, yet again considering this program took place over a span of roughly four years (with this initial transfer of ESF funds covering a period of one year), ending in 2007 before the Taliban resurgence and deterioration of the security situation. A 2009 annual report by the AIHRC noted that the human rights situation in Afghanistan "remains bleak," citing a weak rule of law, persistent culture of impunity, and abuse of power by government officials as well as a weak judicial system as major obstacles to achieving the AIHRC's objectives (AIHRC 2009, 7).

As this chapter attempts to catalogue and highlight the major themes of USAID's efforts at statecraft in Afghanistan and Pakistan, we see that both human rights approaches and the prioritization of rights within programming are haphazard at best, and secondary to the strategic objective to expand the reach of the state to mitigate threats and manage risks. This very brief section is primarily to highlight this point, which underscores the issue of legibility in the example of USAID's statecraft. As the call for the establishment and implementation of HRBAs to development programming has taken place largely since 9/11, we can see that while aspects of these approaches are inherent within statecraft, they do not shape donor strategy for building the capacity of states.

Conclusion

Providing an adequate review of donor statecraft through an examination of USAID in Afghanistan and Pakistan in this chapter was admittedly a huge undertaking. There are a few major themes that the USAID example shows us that emerge with regard to how donor institutions engage in statecraft. First, there is a *general concurrence of statebuilding and market building activities* in most projects to (1) build government infrastructure, (2) strengthen public–private partnerships, (3) counter radicalism, (4) stimulate economic growth, and (5) more generally respond to the needs of society. *The four donor-targeted functions of governance*—specifically the provision of services and the facilitation of democratic processes—*also exist and are actively pursued outside the domain of state*. Donors attempt to strengthen functions of governance and build state legitimacy through the realms of private sector and civil society. Additionally, there are elements within the objectives of most projects explicitly surrounding the strengthening of subnational/national linkages, which is one of the greatest challenges of donor statecraft projects, because donors lack legitimacy and social power at the subnational scale.

It is also necessary to address that this section has been more heavily focused on the task of statecraft in Afghanistan, as it is a far more intrusive and complex pursuit by donors than in Pakistan. This is because it involves an almost complete reconstruction and redefining of state infrastructure. The subnational/national tensions that exist in Afghanistan also exist in Pakistan and provide the same challenges to development projects. These instances demonstrate the *consistency* of challenges faced by donors from subnational/transnational networks as well as to display the way in which donor positioning is inherently situated in (and limited by) relation to the central government.

Furthermore, while there has been a greater institutionalization of methodological tools to conduct preaward assessments and to conduct monitoring and evaluation in practice, the actual tactics of donor statecraft have not evolved significantly over the past four decades. Evaluations during the Soviet period note the same kinds of issues that plague projects today—notably, (1) relatively autonomous tribes who had traditionally been hostile to intrusions of the state, and foreigners affiliated with it, (2) issues with donor coordination, knowledge of important cultural codes that surround the definition of relationships, and other already existing systems of authority and governance. Yet, donors continue to attempt to build superficial forms of social power to expand the legibility of the state to ultimately manage affairs and contain threats within the territorial confines of the state, in spite of the fact that the state's institutional reach has never actually permeated the extent of its demarcated colonial boundaries.

Projects of development, funded by donor institutions, invest in the *sustainability* of the organizations (both of the state and nonstate) to continue carrying out projects of statecraft after donors leave. These projects involve state simplifications in order to provide state organizations with information for development schemes to better manage the affairs of societies within the territory of the state. The process of state simplification, and projects to further state simplification processes, involve battles for "social capital" to gain legibility for the state. These battles for legibility are fought with donor-institutionalized performance-based methodologies designed to build the capacity of individuals and organizations through exchange-based relationships to gain social power at all scales of the enabling environment, although they are typically skewed toward those individuals and organizations in closer proximity to the centralized government as that is the scale donor networks have greatest access to. As I noted in the introduction to this section, the actual battle for legibility takes place at subnational and transnational scales of the enabling environment where the central government lacks influence to carry out projects of statecraft.

In Figure 6.3, I visually display how the statecraft of donors attempts to impose fixed positionings upon the reality of a multiscalar social environment, in order to reinforce the hierarchical nature of the development apparatus. I break down the process by which donor institutions target *scales* of the enabling (or disabling) environment for projects to enhance functions of governance. I display the *attributes* of capacity development identified in Chapter 3, focusing on the enabling environment as the target *object* of capacity development efforts. Each scale of the enabling environment defines the context of capacity development, as well as the varying dynamics of social power that enable the ownership of development processes that capacity development efforts seek to impart upon beneficiaries.

It is also crucial to note that the scales of the enabling environment are not limited to those I present in the figure. Subnational and transnational scales of context can be broken down even further to demonstrate the familial, district, tribal, and provincial dynamics of social power and ownership of political and economic processes. I address

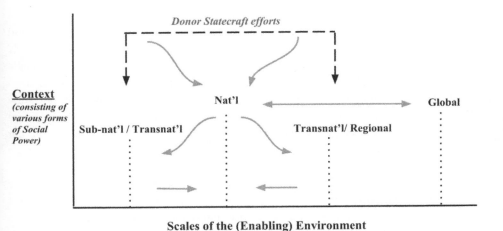

Figure 6.3 Statecraft and Capacity Development of the Enabling Environment.

some of these dynamics in Chapter 2 and do not expand upon them further here in order to contain my argument. With that said, while donor statecraft really only targets the subnational/transnational and national scales of the environment, projects themselves are limited by the scale of the state's operation. This is largely because the national scale is that of the central government—the scale to which donors have the greatest access. Through targeting statecraft from a national framework, donors attempt to impose a hierarchy of governance surrounding political and economic relationships to reinforce the production processes of the development apparatus upon networks that operate relatively autonomously at subnational/transnational scales. Furthermore, with projects that ascribe a reinforcement of the state, donor statecraft attempts to facilitate national–regional–global relationships that legitimize the state and facilitate the expansion of global capitalism.

In this figure, the arrows represent networks and linkages of development. Donors primarily have access to state networks and try to build linkages with subnational spaces to manage transnational threats through these state linkages. They also try to integrate subnational spaces into regional and global governance networks (e.g., trade agreements, WTO accession). We see in this figure a display of how the context (which is constituted of varying forms of social power) of the environment varies at different scales of the environment. It is within this framework that development occurs. In this particular instance, I use development loosely. The context of social power will continue to evolve and change form with the passage of time and in that sense continues to "develop," but the *project* of development and of statecraft will always have to adapt to the context of the relationships and networks that define the social power at the varying scales of environment. It is here that donors face a nearly impossible challenge as in their very nature of *belonging* to and *being* of a scale of context so far distanced and removed from the realities of subnational and transnational networks that the task of statecraft inherently becomes an act of neo-imperialism.

There are cultural, political, and economic components to each function of government targeted by projects of statecraft: in the provision of services, facilitating and enabling trade and economic opportunity, establishing rule of law and security, and establishing democratic political processes and institutions. Statebuilding is not merely a matter of defining components and the pursuit of systemization; it requires strategic resource allocation and investment that takes into account (1) ripeness for investment to "stick" or leave lasting impact beyond the lifespan of the project and more importantly (2) the actual needs of the population on the ground. Building roads and vocational training aimed at building infrastructure for trade is irrelevant if every convoy entering a village requires an armed escort to pay off militants to prevent attacks and where those who are injured do not have access to medical care. The task of thoroughly surveying populations, identifying the needs of remote communities—which are required for statebuilding, systemization, and enhancing the legitimacy of the state—requires a level of infiltration and resources too great for the international community of states and institutions seeking to extend the arm of global governance.

There are some important trends to recognize in looking at projects over the past four decades in Afghanistan and Pakistan. First, the issues that plague development projects have become exacerbated with the rise of transnational networks of resistance, but the tactics employed by donors to address them, while in name have changed, do not reflect changes in donor strategy. Moreover, the evolution of capacity building/development displays a discursive transformation in how donors frame issues but not actually a methodological transformation in understanding the systemic nature of these issues. This is in part due to the positioning of the donor within the broader context of bilateral relationships and the continued reproduction of development and military activities in different forms.

This methodological weakness of capacity development is most highlighted in the "enabling" environment, which operates at multiple scales within subnational spaces that harbor transnational networks consistently eluding the reach of state governance, as well as the donor community that seeks to manage it. The methodological tactic of conducting assessments in order to gain knowledge for donor and state management schemes is weak at best and demonstrates the actual distance between the international networks of donors operating predominantly in spaces of the Global North and of the subnational spaces housing transnational networks of militants. Furthermore, this has implications for donors attempting to build state in any context where the boundaries of communities and movements extend beyond the political boundaries of the state. The challenge of donors' statecraft is ultimately a confrontation with the colonial heritage of donor states and a challenge over the ownership of local development.

Finally, it is important to problematize this concept of "capacity" within this context of donor statecraft. Are USAID's projects actually training people and strengthening institutions in ways that actually enhance their capacity? And capacity for what? As previously mentioned, donors examine capacity at the scale of the individual, the organization, and the environment (though the latter rather weakly). Based on this chapter's examination of projects, USAID projects are generally not succeeding in cultivating sustainable and operational networks *or* in shifting local and transnational social networks to accommodate central democratic governance and capitalist expansion.

Further, USAID and other donors' attempts at building the capacity of states have in many cases fueled conflict—supporting warlords, poorly conceiving of actual needs, and hastily implementing projects within unstable communities not receptive to foreign occupiers. To be clear, this does not mean that there have been no positive outcomes to development projects. Rather, USAID's model of statecraft has been to enhance the capacity of state managers as well as private sector actors and workers—to ideally enhance the capacity of the organizations and institutions of the private sector and the state. As I demonstrate in my analysis of USAID's *statecraft*, donor attempts at enhancing the capacity of the state to be operational within the territorial boundaries of these states have largely failed—particularly given haphazard implementation, the short time span of projects, and the embedded resilience of the Taliban, Haqqani Network, TTP, and other insurgent groups with the transnational infrastructure.

The overarching issue that consumes all of the aforementioned is the short-term nature of foreign intervention and statebuilding compared to actual historical processes of state formation, which as discussed in the previous chapter is lengthy. While the donor community has invested in Afghanistan for the better part of two decades as of this writing, that was not the original plan. As donors conceived plans upon timelines that kept getting extended, donor mistakes and Taliban's resurgence provided justifications for the continued extension of plans. USAID's attempts to build capacity have actually *not* resulted in the enhanced freedom or autonomy of Afghans and has in many cases made them more vulnerable to coercive insurgent and kinship-based forces while also reinforcing networks of dependency upon donor funding. Moving into the final chapter, as we consider the impact of this seemingly never-ending conflict, we must collectively face tough questions about how international, transnational, and global networks of states and institutions engage in statebuilding and the *crafting* of states. We must recognize this general failure of capacity development efforts to cultivate systems of governance based upon relationships and networks of empowerment and autonomy, and not violence, capital, and coercion.

Chapter Seven

DEVELOPING CAPACITY TO MANAGE GLOBAL THREATS: *STATEMAKING, THE MILITARIZATION OF DEVELOPMENT, AND HUMAN RIGHTS APPROACHES*

How local national staff managed to implement project activities in these areas (… with only a token security apparatus and no functional district government) … is still an open question … The explanation given, that they were able to leverage local knowledge and contacts, is in and of itself not a sufficient explanation. How *they leveraged local knowledge and contacts is more to the point. This has not been sufficiently answered to allow for practical lessons learned and to help in establishing best practices for program delivery in insurgent controlled areas …*
> —*USAID Stability in Key Areas (SIKA) Final Performance Evaluation* (USAID 2015b, 2)

Now the great desire of the trans-border tribesman is, I take it, to maintain his religion and his independence. The British Government have not the smallest desire to interfere with either … The policy of the Government of India towards the trans-border men is very simple, and it is this. We have no wish to seize your territory or interfere with your independence. If you go on worrying and raiding and attacking, there comes a time when we say, This thing must be put an end to: and if the tribes will not help us do it, then we must do it ourselves. *The matter is thus almost entirely in your own hands. You are the keepers of your own house. We are ready enough to leave you in possession. But if you dart out from behind the shelter of your door to harass and pillage and slay, then you must not be surprised if we return quickly and batter the door in.*
> —Lord Curzon, British viceroy and governor-general of India
> (1898–1905) (Curzon 1906, 422)

This project addresses a series of complex questions around how concepts such as capacity gain salience in donor spaces, the foreign policy priorities of donor states, and the rise of transnational militancy. By examining the transformation of capacity within the example of USAID frameworks and projects, I expose conceptual and discursive shifts that mask the political project of development, particularly as it pertains to threats to global security. Capacity development is now a permanent part of the lexicon of the development space. Amid the growing prevalence of capacity development specialists, institutional trainings on capacity development work, and calls for the need to build the capacity of developing countries, one gets the sense that all at once capacity means everything and nothing.

In this project I have deconstructed this concept in tracing its transformation within one of the oldest and most influential development agencies, USAID. The task of developing state capacity in Afghanistan and Pakistan within the context of the rise of Islamic militancy steeped in transnational networks of resistance has presented an especially unsettling challenge for donors, given the promulgation of Islamic militant groups. How can we reconcile (1) the decades of international dialogue, conferences, and global agendas for action and (2) the subsequent attempts by cadres of trained "specialists," by development institutions and agencies, by those willing and vested recipients with the rise and expansion of Islamic militant networks and the ultimate failure of capacity-building efforts in one of the most challenging geopolitical terrains?

I approached this task in Chapter 2 first through an examination of the spaces within which donors operate and produce strategy and agendas for aid. The dynamics of this space are distinct from the dynamics of recipient spaces and dictate the way in which concepts of practice, such as capacity, gain salience. Furthermore, the architecture of donor institutions and agencies that constitute official development assistance (ODA) carries with it a heritage of political and economic ideologies of modernization that justifies interventionism with a tone of altruistic objectivity. The epistemological and professional dynamics of this space (see Figure 2.1) continues to impact and influence knowledge production processes, as well as which voices gain recognition in the fields of policy and practice.

While private aid and donors from the Global South are increasing their presence within this global space of donors, the modern architecture of ODA largely financed by the countries of the Global North continues to steer development efforts, particularly in challenging contexts that carry security risks for aid workers (e.g., in so-called fragile states). I detail this donor architecture in the third section of Chapter 2 (see Figure 2.2 on donor systems). As supranational governing bodies such as the UN or OECD organize conferences to create agendas to prioritize and address global issues, bilateral development agencies such as the USAID develop strategies that integrate global agendas for progress alongside the donor state's foreign policy objectives. The example of how capacity has gained salience within these discourses demonstrates how concepts gain salience within this space (see Figure 2.4).

To provide further substance to this examination of capacity, I examine the transformation of the concept within USAID's policy and practice in Chapter 3. In my review of USAID's usage and conceptualizations of capacity in this chapter, some important questions emerge regarding the very nature of development. The objectives of capacity development within donors' agendas are wide ranging and grand in scope. While methodologies are implemented on the project level, donors' objectives are ultimately tied to building state capacity to manage subnational spaces of exclusion that harbor transnational threats. From my examination, I find that while there are references within evaluations, assessments, and subsequent strategy and methodologies highlighting the importance of local ownership, building upon already existing capacities, and preventing the creation of duplicate systems, ultimately the theories of change and transformation behind capacity development largely come from a Western framework.

Decades removed from the heyday of the modernization theorists, and even from the post-Washington Consensus frameworks for emerging markets, USAID's (2010c) capacity development framework adapts a Harvard business model for private sector transformation to public sector institutions in developing countries. Furthermore, as the issue of global security and concern over terrorism has become more prevalent within the literature on so-called fragile states and on counterinsurgency, we see the influence of military frameworks in defining the capacities of governance for development purposes. Moreover, as capacity becomes intertwined with issues of sustainability, we must ask what cultivating resilience requires? Why have capacity development efforts failed to strengthen state capacity? Relatedly, what does *ownership* of development processes truly mean and whose *ownership* matters, particularly in the context of combating insurgency and transnational militancy? These are sticky questions that become more complex as issues of capacity become attributed to reasons for state "fragility" and as part of donor states' counterinsurgency strategies. We see from this conceptual transformation that capacity not only reveals epistemological and professional tensions within the development space but also exposes pertinent questions about the very role of development in the context of foreign invasion (or intervention), subnational conflict, and statemaking.

This point is further highlighted in Chapter 4 as an examination of sociological frameworks for the capacity project. Capacity-building projects evolved out of community-building programs in the Global North. These examples bring to light major themes of the capacity project (state power, community, and social capital) that also underscore the conceptual limitations when applied as a project of statebuilding by foreign donors, particularly in how donors conceptualize social capital in an attempt to cultivate community and state power through development projects. While the development agency's involvement (particularly USAID's) in projects of statebuilding (and relatedly, counterinsurgency) is not a recent phenomenon, the emergence of "fragility" as a discursive label has served to further the discursive reach of "capacity," especially within military frameworks for development. Yet while this new century defined by post-9/11 geopolitics has catapulted a global security paradigm for development, DAC donors have at least nominally reaffirmed commitments to evolving HRBAs to development programming. The discursive framing of capacity (and different types of capacity) within USAID's frameworks for engaging in fragile states, responding to insurgency, and promoting HRBA illuminates this tension within institutional approaches as well as raises important questions for those considering how to evolve HRBA to development programming in situations of counterinsurgency within fragile states.

In Chapter 5, I situate these questions surrounding the capacity development and donor-driven statemaking within the context of Afghanistan and Pakistan. I frame the challenges of development efforts as steeped in the colonial partitioning of the border between Afghanistan and Pakistan by the British and provide some basic context for tribal dynamics and governance of this region. I do not go into depth on these issues as a full examination is outside the parameters of this project. That said, while the border itself is not a primary focus of the insurgencies today, the heritage of conflict from this partitioning is particularly relevant in considering the context that enabled the rise of transnational terrorism and also in explaining the history of tension between Afghanistan and Pakistan (see Figures 5.1, 5.2, and 5.3). During the Cold War, the United States and Soviet Union played upon these tensions—the Soviets in pursuit of the communist experiment and the Americans in an effort to contain its expansion.

As the Soviet experiment turned into a subsequent invasion and occupation of Afghanistan, Western humanitarian and military assistance to the Mujahideen through

Pakistan facilitated relationships and networks that made up a convoluted transnational architecture of resistance (see Figures 5.6 and 5.7) involving covert relationships among state actors, militants seeking to subvert state, and ideological Arab migrants. The unique circumstances surrounding this collaboration established a *transnational political terrain* that encompasses elements within the state, operates relatively autonomously between states, whose grasp is just beyond the state, and has enabled the flourishing of global terrorist networks of the present day (see Figures 5.8 and 5.9). The very task of establishing the authority and imbuing the legitimacy of the state within spaces that are subnational *within the context of the state* but transnational in scope exposes a fundamental challenge facing international efforts in statecraft.

In Chapter 6, I expand upon this examination of donor efforts through an analysis of USAID's statecraft in Afghanistan and Pakistan. Based upon my examination of USAID projects, I identify four primary components or broad program areas of governance that development projects work toward developing the capacity of: the provision of basic services, the establishment of the rule of law and security, political processes and institutions, as well as trade and economic opportunity. However, as donors reduce relationships of power and influence to "social capital" to be gained through projects, they misunderstand (or perhaps lack the capacity) to construct relationships steeped in trust, shared experience, and continuity as opposed to what Tilly (1992) might call relationships steeped in *capital* or *coercion*. This is fundamentally an issue with regard to how donors are situated in relation to the recipients of aid, particularly in the context of statecraft, and is an element that is surprisingly largely absent in the methodologies on capacity development. The development of state capacity (at any scale) ultimately hinges on the strength of relationships and networks that legitimize and extend the arm of the state. Donors such as USAID seek to ideally extend this arm through projects into the subnational spaces that harbor insurgencies in order to manage threats not only to the state but also the broader community of states. In this final chapter, I summarize and present my findings in two figures to demonstrate the conceptual transformation of capacity, engage in a discussion on the inherent limitations of donor spaces of operation within the context of statecraft or statemaking, and offer suggestions for scholars and practitioners.

The Transformation of Capacity in Donor Spaces

The first question I present in this project is, what is capacity? I ask how and why it has gained salience, what we can learn about donor methodologies, and how it relates to the management of global threats. I also question what it masks. What are the ideological discourses that lurk behind this term that has come to account for every development activity under the sun? Throughout the first four chapters of this project, I contend with varying definitions and scholarly frameworks, highlight its transformations within policy and practice, the processes within which the concept has gained salience in donor discourses and global agendas for aid, as well as highlight major themes and discursive relationships that carry ideological shifts behind capacity.

The condensed answer is that capacity, as a concept of practice in the international development of states, is a discursive tool of statemaking. In individual projects, capacity is

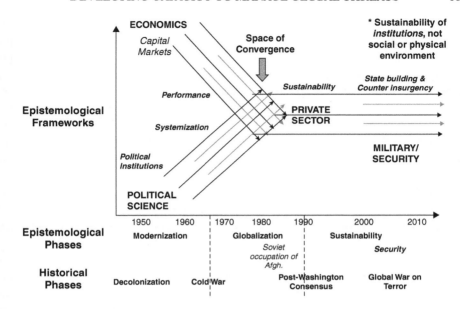

Figure 7.1 Phases of Capacity Transformation.

given substance and tied to very specific tasks and objectives, such as training individuals, but the capacity project is broader than any individual project designated to build any specific kind of capacity. As donors such as USAID engage in the practice of developing capacity, they embark on experiments of statecraft. Capacity has evolved alongside major shifts in the geopolitical environment, from the post-World War II years, through the Cold War, the post-Washington Consensus, and now the US-led War on Terror. This transformation has involved carrying the heritage of imperialistic ideas through altruistic and interventionist discourse, while simultaneously masking and building upon the epistemological influences of the past. This is a complex discursive metamorphosis and, in Figure 7.1, I display this conceptual transformation to visually map these epistemological influences and phases, as well as the major points of convergence (and emergence) within the capacity-building discourse in USAID literature.

This figure condenses a significant transformation. To simplify, of the four major attributes of capacity that I identify in Chapter 3 (*sites, ownership, processes,* and *context*), this figure displays the latter two: the donors' framing of *processes* to build capacity juxtaposed against the *context* within which they were conceived. I highlight three influential macro-variables on the y-axis that shape the *context* within which the transformation of capacity has taken place: (1) epistemological frameworks, (2) epistemological phases, and (3) historical phases. The arrows represent the direction of the discourse over time, with the terms above each arrow serving as discursive beacons for the emergence and transformation of capacity. *Performance, systemization, sustainability, statebuilding, and counterinsurgency* are all discursive relatives of capacity. They either call for capacity or have become conflated with it.

The first references to capacity within development come from political sciences and economics frameworks during the period of modernization, carried forth by the MIT scholars like Lucian Pye and his colleagues. We find references to the political development of states requiring strengthening the capacity of political institutions and calls for *systemization* to carry out projects and state planning schemes (requiring what Scott [1999] would call "state simplifications") to conduct projects. Capacity is also referenced in relation to *performance* to build industries, improve production processes, and construct national markets. These two frameworks converged during the period of globalization, and we begin to see a discursive shift in focus to "building capacity for *sustainability*" come to the fore in the literature. Particularly post-Washington Consensus, projects to build capacity for improved *performance* and *systemization* to strengthen political institutions, as well as industry and markets, were for the purpose of ensuring *sustainability*.

This convergence and the subsequent shift to *sustainability* resulted in the introduction and application of *private sector performance-based models* for organizational growth (designed to improve the performance of companies in developed, first-world markets) to *all* forms of organizations and institutions in developing countries (from nonstate, nonindustry— e.g., community-building organizations, PVOs, NGOs, etc., to public sector institutions and private industry). Adaptations of these first-world private sector methodologies continue to be used in present-day capacity development methodologies, as we see with USAID's *Human and Institutional Capacity Development Handbook* (2010c).

An important point to note is that the usage of *sustainability* is in reference to institutions, not of the environment. While environmental sustainability is an issue of development, it did not emerge within the context of issues of capacity and is not a key attribute of the capacity development discourse. That said, within the context of *sustainability*, the usage of capacity has become conflated with processes of *statebuilding* and highlighted within *counterinsurgency* strategies to combat violent extremism in so-called fragile states. This has led to a greater sense of urgency for the need to build state capacity. Not only did it become imperative for donors to invest in and develop centralized institutions that were actually sustainable, but these institutions should support a state system that would be capable of quelling insurgency—maintaining security and managing various threats to the state system. This has contributed to justifications for the continued and increased integration of security and development activities (e.g., PRTs), particularly in Afghanistan, where the US and other donor governments have justified international military intervention, and kindred transnational US executive branch and CIA programs (see, e.g., Dale and Samara, 2008) to combat the spread of global terrorist networks.

The transformation of capacity reveals an important aspect of the donor's framework for networks and relationships as they relate to the *processes* targeted for development and, more specifically, attempts to craft the state. As *processes* to improve *performance*, enhance *systemization*, increase the likelihood of *sustainability*, and maintain *security* became integrated into the vernacular surrounding the discourses on capacity building, the concept gained salience within broader donor narratives of development. This discursive transformation displays the ways in which imperialistic scholarly, private sector, and military frameworks have shaped the development discourse, carrying forth Cold War era capital-centric frameworks for conceiving and coercing relationships of development that mask ideological motivations for intervention.

Relationships of Development: Capital, Autonomy, and Recipient Ownership

In the introductory quote of this chapter, an evaluation of USAID's Stability in Key Areas (SIKA) program questions just how local staff managed to implement project activities. The evaluator comments, "leveraging local knowledge and contacts" is an *insufficient* explanation for USAID to systematically conduct operations in insurgent controlled areas. There is a lot behind this statement. The evaluator asks *how* local national staff leveraged local knowledge and contacts, searching for "practical lessons" to "establish best practices for program delivery" in subnational insurgent spaces. This question misses the point and is at the core of the donors' misunderstanding and also devaluing of the contextual factors that surround the construction of relationships and networks for development.

As the USAID example demonstrates, foreign donor-led statecraft conceives of relationships surrounding networks and systems as *exchange based*. This capital-centric framework that values *transaction* over *loyalty* attempts to systematize and centralize subnational spaces of contention through short-term incentives. It has effectively increased corruption and further legitimized the authority and operations of radical militant groups whose familiarity and proximity to the cultural fabric that characterizes and dictates social relationships and networks of power are far more intimate than that of any development agency, which carries with it the baggage of the colonial and imperial histories of Western donor states.

As I detail through an examination of USAID projects, donor statecraft attempts to build functions and construct units of centralized state systems that require simplifications and formulaic understandings of relationships and networks. In this way, donor frameworks disassociate development activities from the macro-historical context of entrenched donor–recipient relationships. This brings us to how donors target *sites* (individuals, organizations, environment) for capacity development. I discuss the aspect of sites briefly here with regard to the notion of *ownership*, which is perhaps one of the more interesting aspects for understanding capacity.

Local involvement and *ownership* of development projects and processes require some level of *autonomy* for the recipient to partake in exchange-based relationships that favor the strategy and objectives of the development agency and the donor government, and also to justify the legitimacy of the state. Why should communities living in subnational spaces who have maintained a relatively autonomous relationship with the state cooperate with USAID, or other donors for that matter, on any projects? What benefit do these projects bring to them, particularly after the project concludes? Can they really be considered *beneficiaries*? Donor notions of *ownership*, with regard to the sustainability of development projects, are indicative of the *context* of the relationship between the development agency, the donor state(s) funding them, and the recipients' perceptions of the donor state.

It is recognized throughout USAID's literature—reports, assessments, evaluations, and so on—that beneficiary *ownership* is important and necessary for the sustainability of projects. The donor effort to understand and consider contextual factors is demonstrated through entertaining questions of *sustainability*. Environmental factors emerge as a variable of capacity as strategic frameworks defined factors and theorized strategies to make an environment "enabling." However, in practice, donor targeting of the so-called enabling environment as a *site* of capacity development efforts displays an at best superficial, acknowledgment of the contextual factors at work that impact attempts to build capacity. We also see an effort by donors to systematically identify *points of entry* into disabling environments (through individuals and organizations targeted as recipients) to attempt a transformation of the context that hinders capacity development efforts.

There are references throughout the USAID literature regarding *partner selection* and also in conceptualizing and reflecting upon *implementation* with regard to the need to identify so-called change agents, which can take charge of and lead programs, organizations that can withstand shifts in turbulent environments, and of the necessity of local "participation," in development to be managed by state actors and government bureaucrats. The actors and organizations (insurgents and militant organizations) that exercise their autonomy to not comply, or who openly challenge the objectives of projects or donor strategy for development, make it difficult for donors to ensure local *ownership* (for the sustainability) of their project investments. This is not to claim that there are not individuals interested in or vested in the donor vision for development, but that these actors and organizations are often at risk or have alternative motivations for collaborating with donors.

At the methodological level, donor methodologies on capacity development systematize various forms of "assessments" or studies conducted to garner knowledge on systems and capacities already existing so as to avoid duplication and to determine points of entry for donors seeking to build capacity. However, these assessments are still donor initiated and are often superficial at best. Confined to the scope of a project, the donor objective of determining context to carry out project goals inherently strips aspects of agency from recipients attempting to determine a course for their own development. This is not to say that there are not willing partners whose interests and objectives align wholeheartedly with donors, or that methodological attempts to incorporate additional components of knowledge are ill-founded or always ineffective, but that they are inherently constrained by the donor's position of dominance in the donor–recipient relationship.

Thus, in some conflict with the notion of ownership within the *donor's perceived context* of building capacity is that this notion removes *full autonomy* from the recipient. Now, whether or not any recipient has *full autonomy* in any given environment to begin with is certainly questionable, and how recipients define and measure autonomy likely varies considerably. Some recipients are open and willing to sacrifice varying *aspects of their autonomy* to receive compensation or to increase their power and influence in donor-recognized contexts. The myriad of reasons for recipient interest and compliance in development projects, as well as the relationship between these reasons, the operational scale of recipient, and their self-perceptions of their own autonomy is outside the parameters of this project, but is an area of further study that would enhance our understanding of the relationships and networks surrounding statemaking and the cultivation of state capacity.

Those recipients who do not frame collaboration and cooperation with donors as sacrifice or imposition, but as aligned with their vision of development for the country, remain in contention with those, particularly communities at subnational levels, that have led lives not situated by boundaries for centuries, *and* within the very situated transnational networks that have enabled paths to refuge and mobilized resistance when the state has oppressed these communities. Further, the divisions among recipients and nonrecipients often fall along class, ethnic, and tribal cleavages. Thus, recipient compliance with donor notions of project *ownership,* particularly surrounding the cultivation of state capacity and countering insurgencies, often requires recipients to relinquish some rights to self-determination. This relinquishing is required for integration and recognition within the international system of states and demonstrates that not much has actually shifted in donor–recipient relationships throughout the transformation of capacity, as donors continue to build and define the structures of state as the British had in the demarcation of the Durand Line and the partitioning of Pakistan. In considering these relationships of development between donors and recipients in extending the arm of the state governance to reach and manage subnational spaces, there exists a fundamental conflict of frameworks in the defining of trust, legitimacy, and structures of governance.

Consider the spaces within which donors have evolved conceptions of capacity. They are far removed from the realities of communities whose transnational networks have been built upon principles of autonomy, loyalty, and faith—principles and bonds which become particularly strong and entrenched when communities endure decades of conflict and invasion. Moreover, the foreign policy of the donor state, as well as the role and positioning of the donor within the context of broader geopolitical dynamics, is manifest within the social narratives and realities of communities operating in subnational and transnational spaces. With continuous waves of war and foreign invasion, shared narratives emerge surrounding forms of outsiders and common enemies. In the case of Afghanistan, warring tribes have historically unified around the shared desire to expel foreign enemies. This has also contributed to the rise of transnational Islamic militant groups. Further, these narratives do not merely denote positioning (e.g., us-versus-them groupthink mentality) but are also forged from shared notions of customs and traditions, faith, and otherwise shared values, beliefs, meanings, and norms that emerge from shared existences.

That said, insurgent group infighting and competition over land and resources also marginalize and terrorize local populations—but these networks are enduring, withstanding organizational transformation within transnational contexts and tumultuous transitions in state leadership. Consider the lineage of the Afghan and Pakistani militant leaders of the present day. Many trace their history back to fighting with the Soviets, their sons continuing the fight of their fathers and uncles. Even as organizations split into divergent factions (e.g., from former Mujahideen becoming the Northern Alliance and former PDPA and anti-PDPA mullahs joining with ex-Mujahids and JUIP activists to form the Taliban in the 1990s (see Figure 5.8), to disgruntled former Taliban, Haqqani Network, and Tehrik-e Taliban leaders forming the Islamic State of Kandahar Province—ISKP, following the public knowledge of Mullah Omar's death in 2015), these transnational insurgent networks have proved resilient.

When we consider the broad framework from which recipients live out their lives and construct relationships and networks that sustain cycles of donor investment and military intervention we must consider their complexity and capacity for transformation. Consider donor efforts in subnational spaces in Afghanistan and Pakistan. While state officials, private citizens, project managers, and teams interact to build the "capacity" of various institutions and infrastructure for the state, the cultivation of sustainable relationships is strained not only by the tension, trauma, and continued reality and threat of conflict but by the temporary nature of the project engagement.

Projects have a time span, and relationships to foster "social capital" fail to take root and hold real power or sway. Often, those who participate in development projects either already are, or become, targets of insurgent campaigns. Further, particularly when military or security forces are needed to enable project implementation, the context surrounding the activities designed to build sustainable relationships becomes immediately both politicized and militarized. If we are to follow Fallov's (2010) defining of capacity as the adoption of the "regulator" or donor frame among recipients, then the target of capacity development efforts would be to alter the frameworks of (1) those project participants or recipients who are neither strongly allied nor truly loyal to the state or transnational militant group or (2) militants with grievances or who are open to coercion. In either case, the way in which donors frame capital coercion-centric relationships around development projects, the questionable time span of donor investment, and the cases of development agency and military blunders that have exacerbated local tensions make it so that the project is a shaky vessel from which to cultivate strong linkages between the central government and subnational spaces.

That said, I argue it is generally unrealistic to expect a core shifting of frameworks among recipients or to expect local ownership of donor-designed development given the typical life span development projects and the questionable time line of donor commitment. It is also potentially counterproductive when such expectations signal to recipients that they must comply with donors in certain ways in order to receive funding. Further, a fundamental transformation of frameworks may not be the right objective within this context. As my analysis of USAID projects to build capacity in Afghanistan and Pakistan reveals, the donor challenge of crafting states in so-called fragile environments is that donor networks remain largely embedded within the boundaries of their own spaces of operation. As the Afghan state recovers from decades of war and elements within Pakistani state that harbors tangled relationships with insurgent groups carrying out covert state agendas, how can development agencies expect to cultivate substate linkages and facilitate the state management of subnational spaces, particularly when they are often dependent upon state networks for access to these spaces or in the position of having to broker relationships between hostile actors? Can development agencies even play a legitimate role in state efforts to reintegrate or eradicate insurgent networks? I elaborate upon these questions in the following section.

Recipient State Networks and the Scale of Donor Operation

As the example of USAID's efforts in Afghanistan and Pakistan demonstrates, when considering how development agencies craft the state in so-called fragile environments, the dynamics of recipient state networks are critical. These dynamics essentially determine

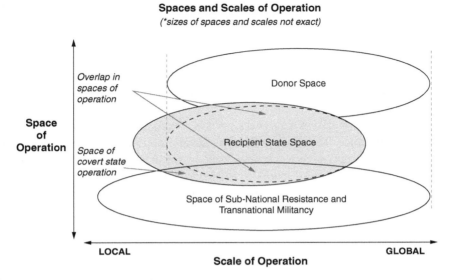

Figure 7.2 Spaces and Scales of Operation.

how donors cultivate linkages that affirm the legitimacy of the state and manage threats from subnational spaces. In the last section, I highlighted the challenges surrounding relationships of development and how donor frameworks for cultivating relationships with and among recipients is limited by capital-centric ideological frameworks. I have detailed throughout this project the context of the spaces within which donors (Chapter 2) and recipients in Afghanistan and Pakistan (Chapter 5) are situated and have constructed infrastructure and narratives that have both enabled and inhibited development efforts. It is clear that donors and recipients operate in distinct spaces. In examining how these spaces connect in the task of crafting the state, we see that the challenge of capacity development exposes the critical role of recipient state networks. In this section, I discuss these dynamics as they relate to the distance between the spaces within which donors and recipients operate in Afghanistan and Pakistan.

Figure 7.2 displays the spaces and scales of the donor, recipient state, and transnational resistance operations for the purpose of demonstrating and defining the spaces between them:

In this figure on the Y-axis we have three distinct spaces of operation: the donor space, the recipient state space, and spaces of resistance and nonstate militancy. Each space encompasses a range of actors and networks that operate along varying scales from local to global along the X-axis. Both the spaces within which donors and transnational militants operate, while distinct spaces, reach global scales of operation. The scope and ambition of some groups, such as al Qaeda (see Figure 5.10) is global in nature, with objectives to establish a global Islamic caliphate and the active development of global networks that operate on a range of scales—including subnationally and transnationally. Whether or not Global Terrorism is truly global is certainly a topic for debate, though one that is outside the realm of this project. I reference it as such here since the presentation of terrorism as a so-called global issue is pervasive throughout policy circles in the donor space. That said, I have constructed the space of transnational militancy as global given the ambition and scope of the operation of some groups and the increasing interconnectedness of insurgent networks, both regionally and globally. Further, an additional important aspect of this figure is that the donor scale of operation does not reach the local and cannot extend further than that of the state—which also does not always reach local scales.

In this project, I've discussed various aspects of the donor space and of transnational networks of resistance. The setting of global agendas and the processes of knowledge production on concepts such as capacity building occur *within* donor spaces and not within recipient state spaces or spaces of resistance. The foreign policies of donor states are also set within this space as are the institutional frameworks of donor agencies and institutions. Furthermore, the recipient's framework for development is largely absent within the processes that determine agendas and frameworks within the development space—*from the global discourse on development, knowledge production processes, agenda setting, and subsequent methodological frameworks for projects regarding the production of "knowledge" by the institutions of development.* The development space encompasses a wide range of epistemological and professional subspaces that influence the production of knowledge, yet recipient networks usually do not have access to these spaces. At the level of global discourse, while nontraditional donors and also voices from donors from the Global South are increasingly gaining space and recognition by OECD/DAC member states within primary spaces of donor collaboration, there is still quite a long way to go until the discourse that sets the global agenda for development is determined by those who are the objects of development processes.

Wendy Wong sheds light on the nature of *agenda-setting powers* in her 2012 work on how the structure of NGOs impacts the political salience of human rights, which also have implications for international development that she does not directly address. In her examination, Wong finds that the centralization of proposal and enforcement (veto) powers enables the salience of human rights *topics*, while the decentralization of implementation powers (or the *tactics* of advocacy) enabled the NGOs to harness the "local capacities and knowledge" necessary to conduct operations within diverse and shifting localized settings. In considering the donor space, these proposal and enforcement (veto) powers largely reside with donor states. They convene to discuss issues and areas involving international collaboration (*conflict and human rights, trade and global finance, military and global security, environment and global sustainability, and global development and aid effectiveness—* see Figure 2.5) in international meetings, workshops, and conferences, which result in the production of declarations, agendas, and agreements for cooperation. I argue in Chapter 2 that it is within these spaces of collaboration that the concept of capacity has gained salience.

There is an important distinction to be made regarding the "implementers" and implementation processes in my case and Wong's. Wong examines NGOs, which are largely singular organizational bodies. While the NGOs she examines have transnational arms (the successful ones for implementation), she focuses on organizational structure as the primary variable for explaining the emergence and salience of human rights topics.

I do not examine USAID's structure or success in developing agendas on topics that gain political salience nor the power dynamics or jockeying that occurs within donor spaces of collaboration in the production of agendas. Instead, I examine the processes behind which a topic (or concept) like capacity has already gained salience, and the way in which it is applied in practice. The agenda implementers, in my case, are multilateral and bilateral development institutions and agencies, such as USAID. These organizations then develop frameworks and strategies for conceptualizing aid relationships and for the execution of projects to implement the agendas formed from donor collaboration, carrying forth topics like capacity, which have gained salience within these spaces. In Chapter 3, I examine the emergence of capacity within USAID's projects and policy and the application of international agendas within these frameworks (though this is most relevant post-2001). As I previously mentioned, the spaces within which agendas for aid are set are not accessible by most recipients of aid. Thus, the agenda-setting powers and processes for development also reflect global macro-historical divisions of power inequity between donors and so-called beneficiaries of aid. These divisions feed into the distance between donor spaces and spaces of subnational resistance.

There are two spaces of overlap on which to focus in Figure 7.2: the overlapping space that exists between donors and recipient states, as well as the overlapping space between recipient states and subnational spaces of transnational operation. Note that donor spaces and subnational spaces do not meet directly. Donors must go through the recipient state in order to access subnational spaces, unless invading the recipient state with the intention of overthrowing the government regime. Further, donor access to state networks *does not guarantee* access to subnational spaces or *compliance* in targeting insurgent networks.[1] Throughout this project, I treat USAID's engagement in Afghanistan and Pakistan broadly as a case study in considering the rise of transnational militancy along their shared border, highlighting important distinctions that impact the context of development in both countries along the way. As the transformation of capacity development demonstrates the limitations of how donors frame relationships and networks, the dynamics of recipient state networks become an incredibly critical variable of capacity development efforts.

Donor and recipient state spaces overlap in the form of *networks* among foreign actors and government officials (and state-recognized private actors), *formal agreements* (between and among states, e.g., Afghanistan navigating WTO ascension), and *integrated activity* (for development, humanitarian, or military/security purposes). Integrated activities facilitate donor–recipient networks, as well as the scale to which this space operates. Donor networks are largely dependent upon the reach of state networks. This is a significant point. Development institutions and agencies as well as exogenous beneficiaries of ODA

---

1. The work of sociologists Alex Veit and Klaus Schlichte (2012) on the "three conflictual arenas" of external statebuilding describes these spaces in different terms: the donor space as the "metropolitan arena"—where agendas are set, the recipient state/donor space overlap as "base camp" where envoys and intermediaries liaise between the "bush" and headquarters, and the recipient state/subnational overlap as "bush office," which provides information for planning to base camp.

conduct development activities through their relationships with recipient state actors, as well as private sector and civil society actors that *interact with and recognize* the state and are *recognized by* the state. While relationships and networks within the recipient state space may have access[2] to subnational spaces that house transnational militant groups, they do not necessarily extend the reach of donor networks. The donor's scale of operation does not (and cannot) extend further than that of the state, unless the donor is attempting to subvert the state, which was the case with US investment in the Mujahideen by way of Pakistan during the Soviet occupation of Afghanistan. Yet even here, this transnational operation and access to subnational spaces was enabled through bilateral relationships among state actors.

The exception to donor dependency on state networks is in cases of military invasion and occupation, when military forces penetrate subnational spaces (of insurgency) that state networks do not govern, effectively circumventing state networks that are deemed problematic or seeking to replace them. In these cases, the details of context matter. Mere occupation is not the extension of state networks nor does it guarantee submission to state authority, and unless occupation is permanent there is no guarantee that the space is actually won. This is where reconstruction, statebuilding, counterinsurgency, and capacity development come in. In both Afghanistan and Pakistan, there is great complexity surrounding the networks and relationships between the central government of the state and those who operate in subnational spaces (both civilians and militant groups). How can development agencies parse out how social power and influence operate within and among networks at varying scales? How can donors know the context of the space within which the recipient state and transnational militants interact? When have transnational networks extended and also limited the scale of donor spaces and reach? In contemplating these questions, particularly in regard to the spaces within which the state and transnational militants overlap, it is important here to make some distinctions between Afghanistan and Pakistan, specifically with regard to *military activity and transnational networks* as these spaces overlap and largely house both overt and covert military and economic networks (much like during the Cold War).

In Afghanistan, foreign militaries have invaded and occupied the country both during the Cold War and now the Global War on Terror. This has fundamentally impacted the mere cultivation of strong state networks as there has never truly been a strong state network in Afghanistan, unless you consider the Taliban. While shifts in power are not uncommon in Pakistan—its history marked by a series of military coups—centralized power has largely shifted among a few primary factions. These factions include established political parties—civilian and military networks—and are largely Punjab dominated. This is not the case in Afghanistan. Central power has shifted among various warring tribes who at some points have unified or created haphazard military alliances, which usually do not sustain. Further, consider Taliban rule prior to the US invasion as an example of somewhat enduring state power in Afghanistan. The Taliban was the only

---

2. By access I mean that the networks of state officials usually include affiliations and relationships (often covert) with nonstate, militant groups and actors.

group capable of quelling the warring Mujahideen commanders after the Soviet with-drawal and maintaining centralized control of the country. The Taliban did not have a strong institutional infrastructure, trained cadres of government bureaucrats, nor did they provide many basic services, access to education, or widespread opportunities for employment. The Taliban provided security and dispute resolution, which actually does not *require* having a strong centralized infrastructure. SIGAR's most recent (2018) report on stabilization in Afghanistan notes this as such, casting a critical lens on US stabiliza-tion strategies that were too broad in scope and did not place priority upon these basic elements of governance that the Taliban had provided (SIGAR 2018, 155).

Further, Afghanistan's foreign-backed civilian administrations continuously struggle to maintain rule of law and command legitimacy outside of major cities. Since the cen-tral government has been the vessel through which foreign invaders have attempted to extend the reach of their operations, foreign donors seeking to build state capacity face fundamental issues of legitimacy that inhibit their task of statecraft. When statemaking is pursued by foreign entities in order to secure the efforts and objectives of interven-tion, and this intervention involves international military presence, it fundamentally inhibits the cultivation of relationships and networks among state actors and leaders within subnational spaces. Further, in the case of Afghanistan it has complicated, rather than facilitated, the strengthening of state networks and the extending of these networks into subnational spaces. In the early years of the US invasion, establishing relationships for control essentially involved paying off warlords, who then went on to terrorize local populations and further undermined the legitimacy of the Afghan state (Jones 2008b, 25).

Moreover, continued foreign (military) presence and development planning blunders often further justify the legitimacy of insurgent groups, further damaging the potential of state to cultivate subnational linkages. This is especially so when state officials engage in corruption, ignoring state line and even competing with insurgents in illicit activities—such as profiting from the cultivation of opium. The closest the Afghan government has come to having a strong and established military to quell "insurgencies" would be the Taliban. While there are many armed militant groups who maintain security and rule of law at local scales, Afghanistan has never had an enduring legitimate military of the state the way that Pakistan has. This point is critical in understanding the relationship between state networks and transnational militant networks, as they are ultimately relationships rooted in the extraction of resources and military alliances.

The situation and role of the military in relation to transnational networks in Pakistan are quite different than in Afghanistan, but there are similar lessons to be gleaned. First of all, the GoP has a strong state apparatus that has shifted between civilian and military regimes since inception. The GoP has generally not allowed foreign military operations on its soil, though there are a few exceptions. While Pakistan has not experienced a foreign invasion and occupation the way Afghanistan has, the Pakistani army occupies and conducts aggressive military operations throughout subnational spaces of con-tention within the country such as the Swat Valley, Dera Bugti, Gilgit-Baltistan, and Pakistan-occupied Kashmir (PoK). This is usually for the purposes of economic devel-opment (resource extraction and establishing trade routes—particularly in Balochistan and Kashmir). Further, while the GoP carries an official line of working to counter insurgency, it is well documented that there are covert relationships among the Pakistani military, ISI, and militant groups to carry out covert state operations such as arms sales and smuggling, training suicide bombers, and offering resources for terrorist attacks against internal and external state targets. These covert state–militant networks reveal cleavages *within* the GoP that ultimately subvert the state—targeting political opponents in Pakistan, India, US and NATO forces, as well as an attempted assassination against former Afghan President Hamid Karzai (Unnithan 2010). That said, these not-so-covert state-insurgent networks have been straining Pakistan's relationships with other states, particularly the United States, and presently GoP state officials seem to be taking a bit of a tougher line with some groups such as the Haqqani Network as they become liabilities in bilateral relationships (Siddique 2017). Whether or not this will be sustained is yet to be seen.

Going back to Figure 7.2, what can be determined about the distance between donor spaces and subnational spaces? Regarding state networks there are a few main points. First, state networks are generally necessary to enable donor access to subnational spaces, unless donors seek to subvert the state through military intervention. Second, where state networks are weak, donor attempts to strengthen the capacity of these networks can be counterproductive in establishing sustainable linkages between state and subnational networks. Finally, state networks do not guarantee the access donors seek, particularly if there are strong elements within state networks that maintain linkages with insurgent groups operating subnationally to carry out covert agendas. In the case of Pakistan, while elements within the state have networks that penetrate insurgent networks operating in subnational spaces, they do not represent the interests of foreign donors and thus do not extend the reach of donor operations. Furthermore, covert state relationships with insurgent groups exacerbate political cleavages within the state, ultimately subverting the strength of the state. In Afghanistan, since the apparatus of the state is largely dependent upon funding by foreign donors and the country has never had strong centralized institutions or infrastructure, state networks do not carry the same weight as they would in Pakistan where the infrastructure of centralized networks are much more established.

A final important point regarding the distance between donor spaces and subnational spaces has to do with the role of militaries in subnational spaces. Pakistan has a strong military—one that has led to the overthrow of civilian administration on more than several occasions. Further, the Pakistani army has occupied subnational spaces in attempts to control resources and facilitate the sale and transfer of weapons. Elements within Pakistan's military and intelligence community also maintain covert ties with insurgent groups tasked with carrying out covert state agendas. Moreover, Pakistan has not endured a wide-scale foreign military invasion and occupation. Donors thus depend on the state for access to subnational spaces, and their access is limited by cleavages among civilian and military elements of the Pakistani state. Afghanistan has never had a strong centralized military institution and the country consists of a wide array of armed militant groups with alliances and loyalties steeped in tribal and ethnic rivalries. Successive waves of foreign invasion and attempts to build state based on Communist or Democratic Capitalist models have damaged the development of strong state networks capable of subduing warring factions and inhibited the cultivation of sustainable state and subnational linkages. Thus, as we attempt to understand how donor states utilize development agencies like USAID, among other entities, to respond to transnational militancy in subnational spaces, we must consider both the role of state networks and also that of military intervention and occupation in donor access to subnational spaces.

Responding to Transnational Militancy: Crafting the State and Militarizing Development

What are some final lessons that can be drawn from this examination of USAID's capacity development efforts in Afghanistan and Pakistan and the rise of transnational militancy along the border of these two countries? There are a few fundamental areas in which this project has implications. The first has to do with state formation processes and the role of capacity development as a variable to this process. In this project, I apply Scott's (1999) term *statecraft* to frame USAID's activities and tease out elements of projects that expose how the development agency defines and constructs units of the state. In order for statebuilding in the abstract to become actionable projects carried out by institutions of development, particularly national development agencies beholden to public opinion and taxpayer funding, planning schemes must be articulated. Charles Tilly (1992[3]) might instead qualify this *statecraft* as a form of "statemaking."

In considering the implications of this project on scholarship regarding state formation processes, it is necessary to address some of the points that Charles Tilly makes in his monumental work on European statemaking (AD 990–1992). Tilly argues that warmaking has become a specialized, professional enterprise that has driven statemaking, leading to different state trajectories in different settings. This is not different from what the United States has done in Vietnam, Iraq, and Afghanistan. Tilly (1992) identifies three primary patterns of state formation: coercion-intensive, capital-intensive, and capitalized-coercion. With regard to so-called Third World nations, Tilly speculates that the post-World War II bipolar order set about a competition between the United States and Soviet Union for the allegiance of these states. This led to bilateral military investments in Third World countries and returns from these investments in the form of commodities (resources such as oil), political support, and sometimes profits from arms sales (Tilly 1992, 220).

The examples of Afghanistan and Pakistan clearly demonstrate this and I outlined this US–USSR donor battle for ideological hegemony in Chapter 4. This is particularly relevant in considering US investment in Pakistan during the Soviet occupation of Afghanistan. The United States made bilateral assistance agreements based upon the premise that investment in economic development would enable the GoP to repay the United States for military aid when it was ultimately the strategic geopolitical positioning of Pakistan that inspired these investments to begin with. Further, these justifications also led to exempting Pakistan from US legislative restrictions prohibiting

---

3. Tilly, Charles. 1992. *Coercion, Capital, and European States, AD 990–1992*. Blackwell Publishing: Oxford.

aid to countries cultivating nuclear capability. What does this example tell us about the role of development (and of *statecraft*) and of the development agency in the context of bilateral relationships? While it would be an exaggeration to call this "statemaking," and this example is nowhere near the scale of donor statebuilding activities in post-9/11 Afghanistan, we still see attempts to shape the fiscal and economic management of the state in order to facilitate the policy objectives of the United States within a bipolar Cold War context.

Tilly goes on to surmise that *great power competition / confrontation* and *intervention* can do no more than to play "*supporting* parts in any particular coup and in the maintenance of any particular military regime" ... (and that) "paths to *civilianization* are two-pronged: either reducing great power competition through militarily strengthening Third World states *or* through insulating these states from the competition" (223). Now, it is necessary to take into account when this work was written and the speculative place of scholarship immediately following a bipolar Cold War context. Around the same time that Tilly's revised edition was published, Huntington advanced the argument that ideological components of conflict and warmaking, such as cultural and religious identity, would be the primary sources of conflict in the post-Cold War era in a "Clash of Civilizations" (1993). Jack Goldstone's (1991) review of Tilly actually highlights ideological issues as a seemingly glaring omission in Tilly's work on statemaking. Further, in addition to contemplating whether or not statemaking is an ideological endeavor, particularly in the context of development, it is also necessary to consider the relevance of statemaking in an increasingly globalized world with a diversity of situated cultural contexts (a topic on which there is rich scholarly debate[4]). My project sheds some light on these complex areas—on intervention, statemaking, and state formation processes, on the role of ideology within these processes, and on the relevance of the state as an institution of governance.

Capacity development has become a critical variable in the donors' formula for statecraft. It was identified as an objective and issue throughout USAID projects even before the term gained salience within discourses on development. It is articulated within global agendas for aid and within the institutional frameworks of development agencies, and also within military counterinsurgency strategy. Efforts are made, however haphazardly, to incorporate capacity development methodologies into project design to build upon already existing institutions, integrate recipient-defined needs into planning, prevent the duplication of efforts and creation of parallel (often superfluous) systems, and assess and measure impact. Through my examination of agendas, institutional frameworks, and projects, we also see that capacity is not merely a technical discourse, but actually central to the ideologies espoused by development institutions that fundamentally shape the statemaking processes of designated fragile states (see Figure 6.1). It is born from the assumption that democratic and capitalist models should be the foundation for foreign-led development and that planning schemes for society should be centralized around state institutions.

---

4. Ohmae (1996), Sassen (1998), Mato (1997), Meyer et al. (1997), McMichael (1996), Strange (1996), Weiss (1997), Soysal (1994).

Furthermore, international intervention is now not instigated by conflict between great powers but due to the perceptions of donor states on what qualifies as so-called global threats coming from nonstate actors and organizations whose operation is transnational and global in reach. International intervention, war-making, and statemaking are ultimately for the purposes of managing these threats. There is also rich dialogue among scholars and policy makers in this area. Donors engage in the crafting of states to manage threats, not for the purpose of cultivating fully functioning and thriving states. I would posit that we cannot understand modern state formation processes, particularly in so-called fragile states without looking at the role of development institutions, and furthermore the militarization of development activity. Given my review of USAID projects, USAID's statecraft employs a Western model of capital-coercion in framing the cultivation of relationships and networks to construct the state. As donor states have come to portray development activity as a necessary element of reconstruction following military intervention to contain the instability and damage caused by foreign invasion, determining how to build *capacity* has become a core component in the task of crafting resilient and sustainable state institutions.

With the 2018 publication by the Special Inspector General for Reconstruction in Afghanistan damning US stabilization strategies between 2002 and 2017, we witness yet again the monumental failure of Western intervention and statemaking. My research leaves us with a few questions for moving forward. First, in considering the task of development in the broadest sense, is the state still a relevant model for governance, particularly with regard to the management of global threats? Relatedly, do transnational insurgent networks fundamentally reject statemaking? If not, what role do they play in it? Further, what would or could a recipient-driven model for development look like, particularly in the context of Afghanistan and Pakistan?

While the theoretical task of defining a recipient framework for development in Afghanistan and Pakistan merits its own exploration and is outside the scope of this project, it is a topic worth addressing. What precisely would development look like to groups operating transnationally within subnational spaces? There are some crucial elements to consider. First, development, in and of itself, is a Western concept. Societies evolve and have evolved as long as humans have been in existence. This evolution has been both progressive and regressive and I make no grand claims about the history of humanity here, but I may go so far as to say that those working in International Development seek to shape this evolution and progression of human societies in the pursuit of global "development," involving reconfigurations of systems of governance and trade centered around the state and capitalist expansion.

Attempting to dissect "indigenous" frameworks for development is a necessary point to address, but fruitless as a task (particularly if this dissection is produced by someone who would not be considered "indigenous."). Any attempt to define development or progress for or on behalf of recipients would only serve to reproduce hierarchies of knowledge production and so I will not do that here. That said, to tread ever so lightly in considering the cases of Afghanistan and Pakistan, "indigenous" systems of authority and trade that have governed life along the tribal belt and beyond have largely been warped by the ideological movements surrounding global conflicts. Considering the question of what Pashtun or Baluchi or Hazara frameworks for "development" looks like is in many ways laughable. Throughout history, these populations have not harbored or acted upon grand imperialistic frameworks for human society outside of their own. They have not determined the outcomes of global conflicts; they have merely endured and absorbed them.

Religious frameworks for governance must also be considered. The situation of bipolar conflict and Soviet occupation brought with it waves of ideologically driven migrants seeking to participate in holy war against Godless Soviets. As Arab and Indian variants of fundamentalist Islam superseded indigenous Sufi frameworks, particularly among the Pashtun population, indigenous forms and infrastructure for nonviolent dispute resolution and political organization were systematically destroyed. As the investment of donor funds ascribed legitimacy to select tribal leaders, such as Jalaluddin Haqqani or Sayyaf or Hekmatyar (see Figure 4.6 for detail on these leaders), they established a transnational infrastructure and cultivated a globalized brand of Islamic militancy that actively sought the destruction and replacement of generations of tribal leaders and local systems of governance, leaving gaping leadership vacuums in subnational spaces, and terrorizing or coercing local populations into submission. Whatever "indigenous" tribal frameworks for "development" might have existed no longer dictate the power dynamics of authority within subnational spaces.

So do the transnational insurgent networks which have evolved fundamentally resist statemaking and in what ways do they impact processes of statemaking? I argue that it is not that transnational militant networks resist the process of statemaking itself but all that is affiliated with it—Western values, foreign intervention, and situated boundaries. The Taliban did at a point in time maintain authority of the state of Afghanistan and were recognized by a few select countries. That said, controlling the state is not necessarily an objective of these networks, nor is the destruction of the state an explicit objective. Rather, the diversity of transnational insurgent objectives is more greatly aligned with the general disruption of imperialistic and ideological elements (see Figures 4.7 and 4.9), which often reside within the state apparatus. Further, like state actors, transnational insurgents seek control of territory and resources from which to conduct operations and expand the reach of their agendas. Subnational spaces are where this battle takes place, as no state's reach extends fully throughout all the spaces within its boundaries—and the control and regulation of borders has been a continuous struggle for state actors (not only in Afghanistan and Pakistan, but among states in general).

So what does it entail for the state to penetrate the local? Consider the four components I identify in the previous chapter on USAID's *statecraft*—the provision of services, facilitation of economic opportunity, establishment of rule of law and security, as well as political processes and institutions. These are all elements of "governance" that long-standing transnational insurgent networks such as the Taliban or the Haqqani Network have engaged with in one way or another in subnational spaces but through weaving in and out of a transnational framework and a reliance upon transnational mobility and operation. Within a tribal context that places value upon autonomy and loyalty, statemaking cannot be divorced from the cultural frameworks that determine legitimacy. This is not to say that transnational militant groups are (or are not) considered legitimate among the local populations within which they reside—and also often terrorize—but that their relationships and networks are steeped within the social and cultural fabric of generations who have fought the same wars and shared many of the same experiences of foreign invasion and state oppression. Subnational spaces enabling access to transnational mobility have provided not only infrastructure for militancy but also paths to safety and refuge. As Western states navigate the baggage of colonialism, repackaging interventionist policies in the context of rising anti-Western global terrorism, attempts by USAID and other development institutions to strengthen the state often actually undermine this objective.

The state is not irrelevant, but it is also not the only model for governance—nor is it the primary model, particularly in subnational spaces. In Afghanistan and Pakistan, the state may need to cede some authority to those already governing subnational spaces, consider integrated forms of shared governance, and/or seek the reintegration of insurgent elements into the political life of the state. This is actually already happening—both former Afghan president Karzai and current president Ghani have extended offers for peace talks to the Taliban. As of this writing, these highly anticipated talks between Afghan politicians and civil society leaders and the Taliban delegation in Qatar were abruptly cancelled due to disagreements about the size and composition of the Afghan delegation, demonstrating how incredibly fragile these processes are (RFE/RL 2019). The talks were actually encouraged by the Trump administration and were to include women, which is significant given the Taliban's conservative hardliner stances. Yet, in spite of the cancellation by the Afghan delegation, the United States continues bilateral negotiations with the Taliban in Qatar—begging questions about what potential resolution to this decades-long war may be brokered when the dialogue excludes state actors, very much subverting the very central notion of state the United States (and Soviets) have spent decades trying to build. In the case of Pakistan, the GoP has somewhat ceded and decentralized provisional governance to the district and tehsil scale. Future research might focus on examining the various forms of ceded or shared governance, as well as patterns among peace talks and strategies for insurgent reintegration in order to shed light on how states navigate governance in subnational spaces with transnational insurgent networks.

As we consider the transformation of capacity within donor frameworks, USAID's capacity development efforts in Afghanistan and Pakistan, and the rise of transnational militancy along the border of these two countries, we must acknowledge some truths about the reality of development. Capacity development *masks* Western ideological frameworks for development. It is increasingly being used within donor and military frameworks and serves to justify interventionist policy. Scholars and practitioners need to pay more attention to the way in which language is used in institutional strategies, in devising methodologies for projects and broad policy initiatives, and within projects themselves. This is particularly the case when it comes to the most pervasive concepts—capacity. The term "capacity" is so overused that it seemingly means everything, and thus nothing, at once. Finally, as donor governments continue to frame development within the context of managing global threats, development *cannot* be studied outside of the context of bilateral relationships, the foreign policies of donor states, and the military frameworks and activities of these states.

Considering Human Rights and Security in Development: Recommendations and Next Steps for Scholars and Practitioners

The focus of this project is on the transformation of a concept, yet this transformation touches upon many areas of development work, scholarship, and policy, and illuminates complex dynamics and aspects of the development profession and industry. A common critique scholarly works receive by those in the world of practice is that while the work may be informative, it is perhaps not directly relatable to the experience of the practitioner, calls for shifts that are too radical, and is often lacking in clear actionable next steps. This final section attempts to address this critique by providing a very basic framework for next steps, recommendations, and considerations for the various audiences who may be interested in different aspects of this work, but with particular focus paid to those whose work is focused on development, security and advancing HRBAs. Since the epistemological frameworks and professional backgrounds of those who work and study development is very diverse, I provide suggestions more broadly on development and globalization with some specific recommendations regarding the advancement of HRBAs, particularly within the context of security frameworks. I divide my recommendations into two sections: for scholars and practitioners.

This first recommendation is intended for scholars whose primary occupation is within the university, particularly those whose focus is on globalization or development, regardless of disciplinary background. My main suggestion is to engage with the literature produced by practitioners, policy makers, and institutions. There is a tendency, especially among critical scholars, to dismiss the literature produced by policy makers and practitioners almost as propaganda of institutions or too narrowly issue oriented. This only serves to further marginalize the academy from the world of practice and makes it so that critical voices only operate in echo chambers. Scholars need to conduct research to build bridges across disciplines and between the academy and the worlds of policy and practice, and the discursive examination of institutional literature is one way to do so.

The privilege of the scholar's positioning is that they are able to apply scrupulous methodological lenses to the work of practitioners and policy makers, rigor and time typically not afforded by institutional and government budgets. This encouragement on my part is in no ways blind to the ways in which the scholar–practitioner–policy maker nexus has operated to promote the imperialistic modernist frameworks of the past, but this is not a valid excuse for critical scholars to eschew engagement, evade networks of power, or to only consort among intellectual elites. Power will continue to operate in unsavory ways, but critical scholarly voices will be drowned out if they refuse to engage in spaces and venues outside and beyond the academy or harbor impatience or indignation at those whose occupations serve the interests of institutions. The author believes that this may be one of the ways in which to reestablish the relevance and importance of the academy as universities are continually privatized and increasingly subject to corporate influence.

For students whose futures are unclear and may be budding scholars, practitioners, or policy makers, conduct interdisciplinary work and make sure that your base of knowledge includes voices from the Global South and the places you are actually studying. Read about development across disciplines and do not be seduced by those whose voices seem the loudest or most prominent. There is a vast reservoir of scholarship that exists and much is buried, but that does not mean that the work itself is not valuable or that it will not later be discovered and illuminated in innovative ways—consider unlikely connections between works and entertain the potential of new paths for the direction of knowledge. Sociologists, anthropologists, political scientists, economists, historians, philosophers, as well as authors of fictional works and literary scholars will all have different frameworks for explaining development and progress. It will enhance your understanding of how our world is progressing and open new frameworks for conceptualizing the complexity of the increasingly globalized world we live in.

This final part provides some thoughts for consideration for practitioners. I make both abstract and concrete recommendations in this section both regarding HRBAs and development practice more broadly with the understanding that some of these suggestions require shifts in how institutions operate, and are not quick fixes. This project is an inherently critical work, but it does not deny or attempt to dismiss the individuals, organizations, and institutions involved in the work of development and whose driving force behind their occupations is to create a more peaceful, stable world through relationships based upon trade and the expansion of markets and political alliances.

Broadly, I would encourage practitioners and policy makers to consider how to build political, economic, and social relationships outside of Capitalist frameworks. The transformation of the methodologies behind the capacity project demonstrates that this framework is inherently limiting for conceiving of relationships and networks around development projects and actually inhibits the facilitation of relationships and networks for sustainable development, particularly in fragile states or development within the context of counterinsurgency. Furthermore, advancing HRBA to development requires this since Capitalist development has largely involved the displacement and subjugation of local and indigenous populations in the postcolonial countries of the Global South. There is more than one framework for progress, and it is the obligation of donors who claim commitment to the eradication of poverty, human rights, and sustainable peace to prevent the infiltration of the governing institutions of our world by those whose primary considerations are profits over humanity. What could this look like in practice?

When setting the global agendas for aid, in order to encourage local ownership and alternative frameworks for development by the Global South, the voices of those who are the so-called recipients and beneficiaries of development must be present at the conferences and meetings that set global agendas for aid. In addition to being present, they must be given platforms to vocalize priorities and concerns and their voices should be taken seriously. Furthermore, nontraditional actors and organizations (aside from the large institutions and private donors) should be more present as well. This diversification is already happening as discussed in Chapter 2 of this book, as we see with the OECD High Level Fora conferences, but in the planning of global conferences and meetings, inclusivity and diversity should be prioritized. This is not a new or groundbreaking suggestion, but this is still a very real area to increase the ownership of development processes by those who are the recipients of aid.

Finally, consider who projects are building relationships and networks with. A major theme of this work and finding about the failure of capacity development in Afghanistan and Pakistan is steeped in donor's superficial framing of relationships and networks surrounding development projects. In an increasingly globalized world, threats that may be written off as marginal, local, and subnational can easily become globalized and spread across borders. This is not only seen by the example of global terror stemming from the borders of Afghanistan and Pakistan but across North America and Europe as white nationalists become increasingly connected, emboldened, and empowered. Responses to these global security threats require human rights approaches to progress—building stronger linkages among local, regional, national, transnational, and international scales—and preventing the marginalization and stigmatization of groups that are socioeconomically disadvantaged.

As many projects attempt to build relationships through trade, considering context is critical. This is not new or especially groundbreaking advice. The emphasis on the importance of the environment, of context, or "enabling" conditions is rampant throughout the literature on capacity development. If donor approaches to understanding context and building relationships are superficial, and actual relationships that are steeped in and impacted by complex macro-political relationships are treated lightly, the relationships and networks projects seek to cultivate will not be enduring or sustainable. Training and exchange of knowledge need to go both ways. Pre-project assessments should involve feasibility studies on already existing infrastructure, networks, and forms of relationships. These studies should be inherently collaborative and be driven by local knowledge and not outside perspectives or foreign donor-driven agendas. They should determine actual gaps, places for improvement and strengthening, and perhaps avenues for the construction of new structures. Again, these determinations should be locally driven and donors must do their due diligence in making sure they actually know who they are building relationships with, particularly in the context of statebuilding in spaces where security is an issue and territory is contested. Projects should not commence until feasibility studies determine that the project makes sense and is highly likely to create impact. Impact is not impossible to predict, and the waste of donor resources should not be discovered in postproject evaluations or assessments when in many cases better planning and coordination can determine outcomes. This is supported by findings within program evaluations and assessments I examined spanning the past 40 years of projects in Afghanistan and Pakistan.

Feasibility studies are not uncommon, particularly for technical and agricultural projects. They should also be conducted when considering projects to build markets, civil society, legal and judicial infrastructure, and other much needed projects to expand access to public services, particularly in remote or contested areas. Of course, this requires pre-project investment, but it is investment to prevent millions lost and encourages a thoughtful HRBA to development that could lead to more sustainable and enduring relationships. So many evaluations and assessments note poor planning and conceptualization, lack of strategic focus or clear objectives, and lack of knowledge about localities. This is not to say that conducting pre-project feasibility studies across the board would resolve ingrained macro-historical tension between donors and recipients, but it would be a way to improve institutional methodology for projects to build more genuine and lasting relationships around development projects. Human rights-based frameworks actually call for assessments before engagement, but these frameworks are not actually integrated in practice.

Part of the challenge in advancing HRBA is that the frameworks that do exist by OECD/DAC donor institutions do not actually provide explicit operating definitions of a common conceptual approach to human rights. Derek Evans (2009) writes about this extensively, noting that human rights appear to be associated with very specific issues, such as *social inclusion, participation of minority groups,* and *democratic governance,* but that a coherent approach or integrated perspective is not articulated (182–83). When it comes to HRBA to development specifically, my suggestion to practitioners may seem contradictory given the critical context of this work regarding the infiltration of military frameworks in development agendas.

My suggestion is this: those interested in advancing the HRBA agenda should adopt some of the language prominent in security-based frameworks to advance these approaches and create approaches specifically on the topics of statebuilding and development in fragile states, especially cases of counterinsurgency. While development institutions such as USAID have literature research and frameworks on HRBA, including thorough assessment guides for developing strategies, there is a lack of institutional literature and frameworks on HRBA on statebuilding, engagement in fragile states,[5] and particularly in cases of counterinsurgency. There is some scholarly literature on these topics, but there is a huge void within the frameworks of development agencies and institutions.

Those institutional frameworks that do exist and consider HRBA to fragile states often do not refer to fragility explicitly, and usually not in the title of the framework, even if the content does actually consider situations of fragility. We see this in USAID's DRG framework (2013d), DAC's Action-Oriented Policy Paper on Human Rights and Development (2007), and OECD's Integrating Human Rights into Development (2006c; 2013). An exception is a 2012 report by the World Bank's Nordic Trust Fund group on Development, Fragility, and Human Rights, which provides the most comprehensive framework for HRBA in cases of fragility among traditional donors, but there is no language on statebuilding or counterinsurgency specifically. This is a huge omission on the part of those working to advance HRBA. While there is plenty of institutional literature on statebuilding, there is almost nothing on HRBA for statebuilding. It is perhaps more understandable that frameworks for approaching situations of counterinsurgency would not come from development institutions, but situations of counterinsurgency winds up being the reality of development in many cases, particularly when military intervention is involved. These discursive differences in frameworks matter, particularly when it comes to coordination on the donor end.

Consider PRTs—when development practitioners, government officials, military, and local security forces have to agree on strategic visions and work together, jockeying for

---

5. Evans (2009) also highlights that there is no comprehensive definition of how to apply HRBA to "fragile" states.

position to influence strategy differences in language and terminology, even when referring to the same thing, contributes to competing frameworks and narratives that can shift short- and long-term objectives and also cause mistakes and miscommunication, especially in complex situations. It may be in the interest of development practitioners to start working toward developing explicit frameworks for cooperation and HRBA to statebuilding, development in fragile states, and counterinsurgency operations or, as the Nordic Trust Fund report broadly terms it, "development interventions." This is not to say that explicit HRBA frameworks on these topics would resolve all tensions and issues, but it would certainly provide some clarity and perhaps ease some of the disconnection surrounding the competing frameworks by the diverse set of actors involved in such situations.

I also suggest that it would be particularly important for HRBA approaches to statebuilding, development in fragile states, and in cases of counterinsurgency to be produced by development institutions and not militaries or private security groups in order to superimpose a development lens upon the issue of security, which has traditionally been guided by military frameworks. Since the UN's Common Understanding (2003) calls for the broad-scale integration of HRBA by donors, some development institutions have built out infrastructural arms (e.g., the DRG Center at USAID, the Nordic Trust Fund at the World Bank) that have strong learning and research elements as part of their mandates. These are ripe spaces for the production of these frameworks, and so are the annual meetings and conferences of large donor institutions. Development institutions do not use the language of "counterinsurgency," as this is more of a military framework for developing tactics to respond to groups that cause instability and threaten the cultivation of governance capacity. If development institutions began using this language, it could broaden the scope and reach of those who advocate for HRBA to development as opposed to being subject to the influence of military strategists directing the foreign policies of donor states.

This is in certain ways a discursive battle steeped in the epistemological and professional backgrounds of the actors involved in development in situations of counterinsurgency in fragile states and is somewhat a matter of reaching across the aisle and using the language of those from differing epistemological and professional frameworks. Roxborough (2012) notes how there is a need for a sociological approach to statebuilding in his examination of the F-07 Army Manual and military approaches to statebuilding—through the transformation of capacity, we see the same need in advancing HRBA to development in the most precarious of situations. Furthermore, an explicit HRBA to statebuilding, fragility, and counterinsurgency could potentially shift the focus and methods behind statebuilding and how donors try to develop state capacity, potentially conjoining the cultivation of democratic political processes within society alongside the strengthening of institutions designed to protect society. The HRBA already advances more thoughtful approaches to program strategy involving critical assessments to determine factors potentially impacting donor efforts and engagement. Applying this kind of approach in situations of fragility and counterinsurgency would help to mitigate the mistakes the donor community has made, particularly in Afghanistan, and prevent the exacerbation of threats to global security.

It is not the primary preoccupation of the development expert to contemplate what their role should be once the United States or a coalition of donor states justify the military invasion of another state. Nor is it the task of the development practitioner to consider how to conduct projects within the context of counterinsurgency campaigns led either by foreign or domestic actors. Yet, this may be an entry point in shifting the narratives and approaches to statebuilding and development programming, particularly in situations of conflict in fragile states. It is dangerous to leave the task of conceptualizing reconstruction and approaches to development within the context of counterinsurgency to military experts or foreign policy advisors. While their objectives may not be incompatible with sustainable peace and development, short-term security objectives and their professional frameworks for operation may actually inhibit the advancement of these longer term strategic objectives. As we consider the work of development moving forward and acknowledge the reality of the interconnectedness of the foreign policies of donor states and development agendas, we must strive to achieve clarity on the concepts behind development so that the very structures we try to build are not built upon a foundation of discursive ambiguity. In advancing collaborative and coordinated HRBAs to development, this is fundamental to mitigate global threats, ensure the survival of our planet and of humanity.

REFERENCES

Abbas, Hassan. *The Taliban Revival: Violence and Extremism on the Pakistan-Afghanistan Frontier*. New Haven: Yale University Press, 2014.

Abbottabad Commission. "Abbottabad Commission Report on Killing of Osama bin Laden." 2013. Retrieved May 4, 2018. http://arks.princeton.edu/ark:/88435/dsp01jq085k07t.

Academy for Educational Development (AED). "Development Support Training Project." 1991.

Acemoglu, Daron, Tristan Reed, and James A. Robinson. "Chief's: Economic Development and Elite Control of Civil Society in Sierra Leone." *Journal of Political Economy* 122, no. 2 (2014): 319–68.

Adams, David, and Michael Hess. "Community in Public Policy: Fad or Foundation?" *Australian Journal of Public Administration* 60, no. 2 (2001): 13–23.

Adkins, E. H. Jr. "The Police and Resources Control in Counter-Insurgency: A Training Manual for Police." *Development Experience Clearinghouse*. 1964.

Adler, John H. "Absorptive Capacity: The Concept and Its Determinants." *Brookings Institution*. 1965.

Afghan Ministry of Foreign Affairs. "Realizing Self-Reliance: Commitments to Reforms and Renewed Partnership." Accessed October 30, 2017, http://mfa.gov.af/Content/files/Realizing%20Self%20Reliance%20-%2025%20November%202014.pdf., 2014.

Afghanistan Independent Human Rights Commission (AIHRC). "Afghanistan Independent Human Rights Commission Annual Report 2009." Published in 2009. Accessed March 25, 2019, https://www.refworld.org/pdfid/4bb31a012.pdf.

Afghanistan Reconstruction Trust Fund (ARTF). "Public Sector Capacity/Governance." Published in 2010. Accessed February 10, 2018, http://www.artf.af/portfolio/closed-projects/civil-service-capacity-building.

Afsar, Shahid, Chris Samples, and Thomas Wood. "The Taliban: An Organizational Analysis." *Military Review*. Published 2008. Accessed November 10, 2017, https://calhoun.nps.edu/bitstream/handle/10945/38410/Afsar_the_Taliban_MilitaryReview_2008-05.pdf?sequence=1.

Aga Khan Foundation. "Final Report to Agency for International Development on Matching Grant for Aga Khan Rural Support Programme 1985–1988." 1988.

Agence France-Press Kandahar. "Google Maps to Help." Published May 8, 2017. Accessed April 4, 2018, https://www.theguardian.com/world/2017/may/08/google-maps-to-help-settle-afghanistan-pakistan-border-dispute.

Ahsan, Abdullah. "Pakistan since Independence: An Historical Analysis." *Muslim World* 93, nos. 3–4 (2003): 351–71.

Ali, Idrees. "U.S. Aid to Pakistan Shrinks Amid Frustration over Militants." *Reuters*. Published August 26, 2016. Accessed July 19, 2017, http://www.reuters.com/article/us-usa-pakistan-aid/u-s-aid-to-pakistan-shrinks-amid-mounting-frustration-over-militants-idUSKCN1110AQ.

Amini, Mariam. "At Stake in US Military Efforts to Stabilize Afghanistan: At least $3 Trillion in Natural Resources." CNBC. Published August 19, 2017, https://www.cnbc.com/2017/08/18/trumps-afghanistan-strategy-may-unlock-3-trillion-in-natural-resources.html.

Amir Zal, W.A. "Fragility and Capacity Building of Social Capital of Malaysian Fisherman." *Ocean & Coastal Management* 119 (2016): 177–83.

Andersen, Louise Riis, Finn Stepputat, and Bjorn Moller. *Fragile States and Insecure People? Violence Security and Statehood in the Twenty-First Century.* New York: Palgrave Macmillan, 2007.

The Asia Foundation. "An Assessment of Sub-National Governance in Afghanistan." 2007.

Australian Department of Foreign Affairs and Trade. "The OECD." Published in 2017. Retrieved July 19, 2017, http://dfat.gov.au/international-relations/international-organisations/oecd/pages/the-oecd.aspx.

Aziz, Omer. "The ISI's Great Game in Afghanistan." *The Diplomat,* Published June 8, 2014, https://thediplomat.com/2014/06/the-isis-great-game-in-afghanistan/.

Bank Information Center (BiC). "International Financial Institutions." Accessed July 19, 2017, http://www.bankinformationcenter.org/resources/institutions/.

Barakat, Sultan, and Anna Larson. "Fragile States: A Donor-Serving Concept? Issues with Interpretations of Fragile Statehood in Afghanistan." *Journal of Intervention and Statebuilding* 8, no. 1 (2014): 21–41.

Barbara, Julien. "Rethinking Neo-Liberal State Building: Building Post-Conflict Development States." *Development in Practice* 18, no. 3 (2008): 307–18.

Bardach, Eugene. *The Implementation Game: What Happens after a Bill Becomes a Law.* Cambridge, MA: MIT Press, 1977.

Barnett, Michael, and Christopher Zurcher. "The Peacebuilder's Contract: How External State-Building Reinforces Weak Statehood." In Roland Paris and Timothy Sisk (eds.), *The Dilemmas of Statebuilding: Confronting the Contradictions of Postwar Peace Operations.* New York: Routledge, 2009: 23–52

BBC News. "Leader of Afghan mujahideen dies." Published July 24, 2006, http://news.bbc.co.uk/2/hi/south_asia/5211604.stm.

Bergen, Peter. *Holy War, Inc.* New York: Simon & Schuster, 2002.

Berger, Mark T., and Heloise Weber. "Beyond State-Building: Global Governance and the Crisis of the Nation-State System in the 21st Century." *Third World Quarterly* 27, no. 1 (2006): 201–8.

Berger, Peter L., and Thomas Luckmann. *The Social Construction of Reality.* New York: Anchor Books, 1967.

Berkowitz, Daniel, Katharina Pistor, and Jean-Francois Richard. "The Transplant Effect." *The American Journal of Comparative Law* 51, no. 1 (2003): 163–203.

Bever, Barbara. "The Impact of USAID Assistance on Baluchistan 1982–1987." 1987. November 4, 2017. https://pdf.usaid.gov/pdf_docs/PDABL035.pdf.

Bever, James. U.S. Assistance to Pakistan: Hearings before the Subcommittee on National Security and Foreign Affairs Committee on Oversight and Government Reform, House of Representatives, 112th Congress. Testimony of James Bever, Director, USAID Afghanistan Pakistan Taskforce, 2010.

Bhambra, Gurminder K. "Comparative Historical Sociology and the State: Problems of Method." *Cultural Sociology* 10, no. 3 (2016): 335–51.

Bhuiyan, Shahjahan H. "Social Capital and Community Development: An Analysis of Two Cases from India and Bangladesh." *Journal of Asian and African Studies* 46, no. 6 (2011): 533–45.

Blackton, John S. Information Memorandum for the Assistant Administrator for Asia and the Near East: Close-Out Plan for Pakistan, 1994. Accessed November 4, 2017. https://pdf.usaid.gov/pdf_docs/PDABM552.pdf.

Blatt, Darin, Eric Long, Brian Mulheron and Michael Ploskunak. "Tribal Engagement in Afghanistan." Special Warfare January/February: 2009.

Bliesemann de Guevara, Berit. "The State in Times of Statebuilding." *Civil Wars* 10, no. 4 (2008): 350–70.

Bliesemann de Guevara, Berit. "Introduction: Statebuilding and State-Formation." In Berit Bliesemann de Guevara (ed.), *Statebuilding and State-Formation: The Sociology of Intervention.* Routledge: New York, 2010.

Block, Fred. *Revising State Theory.* Philadelphia: Temple University Press, 1987.

Blue, Richard, and Richard Hoffman. "Pakistan Rule of Law Assessment – Final Report." *Management Systems International*, 2008.

Boettke, Peter J., Christopher J. Coyne, and Peter T. Leeson. "Institutional Stickiness and the New Development Economics." *American Journal of Economics and Sociology* 67, no. 2 (2008): 331–58.

Bolger, Joe. "Capacity Development: Why, What and How." *Canadian International Development Agency (CIDA) Policy Branch Capacity Development Occasional Series* 1, no. 1 (2000): 1–8.

Boltanski, Luc. Distant Suffering: Morality, Media, and Politics. Cambridge: Cambridge University Press, 1999.

Boutton, Andrew, David B. Carter. "Fair-Weather Allies? Terrorism and the Allocation of US Foreign Aid." Journal of Conflict Resolution58, No. 7 (2014): 1144–1173.

Brinkerhoff, Derick W. "Enhancing Capacity for Strategic Management of Policy Implementation in Developing Countries." *Management Systems International*, 1996.

Brinkerhoff, Derick W. Capacity Development in Fragile States. Maastricht: European Centre for Development Policy Management, Discussion Paper No. 58D, 2007.

Brown, Lisanne, Anne LaFond, and Kate Macintyre. "Measuring Capacity Building." MEASURE Evaluation,. 2001. Accessed November 4, 2017. https://pdf.usaid.gov/pdf_docs/PNACM119.pdf.

Brown, Michael. "Non-Governmental Organizations and Natural Resources Management: Synthesis Assessment of Capacity-Building Issues in Africa." *USAID*, 1996. Accessed November 4, 2017. https://pdf.usaid.gov/pdf_docs/PNABZ603.pdf.

Brown, Vahid, and Don Rassler. Fountainhead of Jihad the Haqqani nexus, 1973–2012. London: Hurst & Company, 2013.

Bryson, Lois, and Martin Mowbray. "Community: The Spray-On Solution." *Australian Journal of Social Issues* 16, no. 4 (1981): 255–67.

Burby, Raymond J., and Peter J. May. *Making Governments Plan: State Experiments in Managing Land Use.* Baltimore, MD: The Johns Hopkins University Press, 1997.

Burke, Kenneth. *Permanence and Change.* Berkeley: California University Press, 1984 (1935).

Buzan, Barry G., and Ole Waever. *Regions and Powers: The Structure of International Security.* Cambridge: Cambridge University Press, 2003.

Carment, David, John J. Gazo, and Stewart Prest. "Risk Assessment and State Failure." *Global Society* 21, no. 1 (2007): 47–69.

Carter, Lynn. "Afghan Non Governmental Organizations and Their Role in Rehabilitation of Afghanistan." International Rescue Committee, 1991. http://afghandata.org:8080/xmlui/bitstream/handle/azu/4112/azu_acku_pamphlet_hv670_6_z9_c37_1991_w.pdf?sequence=1&isAllowed=y.

Center for Global Development. Aid to Pakistan by the Numbers. Accessed July 19, 2017, https://www.cgdev.org/page/aid-pakistan-numbers.

The Center for Public Integrity. "Winning contractors: U.S. Contractors reap the windfalls of post-war reconstruction." Updated May 19, 2014, https://www.publicintegrity.org/2003/10/30/5628/winning-contractors.

Chandler, David. *Empire in Denial: The Politics of State-Building.* London: Pluto Press, 2006.

Chandrasekaran, Rajiv. "In Marja, It's War the Old-Fashioned Way." *Washington Post.* February 20, 2010, http://www.washingtonpost.com/wp-dyn/content/article/2010/02/19/AR2010021905294.html.

Chesterman, Simon. *You, the People: The United Nations, Transitional Administration, and State-Building.* Oxford: Oxford University Press, 2004.

Coll, Steve. *Ghost Wars.* New York: Penguin Group, 2004.

Comte, Augustus. *System of Positive Polity, vol. 1.* London: Longmans, Green, and Co. 1875 (1851).

Connolly, Eileen, and Aurelie Sicard. "Responding to China–Changing Donor Discourse and Perspectives on Africa?" *Irish Studies in International Affairs* 23 (1875) (2012): 111–24.

Council on Foreign Relations (CFR). "The Taliban." InfoGuide. Published January 21, 2015, https://www.cfr.org/interactives/taliban?cid=marketing_use-taliban_infoguide-012115#!/taliban?cid=marketing_use-taliban_infoguide-012115.

Counterpart International. "2011 Afghanistan Civil Society Assessment." 2011. Accessed November 4, 2017. https://pdf.usaid.gov/pdf_docs/PA00J8VX.pdf.

Cowen, Michael, and Robert Shenton. "The Invention of Development." In J. Crush (ed.), *Power of Development*. New York: Routledge, 1995: 27–43

Craig, David, and Douglas Porter. *Development Beyond Neoliberalism?* London: Simon and Routledge, 2006.

Crush, Jonathan, ed. *Power of Development*. New York: Routledge, 1995.

Curzon, Marquess George Nathaniel. *Lord Curzon in India: Being a Selection from his Speeches as Viceroy & Governor-General of India: 1898–1905*. London: Macmillan and Co., 1906.

Dale, John and Tony Samara. "Legal Pluralism within a Transnational Network of Governance: The Extraordinary Case of Rendition." *Law, Social Justice & Global Development Journal (LGD)*, no. 2 (2008), https://warwick.ac.uk/fac/soc/law/elj/lgd/2008_2/daleandsamara/.

Danaher, Patrick Alan, Linda de George-Walker, Robyn Henderson, Karl J. Matthews, Warren Midgely, Karen Noble, Mark A. Tyles and Catherine H. Arden (eds). *Constructing Capacities: Building Capabilities through Learning and Engagement*. Newcastle upon Tyne: Cambridge Scholars Publishing, 2012.

Darling, Robert. "Analysis of the Insurgency in Thailand and U.S./RTG: Counterinsurgency Strategy and Programs." 1973. Accessed November 4, 2017. https://pdf.usaid.gov/pdf_docs/PBAAB499.pdf.

Della Faille, Dimitri. "Discourse Analysis in International Development Studies: Mapping Some Contemporary Contributions." *Journal of Multicultural Discourses* 6, no. 3 (2011): 215–35.

Democracy International. "U.S. Election Observation Mission to Pakistan General Elections 2008 Final Report." 2008. Accessed November 4, 2017. https://pdf.usaid.gov/pdf_docs/PNADT907.pdf.

Department of Defense (DOD). Foreign Military Sales, Foreign Military Construction Sales and Other Security Cooperation Historical Facts. 2015. Published September 30, 2015, http://www.dsca.mil/sites/default/files/fiscal_year_series_-_30_september_2015.pdf.

Development Experience Clearinghouse (DEC). "About." 2017, https://dec.usaid.gov/dec/About.aspx.

Devolution Trust for Community Empowerment (DTCE). Overview of DTCE. Last Updated on November 29, 2013, http://www.dtce.org.pk/about/over-view.html.

Dietz, Thomas, Robert W. Rycroft. *The Risk Professionals*. New York: Russell Sage Foundation, 1987.

Dietz, Thomas, Paul C. Stern, and Robert W. Rycroft. "Definitions of Conflict and the Legitimation of Resources: The Case of Environmental Risk." *Sociological Forum* 4, no. 1 (1989): 47–70.

Douglas-Jones, Rachel, and Justin Shaffner. "Introduction: Capacity Building in Ethnographic Comparison." *The Cambridge Journal of Anthropology* 35, no. 1 (2017): 1–16.

Dressler, Jeremy. "Afghanistan Report 6: The Haqqani Network." Washington, DC: Institute for the Study of War, 2010.

Druzin, Heath. A Look at How the US-Led Coalition Lost Afghanistan's Marja District to the Taliban. Published January 16, 2016, https://www.stripes.com/news/middle-east/a-look-at-how-the-us-led-coalition-lost-afghanistan-s-marjah-district-to-the-taliban-1.389156.

Duffield, Mark. *Global Governance and the New Wars: The Merging of Development and Security*. New York: Zed Books, 2001.

Durkheim, Emile. *The Division of Labor in Society*. New York: Macmillan, 1893.

Eade, Deborah. *Capacity-Building: An Approach to People-Centred Development*. Oxford: Oxfam, 1997.

Economist. 2017. "A Growing Share of Aid Is Spent by Private Firms, Not Charities." Published 6 May 2017, https://www.economist.com/news/international/21721635-they-need-diversify-growing-share-aid-spent-private-firms-not-charities.

Edwards, David B. *Before Taliban: Genealogies of the Afghan Jihad.* Berkeley: University of California Press, 2003.

Emadi, Hafizullah. "Durand Line and Afghan-Pak Relations." *Economic and Political Weekly* 25, no. 28 (1990): 1515–16.

Engberg-Pedersen, Lars, LouiseAndersen, Finn Stepputat, and Dietrich Jung. "Fragile Situations: Background Papers." DIIS Report. Published in 2008. http://pure.diis.dk/ws/files/61269/R2008_11_Fragile_Situations_Background_papers.pdf.

Escobar, Arturo. "Power and Visibility: The Invention and Management of Development in the Third World." *Cultural Anthropology* 4, no. 4 (1988): 428–43.

Escobar, Arturo. "Imagining a Post-Development Era: Critical Thought, Development and Social Movements." *Social Text*, no. 31–32 (1992): 20–56.

Escobar, Arturo. *The Making and Unmaking of the Third World.* Princeton, New Jersey: Princeton University Press, 1994.

Esteva, Gustavo. "Regenerating People's Space." *Alternatives* 10, no. 3 (1987): 125–52.

European Commission (EC). "Institutional Assessment and Capacity Development: Why, What and How?" Published September 2005, https://ec.europa.eu/europeaid/sites/devco/files/methodology-tools-and-methods-series-institutional-assessment-capacity-development-200509_en_2.pdf.

European Commission (EC). "Toolkit for Capacity Development." Published in 2010, https://ec.europa.eu/europeaid/sites/devco/files/guidelines-toolkit-capacity-development-2010_en.pdf.

European Commission (EC). "Capacity Development." Accessed on July 19, 2017, https://ec.europa.eu/europeaid/capacity-development_en.

European Union (EU). "Capacity4dev: Capacity Development." Accessed on July 19, 2017, https://europa.eu/capacity4dev/topics/capacity-development.

Evans, Derek. G. "Human Rights and State Fragility: Conceptual Foundations and Strategic Directions for State-Building." *Journal of Human Rights Practice* 1, no. 2 (2009): 181–207.

Fabra Mata, Javier, and Sebastian Ziaja. "Users' Guide on Measuring Fragility." Bonn: German Development Institute and UNDP, 2009.

Fairweather, Jack. *The Good War: Why We Couldn't Win the War or the Peace in Afghanistan.* Philadelphia: Basic Books, 2014.

Fallov, Mia Arp. "Community Capacity Building as the Route to Inclusion in Neighbourhood Regeneration?" *International Journal of Urban and Regional Research* 34, no. 4 (2010): 789–804.

Farivar, Masood. *Confessions of a Mullah Warrior.* New York: Atlantic Monthly Press, 2009.

Ferguson, James. *The Anti-Politics Machine: Development, Depoliticization, and Bureaucratic Power in Lesotho.* Minneapolis: University of Minnesota Press, 1994.

Fisher, Max. "40 maps that explain the Middle East." *Vox.* Published March 26, 2015, https://www.vox.com/a/maps-explain-the-middle-east.

Flora, Cornelia Butler, and Jan L. Flora. "Social Capital." In D.L. Brown, and L.E. Swanson (eds.), *Challenges for Rural America in the Twenty-first Century.* University Park, PA: Pennsylvania State University Press, 2005, 214–27.

Flynn, Michael. "State of the Insurgency: Unclassified." ISAF, December 22, 2009.

Fort, Alfredo L. "Technical Report 16: Capacity Building in Training: A Framework and Tool for Measuring Progress." 1999. Accessed November 4, 2017. https://pdf.usaid.gov/pdf_docs/PNACH028.pdf.

Foucault, Michel. "The Subject and Power." In J.D. Faubion (ed.), *Power – Essential Works of Foucault 1954–1984*, vol. 3. London: Penguin, 2000: 326–48.

Fukuyama, Francis. "Nation-Building 101." *The Atlantic.* Published January/February 2004a, https://www.theatlantic.com/magazine/archive/2004/01/nation-building-101/302862/.

Fukuyama, Francis. *State-Building: Governance and World Order in the 21st Century.* New York: Cornell University Press, 2004b.

Fukuyama, Francis. "What is Governance?" *Governance* 26, no. 3 (2013): 347–68.

Fund for Peace. "Fragile States Index." Published in 2017. Accessed on July 19, 2017, http://fundforpeace.org/fsi/.

Gardezi, Hassan N. "The Politics of Religion in Pakistan: Islamic State or Shari'a Rule." South Asia Citizens Web. Published April 14, 2003, http://www.sacw.net/new/Gardezi140403.html.

Gargan, J.J. "Consideration of Local Government Capacity." *Public Administration Review* 41 (1981): 649–58.

Geissler, Paul Wenzel., Henrietta Moore, Branwyn Poleykett, Ruth Jane Prince and Noemi Tousignant. Convenors of Making Scientific Capacity in Africa: An Interdisciplinary Conversation. 13–14 June 2014, Centre for Research in the Arts, Social Sciences and Humanities, Cambridge.

Gilani, Tariq. "US-Pakistan Relations: The Way Forward." *Parameters*, Winter 2006–07: 84–102

Gillies, John, and Felix Alvarado. "Country Systems Strengthening: Beyond Human and Organizational Capacity Development." Published November 2012, http://kdid.org/sites/kdid/files/resource/files/Nov2012_Capacity_Development_Gillies.pdf.

Gilman, Nils. Mandarins of the Future: Modernization Theory in Cold War America. Baltimore: Johns Hopkins University Press, 2003.

Gisselquist, Rachel M. "Introduction: Aid and Institution-Building in Fragile States: What Do We Know? What Can Comparative Analysis Add?" *The Annals of the American Academic of Political and Social Science* 656 (2014): 6–21.

Glenn, Russell W., Colin Holland, Alasdair W.G. Mackie, Brenda Oppermann, Deborah Zubow Prindle, and Myra Speelmans. "Evaluation of USAID's Community Stabilization Program (CSP) in Iraq: Effectiveness of the CSP Model as a Non-Lethal Tool for Counterinsurgency." 2009. Accessed November 4, 2017. https://pdf.usaid.gov/pdf_docs/PDACN461.pdf.

Gnaedinger, Nancy, and Janice Robinson. "Capacity Building in Residential Care at The Lodge at Broadmead, Victoria, British Columbia, Canada." *Healthcare Management Forum* 24, no. 2 (2011): 72–75.

Goffman, Erving. *Frame Analysis*. Cambridge, MA: Harvard University Press, 1974.

Goldstone, Jack. "Reviewed Work(s): Coercion, Capital, and European States, AD 990–1990 by Charles Tilly." *Contemporary Sociology* 20, no. 2 (1991): 176–78.

Goode, Steven. "A Historical Basis for Force Requirements in Counterinsurgency." US Army. Published March 25, 2010, https://www.army.mil/article/36324/a_historical_basis_for_force_requirements_in_counterinsurgency.

Goodhand, Jonathan and Mark Sedra. "Who Owns the Peace? Aid, Reconstruction, and Peacebuilding in Afghanistan." *Disasters* 34, no. 1 (2010): S78–102.

Gopal, Anand. "The Most Deadly US foe in Afghanistan." *Christian Science Monitor*. Published June 1, 2009, https://www.csmonitor.com/World/Asia-South-Central/2009/0601/p10s01-wosc.html.

Green, Dan. "Going Tribal: Enlisting Afghanistan's Tribes." *Special Warfare* 22, no. 4 (2010): 1–8

Grimm, S., John Humphrey, Erik Lundsgaarde, and Sarah-Lea John de Sousa. "European Development Cooperation to 2020: Challenges by New Actors in International Development," no. 4. Published May 2009, http://www.edc2020.eu/fileadmin/Textdateien/EDC2020_WP4_Webversion.pdf.

Gulzad, Zalmay Ahmad. "The History of the Delimitation of the Durand Line and the Development of the Afghan State (1838–1898)." PhD dissertation, Department of History, University of Wisconsin, Madison, 1991.

Hafvenstein, Joel. *Opium Season: A Year on the Afghan Frontier*. Guilford, CT: Lyons Press, 2007.

Hameiri, Shahar. "Capacity and its Fallacies: International State Building as State Transformation." *Journal of International Studies* 38, no. 1 (2009): 55–81.

Hannerz, Ulf. "Cosmopolitans and Locals in World Culture." In M. Featherstone (ed.), *Global Culture: Nationalism, Globalization, and Modernity*. London: Sage, 1990, 237–53.

Harris, Gardiner. "U.S. Gives Military Assistance to Pakistan, with Strings Attached." *New York Times*, August 30. Published 30 August 2017, https://www.nytimes.com/2017/08/30/us/politics/us-aid-pakistan-terror.html.

Haslam, Ian R., Myint Swe Khine, and Issa M. Saleh (eds). *Large Scale School Reform and Social Capital Building*. New York: Routledge, 2013.

Heathershaw, John. "Conclusion: Neither Built Nor Formed – the Transformation of States under International Intervention." In Berit Bliesemann de Guevara (ed.), *Statebuilding and State-Formation: The Sociology of Intervention*. New York: Routledge, 2012: 246–59

Herring, Eric, and Glen Rangwala. *Iraq in Fragments: The Occupation and Its Legacy*. London: Hurst, 2006.

Hershman, M.J., J.W. Good, T. Bernd-Cohen, R.F. Goodwin, and V. Lee Pam Pogue. "The Effectiveness of Coastal Zone Management in the United States." *Coastal Management* 27 (1999): 113–38.

Heymann, Hans. "Seminar on Development and Security in Thailand: Part I, The Insurgency." Santa Monica, CA: RAND Corporation. 1969. https://www.rand.org/pubs/research_memoranda/RM5871.html.

Holtgrave, Peter L., Christie Norrick, James Teufel, and Pat Gilbert. "Building Community and Social Capital by Engaging Capacity-building Volunteers in Intergenerational Programs." *Journal of Intergenerational Relationships* 12, no. 2 (2014): 192–96.

Honadle, George H. "Fishing for Sustainability: The Role of Capacity Building in Development Administration." *Development Alternatives, Inc.* 1981. Accessed November 4, 2017. https://pdf.usaid.gov/pdf_docs/PNAAL358.pdf.

Honadle, George H., and John P. Hannah. "Management Performance for Rural Development: Packaged Training or Capacity Building?" *Development Alternatives, Inc.* 1982. Accessed November 4, 2017. https://pdf.usaid.gov/pdf_docs/PNABA381.pdf.

Honadle, George H., and David D. Gow. "Putting the Cart Behind the Horse: Participation, Decentralization, and Capacity Building for Rural Development." *Development Alternatives, Inc.* 1981. Accessed November 4, 2017. https://pdf.usaid.gov/pdf_docs/PNAAQ303.pdf.

Horký-Hlucháň, Ondřej, and Balázs Szent-Iványi. "Neither Security Nor Development? Czech and Hungarian Identities and Interests in the Provincial Reconstruction Teams in Afghanistan." *East European Politics* 31, no. 4 (2015): 388–406.

Hudson Institute. "About." Accessed on March 11, 2018, https://www.hudson.org/about.

Hudson Institute. The Index of Global Philanthropy and Remittances. Published 2016, https://s3.amazonaws.com/media.hudson.org/files/publications/201703IndexofGlobalPhilanthropyandRemittances2016.pdf.

Hughes, Bryn., Charles T. Hunt and Boris Kondoch. *Making Sense of Peace and Capacity-Building Operations: Rethinking Policing and Beyond*. Leiden: Martinus Nijhoff Publishers, 2010.

Hughes, Christopher. "Conceptualizing the Globalization-Security Nexus in the Asia-Pacific." *Security Dialogue* 32, no. 4 (2001): 407–21.

Huntington, Samuel. "The Change to Change: Modernization, Development, and Politics." *Comparative Politics* 3, no. 3 (1971): 283–322.

Huntington, Samuel. "Democracy's Third Wave." *Journal of Democracy* 2, no. 2 (1991): 12–34.

Idrees, Mohammad Khuram. "Perception of the FATA Residents Regarding the Implementation of the FCR Reforms." DTCE, 2013.

Illitch, Ivan. *Toward a History of Needs*. Berkeley: Heyday Books, 1977.

Immerwahr, Daniel. *Thinking Small: The United States and the Lure of Community Development*. Cambridge: Harvard University Press, 2015.

Inkeles, Alex. "Making Men Modern: On the Causes and Consequences of Individual Change in Six Developing Countries." *American Journal of Sociology* 75, no. 2 (1969): 208–25.

Institute of Public Administration New York City (IPA). "Building Capacity for Local Government Training: Czech Republic and Slovakia." 1993. Accessed November 4, 2017. https://pdf.usaid.gov/pdf_docs/PNABQ776.pdf.

The International Council on Security and Development. "Afghanistan: The Relationship Gap." Published July 2010, https://www.ecoi.net/en/file/local/1160738/1226_1280220908_afghanistan-relationship-gap.pdf.

International Human Rights Network (IHRN), Terre des Hommes International Federation, Action Aid International, and Amnesty International EU Office. "Human Rights-Based Approaches and European Union Development Aid Policies." Published in 2008, https://www.ihrnetwork.org/uploads/files/10.pdf.

International Monetary Fund (IMF). "IMF Executive Directors and Voting Power." Accessed on July 19, 2017 (referred to as 2017a), http://www.imf.org/external/np/sec/memdir/eds.aspx.

Iorio, Mariarosaria. "Global Governance, International Development Discourses and National Policy-Making: Highlights of Critical Issues." International Gender and Trade Network (IGTN). Published in 2012, https://www.wto.org/english/forums_e/ngo_e/posp68_igtn_e.pdf.

Isachenko, Daria. "The Production of Recognized Space: Statebuilding Practices of Northern Cyprus and Transdiestria." *Journal of Intervention and Statebuilding* 2, no. 3 (2008): 353–68.

Jackson, Matthew, and Stuart Gordon. "Rewiring Interventions? UK Provincial Reconstruction Teams and 'Stabilization'." *International Peacekeeping* 14, no. 5 (2007): 647–61.

Janjua, Muhammad Qaiser. "In the Shadow of the Durand Line: Security, Stability and the Future of Pakistan and Afghanistan." Master's Thesis, Defense Analysis, Naval Postgraduate School, Monterey, CA, 2009.

Jochem, Torsten, Ilia Murtazashvili, and Jennifer Murtazashvili. "Establishing Local Government in Fragile States: Experimental Evidence from Afghanistan." *World Development* 77 (2016): 293–310.

Johansen, Robert. "Radical Islam and Nonviolence: A Case Study of Religious Empowerment and Constraint among Pashtuns." *Journal of Peace Research* 34, no. 1 (1997): 53–71.

Jones, Seth G. *Counterinsurgency in Afghanistan.* Arlington, VA: RAND Corporation, 2008a.

Jones, Seth G. "The Rise of Afghanistan's Insurgency: State Failure and Jihad." *International Security* 32, no. 4 (2008b): 7–40.

Jeffalyn Johnson and Associates, Inc. "A Review of United States Development Assistance to Pakistan 1952–1980." Development Experience Clearinghouse. 1981.

Johnson, Charles Michael. Afghanistan Key Oversight Issues for USAID Development Efforts: Hearing before the Subcommittee on National Security, Committee on Oversight and Government Reform, House of Representatives. Statement of Charles Michael Johnson, Jr., Director, International Affairs and Trade, 2014.

Johnson, Thomas H., and Chris M. Mason. *Understanding the Taliban Insurgency in Afghanistan.* Philadelphia, PA, Foreign Policy Research Institute, 2007.

Jones, Seth. *In the Graveyard of Empires.* New York: W. W. Norton, 2009.

Jane's Terrorism and Security Monitor (JTSM). "Unraveling Haqqani's Net." June 30, 2009.

Jung, Minsoo, and K. Viswanath. "Does Community Capacity Influence Self-Rated Health? Multilevel Contextual Effects in Seoul, Korea." *Social Science & Medicine* 77, no. 1 (2013): 60–69.

Kagan, Frederick. "The Two-Front War." Critical Threats Project. Published November 2, 2009, https://www.criticalthreats.org/analysis/the-two-front-war.

Kaplan, Seth D. *Fixing Fragile States: A New Paradigm for Development.* Westport, CT: Praeger Security International, 2008.

Kapstein, Ethan B. "Aid and Stabilization in Afghanistan." USIP. Published in June 2017, https://www.usip.org/sites/default/files/2017-06/sr405-aid-and-stabilization-in-afghanistan.pdf.

Katzman, Kenneth. "Afghanistan: Post-War Governance, Security, and U.S. Policy." Congressional Research Service, 2008.

Keane, Conor, and Steve Wood. "Bureaucratic Politics, Role Conflict, and the Internal Dynamics of US Provincial Reconstruction Teams in Afghanistan." *Armed Forces & Society* 42, no. 1 (2016): 99–118.

Kelly, Jose Antonio. *State Healthcare and Yanomami Transformations: A Symmetrical Ethnography*. Tucson: The University of Arizona Press, 2011

Khan, Shah Jehan. "The Religious Leadership of the Pushtuns." PhD Dissertation, University of Hawaii, 1999.

Kim, Jinho, Ji-Hye Kim, Vanphanom Sychareun, and Minah Kang. "Recovering Disrupted Social Capital: Insights from Lao DPR Rural Villagers Perceptions of Local Leadership." *BMC Public* 16, no. 1 (2016): 1–10.

King, L.R. and S.G. Olson. "Coastal State Capacity for Marine Resources Management." *Coastal Management* 16 (1988): 305–18.

Klass, Rosanne. "Afghanistan: The Accords." *Foreign Policy*. Published April 14, 1988, https://www.foreignaffairs.com/articles/asia/1988-06-01/afghanistan-accords.

Klitgaard, Robert. *Tropical Gangsters*. New York: Basic Books, 1990.

Krause, Monika. 2014. *The Good Project: Humanitarian Relief NGOs and the Fragmentation of Reason*. Chicago: University of Chicago, 2014.

Krause, Monika, and Julian Go. *Fielding Transnationalism*. Malden, MA: Wiley Blackwell/The Sociological Review, 2016.

Krogman, Naomi. "Frame Disputes in Wetland Policy: Louisiana's Stakeholders on Regulatory Reform." PhD dissertation, Department of Sociology, Colorado State University, 1995.

Kuhn, Florian. "Risk and externalization in Afghanistan: Why Statebuilding Upends State-Formation." In Berit Bliesemann de Guevara (ed.), *Statebuilding and State-Formation: The Sociology of Intervention*. New York: Routledge, 2012.

Kunder, James D. U.S. Assistance to Pakistan: Hearings before the Senate Committee on Foreign Relations, Senate, 110th Congress. Testimony of James. D. Kunder, Acting Deputy Administrator, USAID, 2007.

Learning Network on Capacity Development (LenCD). A Country-led Approach toward Reform of Technical Cooperation. Published on September 15, 2011 (referred to as 2011a), http://www.lencd.org/event/2011/bangkok.

Learning Network on Capacity Development (LenCD). Cairo Consensus on Capacity Development: Call to Action. Published March 29, 2011 (referred to as 2011b), http://www.lencd.org/event/2011/cairo-workshop-capacity-development-concepts-implementation#document.

Lenzer, Gertrude. (ed.). *Auguste Comte and Positivism: The Essential Writings*. Chicago: University of Chicago Press, 1983.

Lewis, Oscar. "The Culture of Poverty." *American* 215, no. 4 (1966): 19–25.

Leys, Colin. *Market-Driven Politics: Neoliberal Democracy and the Public Interest*. London and New York: Verso, 2001.

Liebl, Vernon. "Pushtuns, Tribalism, Leadership, Islam and Taliban." *Small Wars & Insurgencies* 18, no. 3 (2007): 492–510.

Linnell, Deborah. (ed.). *Evaluation of Capacity Building: Lessons from the Field*. New York: Alliance for Non-profit Management, 2003.

Lipset, Seymour. "Some Social Requisites of Democracy: Economic Development and Political Legitimacy." *The American Political Science Review* 53, no. 1 (1958): 69–105.

List, Friedrich. *The National System of Political Economy*, Philadelphia: J.B. Lippincott. – (1991[1885]), Sampson S. Lloyd, trans.) *The National System of Political Economy*. New York: Augustus M. Kelly, 1856.

MacDonald, Barry. "Memorandum: Afghanistan Close-Out Plan." *Development Experience Clearinghouse*, 1994.

Mandarano, Lynn. "Civic Engagement Capacity Building." *Journal of Planning Education and Research* 35, no. 2 (2015): 174–87.

Mann, Michael. *The Sources of Social Power: Volume 1, A History of Power from the Beginning to AD 1760*. Cambridge: Cambridge University Press, 1986.

Mann, Michael. *The Sources of Social Power: Volume 2, The Rise of Classes and Nation States 1760–1914*. Cambridge: Cambridge University Press, 1993.

Mantopoulos, Jeannie, Sosena Kebede, Shoba Ramanadhan, and Elizabeth H. Bradley. "Network-Based Social Capital and Capacity-Building Programs: An Example from Ethiopia." *Human Resources for Health* 8, no. 1 (2010): 8–17.

Mapping Militant Organizations. *Stanford University Mapping Militants Project*. Accessed 2017, http://web.stanford.edu/group/mappingmilitants/cgi-bin/.

Marsden, Peter. *The Taliban: War, Religion and the New Order in Afghanistan*. New York: Zed Books Ltd, 1998.

Marx, Karl. "1858, 1875, 1867." In Elster, J. (ed.), *Karl Marx: A Reader*. Cambridge: Cambridge University Press, 1986.

May, Peter J., and Walter Williams. *Disaster Policy Implementation: Managing Programs Under Shared Governance*. New York: Plenum Press, 1986.

Mato, Daniel. "On the Making of Transnational Identities in the Age of Globalization." *Cultural Studies* 12, no. 4 (1997): 598–620.

McGirk, Tim. "A Civil War Among Afghanistan's Insurgents?" *TIME*. Published on March 8, 2010, https://defence.pk/pdf/threads/a-civil-war-among-afghanistans-insurgents.49733/.

McMichael, Philip. "Rethinking Globalization: The Agrarian Question." *Review of International Political Economy* 4, no. 4 (1996): 630–62.

McMichael, Philip. *Development as Social Change: A Global Perspective* (5th ed.).Thousand Oaks, CA: Sage Publications, Inc., 2012.

Meyer, John, John Boli, George M. Thomas and Francisco O. Ramirez. "World Society and the Nation-State." *American Journal of Sociology* 103, no. 1 (1997): 144–81.

Miakhel, Shahmahmood. "A Brief Overview of the Afghanistan Stabilisation Program." Afghan Analysts Network. Published September 7, 2012, https://www.afghanistan-analysts.org/wp-content/uploads/downloads/2012/09/7_Miakhel_A_Brief_Overview_of_the_ASP.pdf.

Mill, John Stuart. "On Liberty." In Max Lerner (ed.), *Essential Works of John Stuart Mill*. New York: Bantam, 1965 [1859].

Miller, Barbara D. *Local Social Organizations and Local Project Capacity*. USAID/Syracuse University, 1980. Accessed November 4, 2017. https://pdf.usaid.gov/pdf_docs/PNAAX638.pdf.

Minkov, Anton, and Gregory Smolynec. "4-D Soviet Style: Defense, Development, Diplomacy, and Disengagement in Afghanistan During the Soviet Period. Part III: Economic Development." *The Journal of Slavic Military Studies* 23, no. 4 (2010): 597–616.

Minority Rights Group International. "Pathans." Accessed September 8, 2017, http://minorityrights.org/minorities/pathans/.

Mishali-Ram, Meirav. "Afghanistan: A Legacy of Violence? Internal and External Factors of the Enduring Violent Conflict." *Comparative Studies of South Asia, Africa and the Middle East* 28, no. 3 (2008): 473–86.

Mitchell, Timothy. "Society, Economy and the State Effect." In George Steinmetz (ed.), *State/Culture: State-Formation After the Cultural Turn*. Ithaca, NY: Cornell University Press, 1999.

Mitchell, Timothy, and Robert Owen. "Defining the State in the Middle East: A Report on the Second of Three Workshops Organized by Social Science Research Council's Joint Committee on the Near and Middle East." *Middle East Studies Association Bulletin* 25, no. 1 (1991): 25–29.

Mitchell, Timothy. *Rule of Experts: Egypt, Techno-Politics, Modernity*. Berkeley: University of California Press, 2002.

Monten, Jonathan. "Intervention and State-Building: Comparative Lessons from Japan, Iraq, and Afghanistan." *The Annals of the American Academic of Political and Social Science* 656 (2014): 173–91.

Morgan, Peter. "Capacity Development – An Introduction." *Emerging Issues in Capacity Development*. Ottawa: Institute on Governance, 1994.

Morton, Melinda, and Nicole Lurie. "Community Resilience and Public Health Practice." *American Journal of Public Health* 103, no. 7 (2013): 1158–60.

Mowbray, Martin. "Community Capacity Building or State Opportunism?" *Community Development Journal* 40, no. 3 (2005): 255–64.

Mullaney, Alexander, and Syeda Amna Hassan. "He Led the CIA to bin Laden – and Unwittingly Fueled a Vaccine Backlash." *National Geographic.* 2015. Published February 27, 2015, https://news.nationalgeographic.com/2015/02/150227-polio-pakistan-vaccination-taliban-osama-bin-laden/#close.

Nair, Sheila. "Governance, Representation and International Aid." *Third World Quarterly* 34, no. 4 (2013): 630–52.

Napoleoni, Loretta. *Modern Jihad: Tracing the Dollars Behind the Terror Networks.* London: Pluto Press, 2003.

Nay, Olivier. "Fragile and Failed States: Critical Perspectives on Conceptual Hybrids." *International Political Science Review* 34, no. 3(2013a): 326–41.

Nay, Olivier. "International Organizations and the Production of Hegemonic Knowledge: How the World Bank and the OECD Helped Invent the Fragile State Concept." *Third World Quarterly* 35, no. 2 (2013b): 210–31.

Naylor, Tristan. "Deconstructing Development: The Use of Power and Pity in the International Development Discourse." *International Studies Quarterly* 55, no. 1 (2011): 177–97.

Nielsen, Rich. "Does Aid Follow Need? Humanitarian Motives in Aid Allocation." Prepared for the Aid Transparency and Development Finance: Lessons from AidData held at University College, Oxford, March 22–25, 2010.

Nojumi, Neamatollah. *The Rise of the Taliban in Afghanistan: Mass Mobilization, Civil War, and the Future of the Region.* London: Oxford University Press, 2002.

Nojumi, Neamatollah. "The Critical Gap Between Local versus International Perspectives on Security and Justice and Its Implications for the U.S.-Led International Intervention in Afghanistan, 2001–2006: Between State-Building and the Global War on Terror." PhD Dissertation, Conflict Analysis and Resolution, George Mason University, 2012.

Norris-Raynbird, Carla. "The Use of Frames Analysis in Evaluating Capacity-Building in Local Coastal Programs in Louisiana." *Rural Sociology* 73, no. 1 (2008): 22–43.

North Atlantic Treaty Organization (NATO). ISAF's mission in Afghanistan (2001–2014) (Archived). Last Updated September 1, 2015, https://www.nato.int/cps/ua/natohq/topics_69366.htm.

Norton, John DeWitt, Philip M. Ritz, Robert M. Waddell, and Marshall K. Wood. "Capacity Expansion Planning Factors: Part 1. Methods and Sources." National Planning Association, 1965. Accessed November 4, 2017. https://pdf.usaid.gov/pdf_docs/PNAAC453.pdf.

Nunan, Timothy. *Humanitarian Invasion: Global Development in Cold War Afghanistan.* Cambridge: Cambridge University Press, 2016.

O'Reilly, K. "Building Capacity, Extracting Labour: The Management of Emotion in NGOs". Paper presented at 'Traces, Tidemarks and Legacies', 110th annual meeting of the American Anthropological Association, Montreal, 16–20 November, 2011.

Ohmae, Ken'ichi. *The End of the Nation State: The Rise of Regional Economies.* New York: The Free Press, 1996.

Organization for Economic Cooperation and Development (OECD). "Rome Declaration on Harmonisation." Published 2003, http://www.oecd.org/dac/effectiveness/31451637.pdf.

OECD. "DAC in Dates: The History of OECD's Development Assistance Committee." Published in 2006 (referred to as 2006a), http://www.oecd.org/dac/1896808.pdf.

OECD. "The Challenge of Capacity Development: Working Toward Good Practice." Published in 2006 (referred to as 2006b), http://www.fao.org/fileadmin/templates/capacitybuilding/pdf/DAC_paper_final.pdf.

OECD. "DAC Action-Oriented Policy Paper on Human Rights and Development." Published in 2007, http://www.oecd.org/dac/governance-development/39350774.pdf.

OECD. "The Accra Agenda for Action." Published in 2008 (referred to as 2008a), http://www.oecd.org/dac/effectiveness/45827311.pdf.

OECD. "The Paris Declaration on Aid Effectiveness: Five Principles for Smart Aid." Published in 2008 (referred to as 2008b), http://www.oecd.org/dac/effectiveness/45827300.pdf.

OECD. "The Paris Declaration on Aid Effectiveness and the Accra Agenda for Action." Published in 2008 (referred to as 2008c), http://www.oecd.org/dac/effectiveness/34428351.pdf.

OECD. "Bonn Workshop on Capacity Development 15–16 May 2008: Consensus Conclusions." Published in 2008 (referred to as 2008d), https://www.oecd.org/site/oecdgfd/40713038.pdf.

OECD. "Bogota Statement Toward Effective and Inclusive Development Partnerships." *The High Level Event on South-South Cooperation and Capacity Development*. Published March 25, 2010 (referred to as 2010a), https://www.oecd.org/development/effectiveness/45497536.pdf.

OECD. "Inventory of Donor Approaches to Capacity Development: What We Are Learning." Updated October 2010 (referred to as 2010b), https://www.eda.admin.ch/content/dam/deza/en/documents/die-deza/strategie/202116-inventory-donor-approaches_EN.pdf.

OECD. "Busan High Level Forum on Aid Effectiveness: Proceedings." Published in 2011, http://www.oecd.org/dac/effectiveness/HLF4%20proceedings%20entire%20doc%20for%20web.pdf.

OECD. "Integrating Human Rights in Development, 2nd ed." Published in 2013, https://openknowledge.worldbank.org/bitstream/handle/10986/12800/9780821396216.pdf.

OECD. "Development Assistance Committee (DAC)." Retrieved July 19, 2017 (referred to as 2017a), http://www.oecd.org/development/developmentassistancecommitteedac.htm.

OECD. "History." Accessed July 19, 2017, http://www.oecd.org/about/history/.

Olsen, Stephen, James Tobey, and Meg Kerr. "A Common Framework for Learning from ICM Experience." *Ocean & Coastal Management* 37, no. 2 (1997): 155–74.

Ong, Aihwa, and Stephen J. Collier. *Global Assemblages: Technology, Politics and Ethics as Anthropological Problems*. Oxford: Blackwell, 2005.

Orlina, Ezekiel Carlo. "Top USAID Contractors for 2015." *Devex*. Published May 27, 2016, https://www.devex.com/news/top-usaid-contractors-for-2015–88181.

Paczynska, Agnieszka. "Development and Counterinsurgency in Afghanistan and Pakistan." The National Bureau of Asian Research: Special Report #19 (2009): 3–16.

Parker, Michelle. "Programming Development Funds to Support a Counterinsurgency. Nangarhar, Afghanistan 2006." 2008. Accessed November 4, 2017. https://pdf.usaid.gov/pdf_docs/PCAAB850.pdf.

Paris, Roland and Timothy J. Sisk. *The Dilemmas of Statebuilding: Confronting the Contradictions of Postwar Peace Operations*. London: Routledge, 2009.

Parsons, Talcott. "Evolutionary Universals in Society." *American Sociological Association* 29, no. 3 (1964): 339–57.

"Pearson Report" (Report of the Commission on International Development). 1969. *International Organizations and the Generation of the Will to Change*. UAI Study Papers INF/5.Retrieved July 19, 2017, (https://www.laetusinpraesens.org/docs/infwill/inf5.php).

Pfotenhauer, Sebastian, Daniel Roos, and Donald Newman. 'Collaborative Strategies for Innovation Capacity-Building: A Study of MIT's International Partnerships'. In P. Teirlinck, F. de Beule and S. Kelchtermans (eds), *Proceedings of the 8th European Conference on Innovation and Entrepreneurship*. Brussels: Belgium, 2013: 498–506.

Pfotenhauer, Sebastien, Danielle Wood, Daniel Roos and Daniel Newman. "Architecting Complex International Science, Technology and Innovation Partnerships (CISTIPs): A Study of Four Global MIT Collaborations." *Technological Forecasting and Social Change* 104 (2016): 38–56.

Polyani, Karl. *The Great Transformation: The Political and Economic Origins of Our Time*. New York: Farrar & Rinehart, 1944.

Poole, Lydia. "Afghanistan: Tracking Major Resource Flows 2002–2010." Relief Web. Published February 16, 2011, http://devinit.org/post/afghanistan-tracking-major-resource-flows-2002–2010/#.

Porter, Doug. "The Homesickness of Development Discourses." In Crush, Jonathan (ed.), *Power of Development*. New York: Routledge, 1995: 63–86

Pratt, Brian, John Hailey, Michela Gallo, Rebecca Shadwick, and Rachel Hayman. "Policy Briefing Paper 31: Understanding Private Donors in International Development." International NGO Training and Research Center (INTRC). Published July 2012, https://www.intrac.org/wpcms/wp-content/uploads/2016/09/Briefing-Paper-31-Understanding-private-donors-in-international-development.pdf.

Pritchard, Kathleen. "Human Rights and Development: Theory and Data." In D.P. Forsythe (ed.), *Human Rights and Development: International Political Economy Series*. London: Palgrave Macmillan, 1989: 329–45

Putland, Christine, Fran Baum, Anna Ziersch, Kathy Arthurson, and Dorota Pomagalska. "Enabling Pathways to Health Equity: Developing a Framework for Implementing Social Capital in Practice." *BMC Public Health* 13, no. 1 (2013): 1–12.

Putnam, Robert D. "The Prosperous Community." *The American Prospect* no. 4 (1993): 35–42.

Pye, Lucian. "The Concept of Political Development." *The ANNALS of the American Academy of Political and Social Science*, 358, no. 1 (1965): 1–13.

Ravi, Thathiah. "Pakistan Army and Regional Peace in South Asia." *Journal of Third World Studies* 23, no. 1 (2006): 119–46.

Rasmussen, Sune Engel. "'Butcher of Kabul' Pardoned in Afghan Peace Deal." *The Guardian*. Published September 22, 2016, https://www.theguardian.com/world/2016/sep/22/butcher-of-kabul-pardoned-in-afghan-peace-deal.

Reyes, Romeo A. "Absorptive Capacity for Foreign Aid." *USAID/Syracuse University: The Maxwell School of Citizenship and Public Affairs*. 1990. Accessed November 4, 2017. https://pdf.usaid.gov/pdf_docs/PNABE619.pdf.

Richmond, Oliver. "The Legacy of State Formation Theory for Peacebuilding and Statebuilding." *International Peacekeeping* 20, no. 3 (2013): 299–315.

Riedel, Bruce. *What We Won: America's Secret War in Afghanistan, 1979–1989*. Washington, DC: Brookings Institution Press, 2014.

Ripps, Evelyn L. "Capacity Utilization: Undervalued Instrument for a More Productive Approach to Development." USAID Reference Center, 1975.

Rist, Gilbert. *The History of Development: From Western Origins to Global Faith*, 2nd ed. London, New York: Zed Books, 2002.

Robinson, William. "Beyond Nation-State Paradigms: Globalization, Sociology, and the Challenge of Transnational Studies." *Sociological Forum* 13, no. 4 (1998): 561–94.

Robinson, William. "Global Capitalism Theory and the Emergence of Transnational Elites." *Critical Sociology* 38, no. 3 (2011): 349–63.

Robinson, William. "Debate on the New Global Capitalism: Transnational Capitalist Class, Transnational State Apparatuses, and Global Crisis." *International Critical Thought* 7, no. 2 (2017): 171–89.

Robinson, William I. *Latin America and Global Capitalism: A Critical Globalization Perspective*. Baltimore: Johns Hopkins University Press, 2008.

Roggio, Bill. "Coalition Targets Haqqani Network Commander, Kills 29 Fighters." *Long War Journal*. Published May 28, 2009.

Roggio, Bill. "Haqqani Took Heavy Losses in Base Assaults." *Long War Journal*. Published August 29, 2010, https://www.longwarjournal.org/archives/2010/08/haqqani_network_took.php.

Romano, Amy. *A Historical Atlas of Afghanistan*. New York: Rosen Publishing Group, 2003.

Rondinelli, Dennis A. "Capacity-Building in Emerging Market Economies: The Second Wave of Reform." *Business and the Contemporary World* 6, no. 3 (1994): 153–67.

Rossmiller, George E. *Systems Approach to Agricultural Sector Development Decision-Making: Building and Institutionalizing an Investigative Capacity.* Michigan State University, 1977. Accessed November 4, 2017. https://pdf.usaid.gov/pdf_docs/PNAAJ941.pdf.

Rostow, Walt. *The Stages of Economic Growth.* Cambridge: Cambridge University Press, 1959.

Roxborough, Ian. "Building other Peoples' States: The Sociology of State-Building." *Comparative Sociology* 11 (2012): 335–51.

Rowell, James. "Abdul Ghaffar Khan: An Islamic Gandhi." *Political Theology* 10, no. 4 (2009): 591–606.

Ruttig, Thomas. "Islamists, Leftists – and a Void in the Center. Afghanistan's Political Parties and Where They Come from (1902–2006)." Konrad Adenauer Stiftung. Published in 2006, https://web.archive.org/web/20130524194344/http://www.kas.de/db_files/dokumente/7_dokument_dok_pdf_9674_2.pdf.

Ryerson, Christie. "The Pacification of Soldiering, and the Militarization of Development: Contradictions Inherent in Provincial Reconstruction in Afghanistan." *Globalizations* 9, no. 1 (2012): 53–71.

Rzehak, Lutz. "Doing Pashto." Published January 2011, http://www.afghanistan-analysts.org/wp-content/uploads/downloads/2012/10/20110321LR-Pashtunwali-FINAL.pdf.

Sachs, Wolfgang (ed.). *The Development Dictionary: A Guide to Knowledge as Power.* London: Zed Books, 1992.

Sassen, Saskia. *Globalization and Its Discontents.* New York: The New Press, 1998.

Sassen, Saskia. *Territory, Authority, Rights: From Medieval to Global Assemblages.* Princeton, NJ: Princeton University Press, 2006.

Sayah, Reza. "Pakistani Taliban Vows to kill bin Laden Doctor." *CNN.* Published 31 May 2012, https://www.cnn.com/2012/05/31/world/asia/pakistan-bin-laden-doctor/index.html.

Schaefer, Peter. "Insurgency and Development" USAID, (1990). https://pdf.usaid.gov/pdf_docs/PNABT727.pdf

Schwartz, Peter. *The Art of the Long View: Planning for the Future in an Uncertain World.* New York: Currency Doubleday, 1991.

Scott, James C. *Seeing Like a State.* New Haven: Yale University Press, 1999.

Shah, Syed Waqar Ali, and Shaista Parveen. "Disintegration of Pakistan – the Role of the Former Union of Soviet Socialist Republic (USSR), an Appraisal." *JRSP* 53, no. 1 (2016): 71–190.

Shannon, Lyle W. "Is Level of Development Related to Capacity for Self-Government?" *American Journal of Economics and Sociology* 17, no. 4 (1958): 367–81.

Sherwell, Philip. "Osama bin Laden Killed: Behind the Scenes of the Deadly Raid." *Telegraph.* Published 7 May 2011, https://www.telegraph.co.uk/news/worldnews/al-qaeda/8500431/Osama-bin-Laden-killed-Behind-the-scenes-of-the-deadly-raid.html.

Shirazi, Nasim Shah., Turkhan Ali Abdul Mannap, and Muhammad Ali. "Effectiveness of Foreign Aid and Human Development." *The Pakistan Development Review* 48, no. 4 (2010): 853–62.

Siddique, Abubakar. "Pakistan's Strained Alliance with the Haqqani Network." *Gandhara.* Published October 25, 2017, https://gandhara.rferl.org/a/pakistan-afghanistan-jalaluddin-haqqani/28814700.html.

Siddique, Abubakar. *The Pashtun Question: The Unresolved Key to the Future of Pakistan and Afghanistan.* London: Hurst & Company, 2014.

Siegle, Joseph. "Stabilising Fragile States." *Global Dialogue* 13, no. 1 (2011): 1–15.

Silver, Solomon. "Counter-Insurgency and Nation Building: A Study with Emphasis on Southeast Asia." 1967. Accessed November 4, 2017. https://pdf.usaid.gov/pdf_docs/PNARE183.pdf.

Simmons, Annie. "Defining Community Capacity Building: Is It Possible?" *Preventative Medicine* 52, no. 3–4 (2011): 193–99.

Smillie, Ian(ed). *Patronage or Partnership: Local Capacity Building in Humanitarian Crises.* Bloomfield, CT: Kumarian Press, Inc., 2001.

Smith, David A., Ismat Shahjehan, and Moin A. Khalid. "NGO Policy Study: A Review of Non-Governmental Organizations in the North-West Frontier Province with Recommendations for Fostering Their Role in Development." 1993. Accessed November 4, 2017. https://pdf.usaid.gov/pdf_docs/PNABU540.pdf.

Smith, Sally. "Capacity Building Deconstructed." *Community Practitioner* 88, no. 11 (2015): 49–52.

Snow, David A., E. Burke Rochford Jr., Steven K. Worden, and Robert D. Benford. "Frame Alignment Processes, Micromobilization, and Movement Participation." *American Sociological Review* no. 51 (1986): 464–81.

Special Inspector General Afghanistan Reconstruction (SIGAR). "Strategy and Resources Needed to Sustain Afghan Electoral Capacity." 2009. Accessed November 4, 2017. https://pdf.usaid.gov/pdf_docs/PCAAC591.pdf.

SIGAR. "Pakistan and Afghanistan October 2010." 2010. Accessed November 4, 2017. https://pdf.usaid.gov/pdf_docs/PDACT165.pdf.

SIGAR. "Stabilization: Lessons from the U.S. Experience in Afghanistan." Published May 2018, https://www.sigar.mil/pdf/lessonslearned/SIGAR-18-48-LL.pdf.

Soysal, Yasemin Nuhoglu. *Limits of Citizenship: Migrants and Postnational Membership in Europe.* Chicago: University of Chicago Press, 1994.

Stewart, Frances, and Graham Brown. "Fragile States." *Center for Research on Inequality, Human Security and Ethnicity (CRISE) Working Paper No. 51.* Published in 2009, retrieved on May 10, 2018, http://archives.cerium.ca/IMG/pdf/workingpaper51_-_Stewart_Brown.pdf.

Strange, Susan. *The Retreat of the State: The Diffusion of Power in the World Economy* Cambridge: Cambridge University Press, 1996.

Suhrke, Astri. *When More Is Less: The International Project in Afghanistan.* New York: Columbia University Press, 2011.

Talentino, Andrea Kathryn. "Nation Building or Nation Splitting? Political Transition and the Dangers of Violence." *Terrorism and Political Violence* no. 21 (2009): 378–400.

Tariq, Mohammad Osman. "Community-based Security and Justice: Arbakai in Afghanistan." *Institute of Development Studies Bulletin* 40, no. 2 (2009): 20–27

Tesky, Graham. "State-Building and Development: Getting Beyond Capacity." *Commonwealth Good Governance.* Published December 2011, http://www.commonwealthgovernance.org/assets/uploads/2014/04/GG11-State-building-and-development-getting-beyond-capacity.pdf.

The East Los Angeles Community Union (TELACU). "Ecuador PVO Program Development Project: Building Capacity for Ecuador's Private and Voluntary Organizations (PVOs)." 1980. Accessed November 4, 2017. https://pdf.usaid.gov/pdf_docs/PDAAJ657.pdf.

Thompson, Mark. US Troops Prepare to Test Obama's Afghan War Plan. *Time.* Published February 9, 2010, http://content.time.com/time/nation/article/0,8599,1962126,00.html.

Tilly, Charles. *Coercion, Capital, and European States, AD 990–1992.* Oxford: Blackwell Publishing, 1992.

Toosi, Nahal. "Haqqani Network Challenges US-Pakistan Relations."*Associated Press,* Published December 29, 2009.

Truman, Harry. Inaugural Address, Washington D.C., 20 January, in *Documents on American Foreign Relations.* New York: Simon and Schuster,. 1967 [1949].

United Nations Assistance Mission to Afghanistan (UNAMA). Mission Statement. Retrieved July 19, 2017, https://unama.unmissions.org/mission-statement.

United Nations Environmental Programme (UNEP). *Capacity Building for Sustainable Development: An Overview of UNEP Environmental Capacity Development Activities.* New York: United Nations Environmental Programme, 2002.

United Nations. UN Charter. Retrieved April 4, 2018, http://www.un.org/en/sections/un-charter/chapter-i/index.html.

UNDP. "SEAL (Support to the Establishment of the Afghan Legislature) Project Evaluation." 2006. Accessed November 4, 2017. https://erc.undp.org/evaluation/evaluations/detail/2172.

United Nations Development Program (UNDP). "Capacity Development Practice Note." Published July 2008, http://www.unpcdc.org/media/8651/pn_capacity_development.pdf.

UNDP. "Capacity Development: A UNDP Primer." Published in 2009 (referred to as 2009a), http://www.undp.org/content/dam/aplaws/publication/en/publications/capacity-development/capacity-development-a-undp-primer/CDG_PrimerReport_final_web.pdf.

UNDP. "Evaluation of the UNDP SEAL II Project." 2010. Accessed November 4, 2017. https://erc.undp.org/evaluation/documents/download/4522.

UNDP. "Our Work." Retrieved 19 July 2017 (referred to as 2017a), http://www.undp.org/content/undp/en/home/ourwork/overview.html.

United Nations Office for the Coordination of Humanitarian Affairs (UNOCHA). "Financial Tracking Service: Tracking Humanitarian Aid Flows." Retrieved July 19, 2017, https://fts.unocha.org.

United Nations Sustainable Development Group (UNSDG). "The Human Rights Based Approach to Development Cooperation: Towards a Common Understanding Among UN Agencies." Published in 2003; Retrieved April 4, 2019, https://undg.org/wp-content/uploads/2016/09/6959-The_Human_Rights_Based_Approach_to_Development_Cooperation_Towards_a_Common_Understanding_among_UN.pdf.

Uphoff, Norman. "Participatory Evaluation of Participatory Development: A Scheme for Measuring and Monitoring Local Capacity." Center for International Studies, Cornell University, 1986.

USAID. "Management Capacity for Agricultural Development." 1976. Accessed November 4, 2017. https://pdf.usaid.gov/pdf_docs/PDAAC985D1.pdf.

USAID. "Strengthen Institutional Capacity to Expand Program for Integrated Rural Development in Selected Latin American Countries." 1977. Accessed November 4, 2017. https://pdf.usaid.gov/pdf_docs/PDFAH905.pdf.

USAID. "Baseline Studies Field Manual: A Conceptual Model and Field Team Procedures for Analysis of Current Capacities and Development Needs of LDC Agricultural Research, Education and Extension Systems." 1978. Accessed November 4, 2017. https://pdf.usaid.gov/pdf_docs/PNAAR431.pdf.

USAID. "Afghanistan Strategy 1994–1995." 1993. Accessed November 4, 2017. https://pdf.usaid.gov/pdf_docs/PNABT686.pdf.

USAID. "Human Capacity Development: People as Change Agents." 1994. Accessed November 4, 2017. https://pdf.usaid.gov/pdf_docs/PNABX315.pdf.

USAID. "Audit of the Close-Out of USAID/Pakistan & Afghanistan." 1995a. Accessed November 4, 2017. https://pdf.usaid.gov/pdf_docs/PDABL473.pdf.

USAID. "Pakistan Non-Government Organization (NGO) Initiative Project No. 391–0516." 1995b. Accessed November 4, 2017. https://pdf.usaid.gov/pdf_docs/PDABK833.pdf.

USAID. "Practical Approaches to PVO/NGO Capacity Building." 1996. Accessed November 4, 2017. https://pdf.usaid.gov/pdf_docs/PNACA755.pdf.

USAID. "Handbook of Democracy and Governance Program Indicators." Published August 1998, Accessed November 4, 2017. https://pdf.usaid.gov/pdf_docs/PNACC390.pdf.

USAID. "Building Trade Capacity in the Developing World." 2003a. Accessed November 4, 2017. https://pdf.usaid.gov/pdf_docs/PDABX241.pdf.

USAID. "USAID/Pakistan Interim Strategic Plan May 2003-September 2006." 2003b. Accessed November 4, 2017. https://pdf.usaid.gov/pdf_docs/PDACK589.pdf.

USAID. "Afghanistan – Governance Advisory Services for the Afghanistan Stabilization Program Final Task Order Report (July-November 2004)." 2004. Accessed November 4, 2017. https://pdf.usaid.gov/pdf_docs/PDACD094.pdf.

USAID. "Afghanistan Civil Society Assessment." 2005a. Accessed November 4, 2017. https://pdf. usaid.gov/pdf_docs/PNADU210.pdf.

USAID. "The USAID Fragile States Assessment Framework." Published on July 27, 2005 (referred to as 2005b), https://pdf.usaid.gov/pdf_docs/Pnady528.pdf.

USAID. "Fragile States Strategy." Published on January 2005 (referred to as 2005c), https://pdf. usaid.gov/pdf_docs/pdaca999.pdf.

USAID. "USAID/OTI Afghanistan Program Final Evaluation." Published on August 15, 2005 (referred to as 2005d), http://www.oecd.org/countries/afghanistan/36134063.pdf.

USAID. "Provincial Reconstruction Teams in Afghanistan: An Interagency Assessment." 2006b. Accessed November 4, 2017. https://pdf.usaid.gov/pdf_docs/PNADG252.pdf.

USAID. "Analysis of USAID's Capacity Development Program (CDP)." 2008a. Accessed November 4, 2017. https://pdf.usaid.gov/pdf_docs/PDACM814.pdf.

USAID. "Audit of USAID/Afghanistan's Capacity Development Program." 2008b. Accessed November 4, 2017. https://pdf.usaid.gov/pdf_docs/PDACM979.pdf.

USAID. "Building Integrated Capacity for Infrastructure (BICI): A Program Design for Sustainable Infrastructure Management in Afghanistan." 2008c. Accessed November 4, 2017. https://pdf. usaid.gov/pdf_docs/PNADO250.pdf.

USAID. "Evaluation of the USAID/Pakistan Legislative Strengthening Project Final Report." 2008d. Accessed November 4, 2017. https://pdf.usaid.gov/pdf_docs/PDACR619.pdf.

USAID. "Final Report Local Governance and Community Development Program (LGCD) Evaluation." 2009. Accessed November 4, 2017. https://pdf.usaid.gov/pdf_docs/ PDACM816.pdf.

USAID. "Audit of USAID/Afghanistan's Oversight of Private Security Contractors in Afghanistan." Published in 2010; retrieved July 19, 2017 (referred to as 2010a), https://oig. usaid.gov/sites/default/files/audit-reports/5-306-10-009-p.pdf.

USAID. "Capacity Building for the FATA Development Program Tenth Quarterly Report: April – June 2010." 2010b. Accessed November 4, 2017. https://pdf.usaid.gov/pdf_docs/PDACT383. pdf.

USAID. "Human and Institutional Capacity Development Handbook." Published October 2010 (referred to as 2010c), http://pdf.usaid.gov/pdf_docs/pnadt442.pdf.

USAID. "Pakistan and Afghanistan Audit Report October 2010." 2010d. Accessed November 4, 2017. https://pdf.usaid.gov/pdf_docs/PDACT165.pdf.

USAID. "Trade and Accession Facilitation for Afghanistan (TAFA) Annual Report: November 2009–November 2010." 2010e. Accessed November 4, 2017. https://pdf.usaid.gov/pdf_ docs/PA00HT99.pdf.

USAID. "The Development Response to Violent Extremism and Insurgency." Published September 2011 (referred to as 2011a), https://pdf.usaid.gov/pdf_docs/Pdacs400.pdf/.

USAID. "Economic Growth and Governance Initiative (EGGI) Annual Report: October 2010– September 2011." 2011b. Accessed November 4, 2017. https://pdf.usaid.gov/pdf_docs/ PA00JHZD.pdf.

USAID. "Incentives Driving Economic Alternatives – North, East, and West (IDEA-NEW) Annual Report No. 3: October 1, 2010–September 30, 2011." 2011c. Accessed November 4, 2017. https://pdf.usaid.gov/pdf_docs/PDACU251.pdf.

USAID. "Trade and Accession Facilitation for Afghanistan (TAFA) Annual Report: November 2010–November 2011." 2011d. Accessed November 4, 2017. https://pdf.usaid.gov/pdf_ docs/PA00M24Z.pdf.

USAID. "ADS Chapter 540: USAID Development Experience Information." Published July 17, 2012 (referred to as 2012a), https://pdf.usaid.gov/pdf_docs/pdact673.pdf.

USAID. "Afghanistan Parliamentary Assistance Program Evaluation Final Report." 2012b. Accessed November 4, 2017. https://pdf.usaid.gov/pdf_docs/PDACU416.pdf.

USAID. "Assistance for Afghanistan's Anti-Corruption Authority (4A) Project Annual Report – Year 2: October 1, 2011–September 30, 2012." 2012c. Accessed November 4, 2017. https://pdf.usaid.gov/pdf_docs/PA00JP3T.pdf.

USAID. "Financial Access for Investing in the Development of Afghanistan (FAIDA) Annual Report 2012." 2012d. Accessed November 4, 2017. https://pdf.usaid.gov/pdf_docs/PA00M94C.pdf.

USAID. "Kabul City Initiative (KCI) Annual Report (Year Two), October 1, 2011–September 30, 2012." 2012e. Accessed November 4, 2017. https://pdf.usaid.gov/pdf_docs/PA00J9PJ.pdf.

USAID. "Rule of Law Stabilization – Formal Sector Component Program Evaluation Final Report." 2012f. Accessed November 4, 2017. https://pdf.usaid.gov/pdf_docs/PDACU496.pdf.

USAID. Capacity Development Program (CDP). Published in 2013 (referred as 2013a), retrieved March 10, 2018, https://www.usaid.gov/node/52036.

USAID. "Pakistan Firms Project." Retrieved on February 26, 2013 (referred to as 2013b), https://www.usaid.gov/sites/default/files/documents/1871/Firms.pdf.

USAID. "USAID Strategy on Democracy, Human Rights, and Governance." Published June 24, 2013 (referred to as 2013d), https://www.usaid.gov/sites/default/files/documents/1866/USAID-DRG_fina-_6-24-31.pdf.

USAID. "Democracy, Human Rights, and Governance Strategic Assessment Framework." September 2014. https://www.usaid.gov/sites/default/files/documents/1866/Master_SAF_FINAL%20Fully%20Edited%209-28-15.pdf.

USAID. "International Election Observation Program Final Report." 2014a. Accessed November 4, 2017. https://pdf.usaid.gov/pdf_docs/PA00KM5J.pdf.

USAID. "Local Systems: A Framework for Supporting Sustained Development." Published April 2014 (referred to as 2014b), http://www.ics.crs.org/node/262-USAID%3A%20Local%20Systems%3A%20A%20Framework%20for%20Supporting%20Sustained%20Development.pdf.

USAID. "The USAID/Afghanistan Plan for Transition 2015–2018." 2014c. Accessed November 4, 2017. https://pdf.usaid.gov/pdf_docs/PBAAE268.pdf.

USAID. "USAID FIRMS PROJECT: Technical Capacity Assessment of Bureau of Statistics, Khyber Pakhtunkhwa." 2014d. Accessed November 4, 2017. https://pdf.usaid.gov/pdf_docs/PA00K7WC.pdf.

USAID. "USAID FIRMS PROJECT: Institutional Reforms of Planning and Development Department, Khyber Pakhtunkhwa." 2014e. Accessed November 4, 2017. https://pdf.usaid.gov/pdf_docs/PA00K7WD.pdf.

USAID. "Organized Crime, Conflict and Fragility: Assessing Relationships Through a Review of USAID Programs." Published September 30, 2015 (referred to as 2015a), https://www.usaid.gov/sites/default/files/documents/1866/Crime-Conflict-and-Fragility-Technical-Report-9-30-2015-FINAL.pdf.

USAID. "Stability in Key Areas (SIKA) Program Final Performance Evaluation." Published in 2015, Retrieved June 4, 2018 (referred to as 2015b), https://www.usaid.gov/sites/default/files/documents/1871/Approved%20PMP%20updated%2010-02-2010.pdf.

USAID. "U.S. Foreign Assistance for Afghanistan: Post Performance Management Plan 2011–2015." 2015c. Accessed November 4, 2017. https://pdf.usaid.gov/pdf_docs/PDACR391.pdf.

USAID. "Gender Integration in Democracy, Human Rights, and Governance (DRG)." June 2016. Accessed November 4, 2017. https://www.usaid.gov/sites/default/files/documents/2496/Gender%20Toolkit.pdf.

USAID. "Human Rights Landscape Analysis Tool." 2016a. Accessed November 4, 2017. https://pdf.usaid.gov/pdf_docs/PBAAE633.pdf.

USAID. "USAID Strong Hubs for Afghan Hope and Resilience (SHAHAR) Annual Report: October 2015–September 2016 (FY 2016). 2016b.Accessed November 4, 2017. https://pdf.usaid.gov/pdf_docs/PA00MXPH.pdf.

USAID. "Mission, Vision and Values." Retrieved July 19, 2017 (referred to as 2017a), https://www.usaid.gov/who-we-are/mission-vision-values.

USAID. "Local Capacity Development Suggested Approaches." Published in 2017, Retrieved March 3, 2018 (referred to as 2017b), https://www.usaid.gov/sites/default/files/documents/2496/Local_Capacity_Development_Suggest_Approaches_1.pdf.

USAID. "Organizational Capacity Development Measurement." Published May 11, 2017 (referred to as 2017d), https://www.usaid.gov/sites/default/files/documents/2496/Capacity_Development_Measurement_Recommendations_Final_Draft_5.11.2017_1.pdf.

USAID. "Office of Afghanistan and Pakistan Affairs." Retrieved July 19, 2017 (referred to as 2017e), https://www.usaid.gov/who-we-are/organization/independent-offices/office-afghanistan-and-pakistan-affairs.

USAID. "Assistance for the Development of Afghan Legal Access and Transparency (ADALAT): 4th Quarterly Report, January–March 2017." 2017g. Accessed November 4, 2017. .https://pdf.usaid.gov/pdf_docs/PA00MPVP.pdf.

USAID. "Struggles from Below: Literature Review on Human Rights Struggles by Domestic Actors." Published February 17, 2017 (referred to as 2017h), https://www.usaid.gov/sites/default/files/documents/2496/Struggles_from_Below_-_Literature_Review_on_Human_Rights_Struggles_by_Domestic_Actors.pdf.

USAID. "User's Guide to DRG Programming." Published March 15, 2019 (referred to as 2019a), https://www.usaid.gov/sites/default/files/documents/1866/DRG-Users-Guide-3.15.2019.pdf.

USAID. "Technical Publications on Democracy, Human Rights and Governance (DRG)." Retrieved April 17, 2019 (referred to as 2019b), https://www.usaid.gov/what-we-do/democracy-human-rights-and-governance/technical-publications.

U.S. Army. *Field Manual 3–07, "Stability Operations"*. 2008. Accessed November 4, 2017. https://www.globalsecurity.org/military/library/policy/army/fm/3–07/fm3-07_2014.pdf.

USDOS Office of the Historian. "A Guide to the United States' History of Recognition, Diplomatic, and Consular Relations, by Country, since 1776: Pakistan." Published in 2017, Retrieved July 19, 2017, https://history.state.gov/countries/pakistan.

U.S. National Archives and Records Administration (NARA). "Foreign Aid and Counterinsurgency: The USAID and other United States Foreign Assistance Agencies in Vietnam, 1950–1967." Published in 2016, https://www.archives.gov/research/foreign-policy/assistance/vietnam.

Unnithan, Sandeep. "Pakistan's Dirty War." *India Today*. Published July 31, 2010, https://www.indiatoday.in/magazine/cover-story/story/20100809-pakistans-dirty-war-743658-2010-07-31.

Veblen, Thorstein. *The Higher Learning in America*. New York: Sagamore Press, 1918.

Veblen, Thorstein. *The Instinct of Workmanship and the State of the Industrial Arts*. New York: Macmillan, 1914.

Veit, Alex and Klaus Schlichte. Three Arenas: The Conflictive Logic of External Statebuilding. In Berit Bliesemann de Guevara (ed.), *Statebuilding and State-Formation: The Sociology of Intervention*. New York: Routledge, 2012.

Verkoren, Willemijn, and Bertine Kamphuis. "State Building in a Rentier State: How Development Policies Fail to Promote Democracy in Afghanistan." *Development and Change* 44, no. 3 (2013): 501–26.

Wais, Erin. "Trained Incapacity: Thorstein Veblen and Kenneth Burke." *KB Journal* 2, no. 1 (2005): 1–8.

Wallerstein, Immanuel. "The Rise and Future Demise of the World Capitalist System: Concepts for Comparative Analysis." *Comparative Studies in Society and History* 16, no. 4 (1974): 387–415.

Wallerstein, Immanuel. "The West, Capitalism, and the Modern World System." *Review (Fernand Braudel Center)* 15, no. 4 (1992): 561–619. https://www.jstor.org/stable/pdf/40241239.pdf?seq=1#page_scan_tab_contents

Walt, Stephen M. "Beyond bin Laden: Reshaping U.S. Foreign Policy." *International Security* 26, no. 3 (2002): 56–78.

Watts, Michael. "'A New Deal in Emotions' – Theory and Practice and the Crisis of Development." In Crush, Jonathan (ed.), *Power of Development*. New York: Routledge, 1995: 44–62

Weber, Max. *The Protestant Ethic and Spirit of Capitalism*. London: Penguin Books, 2002 [1905].

Weber, Max. "Politics as a Vocation." In Hans Gerth, H., and Mills, C. (eds.), *Max Weber: Essays in Sociology*. Hans Gerth, H. & Mills, C. New York: Oxford University Press, 1948: 77–128.

Wehr, Paul. "Conflict Mapping." In Burgess, G. and Burgess, H. (eds.), *Beyond Intractability*. Eds. Burgess, G & Burgess, H. Conflict Information Consortium. Boulder: University of Colorado, 2006.

Weiss, Linda. *Globalization and the Myth of the Powerless State*. Cambridge: Polity Press, 1997.

West, Paige. *Dispossession and the Environment: Rhetoric and Inequality in Papua New Guinea*. New York: Columbia University Press, 2016.

Williams, Maurice and Ludwig Rudel. *U.S. Economic Assistance to Pakistan: Review of the Period 1982–1987 Final Report*. DEVRES, Inc. 1988. Accessed November 4, 2017. https://pdf.usaid.gov/pdf_docs/XDAAY457A.pdf.

Williams, Maurice, John Kean, and Joann Feldman *Retrospective Review of US Assistance to Afghanistan: 1950–1979*. DEVRES, Inc. 1988. Accessed November 4, 2017. https://pdf.usaid.gov/pdf_docs/PDACQ813.pdf.

Wong, Jocelyn L.N. "Why Social Capital Is Important for Mentoring Capacity Building of Mentors: A Case Study in Hong Kong." *Teachers and Teaching* 25 (2018): 1–13.

Wong, Wendy. *Internal Affairs: How the Structure of NGOs Transforms Human Rights*. Ithaca, New York: Cornell University Press, 2012.

World Bank. "What We Do." Retrieved July 19, 2017 (referred to as 2017a), http://www.worldbank.org/en/about/what-we-do.

World Bank. "Voting Powers." Retrieved July 19, 2017 (referred to as 2017b), http://www.worldbank.org/en/about/leadership/votingpowers.

World Future Fund. "Afghanistan and Pakistan Historical Maps." Retrieved March 11, 2018, http://www.worldfuturefund.org/wffmaster/Reading/Maps/afghan.map.htm.

Zaum, Dominik. *The Sovereignty Paradox: The Norms and Politics of International Statebuilding*. Oxford: Oxford University Press, 2007.

Zea, Maria, and Faye Belgrave. "Mentoring and Research Capacity-Building Experiences: Acculturating to Research from the Perspective of the Trainee." *American Journal of Public Health* 99, no. S1 (2009): S16–19.

Zurecher, Christopher. "Conflict, State Fragility and Aid Effectiveness: Insights from Afghanistan." *Conflict, Security & Development* 12, no. 5 (2012): 461–80.

INDEX

Lightning Source UK Ltd.
Milton Keynes UK
UKHW011843210220
359140UK00001B/36